"A study of great vitality on one of the crucial questions in economics and political economy."
—Gary S. Becker, Nobel laureate in economics, 1992

"Important and insightful book ... This is important analysis not to be missed."
—Peter Diamond, Nobel laureate in economics, 2010

"*The Wealth of Nations* is still being read today. With the same perspicacity and with the same broad historical perspective, Acemoglu and Robinson have re-tackled this same question for our own times. Two centuries from now our great-great- ... -great grandchildren will be, similarly, reading *Why Nations Fail*."
—George Akerlof, Nobel Laureate in Economics, 2001

"This is not only a fascinating and interesting book: it is a really important one ... in a highly accessible, indeed riveting form. Those who pick this book up and start reading will have trouble putting it down."
—Michael Spence, Nobel laureate in economics, 2001

Daron Acemoglu is the Killian Professor of Economics at MIT. He received the John Bates Clark Medal, awarded every two years to the economist under forty judged to have made the most significant contribution to economic thought and knowledge.

James A. Robinson is a political scientist and economist and the David Florence Professor of Government at Harvard University, and a world-renowned expert on Latin America and Africa.

They are the authors of *Economic Origins of Dictatorship and Democracy,* which won numerous prizes. *Why Nations Fail* was shortlisted for the *Financial Times* and Goldman Sachs Business Book of the Year Award 2012.

Why Nations Fail

THE ORIGINS OF POWER,
PROSPERITY, AND POVERTY

Daron Acemoglu and
James A. Robinson

P

PROFILE BOOKS

This paperback edition published in 2013

First published in Great Britain in 2012 by
PROFILE BOOKS LTD
3A Exmouth House
Pine Street
London ECIR OJH
www.profilebooks.com

First published in the United States of America in 2012 by
Crown Publishers, a division of Random House Inc.

3 5 7 9 10 8 6 4 2

Book design by Leonard Henderson
Maps by Melissa Dell

Printed and bound in Great Britain by
CPI Group (UK) Ltd, Croydon CR0 4YY

A CIP catalogue record for this book is available from the British Library.

ISBN 978 1 84668 430 2
eISBN 978 1 84765 461 8

For Arda and Asu—DA

Para María Angélica, mi vida y mi alma—JR

CONTENTS

PREFACE

THIS BOOK IS about the huge differences in incomes and standards of living that separate the rich countries of the world, such as the United States, Great Britain, and Germany, from the poor, such as those in sub-Saharan Africa, Central America, and South Asia.

As we write this preface, North Africa and the Middle East have been shaken by the "Arab Spring" started by the so-called Jasmine Revolution, which was initially ignited by public outrage over the self-immolation of a street vendor, Mohamed Bouazizi, on December 17, 2010. By January 14, 2011, President Zine El Abidine Ben Ali, who had ruled Tunisia since 1987, had stepped down, but far from abating, the revolutionary fervor against the rule of privileged elites in Tunisia was getting stronger and had already spread to the rest of the Middle East. Hosni Mubarak, who had ruled Egypt with a tight grip for almost thirty years, was ousted on February 11, 2011. The fates of the regimes in Bahrain, Libya, Syria, and Yemen are unknown as we complete this preface.

The roots of discontent in these countries lie in their poverty. The average Egyptian has an income level of around 12 percent of the average citizen of the United States and can expect to live ten fewer years; 20 percent of the population is in dire poverty. Though these differences are significant, they are actually quite small compared with those between the United States and the poorest countries in the world, such as North Korea, Sierra Leone, and Zimbabwe, where well over half the population lives in poverty.

Why is Egypt so much poorer than the United States? What are the constraints that keep Egyptians from becoming more prosperous? Is the poverty of Egypt immutable, or can it be eradicated? A natural way to start thinking about this is to look at what the Egyptians themselves are saying about the problems they face and why they rose up against the Mubarak regime. Noha Hamed, twenty-four, a worker at an advertising agency in Cairo, made her views clear as she demonstrated in Tahrir Square: "We are suffering from corruption, oppression and bad education. We are living amid a corrupt system which has to change." Another in the square, Mosaab El Shami, twenty, a pharmacy student, concurred: "I hope that by the end of this year we will have an elected government and that universal freedoms are applied and that we put an end to the corruption that has taken over this country." The protestors in Tahrir Square spoke with one voice about the corruption of the government, its inability to deliver public services, and the lack of equality of opportunity in their country. They particularly complained about repression and the absence of political rights. As Mohamed ElBaradei, former director of the International Atomic Energy Agency, wrote on Twitter on January 13, 2011, "Tunisia: repression + absence of social justice + denial of channels for peaceful change = a ticking bomb." Egyptians and Tunisians both saw their economic problems as being fundamentally caused by their lack of political rights. When the protestors started to formulate their demands more systematically, the first twelve immediate demands posted by Wael Khalil, the software engineer and blogger who emerged as one of the leaders of the Egyptian protest movement, were all focused on political change. Issues such as raising the minimum wage appeared only among the transitional demands that were to be implemented later.

To Egyptians, the things that have held them back include an ineffective and corrupt state and a society where they cannot use their talent, ambition, ingenuity, and what education they can get. But they also recognize that the roots of these problems are political. All the economic impediments they face stem from the way political power in Egypt is exercised and monopolized by a narrow elite. This, they understand, is the first thing that has to change.

Yet, in believing this, the protestors of Tahrir Square have sharply diverged from the conventional wisdom on this topic. When they reason about why a country such as Egypt is poor, most academics and commentators emphasize completely different factors. Some stress that Egypt's poverty is determined primarily by its geography, by the fact that the country is mostly a desert and lacks adequate rainfall, and that its soils and climate do not allow productive agriculture. Others instead point to cultural attributes of Egyptians that are supposedly inimical to economic development and prosperity. Egyptians, they argue, lack the same sort of work ethic and cultural traits that have allowed others to prosper, and instead have accepted Islamic beliefs that are inconsistent with economic success. A third approach, the one dominant among economists and policy pundits, is based on the notion that the rulers of Egypt simply don't know what is needed to make their country prosperous, and have followed incorrect policies and strategies in the past. If these rulers would only get the right advice from the right advisers, the thinking goes, prosperity would follow. To these academics and pundits, the fact that Egypt has been ruled by narrow elites feathering their nests at the expense of society seems irrelevant to understanding the country's economic problems.

In this book we'll argue that the Egyptians in Tahrir Square, not most academics and commentators, have the right idea. In fact, Egypt is poor precisely because it has been ruled by a narrow elite that have organized society for their own benefit at the expense of the vast mass of people. Political power has been narrowly concentrated, and has been used to create great wealth for those who possess it, such as the $70 billion fortune apparently accumulated by ex-president Mubarak. The losers have been the Egyptian people, as they only too well understand.

We'll show that this interpretation of Egyptian poverty, the people's interpretation, turns out to provide a general explanation for why poor countries are poor. Whether it is North Korea, Sierra Leone, or Zimbabwe, we'll show that poor countries are poor for the same reason that Egypt is poor. Countries such as Great Britain and the United States became rich because their citizens overthrew the elites who controlled power and created a society where political rights were much more broadly distributed, where the government was accountable and responsive to citizens, and where the great mass of people could take advantage of economic opportunities. We'll show that to understand why there is such inequality in the world today we have to delve into the past and study the historical dynamics of societies. We'll see that the reason that Britain is richer than Egypt is because in 1688, Britain (or England, to be exact) had a revolution that transformed the politics and thus the economics of the nation. People fought for and won more political rights, and they used them to expand their economic opportunities. The result was a fundamentally different political and economic trajectory, culminating in the Industrial Revolution.

The Industrial Revolution and the technologies it unleashed didn't spread to Egypt, as that country was under the control of the Ottoman Empire, which treated Egypt in rather the same way as the Mubarak family later did. Ottoman rule in Egypt was overthrown by Napoleon Bonaparte in 1798, but the country then fell under the control of British colonialism, which had as little interest as the Ottomans in promoting Egypt's prosperity. Though the Egyptians shook off the Ottoman and British empires and, in 1952, overthrew their monarchy, these were not revolutions like that of 1688 in England, and rather than fundamentally transforming politics in Egypt, they brought to power another elite as disinterested in achieving prosperity for ordinary Egyptians as the Ottoman and British had been. In consequence, the basic structure of society did not change, and Egypt stayed poor.

In this book we'll study how these patterns reproduce themselves over time and why sometimes they are altered, as they were in England in 1688 and in France with the revolution of 1789. This will help us to understand if the situation in Egypt has changed today and whether the revolution that overthrew Mubarak will lead to a new set of institutions capable of bringing prosperity to ordinary Egyptians. Egypt has had revolutions in the past that did not change things, because those who mounted the revolutions simply took over the reins from those they'd deposed and re-created a similar system. It is indeed difficult for ordinary citizens to acquire real political power and change the way their society works. But it is possible, and we'll see how this happened in England, France, and the United States, and also in Japan, Botswana, and Brazil. Fundamentally it is a political transformation of this sort that is required for a poor society to become rich. There is evidence that this may be happening in Egypt. Reda Metwaly, another protestor in Tahrir Square, argued, "Now you see Muslims and Christians together, now you see old and young together, all wanting the same thing." We'll see that such a broad movement in society was a key part of what happened in these other political transformations. If we understand when and why such transitions occur, we will be in a better position to evaluate when we expect such movements to fail as they have often done in the past and when we may hope that they will succeed and improve the lives of millions.

1.

So Close and Yet So Different

The Economics of the Rio Grande

THE CITY OF NOGALES is cut in half by a fence. If you stand by it and look north, you'll see Nogales, Arizona, located in Santa Cruz County. The income of the average household there is about $30,000 a year. Most teenagers are in school, and the majority of the adults are high school graduates. Despite all the arguments people make about how deficient the U.S. health care system is, the population is relatively healthy, with high life expectancy by global standards. Many of the residents are above age sixty-five and have access to Medicare. It's just one of the many services the government provides that most take for granted, such as electricity, telephones, a sewage system, public health, a road network linking them to other cities in the area and to the rest of the United States, and, last but not least, law and order. The people of Nogales, Arizona, can go about their daily activities without fear for life or safety and not constantly afraid of theft, expropriation, or other things that might jeopardize their investments in their businesses and houses. Equally important, the residents of Nogales, Arizona, take it for granted that, with all its inefficiency and occasional corruption, the government is their agent. They can vote to replace their mayor, congressmen, and senators; they vote in the presidential elections that determine who will lead their country. Democracy is second nature to them.

Life south of the fence, just a few feet away, is rather different. While the residents of Nogales, Sonora, live in a relatively prosperous part of Mexico, the income of the average household there is about one-third that in Nogales, Arizona. Most adults in Nogales, Sonora, do not have a high school degree, and many teenagers are not in school. Mothers have to worry about high rates of infant mortality. Poor public health conditions mean it's no surprise that the residents of Nogales, Sonora, do not live as long as their northern neighbors. They also don't have access to many public amenities. Roads are in bad condition south of the fence. Law and order is in worse condition. Crime is high, and opening a business is a risky activity. Not only do you risk robbery, but getting all the permissions and greasing all the palms just to open is no easy endeavor. Residents of Nogales, Sonora, live with politicians' corruption and ineptitude every day.

In contrast to their northern neighbors, democracy is a very recent experience for them. Until the political reforms of 2000, Nogales, Sonora, just like the rest of Mexico, was under the corrupt control of the Institutional Revolutionary Party, or Partido Revolucionario Institucional (PRI).

How could the two halves of what is essentially the same city be so different? There is no difference in geography, climate, or the types of diseases prevalent in the area, since germs do not face any restrictions crossing back and forth between the United States and Mexico. Of course, health conditions are very different, but this has nothing to do with the disease environment; it is because the people south of the border live with inferior sanitary conditions and lack decent health care.

But perhaps the residents are very different. Could it be that the residents of Nogales, Arizona, are grandchildren of migrants from Europe, while those in the south are descendants of Aztecs? Not so. The backgrounds of people on both sides of the border are quite similar. After Mexico became independent from Spain in 1821, the area around "Los dos Nogales" was part of the Mexican state of Vieja California and remained so even after the Mexican-American War of 1846–1848. Indeed, it was only after the Gadsden Purchase of 1853 that the U.S. border was extended into this area. It was Lieutenant N. Michler who, while surveying the border, noted the presence of the "pretty little valley of Los Nogales." Here, on either side of the border, the two cities rose up. The inhabitants of Nogales, Arizona, and Nogales, Sonora, share ancestors, enjoy the same food and the same music, and, we would hazard to say, have the same "culture."

Of course, there is a very simple and obvious explanation for the differences between the two halves of Nogales that you've probably long since guessed: the very border that defines the two halves. Nogales, Arizona, is in the United States. Its inhabitants have access to the economic institutions of the United States, which enable them to choose their occupations freely, acquire schooling and skills, and encourage their employers to invest in the best technology, which leads to higher wages for them. They also have access to political institutions that allow them to take part in the democratic process, to elect their representatives, and replace them if they misbehave. In consequence, politicians provide the basic services (ranging from public health to roads to law and order) that the citizens demand. Those of Nogales, Sonora, are not so lucky. They live in a different world shaped by different institutions. These different institutions create very disparate incentives for the inhabitants of the two Nogaleses and for the entrepreneurs and businesses willing to invest there. These incentives created by the different institutions of the Nogaleses and the countries in which they are situated are the main reason for the differences in economic prosperity on the two sides of the border.

Why are the institutions of the United States so much more conducive to economic success than those of Mexico or, for that matter, the rest of Latin America? The answer to this question lies in the way the different societies formed during the early colonial period. An institutional divergence took place then, with implications lasting into the present day. To understand this divergence we must begin right at the foundation of the colonies in North and Latin America.

The Founding of Buenos Aires

Early in 1516 the Spanish navigator Juan Díaz de Solís sailed into a wide estuary on the Eastern Seaboard of South America. Wading ashore, de Solís claimed the land for Spain, naming the river the Río de la Plata, "River of Silver," since the local people possessed silver. The indigenous peoples on either side of the estuary—the Charrúas in what is now Uruguay, and the Querandí on the plains that were to be known as the Pampas in modern Argentina—regarded the new-comers with hostility. These locals were hunter-gatherers who lived in small groups without strong centralized political authorities. Indeed it was such a band of Charrúas who clubbed de Solís to death as he explored the new domains he had attemped to occupy for Spain.

In 1534 the Spanish, still optimistic, sent out a first mission of set-tlers from Spain under the leadership of Pedro de Mendoza. They founded a town on the site of Buenos Aires in the same year. It should have been an ideal place for Europeans. Buenos Aires, literally meaning "good airs," had a hospitable, temperate climate. Yet the first stay of the Spaniards there was short lived. They were not after good airs, but resources to extract and labor to coerce. The Charrúas and the Querandí were not obliging, however. They refused to provide food to the Spaniards, and refused to work when caught. They at-tacked the new settlement with their bows and arrows. The Spaniards grew hungry, since they had not anticipated having to provide food for themselves. Buenos Aires was not what they had dreamed of. The local people could not be forced into providing labor. The area had no silver or gold to exploit, and the silver that de Solís found had actually come all the way from the Inca state in the Andes, far to the west.

The Spaniards, while trying to survive, started sending out expedi-tions to find a new place that would offer greater riches and popula-tions easier to coerce. In 1537 one of these expeditions, under the leadership of Juan de Ayolas, penetrated up the Paraná River, search-ing for a route to the Incas. On its way, it made contact with the Guaraní, a sedentary people with an agricultural economy based on maize and cassava. De Ayolas immediately realized that the Guaraní were a completely different proposition from the Charrúas and the Querandí. After a brief conflict, the Spanish overcame Guaraní resis-tance and founded a town, Nuestra Señora de Santa María de la Asun-ción, which remains the capital of Paraguay today. The conquistadors married the Guaraní princesses and quickly set themselves up as a new aristocracy. They adapted the existing systems of forced labor and tribute of the Guaraní, with themselves at the helm. This was the kind of colony they wanted to set up, and within four years Buenos Aires was abandoned as all the Spaniards who'd settled there moved to the new town.

Buenos Aires, the "Paris of South America," a city of wide European-style boulevards based on the great agricultural wealth of the Pampas, was not resettled until 1580. The abandonment of Buenos Aires and the conquest of the Guaraní reveals the logic of European colonization of the Americas. Early Spanish and, as we will see, English colonists were not interested in tilling the soil themselves; they wanted others to do it for them, and they wanted riches, gold and silver, to plunder.

From Cajamarca . . .

The expeditions of de Solís, de Mendoza, and de Ayolas came in the wake of more famous ones that followed Christopher Columbus's sighting of one of the islands of the Bahamas on October 12, 1492. Spanish expansion and colonization of the Americas began in earnest with the invasion of Mexico by Hernán Cortés in 1519, the expedition of Francisco Pizarro to Peru a decade and a half later, and the expedition of Pedro de Mendoza to the Río de la Plata just two years after that. Over the next century, Spain conquered and colonized most of central, western, and southern South America, while Portugal claimed Brazil to the east.

The Spanish strategy of colonization was highly effective. First perfected by Cortés in Mexico, it was based on the observation that the best way for the Spanish to subdue opposition was to capture the indigenous leader. This strategy enabled the Spanish to claim the accumulated wealth of the leader and coerce the indigenous peoples to give tribute and food. The next step was setting themselves up as the new elite of the indigenous society and taking control of the existing methods of taxation, tribute, and, particularly, forced labor.

When Cortés and his men arrived at the great Aztec capital of Tenochtitlan on November 8, 1519, they were welcomed by

Moctezuma, the Aztec emperor, who had decided, in the face of much advice from his counselors, to welcome the Spaniards peacefully. What happened next is well described by the account compiled after 1545 by the Franciscan priest Bernardino de Sahagún in his famous Florentine Codices.

> [At] once they [the Spanish] firmly seized Moctezuma . . . then each of the guns shot off . . . Fear prevailed. It was as if everyone had swallowed his heart. Even before it had grown dark, there was terror, there was astonishment, there was apprehension, there was a stunning of the people.
>
> And when it dawned thereupon were proclaimed all the things which [the Spaniards] required: white tortillas, roasted turkey hens, eggs, fresh water, wood, firewood, charcoal . . . This had Moctezuma indeed commanded.
>
> And when the Spaniards were well settled, they thereupon inquired of Moctezuma as to all the city's treasure . . . with great zeal they sought gold. And Moctezuma thereupon went leading the Spaniards. They went surrounding him . . . each holding him, each grasping him.
>
> And when they reached the storehouse, a place called Teocalco, thereupon they brought forth all the brilliant things; the quetzal feather head fan, the devices, the shields, the golden discs . . . the golden nose crescents, the golden leg bands, the golden arm bands, the golden forehead bands.
>
> Thereupon was detached the gold . . . at once they ignited, set fire to . . . all the precious things. They all burned. And the gold the Spaniards formed into separate bars . . . And the Spanish walked everywhere . . . They took all, all that they saw which they saw to be good.
>
> Thereupon they went to Moctezuma's own store-

house . . . at the place called Totocalco . . . they brought forth [Moctezuma's] own property . . . precious things all; the necklaces with pendants, the arm bands with tufts of quetzal feathers, the golden arm bands, the bracelets, the golden bands with shells . . . and the turquoise diadem, the attribute of the ruler. They took it all.

The military conquest of the Aztecs was completed by 1521. Cortés, as governor of the province of New Spain, then began dividing up the most valuable resource, the indigenous population, through the institution of the *encomienda*. The *encomienda* had first appeared in fifteenth-century Spain as part of the reconquest of the south of the country from the Moors, Arabs who had settled during and after the eighth century. In the New World, it took on a much more pernicious form: it was a grant of indigenous peoples to a Spaniard, known as the *encomendero*. The indigenous peoples had to give the *encomendero* tribute and labor services, in exchange for which the *encomendero* was charged with converting them to Christianity.

A vivid early account of the workings of the *encomienda* has come down to us from Bartolomé de las Casas, a Dominican priest who formulated the earliest and one of the most devastating critiques of the Spanish colonial system. De las Casas arrived on the Spanish island of Hispaniola in 1502 with a fleet of ships led by the new governor, Nicolás de Ovando. He became increasingly disillusioned and disturbed by the cruel and exploitative treatment of the indigenous peoples he witnessed every day. In 1513 he took part as a chaplain in the Spanish conquest of Cuba, even being granted an *encomienda* for his service. However, he renounced the grant and began a long campaign to reform Spanish colonial institutions. His efforts culminated in his book *A Short Account of the Destruction of the Indies,* written in 1542, a withering attack on the barbarity of Spanish rule. On the *encomienda* he has this to say in the case of Nicaragua:

Each of the settlers took up residence in the town allotted to him (or encommended to him, as the legal phrase has it), put the inhabitants to work for him, stole their already scarce foodstuffs for himself and took over the lands owned and worked by the natives and on which they traditionally grew their own produce. The settler would treat the whole of the native population—dignitaries, old men, women and children—as members of his household and, as such, make them labor night and day in his own interests, without any rest whatsoever.

For the conquest of New Granada, modern Colombia, de las Casas reports the whole Spanish strategy in action:

To realize their long-term purpose of seizing all the available gold, the Spaniards employed their usual strategy of apportioning among themselves (or encommending, as they have it) the towns and their inhabitants . . . and then, as ever, treating them as common slaves. The man in overall command of the expedition seized the King of the whole territory for himself and held him prisoner for six or seven months, quite illicitly demanding more and more gold and emeralds from him. This King, one Bogotá, was so terrified that, in his anxiety to free himself from the clutches of his tormentors, he consented to the demand that he fill an entire house with gold and hand it over; to this end he sent his people off in search of gold, and bit by bit they brought it along with many precious stones. But still the house was not filled and the Spaniards eventually declared that they would put him to death for breaking his promise. The commander suggested they should bring the case before him, as a representative of the law, and when they did so, entering formal accusations against the King, he sentenced him to torture should he persist in not honoring the bargain. They tortured him with the strappado, put burning tallow on his belly, pinned both his legs to poles with iron hoops and his neck with another and then, with two men holding his hands, proceeded to burn the soles of his feet. From time to time, the commander would look in and repeat that they would torture him to death slowly unless he produced more gold, and this is what they did, the King eventually succumbing to the agonies they inflicted on him.

The strategy and institutions of conquest perfected in Mexico were eagerly adopted elsewhere in the Spanish Empire. Nowhere was this done more effectively than in Pizarro's conquest of Peru. As de las Casas begins his account:

> In 1531 another great villain journeyed with a number of men to the kingdom of Peru. He set out with every intention of imitating the strategy and tactics of his fellow adventurers in other parts of the New World.

Pizarro began on the coast near the Peruvian town of Tumbes and marched south. On November 15, 1532, he reached the mountain town of Cajamarca, where the Inca emperor Atahualpa was encamped with his army. The next day, Atahualpa, who had just vanquished his brother Huáscar in a contest over who would succeed their deceased father, Huayna Capac, came with his retinue to where the Spanish were camped. Atahualpa was irritated because news of atrocities that the Spanish had already committed, such as violating a temple of the Sun God Inti, had reached him. What transpired next is well known. The Spanish laid a trap and sprang it. They killed Atahualpa's guards and retainers, possibly as many as two thousand people, and captured the king. To gain his freedom, Atahualpa had to promise to fill one room with gold and two more of the same size with silver. He did this, but the Spanish, reneging on their promises, strangled him in July 1533. That November, the Spanish captured the Inca capital of Cusco, where the Incan aristocracy received the same treatment as Atahualpa, being imprisoned until they produced gold and silver.

When they did not satisfy Spanish demands, they were burned alive. The great artistic treasures of Cusco, such as the Temple of the Sun, had their gold stripped from them and melted down into ingots.

At this point the Spanish focused on the people of the Inca Empire. As in Mexico, citizens were divided into *encomiendas,* with one going to each of the conquistadors who had accompanied Pizarro. The *encomienda* was the main institution used for the control and organization of labor in the early colonial period, but it soon faced a vigorous contender. In 1545 a local named Diego Gualpa was searching for an indigenous shrine high in the Andes in what is today Bolivia. He was thrown to the ground by a sudden gust of wind and in front of him appeared a cache of silver ore. This was part of a vast mountain of silver, which the Spanish baptized El Cerro Rico, "The Rich Hill." Around it grew the city of Potosí, which at its height in 1650 had a population of 160,000 people, larger than Lisbon or Venice in this period.

To exploit the silver, the Spanish needed miners—a lot of miners. They sent a new viceroy, the chief Spanish colonial official, Francisco de Toledo, whose main mission was to solve the labor problem. De Toledo, arriving in Peru in 1569, first spent five years traveling around and investigating his new charge. He also commissioned a massive survey of the entire adult population. To find the labor he needed, de Toledo first moved almost the entire indigenous population, concentrating them in new towns called *reducciones*—literally "reductions"— which would facilitate the exploitation of labor by the Spanish Crown. Then he revived and adapted an Inca labor institution known as the *mita,* which, in the Incas' language, Quechua, means "a turn." Under their *mita* system, the Incas had used forced labor to run plantations designed to provide food for temples, the aristocracy, and the army. In return, the Inca elite provided famine relief and security. In de Toledo's hands the *mita,* especially the Potosí *mita,* was to become the largest and most onerous scheme of labor exploitation in the Spanish colonial period. De Toledo defined a huge catchment area, running from the middle of modern-day Peru and encompassing most of modern Bolivia. It covered about two hundred thousand square miles. In this area, one-seventh of the male inhabitants, newly arrived in their

Map 1: The Inca Empire, the Inca road network, and the
mining *mita* catchment area

reducciones, were required to work in the mines at Potosí. The Potosí
mita endured throughout the entire colonial period and was abolished only in 1825. Map 1 shows the catchment area of the *mita* su-
perimposed on the extent of the Inca empire at the time of the
Spanish conquest. It illustrates the extent to which the *mita* over-
lapped with the heartland of the empire, encompassing the capital
Cusco.

Remarkably, you still see the legacy of the *mita* in Peru today.
Take the differences between the provinces of Calca and nearby

Acomayo. There appears to be few differences among these provinces. Both are high in the mountains, and each is inhabited by the Quechua-speaking descendants of the Incas. Yet Acomayo is much poorer, with its inhabitants consuming about one-third less than those in Calca. The people know this. In Acomayo they ask intrepid foreigners, "Don't you know that the people here are poorer than the people over there in Calca? Why would you ever want to come here?" Intrepid because it is much harder to get to Acomayo from the regional capital of Cusco, ancient center of the Inca Empire, than it is to get to Calca. The road to Calca is surfaced, the one to Acomayo is in a terrible state of disrepair. To get beyond Acomayo, you need a horse or a mule. In Calca and Acomayo, people grow the same crops, but in Calca they sell them on the market for money. In Acomayo they grow food for their own subsistence. These inequalities, apparent to the eye and to the people who live there, can be understood in terms of the institutional differences between these departments—institutional differences with historical roots going back to de Toledo and his plan for effective exploitation of indigenous labor. The major historical difference between Acomayo and Calca is that Acomayo was in the catchment area of the Potosí *mita*. Calca was not.

In addition to the concentration of labor and the *mita,* de Toledo consolidated the *encomienda* into a head tax, a fixed sum payable by each adult male every year in silver. This was another scheme designed to force people into the labor market and reduce wages for Spanish landowners. Another institution, the *repartimiento de mercancias,* also became widespread during de Toledo's tenure. Derived from the Spanish verb *repartir,* to distribute, this *repartimiento,* literally "the distribution of goods," involved the forced sale of goods to locals at prices determined by Spaniards. Finally, de Toledo introduced the *trajin*—meaning, literally, "the burden"—which used the indigenous people to carry heavy loads of goods, such as wine or coca leaves or textiles, as a substitute for pack animals, for the business ventures of the Spanish elite.

Throughout the Spanish colonial world in the Americas, similar institutions and social structures emerged. After an initial phase of looting, and gold and silver lust, the Spanish created a web of institutions designed to exploit the indigenous peoples. The full gamut of *encomienda, mita, repartimiento,* and *trajin* was designed to force indigenous people's living standards down to a subsistence level and thus extract all income in excess of this for Spaniards. This was achieved by expropriating their land, forcing them to work, offering low wages for labor services, imposing high taxes, and charging high prices for goods that were not even voluntarily bought. Though these institutions generated a lot of wealth for the Spanish Crown and made the conquistadors and their descendants very rich, they also turned Latin America into the most unequal continent in the world and sapped much of its economic potential.

. . . TO JAMESTOWN

As the Spanish began their conquest of the Americas in the 1490s, England was a minor European power recovering from the devastating effects of a civil war, the Wars of the Roses. She was in no state to take advantage of the scramble for loot and gold and the opportunity to exploit the indigenous peoples of the Americas. Nearly one hundred years later, in 1588, the lucky rout of the Spanish Armada, an attempt by King Philip II of Spain to invade England, sent political shockwaves around Europe. Fortunate though England's victory was, it was also a sign of growing English assertiveness on the seas that would enable them to finally take part in the quest for colonial empire.

It is thus no coincidence that the English began their colonization of North America at exactly the same time. But they were already latecomers. They chose North America not because it was attractive, but because it was all that was available. The "desirable" parts of the Americas, where the indigenous population to exploit was plentiful and where the gold and silver mines were located, had already been occupied. The English got the leftovers. When the eighteenth-century English writer and agriculturalist Arthur Young discussed where profitable "staple products," by which he meant exportable agricultural goods, were produced, he noted:

It appears upon the whole, that the staple productions of our colonies decrease in value in proportion to their distance from the sun. In the West Indies, which are the hottest of all, they make to the amount of 8l. 12s. 1d. per head. In the southern continental ones, to the amount of 5l. 10s. In the central ones, to the amount of 9s. 6 1/2d. In the northern settlements, to that of 2s. 6d. This scale surely suggests a most important lesson—to avoid colonizing in northern latitudes.

The first English attempt to plant a colony, at Roanoke, in North Carolina, between 1585 and 1587, was a complete failure. In 1607 they tried again. Shortly before the end of 1606, three vessels, *Susan Constant, Godspeed,* and *Discovery,* under the command of Captain Christopher Newport, set off for Virginia. The colonists, under the auspices of the Virginia Company, sailed into Chesapeake Bay and up a river they named the James, after the ruling English monarch, James I. On May 14, 1607, they founded the settlement of Jamestown.

Though the settlers on board the ships owned by the Virginia Company were English, they had a model of colonization heavily influenced by the template set up by Cortés, Pizarro, and de Toledo. Their first plan was to capture the local chief and use him as a way to get provisions and to coerce the population into producing food and wealth for them.

When they first landed in Jamestown, the English colonists did not know that they were within the territory claimed by the Powhatan Confederacy, a coalition of some thirty polities owing allegiance to a king called Wahunsunacock. Wahunsunacock's capital was at the town of Werowocomoco, a mere twenty miles from Jamestown. The plan of the colonists was to learn more about the lay of the land. If the locals could not be induced to provide food and labor, the colonists might at least be able to trade with them. The notion that the settlers themselves would work and grow their own food seems not to have crossed their minds. That is not what conquerors of the New World did.

Wahunsunacock quickly became aware of the colonists' presence and viewed their intentions with great suspicion. He was in charge of what for North America was quite a large empire. But he had many enemies and lacked the overwhelming centralized political control of the Incas. Wahunsunacock decided to see what the intentions of the English were, initially sending messengers saying that he desired friendly relations with them.

As the winter of 1607 closed in, the settlers in Jamestown began to run low on food, and the appointed leader of the colony's ruling council, Edward Marie Wingfield, dithered indecisively. The situation was rescued by Captain John Smith. Smith, whose writings provide one of our main sources of information about the early development of the colony, was a larger-than-life character. Born in England, in rural Lincolnshire, he disregarded his father's desires for him to go into business and instead became a soldier of fortune. He first fought with English armies in the Netherlands, after which he joined Austrian forces serving in Hungary fighting against the armies of the Ottoman Empire. Captured in Romania, he was sold as a slave and put to work as a field hand. He managed one day to overcome his master and, stealing his clothes and his horse, escape back into Austrian territory. Smith had got himself into trouble on the voyage to Virginia and was imprisoned on the *Susan Constant* for mutiny after defying the orders of Wingfield. When the ships reached the New World, the plan was to put him on trial. To the immense horror of Wingfield, Newport, and other elite colonists, however, when they opened their sealed orders, they discovered that the Virginia Company had nominated Smith to be a member of the ruling council that was to govern Jamestown.

With Newport sailing back to England for supplies and more colonists, and Wingfield uncertain about what to do, it was Smith who saved the colony. He initiated a series of trading missions that secured vital food supplies. On one of these he was captured by Opechancanough, one of Wahunsunacock's younger brothers, and was brought before the king at Werowocomoco. He was the first Englishman to meet Wahunsunacock, and it was at this initial meeting that according to some accounts Smith's life was saved only at the intervention of Wahunsunacock's young daughter Pocahontas. Freed on January 2,

1608, Smith returned to Jamestown, which was still perilously low on food, until the timely return of Newport from England later on the same day.

The colonists of Jamestown learned little from this initial experience. As 1608 proceeded, they continued their quest for gold and precious metals. They still did not seem to understand that to survive, they could not rely on the locals to feed them through either coercion or trade. It was Smith who was the first to realize that the model of colonization that had worked so well for Cortés and Pizarro simply would not work in North America. The underlying circumstances were just too different. Smith noted that, unlike the Aztecs and Incas, the peoples of Virginia did not have gold. Indeed, he noted in his diary, "Victuals you must know is all their wealth." Anas Todkill, one of the early settlers who left an extensive diary, expressed well the frustrations of Smith and the few others on which this recognition dawned:

> "There was no talke, no hope, no worke, but dig gold, refine gold, load gold."

When Newport sailed for England in April 1608 he took a cargo of pyrite, fool's gold. He returned at the end of September with orders from the Virginia Company to take firmer control over the locals. Their plan was to crown Wahunsunacock, hoping this would render him subservient to the English king James I. They invited him to Jamestown, but Wahunsunacock, still deeply suspicious of the colonists, had no intention of risking capture. John Smith recorded Wahunsunacock's reply: "If your King have sent me presents, I also am a King, and this is my land . . . Your father is to come to me, not I to him, nor yet to your fort, neither will I bite at such a bait."

If Wahunsunacock would not "bite at such a bait," Newport and Smith would have to go to Werowocomoco to undertake the coronation. The whole event appears to have been a complete fiasco, with the only thing coming out of it a resolve on the part of Wahunsunacock that it was time to get rid of the colony. He imposed a trade embargo. Jamestown could no longer trade for supplies. Wahunsunacock would starve them out.

Newport set sail once more for England, in December 1608. He took with him a letter written by Smith pleading with the directors of the Virginia Company to change the way they thought about the colony. There was no possibility of a get-rich-quick exploitation of Virginia along the lines of Mexico and Peru. There were no gold or precious metals, and the indigenous people could not be forced to work or provide food. Smith realized that if there were going to be a viable colony, it was the colonists who would have to work. He therefore pleaded with the directors to send the right sort of people: "When you send againe I entreat you rather to send some thirty carpenters, husbandmen, gardeners, fishermen, blacksmiths, masons, and diggers up of trees, roots, well provided, then a thousand of such as we have."

Smith did not want any more useless goldsmiths. Once more Jamestown survived only because of his resourcefulness. He managed to cajole and bully local indigenous groups to trade with him, and when they wouldn't, he took what he could. Back in the settlement, Smith was completely in charge and imposed the rule that "he that will not worke shall not eat." Jamestown survived a second winter.

The Virginia Company was intended to be a moneymaking enterprise, and after two disastrous years, there was no whiff of profit. The directors of the company decided that they needed a new model of governance, replacing the ruling council with a single governor. The first man appointed to this position was Sir Thomas Gates. Heeding some aspects of Smith's warning, the company realized that they had to try something new. This realization was driven home by the events of the winter of 1609/1610—the so-called "starving time." The new mode of governance left no room for Smith, who, disgruntled, returned to England in the autumn of 1609. Without his resourcefulness, and with Wahunsunacock throttling the food supply, the colonists in Jamestown perished. Of the five hundred who entered the winter, only sixty were alive by March. The situation was so desperate that they resorted to cannibalism.

The "something new" that was imposed on the colony by Gates and his deputy, Sir Thomas Dale, was a work regime of draconian severity for English settlers—though not of course for the elite run-

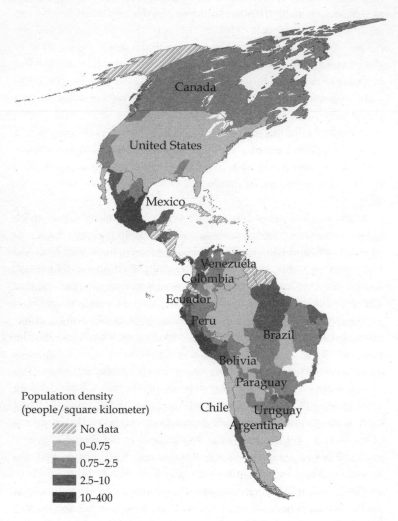

Map 2: Population density in 1500 in the Americas

ning the colony. It was Dale who propagated the "Lawes Divine, Morall and Martiall." This included the clauses

> No man or woman shall run away from the colony to the Indians, upon pain of death.
>
> Anyone who robs a garden, public or private, or a vineyard, or who steals ears of corn shall be punished with death.
>
> No member of the colony will sell or give any commodity of this country to a captain, mariner, master or sailor to transport out of the colony, for his own private uses, upon pain of death.

If the indigenous peoples could not be exploited, reasoned the Virginia Company, perhaps the colonists could. The new model of colonial development entailed the Virginia Company owning all the land. Men were housed in barracks, and given company-determined rations. Work gangs were chosen, each one overseen by an agent of the company. It was close to martial law, with execution as the punishment of first resort. As part of the new institutions for the colony, the first clause just given is significant. The company threatened with death those who ran away. Given the new work regime, running away to live with the locals became more and more of an attractive option for the colonists who had to do the work. Also available, given the low density of even indigenous populations in Virginia at that time, was the prospect of going it alone on the frontier beyond the control of the Virginia Company. The power of the company in the face of these options was limited. It could not coerce the English settlers into hard work at subsistence rations.

Map 2 (opposite) shows an estimate of the population density of different regions of the Americas at the time on the Spanish conquest. The population density of the United States, outside of a few pockets, was at most three-quarters of a person per square kilometre. In central Mexico or Andean Peru, the population density was as high as four hundred people per square kilometre, more than five hundred times higher. What was possible in Mexico or Peru was not feasible in Virginia.

It took the Virginia Company some time to recognize that its initial model of colonization did not work in Virginia, and it took a while, too, for the failure of the "Lawes Divine, Morall and Martiall" to sink in. Starting in 1618, a dramatically new strategy was adopted. Since it was possible to coerce neither the locals nor the settlers, the only alternative was to give the settlers incentives. In 1618 the company began the "headright system," which gave each male settler fifty acres of land and fifty more acres for each member of his family and for all servants that a family could bring to Virginia. Settlers were given their houses and freed from their contracts, and in 1619 a General Assembly was introduced that effectively gave all adult men a say in the laws and institutions governing the colony. It was the start of democracy in the United States.

It took the Virginia Company twelve years to learn its first lesson that what had worked for the Spanish in Mexico and in Central and South America would not work in the north. The rest of the seventeenth century saw a long series of struggles over the second lesson: that the only option for an economically viable colony was to create institutions that gave the colonists incentives to invest and to work hard.

As North America developed, English elites tried time and time again to set up institutions that would heavily restrict the economic and political rights for all but a privileged few of the inhabitants of the colony, just as the Spanish did. Yet in each case this model broke down, as it had in Virginia.

One of the most ambitious attempts began soon after the change in strategy of the Virginia Company. In 1632 ten million acres of land on the upper Chesapeake Bay were granted by the English king Charles I to Cecilius Calvert, Lord Baltimore. The Charter of Maryland gave Lord Baltimore complete freedom to create a government along any lines he wished, with clause VII noting that Baltimore had "for the good and happy Government of the said Province, free, full, and absolute Power, by the Tenor of these Presents, to Ordain, Make, and Enact Laws, of what Kind soever."

Baltimore drew up a detailed plan for creating a manorial society, a North American variant of an idealized version of seventeenth-century rural England. It entailed dividing the land into plots of thousands of acres, which would be run by lords. The lords would recruit tenants, who would work the lands and pay rents to the privileged elite controlling the land. Another similar attempt was made later in 1663, with the founding of Carolina by eight proprietors, including Sir Anthony Ashley-Cooper. Ashley-Cooper, along with his secretary, the great English philosopher John Locke, formulated the Fundamental Constitutions of Carolina. This document, like the Charter of Maryland before it, provided a blueprint for an elitist, hierarchical society based on control by a landed elite. The preamble noted that "the government of this province may be made most agreeable to the monarchy under which we live and of which this province is a part; and that we may avoid erecting a numerous democracy."

The clauses of the Fundamental Constitutions laid out a rigid social structure. At the bottom were the "leet-men," with clause 23 noting, "All the children of leet-men shall be leet-men, and so to all generations." Above the leet-men, who had no political power, were the landgraves and caziques, who were to form the aristocracy. Landgraves were to be allocated forty-eight thousand acres of land each, and caziques twenty-four thousand acres. There was to be a parliament, in which landgraves and caziques were represented, but it would be permitted to debate only those measures that had previously been approved by the eight proprietors.

Just as the attempt to impose draconian rule in Virginia failed, so did the plans for the same type of institutions in Maryland and Carolina. The reasons were similar. In all cases it proved to be impossible to force settlers into a rigid hierarchical society, because there were simply too many options open to them in the New World. Instead, they had to be provided with incentives for them to want to work. And soon they were demanding more economic freedom and further political rights. In Maryland, too, settlers insisted on getting their own land, and they forced Lord Baltimore into creating an assembly. In 1691 the assembly induced the king to declare Maryland a Crown colony, thus removing the political privileges of Baltimore and his great lords. A similar protracted struggle took place in the Carolinas, again with the proprietors losing. South Carolina became a royal colony in 1729.

By the 1720s, all the thirteen colonies of what was to become the United States had similar structures of government. In all cases there was a governor, and an assembly based on a franchise of male property holders. They were not democracies; women, slaves, and the propertyless could not vote. But political rights were very broad compared with contemporary societies elsewhere. It was these assemblies and their leaders that coalesced to form the First Continental Congress in 1774, the prelude to the independence of the United States. The assemblies believed they had the right to determine both their own membership and the right to taxation. This, as we know, created problems for the English colonial government.

A TALE OF TWO CONSTITUTIONS

It should now be apparent that it is not a coincidence that the United States, and not Mexico, adopted and enforced a constitution that espoused democratic principles, created limitations on the use of political power, and distributed that power broadly in society. The document that the delegates sat down to write in Philadelphia in May 1787 was the outcome of a long process initiated by the formation of the General Assembly in Jamestown in 1619.

The contrast between the constitutional process that took place at the time of the independence of the United States and the one that took place a little afterward in Mexico is stark. In February 1808, Napoleon Bonaparte's French armies invaded Spain. By May they had taken Madrid, the Spanish capital. By September the Spanish king Ferdinand had been captured and had abdicated. A national junta, the Junta Central, took his place, taking the torch in the fight against the French. The Junta met first at Aranjuez, but retreated south in the face of the French armies. Finally it reached the port of Cádiz, which, though besieged by Napoleonic forces, held out. Here the Junta formed a parliament, called the Cortes. In 1812 the Cortes produced what became known as the Cádiz Constitution, which called for the introduction of a constitutional monarchy based on notions of popular sovereignty. It also called for the end of special privileges and the introduction of equality before the law. These demands were all anathema to the elites of South America, who were still ruling an institutional environment shaped by the *encomienda,* forced labor, and absolute power vested in them and the colonial state.

The collapse of the Spanish state with the Napoleonic invasion created a constitutional crisis throughout colonial Latin America. There was much dispute about whether to recognize the authority of the Junta Central, and in response, many Latin Americans began to form their own juntas. It was only a matter of time before they began to sense the possibility of becoming truly independent from Spain. The first declaration of independence took place in La Paz, Bolivia, in 1809, though it was quickly crushed by Spanish troops sent from Peru. In Mexico the political attitudes of the elite had been shaped by the 1810 Hidalgo Revolt, led by a priest, Father Miguel Hidalgo. When Hidalgo's army sacked Guanajuato on September 23, they killed the intendant, the senior colonial official, and then started indiscriminately to kill white people. It was more like class or even ethnic warfare than an independence movement, and it united all the elites in opposition. If independence allowed popular participation in politics, the local elites, not just Spaniards, were against it. Consequentially, Mexican elites viewed the Cádiz Constitution, which opened the way to popular participation, with extreme skepticism; they would never recognize its legitimacy.

In 1815, as Napoleon's European empire collapsed, King Ferdinand VII returned to power and the Cádiz Constitution was abrogated. As the Spanish Crown began trying to reclaim its American colonies, it did not face a problem with loyalist Mexico. Yet, in 1820, a Spanish army that had assembled in Cádiz to sail to the Americas to help restore Spanish authority mutinied against Ferdinand VII. They were soon joined by army units throughout the country, and Ferdinand was forced to restore the Cádiz Constitution and recall the Cortes. This Cortes was even more radical than the one that had written the Cádiz Constitution, and it proposed abolishing all forms of labor coercion. It also attacked special privileges—for example, the right of the military to be tried for crimes in their own courts. Faced finally with the imposition of this document in Mexico, the elites there decided that it was better to go it alone and declare independence.

This independence movement was led by Augustín de Iturbide, who had been an officer in the Spanish army. On February 24, 1821, he published the Plan de Iguala, his vision for an independent Mexico. The plan featured a constitutional monarchy with a Mexican emperor, and removed the provisions of the Cádiz Constitution that Mexican elites found so threatening to their status and privileges. It received instantaneous support, and Spain quickly realized that it could not stop the inevitable. But Iturbide did not just organize Mexican secession. Recognizing the power vacuum, he quickly took advantage of his military backing to have himself declared emperor, a position that the great leader of South American independence Simón Bolivar described as "by the grace of God and of bayonets." Iturbide was not constrained by the same political institutions that constrained presidents of the United States; he quickly made himself a dictator, and by October 1822 he had dismissed the constitutionally sanctioned congress and replaced it with a junta of his choosing. Though Iturbide did not last long, this pattern of events was to be repeated time and time again in nineteenth-century Mexico.

The Constitution of the United States did not create a democracy by modern standards. Who could vote in elections was left up to the individual states to determine. While northern states quickly conceded the vote to all white men irrespective of how much income they earned or property they owned, southern states did so only gradually. No state enfranchised women or slaves, and as property and wealth restrictions were lifted on white men, racial franchises explicitly disenfranchising black men were introduced. Slavery, of course, was deemed constitutional when the Constitution of the United States was written in Philadelphia, and the most sordid negotiation concerned the division of the seats in the House of Representatives among the states. These were to be allocated on the basis of a state's population, but the congressional representatives of southern states then demanded that the slaves be counted. Northerners objected. The compromise was that in apportioning seats to the House of Representatives, a slave would count as three-fifths of a free person. The conflicts between the North and South of the United States were repressed during the constitutional process as the three-fifths rule and other compromises were worked out. New fixes were added over time—for example, the Missouri Compromise, an arrangement where one proslavery and one antislavery state were always added to the union together, to keep the balance in the Senate between those for and those against slavery. These fudges kept the political institutions of the United States working peacefully until the Civil War finally resolved the conflicts in favor of the North.

The Civil War was bloody and destructive. But both before and after it there were ample economic opportunities for a large fraction of the population, especially in the northern and western United States. The situation in Mexico was very different. If the United States experienced five years of political instability between 1860 and 1865, Mexico experienced almost nonstop instability for the first fifty years of independence. This is best illustrated via the career of Antonio López de Santa Ana.

Santa Ana, son of a colonial official in Veracruz, came to prominence as a soldier fighting for the Spanish in the independence wars. In 1821 he switched sides with Iturbide and never looked back. He became president of Mexico for the first time in May of 1833, though he exercised power for less than a month, preferring to let Valentín Gómez Farías act as president. Gómez Farías's presidency lasted fifteen days, after which Santa Ana retook power. This was as brief as his first spell, however, and he was again replaced by Gómez Farías, in early July. Santa Ana and Gómez Farías continued this dance until the middle of 1835, when Santa Ana was replaced by Miguel Barragán. But Santa Ana was not a quitter. He was back as president in 1839, 1841, 1844, 1847, and, finally, between 1853 and 1855. In all, he was president eleven times, during which he presided over the loss of the Alamo and Texas and the disastrous Mexican-American War, which led to the loss of what became New Mexico and Arizona. Between 1824 and 1867 there were fifty-two presidents in Mexico, few of whom assumed power according to any constitutionally sanctioned procedure.

The consequence of this unprecedented political instability for economic institutions and incentives should be obvious. Such instability led to highly insecure property rights. It also led to a severe weakening of the Mexican state, which now had little authority and little ability to raise taxes or provide public services. Indeed, even though Santa Ana was president in Mexico, large parts of the country were not under his control, which enabled the annexation of Texas by the United States. In addition, as we just saw, the motivation behind the Mexican declaration of independence was to protect the set of economic institutions developed during the colonial period, which had made Mexico, in the words of the great German explorer and geographer of Latin America Alexander von Humbolt, "the country of inequality." These institutions, by basing the society on the exploitation of indigenous people and the creation of monopolies, blocked the economic incentives and initiatives of the great mass of the population. As the United States began to experience the Industrial Revolution in the first half of the nineteenth century, Mexico got poorer.

HAVING AN IDEA, STARTING A FIRM, AND GETTING A LOAN

The Industrial Revolution started in England. Its first success was to revolutionize the production of cotton cloth using new machines powered by water wheels and later by steam engines. Mechanization of cotton production massively increased the productivity of workers in, first, textiles and, subsequently, other industries. The engine of technological breakthroughs throughout the economy was innovation, spearheaded by new entrepreneurs and businessmen eager to apply their new ideas. This initial flowering soon spread across the North Atlantic to the United States. People saw the great economic opportunities available in adopting the new technologies developed in England. They were also inspired to develop their own inventions.

We can try to understand the nature of these inventions by looking at who was granted patents. The patent system, which protects property rights in ideas, was systematized in the Statute of Monopolies legislated by the English Parliament in 1623, partially as an attempt to stop the king from arbitrarily granting "letters patent" to whomever he wanted—effectively granting exclusive rights to undertake certain activities or businesses. The striking thing about the evidence on patenting in the United States is that people who were granted patents came from all sorts of backgrounds and all walks of life, not just the rich and the elite. Many made fortunes based on their patents. Take Thomas Edison, the inventor of the phonogram and the lightbulb and the founder of General Electric, still one of the world's largest companies. Edison was the last of seven children. His father, Samuel Edison, followed many occupations, from splitting shingles for roofs to tailoring to keeping a tavern. Thomas had little formal schooling but was homeschooled by his mother.

Between 1820 and 1845, only 19 percent of patentees in the United States had parents who were professionals or were from recognizable major landowning families. During the same period, 40 percent of those who took out patents had only primary schooling or less, just like Edison. Moreover, they often exploited their patent by starting a firm, again like Edison. Just as the United States in the nineteenth century was more democratic politically than almost any other nation in the world at the time, it was also more democratic than others when it came to innovation. This was critical to its path to becoming the most economically innovative nation in the world.

If you were poor with a good idea, it was one thing to take out a patent, which was not so expensive, after all. It was another thing entirely to use that patent to make money. One way, of course, was to sell the patent to someone else. This is what Edison did early on, to raise some capital, when he sold his Quadruplex telegraph to Western Union for $10,000. But selling patents was a good idea only for someone like Edison, who had ideas faster than he could put them to practice. (He had a world-record 1,093 patents issued to him in the United States and 1,500 worldwide.) The real way to make money from a patent was to start your own business. But to start a business, you need capital, and you need banks to lend the capital to you.

Inventors in the United States were once again fortunate. During the nineteenth century there was a rapid expansion of financial intermediation and banking that was a crucial facilitator of the rapid growth and industrialization that the economy experienced. While in 1818 there were 338 banks in operation in the United States, with total assets of $160 million, by 1914 there were 27,864 banks, with total assets of $27.3 billion. Potential inventors in the United States had ready access to capital to start their businesses. Moreover, the intense competition among banks and financial institutions in the United States meant that this capital was available at fairly low interest rates.

The same was not true in Mexico. In fact, in 1910, the year in which the Mexican Revolution started, there were only forty-two banks in Mexico, and two of these controlled 60 percent of total banking assets. Unlike in the United States, where competition was fierce, there was practically no competition among Mexican banks. This lack of competition meant that the banks were able to charge their customers very high interest rates, and typically confined lending to the privileged and the already wealthy, who would then use their access to credit to increase their grip over the various sectors of the economy.

The form that the Mexican banking industry took in the nineteenth and twentieth centuries was a direct result of the postindependence political institutions of the country. The chaos of the Santa Ana era was followed by an abortive attempt by the French government of Emperor Napoleon III to create a colonial regime in Mexico under Emperor Maximilian between 1864 and 1867. The French were expelled, and a new constitution was written. But the government formed first by Benito Juárez and, after his death, by Sebastián Lerdo de Tejada was soon challenged by a young military man named Porfirio Díaz. Díaz had been a victorious general in the war against the French and had developed aspirations of power. He formed a rebel army and, in November of 1876, defeated the army of the government at the Battle of Tecoac. In May of the next year, he had himself elected president. He went on to rule Mexico in a more or less unbroken and increasingly authoritarian fashion until his overthrow at the outbreak of the revolution thirty-four years later.

Like Iturbide and Santa Ana before him, Díaz started life as a military commander. Such a career path into politics was certainly known in the United States. The first president of the United States, George Washington, was also a successful general in the War of Independence. Ulysses S. Grant, one of the victorious Union generals of the Civil War, became president in 1869, and Dwight D. Eisenhower, the supreme commander of the Allied Forces in Europe during the Second World War, was president of the United States between 1953 and 1961. Unlike Iturbide, Santa Ana, and Díaz, however, none of these military men used force to get into power. Nor did they use force to avoid having to relinquish power. They abided by the Constitution. Though Mexico had constitutions in the nineteenth century, they put few constraints on what Iturbide, Santa Ana, and Díaz could do. These men could be removed from power only the same way they had attained it: by the use of force.

Díaz violated people's property rights, facilitating the expropriation of vast amounts of land, and he granted monopolies and favors to his supporters in all lines of business, including banking. There was nothing new about this behavior. This is exactly what Spanish conquistadors had done, and what Santa Ana did in their footsteps.

The reason that the United States had a banking industry that was radically better for the economic prosperity of the country had nothing to do with differences in the motivation of those who owned the banks. Indeed, the profit motive, which underpinned the monopolistic nature of the banking industry in Mexico, was present in the United States, too. But this profit motive was channeled differently because of the radically different U.S. institutions. The bankers faced different economic institutions, institutions that subjected them to much greater competition. And this was largely because the politicians who wrote the rules for the bankers faced very different incentives themselves, forged by different political institutions. Indeed, in the late eighteenth century, shortly after the Constitution of the United States came into operation, a banking system looking similar to that which subsequently dominated Mexico began to emerge. Politicians tried to set up state banking monopolies, which they could give to their friends and partners in exchange for part of the monopoly profits. The banks also quickly got into the business of lending money to the politicians who regulated them, just as in Mexico. But this situation was not sustainable in the United States, because the politicians who attempted to create these banking monopolies, unlike their Mexican counterparts, were subject to election and reelection. Creating banking monopolies and giving loans to politicians is good business for politicians, if they can get away with it. It is not particularly good for the citizens, however. Unlike in Mexico, in the United States the citizens could keep politicians in check and get rid of ones who would use their offices to enrich themselves or create monopolies for their cronies. In consequence, the banking monopolies crumbled. The broad distribution of political rights in the United States, especially when compared to Mexico, guaranteed equal access to finance and loans. This in turn ensured that those with ideas and inventions could benefit from them.

PATH-DEPENDENT CHANGE

The world was changing in the 1870s and '80s. Latin America was no exception. The institutions that Porfirio Díaz established were not identical to those of Santa Ana or the Spanish colonial state. The world economy boomed in the second half of the nineteenth century, and innovations in transportation such as the steamship and the railway led to a huge expansion of international trade. This wave of globalization meant that resource-rich countries such as Mexico—or, more appropriately, the elites in such countries—could enrich themselves by exporting raw materials and natural resources to industrializing North America or Western Europe. Díaz and his cronies thus found themselves in a different and rapidly evolving world. They realized that Mexico had to change, too. But this didn't mean uprooting the colonial institutions and replacing them with institutions similar to those in the United States. Instead, theirs was "path-dependent" change leading only to the next stage of the institutions that had already made much of Latin America poor and unequal.

Globalization made the large open spaces of the Americas, its "open frontiers," valuable. Often these frontiers were only mythically open, since they were inhabited by indigenous peoples who were brutally dispossessed. All the same, the scramble for this newly valuable resource was one of the defining processes of the Americas in the second half of the nineteenth century. The sudden opening of this valuable frontier led not to parallel processes in the United States and Latin America, but to a further divergence, shaped by the existing institutional differences, especially those concerning who had access to the land. In the United States a long series of legislative acts, ranging from the Land Ordinance of 1785 to the Homestead Act of 1862, gave broad access to frontier lands. Though indigenous peoples had been sidelined, this created an egalitarian and economically dynamic frontier. In most Latin American countries, however, the political institutions there created a very different outcome. Frontier lands were allocated to the politically powerful and those with wealth and contacts, making such people even more powerful.

Díaz also started to dismantle many of the specific colonial institutional legacies preventing international trade, which he anticipated could greatly enrich him and his supporters. His model, however, continued to be not the type of economic development he saw north of the Rio Grande but that of Cortés, Pizarro, and de Toledo, where the elite would make huge fortunes while the rest were excluded. When the elite invested, the economy would grow a little, but such economic growth was always going to be disappointing. It also came at the expense of those lacking rights in this new order, such as the Yaqui people of Sonora, in the hinterland of Nogales. Between 1900 and 1910, possibly thirty thousand Yaqui were deported, essentially enslaved, and sent to work in the henequen plantations of Yucatán. (The fibers of the henequen plant were a valuable export, since they could be used to make rope and twine.)

The persistence into the twentieth century of a specific institutional pattern inimical to growth in Mexico and Latin America is well illustrated by the fact that, just as in the nineteenth century, the pattern generated economic stagnation and political instability, civil wars and coups, as groups struggled for the benefits of power. Díaz finally lost power to revolutionary forces in 1910. The Mexican Revolution was followed by others in Bolivia in 1952, Cuba in 1959, and Nicaragua in 1979. Meanwhile, sustained civil wars raged in Colombia, El Salvador, Guatemala, and Peru. Expropriation or the threat of expropriation of assets continued apace, with mass agrarian reforms (or attempted reforms) in Bolivia, Brazil, Chile, Colombia, Guatemala, Peru, and Venezuela. Revolutions, expropriations, and political instability came along with military governments and various types of dictatorships. Though there was also a gradual drift toward greater political rights, it was only in the 1990s that most Latin American countries became democracies, and even then they remained mired in instability.

This instability was accompanied by mass repression and murder. The 1991 National Commission for Truth and Reconciliation Report in Chile determined that 2,279 persons were killed for political reasons during the Pinochet dictatorship between 1973 and 1990. Possibly 50,000 were imprisoned and tortured, and hundreds of thousands of people were fired from their jobs. The Guatemalan Commission for Historical Clarification Report in 1999 identified a total of 42,275 named victims, though others have claimed that as many as 200,000 were murdered in Guatemala between 1962 and 1996, 70,000 during the regime of General Efrain Ríos Montt, who was able to commit these crimes with such impunity that he could run for president in 2003; fortunately he did not win. The National Commission on the Disappearance of Persons in Argentina put the number of people murdered by the military there at 9,000 persons from 1976 to 1983, although it noted that the actual number could be higher. (Estimates by human rights organizations usually place it at 30,000.)

MAKING A BILLION OR TWO

The enduring implications of the organization of colonial society and those societies' institutional legacies shape the modern differences between the United States and Mexico, and thus the two parts of Nogales. The contrast between how Bill Gates and Carlos Slim became the two richest men in the world—Warren Buffett is also a contender—illustrates the forces at work. The rise of Gates and Microsoft is well known, but Gates's status as the world's richest person and the founder of one of the most technologically innovative companies did not stop the U.S. Department of Justice from filing civil actions against the Microsoft Corporation on May 8, 1998, claiming that Microsoft had abused monopoly power. Particularly at issue was the way that Microsoft had tied its Web browser, Internet Explorer, to its Windows operating system. The government had been keeping an eye on Gates for quite some time, and as early as 1991, the Federal Trade Commission had launched an inquiry into whether Microsoft was abusing its monopoly on PC operating systems. In November 2001, Microsoft reached a deal with the Justice Department. It had its wings clipped, even if the penalties were less than many demanded.

In Mexico, Carlos Slim did not make his money by innovation. Initially he excelled in stock market deals, and in buying and revamping unprofitable firms. His major coup was the acquisition of Telmex, the Mexican telecommunications monopoly that was privatized by President Carlos Salinas in 1990. The government announced its intention to sell 51 percent of the voting stock (20.4 percent of total stock) in the company in September 1989 and received bids in November 1990. Even though Slim did not put in the highest bid, a consortium led by his Grupo Carso won the auction. Instead of paying for the shares right away, Slim managed to delay payment, using the dividends of Telmex itself to pay for the stock. What was once a public monopoly now became Slim's monopoly, and it was hugely profitable.

The economic institutions that made Carlos Slim who he is are very different from those in the United States. If you're a Mexican entrepreneur, entry barriers will play a crucial role at every stage of your career. These barriers include expensive licenses you have to obtain, red tape you have to cut through, politicians and incumbents who will stand in your way, and the difficulty of getting funding from a financial sector often in cahoots with the incumbents you're trying to compete against. These barriers can be either insurmountable, keeping you out of lucrative areas, or your greatest friend, keeping your competitors at bay. The difference between the two scenarios is of course whom you know and whom you can influence—and yes, whom you can bribe. Carlos Slim, a talented, ambitious man from a relatively modest background of Lebanese immigrants, has been a master at obtaining exclusive contracts; he managed to monopolize the lucrative telecommunications market in Mexico, and then to extend his reach to the rest of Latin America.

There have been challenges to Slim's Telmex monopoly. But they have not been successful. In 1996 Avantel, a long-distance phone provider, petitioned the Mexican Competition Commission to check whether Telmex had a dominant position in the telecommunications market. In 1997 the commission declared that Telmex had substantial monopoly power with respect to local telephony, national long-distance calls, and international long-distance calls, among other things. But attempts by the regulatory authorities in Mexico to limit these monopolies have come to nothing. One reason is that Slim and Telmex can use what is known as a *recurso de amparo,* literally an "appeal for protection." An *amparo* is in effect a petition to argue that a particular law does not apply to you. The idea of the *amparo* dates back to the Mexican constitution of 1857 and was originally intended as a safeguard of individual rights and freedoms. In the hands of Telmex and other Mexican monopolies, however, it has become a formidable tool for cementing monopoly power. Rather than protecting people's rights, the *amparo* provides a loophole in equality before the law.

Slim has made his money in the Mexican economy in large part thanks to his political connections. When he has ventured into the United States, he has not been successful. In 1999 his Grupo Carso bought the computer retailer CompUSA. At the time, CompUSA had given a franchise to a firm called COC Services to sell its merchandise in Mexico. Slim immediately violated this contract with the intention of setting up his own chain of stores, without any competition from COC. But COC sued CompUSA in a Dallas court. There are no *amparos* in Dallas, so Slim lost, and was fined $454 million. The lawyer for COC, Mark Werner, noted afterward that "the message of this verdict is that in this global economy, firms have to respect the rules of the United States if they want to come here." When Slim was subject to the institutions of the United States, his usual tactics for making money didn't work.

TOWARD A THEORY OF WORLD INEQUALITY

We live in an unequal world. The differences among nations are similar to those between the two parts of Nogales, just on a larger scale. In rich countries, individuals are healthier, live longer, and are much better educated. They also have access to a range of amenities and options in life, from vacations to career paths, that people in poor countries can only dream of. People in rich countries also drive on roads without potholes, and enjoy toilets, electricity, and running water in their houses. They also typically have governments that do not arbitrarily arrest or harass them; on the contrary, the governments provide services, including education, health care, roads, and law and order. Notable, too, is the fact that the citizens vote in elections and have some voice in the political direction their countries take.

The great differences in world inequality are evident to everyone, even to those in poor countries, though many lack access to television or the Internet. It is the perception and reality of these differences that drive people to cross the Rio Grande or the Mediterranean Sea illegally to have the chance to experience rich-country living standards and opportunities. This inequality doesn't just have consequences for the lives of individual people in poor countries; it also causes grievances and resentment, with huge political consequences in the United States and elsewhere. Understanding why these differences exist and what causes them is our focus in this book. Developing such an understanding is not just an end in itself, but also a first step toward generating better ideas about how to improve the lives of billions who still live in poverty.

The disparities on the two sides of the fence in Nogales are just the tip of the iceberg. As in the rest of northern Mexico, which benefits from trade with the United States, even if not all of it is legal, the residents of Nogales are more prosperous than other Mexicans, whose average annual household income is around $5,000. This greater relative prosperity of Nogales, Sonora, comes from maquiladora manufacturing plants centered in industrial parks, the first of which was started by Richard Campbell, Jr., a California basket manufacturer. The first tenant was Coin-Art, a musical instrument company owned by Richard Bosse, owner of the Artley flute and saxophone company in Nogales, Arizona. Coin-Art was followed by Memorex (computer wiring); Avent (hospital clothing); Grant (sunglasses); Chamberlain (a manufacturer of garage door openers for Sears); and Samsonite (suitcases). Significantly, all are U.S.-based businesses and businessmen, using U.S. capital and know-how. The greater prosperity of Nogales, Sonora, relative to the rest of Mexico, therefore, comes from outside.

The differences between the United States and Mexico are in turn small compared with those across the entire globe. The average citizen of the United States is seven times as prosperous as the average Mexican and more than ten times as the resident of Peru or Central America. She is about twenty times as prosperous as the average inhabitant of sub-Saharan Africa, and almost forty times as those living in the poorest African countries such as Mali, Ethiopia, and Sierra Leone. And it's not just the United States. There is a small but growing group of rich countries—mostly in Europe and North America, joined by Australia, Japan, New Zealand, Singapore, South Korea, and Taiwan—whose citizens enjoy very different lives from those of the inhabitants of the rest of the globe.

The reason that Nogales, Arizona, is much richer than Nogales, Sonora, is simple; it is because of the very different institutions on the two sides of the border, which create very different incentives for the inhabitants of Nogales, Arizona, versus Nogales, Sonora. The United States is also far richer today than either Mexico or Peru because of the way its institutions, both economic and political, shape the incentives of businesses, individuals, and politicians. Each society functions with a set of economic and political rules created and enforced by the state and the citizens collectively. Economic institutions shape economic incentives: the incentives to become educated, to save and invest, to innovate and adopt new technologies, and so on. It is the political process that determines what economic institutions people live under, and it is the political institutions that determine how this process works. For example, it is the political institutions of a nation that determine the ability of citizens to control politicians and influence how they behave. This in turn determines whether politicians are agents of the citizens, albeit imperfect, or are able to abuse the power entrusted to them, or that they have usurped, to amass their own fortunes and to pursue their own agendas, ones detrimental to those of the citizens. Political institutions include but are not limited to written constitutions and to whether the society is a democracy. They include the power and capacity of the state to regulate and govern society. It is also necessary to consider more broadly the factors that determine how political power is distributed in society, particularly the ability of different groups to act collectively to pursue their objectives or to stop other people from pursuing theirs.

As institutions influence behavior and incentives in real life, they forge the success or failure of nations. Individual talent matters at every level of society, but even that needs an institutional framework to transform it into a positive force. Bill Gates, like other legendary figures in the information technology industry (such as Paul Allen, Steve Ballmer, Steve Jobs, Larry Page, Sergey Brin, and Jeff Bezos), had immense talent and ambition. But he ultimately responded to incentives. The schooling system in the United States enabled Gates and others like him to acquire a unique set of skills to complement their talents. The economic institutions in the United States enabled these men to start companies with ease, without facing insurmountable barriers. Those institutions also made the financing of their projects feasible. The U.S. labor markets enabled them to hire qualified personnel, and the relatively competitive market environment enabled them to expand their companies and market their products. These entrepreneurs were confident from the beginning that their dream projects could be implemented: they trusted the institutions and the rule of law that these generated and they did not worry about the security of their property rights. Finally, the political institutions ensured stability and continuity. For one thing, they made sure that there was no risk of a dictator taking power and changing the rules of the game, expropriating their wealth, imprisoning them, or threatening their lives and livelihoods. They also made sure that no particular interest in society could warp the government in an economically disastrous direction, because political power was both limited and distributed sufficiently broadly that a set of economic institutions that created the incentives for prosperity could emerge.

This book will show that while economic institutions are critical for determining whether a country is poor or prosperous, it is politics and political institutions that determine what economic institutions a country has. Ultimately the good economic institutions of the United States resulted from the political institutions that gradually emerged after 1619. Our theory for world inequality shows how political and economic institutions interact in causing poverty or prosperity, and how different parts of the world ended up with such different sets of institutions. Our brief review of the history of the Americas begins to give a sense of the forces that shape political and economic institutions. Different patterns of institutions today are deeply rooted in the past because once society gets organized in a particular way, this tends to persist. We'll show that this fact comes from the way that political and economic institutions interact.

This persistence and the forces that create it also explain why it is so difficult to remove world inequality and to make poor countries prosperous. Though institutions are the key to the differences between the two Nogaleses and between Mexico and the United States, that doesn't mean there will be a consensus in Mexico to change institutions. There is no necessity for a society to develop or adopt the institutions that are best for economic growth or the welfare of its citizens, because other institutions may be even better for those who control politics and political institutions. The powerful and the rest of society will often disagree about which set of institutions should remain in place and which ones should be changed. Carlos Slim would not have been happy to see his political connections disappear and the entry barriers protecting his businesses fizzle—no matter that the entry of new businesses would enrich millions of Mexicans. Because there is no such consensus, what rules society ends up with is determined by politics: who has power and how this power can be exercised. Carlos Slim has the power to get what he wants. Bill Gates's power is far more limited. That's why our theory is about not just economics but also politics. It is about the effects of institutions on the success and failure of nations—thus the economics of poverty and prosperity; it is also about how institutions are determined and change over time, and how they fail to change even when they create poverty and misery for millions—thus the politics of poverty and prosperity.

2.

THEORIES THAT DON'T WORK

THE LAY OF THE LAND

THE FOCUS OF our book is on explaining world inequality and also some of the easily visible broad patterns that nest within it. The first country to experience sustained economic growth was England—or Great Britain, usually just Britain, as the union of England, Wales, and Scotland after 1707 is known. Growth emerged slowly in the second half of the eighteenth century as the Industrial Revolution, based on major technological breakthroughs and their application in industry, took root. Industrialization in England was soon followed by industrialization in most of Western Europe and the United States. English prosperity also spread rapidly to Britain's "settler colonies" of Canada, Australia, and New Zealand. A list of the thirty richest countries today would include them, plus Japan, Singapore, and South Korea. The prosperity of these latter three is in turn part of a broader pattern in which many East Asian nations, including Taiwan and subsequently China, have experienced recent rapid growth.

The bottom of the world income distribution paints as sharp and as distinctive a picture as the top. If you instead make a list of the poorest thirty countries in the world today, you will find almost all of them in sub-Saharan Africa. They are joined by countries such as Afghanistan, Haiti, and Nepal, which, though not in Africa, all share something critical with African nations, as we'll explain. If you went back fifty years, the countries in the top and bottom thirty wouldn't be greatly different. Singapore and South Korea would not be among the richest countries, and there would be several different countries in the bottom thirty, but the overall picture that emerged would be remarkably consistent with what we see today. Go back one hundred years, or a hundred and fifty, and you'd find nearly the same countries in the same groups.

Map 3 (opposite) shows the lay of the land in 2008. The countries shaded in the darkest color are the poorest in the world, those where average per-capita incomes (called by economists GDP, gross domestic product) are less than $2,000 annually. Most of Africa is in this color, as are Afghanistan, Haiti, and parts of Southeast Asia (for example, Cambodia and Laos). North Korea is also among this group of countries. The countries in white are the richest, those with annual income per-capita of $20,000 or more. Here we find the usual suspects: North America, western Europe, Australasia, and Japan.

Another interesting pattern can be discerned in the Americas. Make a list of the nations in the Americas from richest to poorest. You will find that at the top are the United States and Canada, followed by Chile, Argentina, Brazil, Mexico, and Uruguay, and maybe also Venezuela, depending on the price of oil. After that you have Colombia, the Dominican Republic, Ecuador, and Peru. At the bottom there is another distinct, much poorer group, comprising Bolivia, Guatemala, and Paraguay. Go back fifty years, and you'll find an identical ranking. One hundred years: same thing. One hundred and fifty years: again the same. So it is not just that the United States and Canada are richer than Latin America; there is also a definite and persistent divide between the rich and poor nations within Latin America.

A final interesting pattern is in the Middle East. There we find oil-rich nations such as Saudi Arabia and Kuwait, which have income levels close to those of our top thirty. Yet if the oil price fell, they would quickly fall back down the table. Middle Eastern countries with little or no oil, such as Egypt, Jordan, and Syria, all cluster around a level of income similar to that of Guatemala or Peru. Without oil, Middle Eastern countries are also all poor, though, like those in Central America and the Andes, not so poor as those in sub-Saharan Africa.

While there is a lot of persistence in the patterns of prosperity we see around us today, these patterns are not unchanging or immutable. First, as we have already emphasized, most of current world inequal-

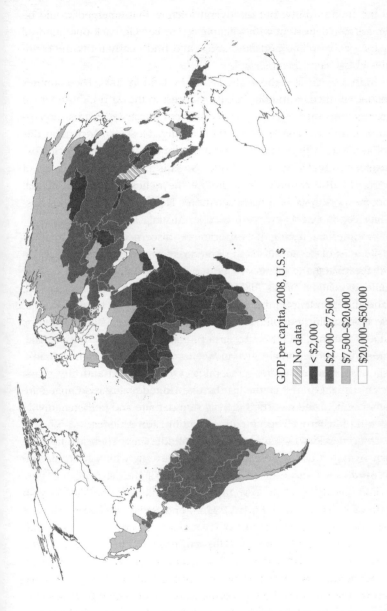

GDP per capita, 2008, U.S. $

No data
< $2,000
$2,000–$7,500
$7,500–$20,000
$20,000–$50,000

Map 3: Prosperity around the world in 2008

ity emerged since the late eighteenth century, following on the tails of the Industrial Revolution. Not only were gaps in prosperity much smaller as late as the middle of the eighteenth century, but the rankings which have been so stable since then are not the same when we go further back in history. In the Americas, for example, the ranking we see for the last hundred and fifty years was completely different five hundred years ago. Second, many nations have experienced several decades of rapid growth, such as much of East Asia since the Second World War and, more recently, China. Many of these subsequently saw that growth go into reverse. Argentina, for example, grew rapidly for five decades up until 1920, becoming one of the richest countries in the world, but then started a long slide. The Soviet Union is an even more noteworthy example, growing rapidly between 1930 and 1970, but subsequently experiencing a rapid collapse.

What explains these major differences in poverty and prosperity and the patterns of growth? Why did Western European nations and their colonial offshoots filled with European settlers start growing in the nineteenth century, scarcely looking back? What explains the persistent ranking of inequality within the Americas? Why have sub-Saharan African and Middle Eastern nations failed to achieve the type of economic growth seen in Western Europe, while much of East Asia has experienced breakneck rates of economic growth?

One might think that the fact that world inequality is so huge and consequential and has such sharply drawn patterns would mean that it would have a well-accepted explanation. Not so. Most hypotheses that social scientists have proposed for the origins of poverty and prosperity just don't work and fail to convincingly explain the lay of the land.

THE GEOGRAPHY HYPOTHESIS

One widely accepted theory of the causes of world inequality is the geography hypothesis, which claims that the great divide between rich and poor countries is created by geographical differences. Many poor countries, such as those of Africa, Central America, and South Asia, are between the tropics of Cancer and Capricorn. Rich nations, in contrast, tend to be in temperate latitudes. This geographic concentration of poverty and prosperity gives a superficial appeal to the geography hypothesis, which is the starting point of the theories and views of many social scientists and pundits alike. But this doesn't make it any less wrong.

As early as the late eighteenth century, the great French political philosopher Montesquieu noted the geographic concentration of prosperity and poverty, and proposed an explanation for it. He argued that people in tropical climates tended to be lazy and to lack inquisitiveness. As a consequence, they didn't work hard and were not innovative, and this was the reason why they were poor. Montesquieu also speculated that lazy people tended to be ruled by despots, suggesting that a tropical location could explain not just poverty but also some of the political phenomena associated with economic failure, such as dictatorship.

The theory that hot countries are intrinsically poor, though contradicted by the recent rapid economic advance of countries such as Singapore, Malaysia, and Botswana, is still forcefully advocated by some, such as the economist Jeffrey Sachs. The modern version of this view emphasizes not the direct effects of climate on work effort or thought processes, but two additional arguments: first, that tropical diseases, particularly malaria, have very adverse consequences for health and therefore labor productivity; and second, that tropical soils do not allow for productive agriculture. The conclusion, though, is the same: temperate climates have a relative advantage over tropical and semitropical areas.

World inequality, however, cannot be explained by climate or diseases, or any version of the geography hypothesis. Just think of Nogales. What separates the two parts is not climate, geography, or disease environment, but the U.S.-Mexico border.

If the geography hypothesis cannot explain differences between the north and south of Nogales, or North and South Korea, or those between East and West Germany before the fall of the Berlin Wall, could it still be a useful theory for explaining differences between North and South America? Between Europe and Africa? Simply, no.

History illustrates that there is no simple or enduring connection between climate or geography and economic success. For instance, it is not true that the tropics have always been poorer than temperate latitudes. As we saw in the last chapter, at the time of the discovery of the Americas by Columbus, the areas south of the Tropic of Cancer and north of the Tropic of Capricorn, which today include Mexico, Central America, Peru, and Bolivia, held the great Aztec and Inca civilizations. These empires were politically centralized and complex, built roads, and provided famine relief. The Aztecs had both money and writing, and the Incas, even though they lacked both these two key technologies, recorded vast amounts of information on knotted ropes called quipus. In sharp contrast, at the time of the Aztecs and Incas, the north and south of the area inhabited by the Aztecs and Incas, which today includes the United States, Canada, Argentina, and Chile, were mostly inhabited by Stone Age civilizations lacking these technologies. The tropics in the Americas were thus much richer than the temperate zones, suggesting that the "obvious fact" of tropical poverty is neither obvious nor a fact. Instead, the greater riches in the United States and Canada represent a stark reversal of fortune relative to what was there when the Europeans arrived.

This reversal clearly had nothing to do with geography and, as we have already seen, something to do with the way these areas were colonized. This reversal was not confined to the Americas. People in South Asia, especially the Indian subcontinent, and in China were more prosperous than those in many other parts of Asia and certainly more than the peoples inhabiting Australia and New Zealand. This, too, was reversed, with South Korea, Singapore, and Japan emerging as the richest nations in Asia, and Australia and New Zealand surpassing almost all of Asia in terms of prosperity. Even within sub-Saharan Africa there was a similar reversal. More recently, before the start of intense European contact with Africa, the southern Africa region was the most sparsely settled and the farthest from having developed states with any kind of control over their territories. Yet South Africa is now one of the most prosperous nations in sub-Saharan Africa. Further back in history we again see much prosperity in the tropics; some of the great premodern civilizations, such as Angkor in modern Cambodia, Vijayanagara in southern India, and Aksum in Ethiopia, flourished in the tropics, as did the great Indus Valley civilizations of Mohenjo Daro and Harappa in modern Pakistan. History thus leaves little doubt that there is no simple connection between a tropical location and economic success.

Tropical diseases obviously cause much suffering and high rates of infant mortality in Africa, but they are not the reason Africa is poor. Disease is largely a consequence of poverty and of governments being unable or unwilling to undertake the public health measures necessary to eradicate them. England in the nineteenth century was also a very unhealthy place, but the government gradually invested in clean water, in the proper treatment of sewage and effluent, and, eventually, in an effective health service. Improved health and life expectancy were not the cause of England's economic success but one of the fruits of its previous political and economic changes. The same is true for Nogales, Arizona.

The other part of the geography hypothesis is that the tropics are poor because tropical agriculture is intrinsically unproductive. Tropical soils are thin and unable to maintain nutrients, the argument goes, and emphasizes how quickly these soils are eroded by torrential rains. There certainly is some merit in this argument, but as we'll show, the prime determinant of why agricultural productivity—agricultural output per acre—is so low in many poor countries, particularly in sub-Saharan Africa, has little to do with soil quality. Rather, it is a consequence of the ownership structure of the land and the incentives that are created for farmers by the governments and institutions under which they live. We will also show that world inequality cannot be explained by differences in agricultural productivity. The great inequality of the modern world that emerged in the nineteenth century was caused by the uneven dissemination of industrial technologies and manufacturing production. It was not caused by divergence in agricultural performance.

Another influential version of the geography hypothesis is advanced by the ecologist and evolutionary biologist Jared Diamond. He argues that the origins of intercontinental inequality at the start of the modern period, five hundred years ago, rested in different historical endowments of plant and animal species, which subsequently influenced agricultural productivity. In some places, such as the Fertile Crescent in the modern Middle East, there were a large number of species that could be domesticated by humans. Elsewhere, such as the Americas, there were not. Having many species capable of being domesticated made it very attractive for societies to make the transition from a hunter-gatherer to a farming lifestyle. As a consequence, farming developed earlier in the Fertile Crescent than in the Americas. Population density grew, allowing specialization of labor, trade, urbanization, and political development. Crucially, in places where farming dominated, technological innovation took place much more rapidly than in other parts of the world. Thus, according to Diamond, the differential availability of animal and plant species created differential intensities of farming, which led to different paths of technological change and prosperity across different continents.

Though Diamond's thesis is a powerful approach to the puzzle on which he focuses, it cannot be extended to explain modern world inequality. For example, Diamond argues that the Spanish were able to dominate the civilizations of the Americas because of their longer history of farming and consequent superior technology. But we now need to explain why the Mexicans and Peruvians inhabiting the former lands of the Aztecs and Incas are poor. While having access to wheat, barley, and horses might have made the Spanish richer than the Incas, the gap in incomes between the two was not very large. The average income of a Spaniard was probably less than double that of a citizen of the Inca Empire. Diamond's thesis implies that once the Incas had been exposed to all the species and resulting technologies that they had not been able to develop themselves, they ought quickly to have attained the living standards of the Spanish. Yet nothing of the sort happened. On the contrary, in the nineteenth and twentieth centuries, a much larger gap in incomes between Spain and Peru emerged. Today the average Spaniard is more than six times richer than the average Peruvian. This gap in incomes is closely connected to the uneven dissemination of modern industrial technologies, but this has little to do either with the potential for animal and plant domestication or with intrinsic agricultural productivity differences between Spain and Peru.

While Spain, albeit with a lag, adopted the technologies of steam power, railroads, electricity, mechanization, and factory production, Peru did not, or at best did so very slowly and imperfectly. This technological gap persists today and reproduces itself on a bigger scale as new technologies, in particular those related to information technology, fuel further growth in many developed and some rapidly developing nations. Diamond's thesis does not tell us why these crucial technologies are not diffusing and equalizing incomes across the world and does not explain why the northern half of Nogales is so much richer than its twin just to the south of the fence, even though both were part of the same civilization five hundred years ago.

The story of Nogales highlights another major problem in adapting Diamond's thesis: as we have already seen, whatever the drawbacks of the Inca and Aztec empires were in 1532, Peru and Mexico were undoubtedly more prosperous than those parts of the Americas that went on to become the United States and Canada. North America became more prosperous precisely because it enthusiastically adopted the technologies and advances of the Industrial Revolution. The population became educated and railways spread out across the Great Plains in stark contrast to what happened in South America. This cannot be explained by pointing to differential geographic endowments of North and South America, which, if anything, favored South America.

Inequality in the modern world largely results from the uneven dissemination and adoption of technologies, and Diamond's thesis does include important arguments about this. For instance, he argues, following the historian William McNeill, that the east–west orientation of Eurasia enabled crops, animals, and innovations to spread from the Fertile Crescent into Western Europe, while the north–south orientation of the Americas accounts for why writing systems, which were created in Mexico, did not spread to the Andes or North America. Yet the orientation of continents cannot provide an explanation for today's world inequality. Consider Africa. Though the Sahara Desert did present a significant barrier to the movement of goods and ideas from the north to sub-Saharan Africa, this was not insurmountable. The Portuguese, and then other Europeans, sailed around the coast and eliminated differences in knowledge at a time when gaps in incomes were very small compared with what they are today. Since then, Africa has not caught up with Europe; on the contrary, there is now a much larger income gap between most African and European countries.

It should also be clear that Diamond's argument, which is about continental inequality, is not well equipped to explain variation within continents—an essential part of modern world inequality. For example, while the orientation of the Eurasian landmass might explain how England managed to benefit from the innovations of the Middle East without having to reinvent them, it doesn't explain why the Industrial Revolution happened in England rather than, say, Moldova. In addition, as Diamond himself points out, China and India benefited greatly from very rich suites of animals and plants, and from the orientation of Eurasia. But most of the poor people of the world today are in those two countries.

In fact, the best way to see the scope of Diamond's thesis is in terms of his own explanatory variables. Map 4 (opposite) shows data on the distribution of *Sus scrofa*, the ancestor of the modern pig, and the aurochs, ancestor of the modern cow. Both species were widely distributed throughout Eurasia and even North Africa. Map 5 (page 56) shows the distribution of some of the wild ancestors of modern domesticated crops, such as *Oryza sativa*, the ancestor of Asian cultivated rice, and the ancestors of modern wheat and barley. It demonstrates that the wild ancestor of rice was distributed widely across south and southeast Asia, while the ancestors of barley and wheat were distributed along a long arc from the Levant, reaching through Iran and into Afghanistan and the cluster of "stans" (Turkmenistan, Tajikistan, and Krgyzistan). These ancestral species are present in much of Eurasia. But their wide distribution suggests that inequality within Eurasia cannot be explained by a theory based on the incidence of the species.

The geography hypothesis is not only unhelpful for explaining the origins of prosperity throughout history, and mostly incorrect in its emphasis, but also unable to account for the lay of the land we started this chapter with. One might argue that any persistent pattern, such as

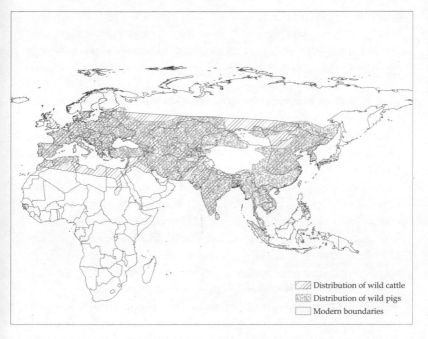

Distribution of wild cattle
Distribution of wild pigs
Modern boundaries

Map 4: The historical distribution of wild cattle and pigs

the hierarchy of incomes within the Americas or the sharp and long-ranging differences between Europe and the Middle East, can be explained by unchanging geography. But this is not so. We have already seen that the patterns within the Americas are highly unlikely to have been driven by geographical factors. Before 1492 it was the civilizations in the central valley of Mexico, Central America, and the Andes that had superior technology and living standards to North America or places such as Argentina and Chile. While the geography stayed the same, the institutions imposed by European colonists created a "reversal of fortune." Geography is also unlikely to explain the poverty of the Middle East for similar reasons. After all, the Middle East led the world in the Neolithic Revolution, and the first towns developed in modern Iraq. Iron was first smelted in Turkey, and as late as the Middle Ages the Middle East was technologically dynamic. It was not the geography of the Middle East that made the Neolithic Revolution

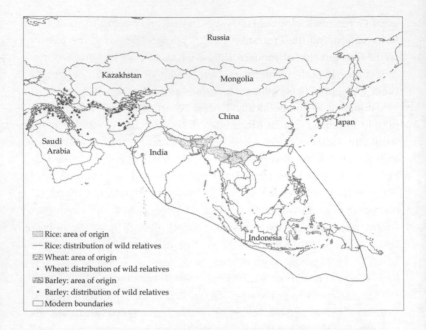

Map 5: The historical distribution of wild rice, wheat, and barley

flourish in that part of the world, as we will see in chapter 5, and it was, again, not geography that made the Middle East poor. Instead, it was the expansion and consolidation of the Ottoman Empire, and it is the institutional legacy of this empire that keeps the Middle East poor today.

Finally, geographic factors are unhelpful for explaining not only the differences we see across various parts of the world today but also why many nations such as Japan or China stagnate for long periods and then start a rapid growth process. We need another, better theory.

THE CULTURE HYPOTHESIS

The second widely accepted theory, the culture hypothesis, relates prosperity to culture. The culture hypothesis, just like the geography hypothesis, has a distinguished lineage, going back at least to the great German sociologist Max Weber, who argued that the Protestant Reformation and the Protestant ethic it spurred played a key role in facilitating the rise of modern industrial society in Western Europe. The culture hypothesis no longer relies solely on religion, but stresses other types of beliefs, values, and ethics as well.

Though it is not politically correct to articulate in public, many people still maintain that Africans are poor because they lack a good work ethic, still believe in witchcraft and magic, or resist new Western technologies. Many also believe that Latin America will never be rich because its people are intrinsically profligate and impecunious, and because they suffer from some "Iberian" or *"mañana"* culture. Of course, many once believed that the Chinese culture and Confucian values were inimical to economic growth, though now the importance of the Chinese work ethic as the engine of growth in China, Hong Kong, and Singapore is trumpeted.

Is the culture hypothesis useful for understanding world inequality? Yes and no. Yes, in the sense that social norms, which are related to culture, matter and can be hard to change, and they also sometimes support institutional differences, this book's explanation for world inequality. But mostly no, because those aspects of culture often emphasized—religion, national ethics, African or Latin values—are just not important for understanding how we got here and why the inequalities in the world persist. Other aspects, such as the extent to which people trust each other or are able to cooperate, are important but they are mostly an outcome of institutions, not an independent cause.

Let us go back to Nogales. As we noted earlier, many aspects of culture are the same north and south of the fence. Nevertheless, there may be some marked differences in practices, norms, and values, though these are not causes but outcomes of the two places' divergent development paths. For example, in surveys Mexicans typically say they trust other people less than the citizens of the United States say they trust others. But it is not a surprise that Mexicans lack trust when their government cannot eliminate drug cartels or provide a functioning unbiased legal system. The same is true with North and South Korea, as we discuss in the next chapter. The South is one of the richest countries in the world, while the North grapples with periodic famine and abject poverty. While "culture" is very different between the South and the North today, it played no role in causing the diverging economic fortunes of these two half nations. The Korean peninsula has a long period of common history. Before the Korean War and the division at the 38th parallel, it had an unprecedented homogeneity in terms of language, ethnicity, and culture. Just as in Nogales, what matters is the border. To the north is a different regime, imposing different institutions, creating different incentives. Any difference in culture between south and north of the border cutting through the two parts of Nogales or the two parts of Korea is thus not a cause of the differences in prosperity but, rather, a consequence.

What about Africa and African culture? Historically, sub-Saharan Africa was poorer than most other parts of the world, and its ancient civilizations did not develop the wheel, writing (with the exception of Ethiopia and Somalia), or the plow. Though these technologies were not widely used until the advent of formal European colonization in the late nineteenth and early twentieth century, African societies knew about them much earlier. Europeans began sailing around the west coast in the late fifteenth century, and Asians were continually sailing to East Africa from much earlier times.

We can understand why these technologies were not adopted from the history of the Kingdom of Kongo at the mouth of the Congo River, which has given its name to the modern Democratic Republic of Congo. Map 6 (opposite) shows where the Kongo was along with another important central African state, the Kuba Kingdom, which we discuss later in the book.

Kongo came into intense contact with the Portuguese after it was first visited by the mariner Diogo Cão in 1483. At the time, Kongo was a highly centralized polity by African standards, whose capital, Mbanza, had a population of sixty thousand, which made it about the same size as the Portuguese capital of Lisbon and larger than London, which had a population of about fifty thousand in 1500. The king of Kongo, Nzinga a Nkuwu, converted to Catholicism and changed his name to João I. Later Mbanza's name was changed to São Salvador. Thanks to the Portuguese, the Kongolese learned about the wheel

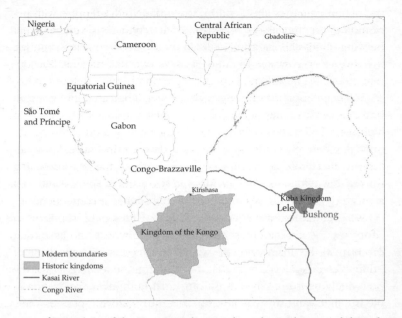

Map 6: Kingdom of the Kongo, Kuba Kingdom, the Bushong, and the Lele

and the plow, and the Portuguese even encouraged their adoption with agricultural missions in 1491 and 1512. But all these initiatives failed. Still, the Kongolese were far from averse to modern technologies in general. They were very quick to adopt one venerable Western innovation: the gun. They used this new and powerful tool to respond to market incentives: to capture and export slaves. There is no sign here that African values or culture prevented the adoption of new technologies and practices. As their contacts with Europeans deepened, the Kongolese adopted other Western practices: literacy, dress styles, and house designs. In the nineteenth century, many African societies also took advantage of the rising economic opportunities created by the Industrial Revolution by changing their production patterns. In West Africa there was rapid economic development based on the export of palm oil and ground nuts; throughout southern Africa, Africans developed exports to the rapidly expanding industrial and mining areas of the Rand in South Africa. Yet these promising economic experiments were obliterated not by African culture or the inability of ordinary Africans to act in their own self-interest, but first by European colonialism and then by postindependence African governments.

The real reason that the Kongolese did not adopt superior technology was because they lacked any incentives to do so. They faced a high risk of all their output being expropriated and taxed by the all-powerful king, whether or not he had converted to Catholicism. In fact, it wasn't only their property that was insecure. Their continued existence was held by a thread. Many of them were captured and sold as slaves—hardly the environment to encourage investment to increase long-term productivity. Neither did the king have incentives to adopt the plow on a large scale or to make increasing agricultural productivity his main priority; exporting slaves was so much more profitable.

It might be true today that Africans trust each other less than people in other parts of the world. But this is an outcome of a long history of institutions which have undermined human and property rights in Africa. The potential to be captured and sold as a slave no doubt influenced the extent to which Africans trusted others historically.

What about Max Weber's Protestant ethic? Though it may be true that predominantly Protestant countries, such as the Netherlands and England, were the first economic successes of the modern era, there is little relationship between religion and economic success. France, a predominantly Catholic country, quickly mimicked the economic performance of the Dutch and English in the nineteenth century, and Italy is as prosperous as any of these nations today. Looking farther east, you'll see that none of the economic successes of East Asia have anything to do with any form of Christian religion, so there is not much support for a special relationship between Protestantism and economic success there, either.

Let's turn to a favorite area for the enthusiasts of the culture hypothesis: the Middle East. Middle Eastern countries are primarily Islamic, and the non–oil producers among them are very poor, as we have already noted. Oil producers are richer, but this windfall of wealth has done little to create diversified modern economies in Saudi Arabia or Kuwait. Don't these facts show convincingly that religion matters? Though plausible, this argument is not right, either. Yes, countries such as Syria and Egypt are poor, and their populations are primarily Muslim. But these countries also systemically differ in other ways that are far more important for prosperity. For one, they were all provinces of the Ottoman Empire, which heavily, and adversely, shaped the way they developed. After Ottoman rule collapsed, the Middle East was absorbed into the English and French colonial empires, which, again, stunted their possibilities. After independence, they followed much of the former colonial world by developing hierarchical, authoritarian political regimes with few of the political and economic institutions that, we will argue, are crucial for generating economic success. This development path was forged largely by the history of Ottoman and European rule. The relationship between the Islamic religion and poverty in the Middle East is largely spurious.

The role of these historical events, rather than cultural factors, in shaping the Middle East's economic trajectory is also seen in the fact that the parts of the Middle East that temporarily broke away from the hold of the Ottoman Empire and the European powers, such as Egypt between 1805 and 1848 under Muhammad Ali, could embark on a path of rapid economic change. Muhammad Ali usurped power following the withdrawal of the French forces that had occupied Egypt under Napoleon Bonaparte. Exploiting the weakness of the Ottoman hold over the Egyptian territory at the time, he was able to found his own dynasty, which would, in one form or another, rule until the Egyptian Revolution under Nasser in 1952. Muhammad Ali's reforms, though coercive, did bring growth to Egypt as the state bureaucracy, the army, and the tax system were modernized and there was growth in agriculture and industry. Nevertheless, this process of modernization and growth came to an end after Ali's death, as Egypt fell under European influence.

But perhaps this is the wrong way to think about culture. Maybe the cultural factors that matter are not tied to religion but rather to particular "national cultures." Perhaps it is the influence of English culture that is important and explains why countries such as the United States, Canada, and Australia are so prosperous? Though this idea sounds initially appealing, it doesn't work, either. Yes, Canada and the United States were English colonies, but so were Sierra Leone and Nigeria. The variation in prosperity within former English colonies is as great as that in the entire world. The English legacy is not the reason for the success of North America.

There is yet one more version of the culture hypothesis: perhaps it is not English versus non-English that matters but, rather, European versus non-European. Could it be that Europeans are superior somehow because of their work ethic, outlook on life, Judeo-Christian values, or Roman heritage? It is true that Western Europe and North America, filled primarily by people of European descent, are the most prosperous parts of the world. Perhaps it is the superior European cultural legacy that is at the root of prosperity—and the last refuge of the culture hypothesis. Alas, this version of the culture hypothesis has as little explanatory potential as the others. A greater proportion of the population of Argentina and Uruguay, compared with the population of Canada and the United States, is of European descent, but Argentina's and Uruguay's economic performance leaves much to be desired. Japan and Singapore never had more than a sprinkling of inhabitants of European descent, yet they are as prosperous as many parts of Western Europe.

China, despite many imperfections in its economic and political system, has been the most rapidly growing nation of the past three decades. Chinese poverty until Mao Zedong's death had nothing to do with Chinese culture; it was due to the disastrous way Mao organized the economy and conducted politics. In the 1950s, he promoted the Great Leap Forward, a drastic industrialization policy that led to mass starvation and famine. In the 1960s, he propagated the Cultural Revolution, which led to the mass persecution of intellectuals and educated people—anyone whose party loyalty might be doubted. This again led to terror and a huge waste of the society's talent and resources. In the same way, current Chinese growth has nothing to do with Chinese values or changes in Chinese culture; it results from a process of economic transformation unleashed by the reforms implemented by Deng Xiaoping and his allies, who, after Mao Zedong's death, gradually abandoned socialist economic policies and institutions, first in agriculture and then in industry.

Just like the geography hypothesis, the culture hypothesis is also unhelpful for explaining other aspects of the lay of the land around us today. There are of course differences in beliefs, cultural attitudes, and values between the United States and Latin America, but just like those that exist between Nogales, Arizona, and Nogales, Sonora, or those between South and North Korea, these differences are a consequence of the two places' different institutions and institutional histories. Cultural factors that emphasize how "Hispanic" or "Latin" culture molded the Spanish Empire can't explain the differences within Latin America—for example, why Argentina and Chile are more prosperous than Peru and Bolivia. Other types of cultural arguments—for instance, those that stress contemporary indigenous culture—fare equally badly. Argentina and Chile have few indigenous people compared with Peru and Bolivia. Though this is true, indigenous culture as an explanation does not work, either. Colombia, Ecuador, and Peru have similar income levels, but Colombia has very few indigenous people today, while Ecuador and Peru have many. Finally, cultural attitudes, which are in general slow to change, are unlikely to account by themselves for the growth miracles in East Asia and China. Though institutions are persistent, too, in certain circumstances they do change rapidly, as we'll see.

THE IGNORANCE HYPOTHESIS

The final popular theory for why some nations are poor and some are rich is the ignorance hypothesis, which asserts that world inequality exists because we or our rulers do not know how to make poor countries rich. This idea is the one held by most economists, who take their cue from the famous definition proposed by the English economist

Lionel Robbins in 1935 that "economics is a science which studies human behavior as a relationship between ends and scarce means which have alternative uses."

It is then a small step to conclude that the science of economics should focus on the best use of scarce means to satisfy social ends. Indeed, the most famous theoretical result in economics, the so-called First Welfare Theorem, identifies the circumstances under which the allocation of resources in a "market economy" is socially desirable from an economic point of view. A market economy is an abstraction that is meant to capture a situation in which all individuals and firms can freely produce, buy, and sell any products or services that they wish. When these circumstances are not present there is a "market failure." Such failures provide the basis for a theory of world inequality, since the more that market failures go unaddressed, the poorer a country is likely to be. The ignorance hypothesis maintains that poor countries are poor because they have a lot of market failures and because economists and policymakers do not know how to get rid of them and have heeded the wrong advice in the past. Rich countries are rich because they have figured out better policies and have successfully eliminated these failures.

Could the ignorance hypothesis explain world inequality? Could it be that African countries are poorer than the rest of the world because their leaders tend to have the same mistaken views of how to run their countries, leading to the poverty there, while Western European leaders are better informed or better advised, which explains their relative success? While there are famous examples of leaders adopting disastrous policies because they were mistaken about those policies' consequences, ignorance can explain at best a small part of world inequality.

On the face of it, the sustained economic decline that soon set in in Ghana after independence from Britain was caused by ignorance. The British economist Tony Killick, then working as an adviser for the government of Kwame Nkrumah, recorded many of the problems in great detail. Nkrumah's policies focused on developing state industry, which turned out to be very inefficient. Killick recalled:

The footwear factory . . . that would have linked the meat factory in the North through transportation of the hides to the South (for a distance of over 500 miles) to a tannery (now abandoned); the leather was to have been backhauled to the footwear factory in Kumasi, in the center of the country and about 200 miles north of the tannery. Since the major footwear market is in the Accra metropolitan area, the shoes would then have to be transported an additional 200 miles back to the South.

Killick somewhat understatedly remarks that this was an enterprise "whose viability was undermined by poor siting." The footwear factory was one of many such projects, joined by the mango canning plant situated in a part of Ghana which did not grow mangos and whose output was to be more than the entire world demand for the product. This endless stream of economically irrational developments was not caused by the fact that Nkrumah or his advisers were badly informed or ignorant of the right economic policies. They had people like Killick and had even been advised by Nobel laureate Sir Arthur Lewis, who knew the policies were not good. What drove the form the economic policies took was the fact that Nkrumah needed to use them to buy political support and sustain his undemocratic regime.

Neither Ghana's disappointing performance after independence nor the countless other cases of apparent economic mismanagement can simply be blamed on ignorance. After all, if ignorance were the problem, well-meaning leaders would quickly learn what types of policies increased their citizens' incomes and welfare, and would gravitate toward those policies.

Consider the divergent paths of the United States and Mexico. Blaming this disparity on the ignorance of the leaders of the two nations is, at best, highly implausible. It wasn't differences in knowledge or intentions between John Smith and Cortés that laid the seeds of divergence during the colonial period, and it wasn't differences in knowledge between later U.S. presidents, such as Teddy Roosevelt or Woodrow Wilson, and Porfirio Díaz that made Mexico choose economic institutions that enriched elites at the expense of the rest of society at the end of the nineteenth and beginning of the twentieth centuries while Roosevelt and Wilson did the opposite. Rather, it was the differences in the institutional constraints the countries' presidents and elites were facing. Similarly, leaders of African nations that have languished over the last half century under insecure property rights and economic institutions, impoverishing much of their populations, did not allow this to happen because they thought it was good economics; they did so because they could get away with it and enrich · themselves at the expense of the rest, or because they thought it was good politics, a way of keeping themselves in power by buying the support of crucial groups or elites.

The experience of Ghana's prime minister in 1971, Kofi Busia, illustrates how misleading the ignorance hypothesis can be. Busia faced a dangerous economic crisis. After coming to power in 1969, he, like Nkrumah before him, pursued unsustainable expansionary economic policies and maintained various price controls through marketing boards and an overvalued exchange rate. Though Busia had been an opponent of Nkrumah, and led a democratic government, he faced many of the same political constraints. As with Nkrumah, his economic policies were adopted not because he was "ignorant" and believed that these policies were good economics or an ideal way to develop the country. The policies were chosen because they were good politics, enabling Busia to transfer resources to politically powerful groups, for example in urban areas, who needed to be kept contented. Price controls squeezed agriculture, delivering cheap food to the urban constituencies and generating revenues to finance government spending. But these controls were unsustainable. Ghana was soon suffering from a series of balance-of-payment crises and foreign exchange shortages. Faced with these dilemmas, on December 27, 1971, Busia signed an agreement with the International Monetary Fund that included a massive devaluation of the currency.

The IMF, the World Bank, and the entire international community put pressure on Busia to implement the reforms contained in the agreement. Though the international institutions were blissfully un-aware, Busia knew he was taking a huge political gamble. The im-mediate consequence of the currency's devaluation was rioting and discontent in Accra, Ghana's capital, that mounted uncontrollably until Busia was overthrown by the military, led by Lieutenant Colonel Acheampong, who immediately reversed the devaluation.

The ignorance hypothesis differs from the geography and culture hypotheses in that it comes readily with a suggestion about how to "solve" the problem of poverty: if ignorance got us here, enlightened and informed rulers and policymakers can get us out and we should be able to "engineer" prosperity around the world by providing the right advice and by convincing politicians of what is good economics. Yet Busia's experience underscores the fact that the main obstacle to the adoption of policies that would reduce market failures and en-courage economic growth is not the ignorance of politicians but the incentives and constraints they face from the political and economic institutions in their societies.

Although the ignorance hypothesis still rules supreme among most economists and in Western policymaking circles—which, almost to the exclusion of anything else, focus on how to engineer prosperity—it is just another hypothesis that doesn't work. It explains neither the origins of prosperity around the world nor the lay of the land around us—for example, why some nations, such as Mexico and Peru, but not the United States or England, adopted institutions and policies that would impoverish the majority of their citizens, or why almost all sub-Saharan Africa and most of Central America are so much poorer than Western Europe or East Asia.

When nations break out of institutional patterns condemning them to poverty and manage to embark on a path to economic growth, this is not because their ignorant leaders suddenly have become better informed or less self-interested or because they've received advice from better economists. China, for example, is one of the countries that made the switch from economic policies that caused poverty and the starvation of millions to those encourag-ing economic growth. But, as we will discuss in greater detail later, this did not happen because the Chinese Communist Party finally

understood that the collective ownership of agricultural land and industry created terrible economic incentives. Instead, Deng Xiaoping
and his allies, who were no less self-interested than their rivals but
who had different interests and political objectives, defeated their
powerful opponents in the Communist Party and masterminded a
political revolution of sorts, radically changing the leadership and
direction of the party. Their economic reforms, which created market incentives in agriculture and then subsequently in industry, followed from this political revolution. It was politics that determined
the switch from communism and toward market incentives in China,
not better advice or a better understanding of how the economy
worked.

WE WILL ARGUE that to understand world inequality we have to
understand why some societies are organized in very inefficient and
socially undesirable ways. Nations sometimes do manage to adopt
efficient institutions and achieve prosperity, but alas, these are the
rare cases. Most economists and policymakers have focused on "getting it right," while what is really needed is an explanation for why
poor nations "get it wrong." Getting it wrong is mostly not about
ignorance or culture. As we will show, poor countries are poor because those who have power make choices that create poverty. They
get it wrong not by mistake or ignorance but on purpose. To understand this, you have to go beyond economics and expert advice on
the best thing to do and, instead, study how decisions actually get
made, who gets to make them, and why those people decide to do
what they do. This is the study of politics and political processes.
Traditionally economics has ignored politics, but understanding politics is crucial for explaining world inequality. As the economist Abba
Lerner noted in the 1970s, "Economics has gained the title Queen
of the Social Sciences by choosing solved political problems as its
domain."

We will argue that achieving prosperity depends on solving some
basic political problems. It is precisely because economics has as-

sumed that political problems are solved that it has not been able to come up with a convincing explanation for world inequality. Explaining world inequality still needs economics to understand how different types of policies and social arrangements affect economic incentives and behavior. But it also needs politics.

3.

THE MAKING OF PROSPERITY AND POVERTY

THE ECONOMICS OF THE 38TH PARALLEL

I N THE SUMMER OF 1945, as the Second World War was drawing to a close, the Japanese colony in Korea began to collapse. Within a month of Japan's August 15 unconditional surrender, Korea was divided at the 38th parallel into two spheres of influence. The South was administered by the United States. The North, by Russia. The uneasy peace of the cold war was shattered in June 1950 when the North Korean army invaded the South. Though initially the North Koreans made large inroads, capturing the capital city, Seoul, by the autumn, they were in full retreat. It was then that Hwang Pyŏng-Wŏn and his brother were separated. Hwang Pyŏng-Wŏn managed to hide and avoid being drafted into the North Korean army. He stayed in the South and worked as a pharmacist. His brother, a doctor working in Seoul treating wounded soldiers from the South Korean army, was taken north as the North Korean army retreated. Dragged apart in 1950, they met again in 2000 in Seoul for the first time in fifty years, after the two governments finally agreed to initiate a limited program of family reunification.

As a doctor, Hwang Pyŏng-Wŏn's brother had ended up working for the air force, a good job in a military dictatorship. But even those with privileges in North Korea don't do that well. When the brothers met, Hwang Pyŏng-Wŏn asked about how life was north of the 38th parallel. He had a car, but his brother didn't. "Do you have a telephone?" he asked his brother. "No," said his brother. "My daughter, who works at the Foreign Ministry, has a phone, but if you don't know the code you can't call." Hwang Pyŏng-Wŏn recalled how all the people from the North at the reunion were asking for money, so he offered some to his brother. But his brother said, "If I go back with money the government will say, 'Give that money to us,' so keep it." Hwang Pyŏng-Wŏn noticed his brother's coat was threadbare: "Take off that coat and leave it, and when you go back wear this one," he suggested. "I can't do that," his brother replied. "This is just borrowed from the government to come here." Hwang Pyŏng-Wŏn recalled how when they parted, his brother was ill at ease and always nervous as though someone were listening. He was poorer than Hwang Pyŏng-Wŏn imagined. His brother said he lived well, but Hwang Pyŏng-Wŏn thought he looked awful and was thin as a rake.

The people of South Korea have living standards similar to those of Portugal and Spain. To the north, in the so-called Democratic People's Republic of Korea, or North Korea, living standards are akin to those of a sub-Saharan African country, about one-tenth of average living standards in South Korea. The health of North Koreans is in an even worse state; the average North Korean can expect to live ten years less than his cousins south of the 38th parallel. Map 7 (page 72) illustrates in a dramatic way the economic gap between the Koreas. It plots data on the intensity of light at night from satellite images. North Korea is almost completely dark due to lack of electricity; South Korea is blazing with light.

These striking differences are not ancient. In fact, they did not exist prior to the end of the Second World War. But after 1945, the different governments in the North and the South adopted very different ways of organizing their economies. South Korea was led, and its early economic and political institutions were shaped, by the Harvard- and Princeton-educated, staunchly anticommunist Syngman Rhee, with significant support from the United States. Rhee was elected president in 1948. Forged in the midst of the Korean War and against the threat of communism spreading to the south of the 38th parallel, South Korea was no democracy. Both Rhee and his equally famous successor, General Park Chung-Hee, secured their places in history as authoritarian presidents. But both governed a market economy where

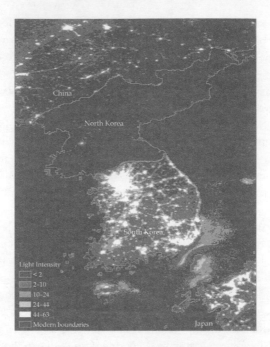

Map 7: Lights in South Korea and darkness in the North

private property was recognized, and after 1961, Park effectively threw the weight of the state behind rapid economic growth, channeling credit and subsidies to firms that were successful.

The situation north of the 38th parallel was different. Kim Il-Sung, a leader of anti-Japanese communist partisans during the Second World War, established himself as dictator by 1947 and, with the help of the Soviet Union, introduced a rigid form of centrally planned economy as part of the so-called Juche system. Private property was outlawed, and markets were banned. Freedoms were curtailed not only in the marketplace, but in every sphere of North Koreans' lives— except for those who happened to be part of the very small ruling elite around Kim Il-Sung and, later, his son and successor Kim Jong-Il.

It should not surprise us that the economic fortunes of South and North Korea diverged sharply. Kim Il-Sung's command economy and the Juche system soon proved to be a disaster. Detailed statistics are not available from North Korea, which is a secretive state, to say the least. Nonetheless, available evidence confirms what we know from the all-too-often recurring famines: not only did industrial production fail to take off, but North Korea in fact experienced a collapse in agricultural productivity. Lack of private property meant that few people had incentives to invest or to exert effort to increase or even maintain productivity. The stifling, repressive regime was inimical to innovation and the adoption of new technologies. But Kim Il-Sung, Kim Jong-Il, and their cronies had no intention of reforming the system, or introducing private property, markets, private contracts, or changing economic and political institutions. North Korea continues to stagnate economically.

Meanwhile, in the South, economic institutions encouraged investment and trade. South Korean politicians invested in education, achieving high rates of literacy and schooling. South Korean companies were quick to take advantage of the relatively educated population, the policies encouraging investment and industrialization, exports, and the transfer of technology. South Korea quickly became one of East Asia's "Miracle Economies," one of the most rapidly growing nations in the world.

By the late 1990s, in just about half a century, South Korean growth and North Korean stagnation led to a tenfold gap between the two halves of this once-united country—imagine what a difference a couple of centuries could make. The economic disaster of North Korea, which led to the starvation of millions, when placed against the South Korean economic success, is striking: neither culture nor geography nor ignorance can explain the divergent paths of North and South Korea. We have to look at institutions for an answer.

EXTRACTIVE AND INCLUSIVE ECONOMIC INSTITUTIONS

Countries differ in their economic success because of their different institutions, the rules influencing how the economy works, and the incentives that motivate people. Imagine teenagers in North and South

Korea and what they expect from life. Those in the North grow up in poverty, without entrepreneurial initiative, creativity, or adequate education to prepare them for skilled work. Much of the education they receive at school is pure propaganda, meant to shore up the legitimacy of the regime; there are few books, let alone computers. After finishing school, everyone has to go into the army for ten years. These teenagers know that they will not be able to own property, start a business, or become more prosperous even if many people engage illegally in private economic activities to make a living. They also know that they will not have legal access to markets where they can use their skills or their earnings to purchase the goods they need and desire. They are even unsure about what kind of human rights they will have.

Those in the South obtain a good education, and face incentives that encourage them to exert effort and excel in their chosen vocation. South Korea is a market economy, built on private property. South Korean teenagers know that, if successful as entrepreneurs or workers, they can one day enjoy the fruits of their investments and efforts; they can improve their standard of living and buy cars, houses, and health care.

In the South the state supports economic activity. So it is possible for entrepreneurs to borrow money from banks and financial markets, for foreign companies to enter into partnerships with South Korean firms, for individuals to take up mortgages to buy houses. In the South, by and large, you are free to open any business you like. In the North, you are not. In the South, you can hire workers, sell your products or services, and spend your money in the marketplace in whichever way you want. In the North, there are only black markets. These different rules are the institutions under which North and South Koreans live.

Inclusive economic institutions, such as those in South Korea or in the United States, are those that allow and encourage participation by the great mass of people in economic activities that make best use of their talents and skills and that enable individuals to make the choices they wish. To be inclusive, economic institutions must feature secure private property, an unbiased system of law, and a provision of public services that provides a level playing field in which people can exchange and contract; it also must permit the entry of new businesses and allow people to choose their careers.

THE CONTRAST OF South and North Korea, and of the United States and Latin America, illustrates a general principle. Inclusive economic institutions foster economic activity, productivity growth, and economic prosperity. Secure private property rights are central, since only those with such rights will be willing to invest and increase productivity. A businessman who expects his output to be stolen, expropriated, or entirely taxed away will have little incentive to work, let alone any incentive to undertake investments and innovations. But such rights must exist for the majority of people in society.

In 1680 the English government conducted a census of the population of its West Indian colony of Barbados. The census revealed that of the total population on the island of around 60,000, almost 39,000 were African slaves who were the property of the remaining one-third of the population. Indeed, they were mostly the property of the largest 175 sugar planters, who also owned most of the land. These large planters had secure and well-enforced property rights over their land and even over their slaves. If one planter wanted to sell slaves to another, he could do so and expect a court to enforce such a sale or any other contract he wrote. Why? Of the forty judges and justices of the peace on the island, twenty-nine of them were large planters. Also, the eight most senior military officials were all large planters. Despite well-defined, secure, and enforced property rights and contracts for the island's elite, Barbados did not have inclusive economic institutions, since two-thirds of the population were slaves with no access to education or economic opportunities, and no ability or incentive to use their talents or skills. Inclusive economic institutions require secure property rights and economic opportunities not just for the elite but for a broad cross-section of society.

Secure property rights, the law, public services, and the freedom to contract and exchange all rely on the state, the institution with the coercive capacity to impose order, prevent theft and fraud, and enforce contracts between private parties. To function well, society also needs other public services: roads and a transport network so that goods can be transported; a public infrastructure so that economic activity can flourish; and some type of basic regulation to prevent fraud and malfeasance. Though many of these public services can be provided by markets and private citizens, the degree of coordination necessary to do so on a large scale often eludes all but a central authority. The state is thus inexorably intertwined with economic institutions, as the enforcer of law and order, private property, and contracts, and often as a key provider of public services. Inclusive economic institutions need and use the state.

The economic institutions of North Korea or of colonial Latin America—the *mita, encomienda,* or *repartimiento* described earlier—do not have these properties. Private property is nonexistent in North Korea. In colonial Latin America there was private property for Spaniards, but the property of the indigenous peoples was highly insecure. In neither type of society was the vast mass of people able to make the economic decisions they wanted to; they were subject to mass coercion. In neither type of society was the power of the state used to provide key public services that promoted prosperity. In North Korea, the state built an education system to inculcate propaganda, but was unable to prevent famine. In colonial Latin America, the state focused on coercing indigenous peoples. In neither type of society was there a level playing field or an unbiased legal system. In North Korea, the legal system is an arm of the ruling Communist Party, and in Latin America it was a tool of discrimination against the mass of people. We call such institutions, which have opposite properties to those we call inclusive, extractive economic institutions—extractive because such institutions are designed to extract incomes and wealth from one subset of society to benefit a different subset.

ENGINES OF PROSPERITY

Inclusive economic institutions create inclusive markets, which not only give people freedom to pursue the vocations in life that best suit their talents but also provide a level playing field that gives them the opportunity to do so. Those who have good ideas will be able to start businesses, workers will tend to go to activities where their productivity is greater, and less efficient firms can be replaced by more efficient ones. Contrast how people choose their occupations under inclusive markets to colonial Peru and Bolivia, where under the *mita,* many were forced to work in silver and mercury mines, regardless of their skills or whether they wanted to. Inclusive markets are not just free markets. Barbados in the seventeenth century also had markets. But in the same way that it lacked property rights for all but the narrow planter elite, its markets were far from inclusive; markets in slaves were in fact one part of the economic institutions systematically coercing the majority of the population and robbing them of the ability to choose their occupations and how they should utilize their talents.

Inclusive economic institutions also pave the way for two other engines of prosperity: technology and education. Sustained economic growth is almost always accompanied by technological improvements that enable people (labor), land, and existing capital (buildings, existing machines, and so on) to become more productive. Think of our great-great-grandparents, just over a century ago, who did not have access to planes or automobiles or most of the drugs and health care we now take for granted, not to mention indoor plumbing, air-conditioning, shopping malls, radio, or motion pictures; let alone information technology, robotics, or computer-controlled machinery. And going back a few more generations, the technological know-how and living standards were even more backward, so much so that we would find it hard to imagine how most people struggled through life. These improvements follow from science and from entrepreneurs such as Thomas Edison, who applied science to create profitable businesses. This process of innovation is made possible by economic institutions that encourage private property, uphold contracts, create a level playing field, and encourage and allow the entry of new businesses that can bring new technologies to life. It should therefore be no surprise that it was U.S. society, not Mexico or Peru, that produced Thomas Edison, and that it was South Korea, not North Korea, that today produces technologically innovative companies such as Samsung and Hyundai.

Intimately linked to technology are the education, skills, competencies, and know-how of the workforce, acquired in schools, at home, and on the job. We are so much more productive than a century ago not just because of better technology embodied in machines but also because of the greater know-how that workers possess. All the technology in the world would be of little use without workers who knew how to operate it. But there is more to skills and competencies than just the ability to run machines. It is the education and skills of the workforce that generate the scientific knowledge upon which our progress is built and that enable the adaptation and adoption of these technologies in diverse lines of business. Though we saw in chapter 1 that many of the innovators of the Industrial Revolution and afterward, like Thomas Edison, were not highly educated, these innovations were much simpler than modern technology. Today technological change requires education both for the innovator and the worker. And here we see the importance of economic institutions that create a level playing field. The United States could produce, or attract from foreign lands, the likes of Bill Gates, Steve Jobs, Sergey Brin, Larry Page, and Jeff Bezos, and the hundreds of scientists who made fundamental discoveries in information technology, nuclear power, biotech, and other fields upon which these entrepreneurs built their businesses. The supply of talent was there to be harnessed because most teenagers in the United States have access to as much schooling as they wish or are capable of attaining. Now imagine a different society, for example the Congo or Haiti, where a large fraction of the population has no means of attending school, or where, if they manage to go to school, the quality of teaching is lamentable, where teachers do not show up for work, and even if they do, there may not be any books.

The low education level of poor countries is caused by economic institutions that fail to create incentives for parents to educate their children and by political institutions that fail to induce the government to build, finance, and support schools and the wishes of parents and children. The price these nations pay for low education of their population and lack of inclusive markets is high. They fail to mobilize their nascent talent. They have many potential Bill Gateses and perhaps one or two Albert Einsteins who are now working as poor, un-educated farmers, being coerced to do what they don't want to do or being drafted into the army, because they never had the opportunity to realize their vocation in life.

The ability of economic institutions to harness the potential of in-clusive markets, encourage technological innovation, invest in people, and mobilize the talents and skills of a large number of individuals is critical for economic growth. Explaining why so many economic in-stitutions fail to meet these simple objectives is the central theme of this book.

EXTRACTIVE AND INCLUSIVE POLITICAL INSTITUTIONS

All economic institutions are created by society. Those of North Korea, for example, were forced on its citizens by the communists who took over the country in the 1940s, while those of colonial Latin America were imposed by Spanish conquistadors. South Korea ended up with very different economic institutions than the North because different people with different interests and objectives made the decisions about how to structure society. In other words, South Korea had dif-ferent politics.

Politics is the process by which a society chooses the rules that will govern it. Politics surrounds institutions for the simple reason that while inclusive institutions may be good for the economic prosperity of a nation, some people or groups, such as the elite of the Commu-nist Party of North Korea or the sugar planters of colonial Barbados, will be much better off by setting up institutions that are extractive. When there is conflict over institutions, what happens depends on which people or group wins out in the game of politics—who can get more support, obtain additional resources, and form more effective alliances. In short, who wins depends on the distribution of political power in society.

The political institutions of a society are a key determinant of the outcome of this game. They are the rules that govern incentives in politics. They determine how the government is chosen and which part of the government has the right to do what. Political institutions determine who has power in society and to what ends that power can be used. If the distribution of power is narrow and unconstrained, then the political institutions are absolutist, as exemplified by the absolutist monarchies reigning throughout the world during much of history. Under absolutist political institutions such as those in North Korea and colonial Latin America, those who can wield this power will be able to set up economic institutions to enrich themselves and augment their power at the expense of society. In contrast, political institutions that distribute power broadly in society and subject it to constraints are pluralistic. Instead of being vested in a single individual or a narrow group, political power rests with a broad coalition or a plurality of groups.

There is obviously a close connection between pluralism and inclusive economic institutions. But the key to understanding why South Korea and the United States have inclusive economic institutions is not just their pluralistic political institutions but also their sufficiently centralized and powerful states. A telling contrast is with the East African nation of Somalia. As we will see later in the book, political power in Somalia has long been widely distributed—almost pluralistic. Indeed there is no real authority that can control or sanction what anyone does. Society is divided into deeply antagonistic clans that cannot dominate one another. The power of one clan is constrained only by the guns of another. This distribution of power leads not to inclusive institutions but to chaos, and at the root of it is the Somali state's lack of any kind of political centralization, or state centralization, and its inability to enforce even the minimal amount of law and order to support economic activity, trade, or even the basic security of its citizens.

Max Weber, who we met in the previous chapter, provided the most famous and widely accepted definition of the state, identifying it with the "monopoly of legitimate violence" in society. Without such a monopoly and the degree of centralization that it entails, the state cannot play its role as enforcer of law and order, let alone provide public services and encourage and regulate economic activity. When the state fails to achieve almost any political centralization, society sooner or later descends into chaos, as did Somalia.

We will refer to political institutions that are sufficiently centralized and pluralistic as inclusive political institutions. When either of these conditions fails, we will refer to the institutions as extractive political institutions.

There is strong synergy between economic and political institutions. Extractive political institutions concentrate power in the hands of a narrow elite and place few constraints on the exercise of this power. Economic institutions are then often structured by this elite to extract resources from the rest of the society. Extractive economic institutions thus naturally accompany extractive political institutions. In fact, they must inherently depend on extractive political institutions for their survival. Inclusive political institutions, vesting power broadly, would tend to uproot economic institutions that expropriate the resources of the many, erect entry barriers, and suppress the functioning of markets so that only a few benefit.

In Barbados, for example, the plantation system based on the exploitation of slaves could not have survived without political institutions that suppressed and completely excluded the slaves from the political process. The economic system impoverishing millions for the benefit of a narrow communist elite in North Korea would also be unthinkable without the total political domination of the Communist Party.

This synergistic relationship between extractive economic and political institutions introduces a strong feedback loop: political institutions enable the elites controlling political power to choose economic institutions with few constraints or opposing forces. They also enable the elites to structure future political institutions and their evolution. Extractive economic institutions, in turn, enrich the same elites, and their economic wealth and power help consolidate their political dominance. In Barbados or in Latin America, for example, the colonists were able to use their political power to impose a set of economic institutions that made them huge fortunes at the expense of the rest of the population. The resources these economic institutions generated enabled these elites to build armies and security forces to defend their absolutist monopoly of political power. The implication of course is that extractive political and economic institutions support each other and tend to persist.

There is in fact more to the synergy between extractive economic and political institutions. When existing elites are challenged under extractive political institutions and the newcomers break through, the newcomers are likewise subject to only a few constraints. They thus have incentives to maintain these political institutions and create a similar set of economic institutions, as Porfirio Díaz and the elite surrounding him did at the end of the nineteenth century in Mexico.

Inclusive economic institutions, in turn, are forged on foundations laid by inclusive political institutions, which make power broadly distributed in society and constrain its arbitrary exercise. Such political institutions also make it harder for others to usurp power and undermine the foundations of inclusive institutions. Those controlling political power cannot easily use it to set up extractive economic institutions for their own benefit. Inclusive economic institutions, in turn, create a more equitable distribution of resources, facilitating the persistence of inclusive political institutions.

It was not a coincidence that when, in 1618, the Virginia Company gave land, and freedom from their draconian contracts, to the colonists it had previously tried to coerce, the General Assembly in the following year allowed the colonists to begin governing themselves. Economic rights without political rights would not have been trusted by the colonists, who had seen the persistent efforts of the Virginia Company to coerce them. Neither would these economies have been stable and durable. In fact, combinations of extractive and inclusive institutions are generally unstable. Extractive economic institutions under inclusive political institutions are unlikely to survive for long, as our discussion of Barbados suggests.

Similarly, inclusive economic institutions will neither support nor be supported by extractive political ones. Either they will be transformed into extractive economic institutions to the benefit of the narrow interests that hold power, or the economic dynamism they create will destabilize the extractive political institutions, opening the way for the emergence of inclusive political institutions. Inclusive economic institutions also tend to reduce the benefits the elites can enjoy by ruling over extractive political institutions, since those institutions face competition in the marketplace and are constrained by the contracts and property rights of the rest of society.

WHY NOT ALWAYS CHOOSE PROSPERITY?

Political and economic institutions, which are ultimately the choice of society, can be inclusive and encourage economic growth. Or they can be extractive and become impediments to economic growth. Nations fail when they have extractive economic institutions, supported by extractive political institutions that impede and even block economic growth. But this means that the choice of institutions—that is, the politics of institutions—is central to our quest for understanding the reasons for the success and failure of nations. We have to understand why the politics of some societies lead to inclusive institutions that foster economic growth, while the politics of the vast majority of societies throughout history has led, and still leads today, to extractive institutions that hamper economic growth.

It might seem obvious that everyone should have an interest in creating the type of economic institutions that will bring prosperity. Wouldn't every citizen, every politician, and even a predatory dictator want to make his country as wealthy as possible?

Let's return to the Kingdom of Kongo we discussed earlier. Though this kingdom collapsed in the seventeenth century, it provided the name for the modern country that became independent from Belgian colonial rule in 1960. As an independent polity, Congo experienced almost unbroken economic decline and mounting poverty under the rule of Joseph Mobutu between 1965 and 1997. This decline continued after Mobutu was overthrown by Laurent Kabila. Mobutu created a highly extractive set of economic institutions. The citizens were impoverished, but Mobutu and the elite surrounding him, known as Les Grosses Légumes (the Big Vegetables), became fabulously wealthy. Mobutu built himself a palace at his birthplace, Gbadolite, in the north of the country, with an airport large enough to land a supersonic Concord jet, a plane he frequently rented from Air France for travel to Europe. In Europe he bought castles and owned large tracts of the Belgian capital of Brussels.

Wouldn't it have been better for Mobutu to set up economic institutions that increased the wealth of the Congolese rather than deepening their poverty? If Mobutu had managed to increase the prosperity of his nation, would he not have been able to appropriate even more money, buy a Concord instead of renting one, have more castles and mansions, possibly a bigger and more powerful army? Unfortunately for the citizens of many countries in the world, the answer is no. Economic institutions that create incentives for economic progress may simultaneously redistribute income and power in such a way that a predatory dictator and others with political power may become worse off.

The fundamental problem is that there will necessarily be disputes and conflict over economic institutions. Different institutions have different consequences for the prosperity of a nation, how that prosperity is distributed, and who has power. The economic growth which can be induced by institutions creates both winners and losers. This was clear during the Industrial Revolution in England, which laid the foundations of the prosperity we see in the rich countries of the world today. It centered on a series of pathbreaking technological changes in steam power, transportation, and textile production. Even though mechanization led to enormous increases in total incomes and ultimately became the foundation of modern industrial society, it was bitterly opposed by many. Not because of ignorance or shortsightedness; quite the opposite. Rather, such opposition to economic growth has its own, unfortunately coherent, logic. Economic growth and technological change are accompanied by what the great economist Joseph Schumpeter called creative destruction. They replace the old with the new. New sectors attract resources away from old ones. New firms take business away from established ones. New technologies make existing skills and machines obsolete. The process of economic growth and the inclusive institutions upon which it is based create losers as well as winners in the political arena and in the economic marketplace. Fear of creative destruction is often at the root of the opposition to inclusive economic and political institutions.

European history provides a vivid example of the consequences of creative destruction. On the eve of the Industrial Revolution in the eighteenth century, the governments of most European countries were controlled by aristocracies and traditional elites, whose major source of income was from landholdings or from trading privileges they enjoyed thanks to monopolies granted and entry barriers imposed by monarchs. Consistent with the idea of creative destruction, the spread of industries, factories, and towns took resources away from the land, reduced land rents, and increased the wages that landowners had to pay their workers. These elites also saw the emergence of new businessmen and merchants eroding their trading privileges. All in all, they were the clear economic losers from industrialization. Urbanization and the emergence of a socially conscious middle and working class also challenged the political monopoly of landed aristocracies. So with the spread of the Industrial Revolution the aristocracies weren't just the economic losers; they also risked becoming political losers, losing their hold on political power. With their economic and political power under threat, these elites often formed a formidable opposition against industrialization.

The aristocracy was not the only loser from industrialization. Artisans whose manual skills were being replaced by mechanization likewise opposed the spread of industry. Many organized against it, rioting and destroying the machines they saw as responsible for the decline of their livelihood. They were the Luddites, a word that has today become synonymous with resistance to technological change. John Kay, English inventor of the "flying shuttle" in 1733, one of the first significant improvements in the mechanization of weaving, had his house burned down by Luddites in 1753. James Hargreaves, inventor of the "spinning jenny," a complementary revolutionary improvement in spinning, got similar treatment.

In reality, the artisans were much less effective than the landowners and elites in opposing industrialization. The Luddites did not possess the political power—the ability to affect political outcomes against the wishes of other groups—of the landed aristocracy. In England, industrialization marched on, despite the Luddites' opposition, because aristocratic opposition, though real, was muted. In the Austro-

Hungarian and the Russian empires, where the absolutist monarchs and aristocrats had far more to lose, industrialization was blocked. In consequence, the economies of Austria-Hungary and Russia stalled. They fell behind other European nations, where economic growth took off during the nineteenth century.

The success and failure of specific groups notwithstanding, one lesson is clear: powerful groups often stand against economic progress and against the engines of prosperity. Economic growth is not just a process of more and better machines, and more and better educated people, but also a transformative and destabilizing process associated with widespread creative destruction. Growth thus moves forward only if not blocked by the economic losers who anticipate that their economic privileges will be lost and by the political losers who fear that their political power will be eroded.

Conflict over scarce resources, income and power, translates into conflict over the rules of the game, the economic institutions, which will determine the economic activities and who will benefit from them. When there is a conflict, the wishes of all parties cannot be simultaneously met. Some will be defeated and frustrated, while others will succeed in securing outcomes they like. Who the winners of this conflict are has fundamental implications for a nation's economic trajectory. If the groups standing against growth are the winners, they can successfully block economic growth, and the economy will stagnate.

The logic of why the powerful would not necessarily want to set up the economic institutions that promote economic success extends easily to the choice of political institutions. In an absolutist regime, some elites can wield power to set up economic institutions they prefer. Would they be interested in changing political institutions to make them more pluralistic? In general not, since this would only dilute their political power, making it more difficult, maybe impossible, for them to structure economic institutions to further their own interests. Here again we see a ready source of conflict. The people who suffer from the extractive economic institutions cannot hope for absolutist rulers to voluntarily change political institutions and redistribute power in society. The only way to change these political institutions is to force the elite to create more pluralistic institutions.

In the same way that there is no reason why political institutions should automatically become pluralistic, there is no natural tendency toward political centralization. There would certainly be incentives to create more centralized state institutions in any society, particularly in those with no such centralization whatsoever. For example, in Somalia, if one clan created a centralized state capable of imposing order on the country, this could lead to economic benefits and make this clan richer. What stops this? The main barrier to political centralization is again a form of fear from change: any clan, group, or politician attempting to centralize power in the state will also be centralizing power in their own hands, and this is likely to meet the ire of other clans, groups, and individuals, who would be the political losers of this process. Lack of political centralization means not only lack of law and order in much of a territory but also there being many actors with sufficient powers to block or disrupt things, and the fear of their opposition and violent reaction will often deter many would-be centralizers. Political centralization is likely only when one group of people is sufficiently more powerful than others to build a state. In Somalia, power is evenly balanced, and no one clan can impose its will on any other. Therefore, the lack of political centralization persists.

THE LONG AGONY OF THE CONGO

There are few better, or more depressing, examples of the forces that explain the logic of why economic prosperity is so persistently rare under extractive institutions or that illustrate the synergy between extractive economic and political institutions than the Congo. Portuguese and Dutch visitors to Kongo in the fifteenth and sixteenth centuries remarked on the "miserable poverty" there. Technology was rudimentary by European standards, with the Kongolese having neither writing, the wheel, nor the plow. The reason for this poverty, and the reluctance of Kongolese farmers to adopt better technologies when they learned of them, is clear from existing historical accounts. It was due to the extractive nature of the country's economic institutions.

As we have seen, the Kingdom of Kongo was governed by the king in Mbanza, subsequently São Salvador. Areas away from the capital were ruled by an elite who played the roles of governors of different parts of the kingdom. The wealth of this elite was based on slave plantations around São Salvador and the extraction of taxes from the rest of the country. Slavery was central to the economy, used by the elite to supply their own plantations and by Europeans on the coast. Taxes were arbitrary; one tax was even collected every time the king's beret fell off. To become more prosperous, the Kongolese people would have had to save and invest—for example, by buying plows. But it would not have been worthwhile, since any extra output that they produced using better technology would have been subject to expropriation by the king and his elite. Instead of investing to increase their productivity and selling their products in markets, the Kongolese moved their villages away from the market; they were trying to be as far away from the roads as possible, in order to reduce the incidence of plunder and to escape the reach of slave traders.

The poverty of the Kongo was therefore the result of extractive economic institutions that blocked all the engines of prosperity or even made them work in reverse. The Kongo's government provided very few public services to its citizens, not even basic ones, such as secure property rights or law and order. On the contrary, the government was itself the biggest threat to its subjects' property and human rights. The institution of slavery meant that the most fundamental market of all, an inclusive labor market where people can choose their occupation or jobs in ways that are so crucial for a prosperous economy, did not exist. Moreover, long-distance trade and mercantile activities were controlled by the king and were open only to those associated with him. Though the elite quickly became literate after the Portuguese introduced writing, the king made no attempt to spread literacy to the great mass of the population.

Nevertheless, though "miserable poverty" was widespread, the Kongolese extractive institutions had their own impeccable logic:

they made a few people, those with political power, very rich. In the sixteenth century, the king of Kongo and the aristocracy were able to import European luxury goods and were surrounded by servants and slaves.

The roots of the economic institutions of Kongolese society flowed from the distribution of political power in society and thus from the nature of political institutions. There was nothing to stop the king from taking people's possessions or bodies, other than the threat of revolt. Though this threat was real, it was not enough to make people or their wealth secure. The political institutions of Kongo were truly absolutist, making the king and the elite subject to essentially no constraints, and it gave no say to the citizens in the way their society was organized.

Of course, it is not difficult to see that the political institutions of Kongo contrast sharply with inclusive political institutions where power is constrained and broadly distributed. The absolutist institutions of Kongo were kept in place by the army. The king had a standing army of five thousand troops in the mid-seventeenth century, with a core of five hundred musketeers—a formidable force for its time. Why the king and the aristocracy so eagerly adopted European firearms is thus easy to understand.

There was no chance of sustained economic growth under this set of economic institutions and even incentives for generating temporary growth were highly limited. Reforming economic institutions to improve individual property rights would have made the Kongolese society at large more prosperous. But it is unlikely that the elite would have benefited from this wider prosperity. First, such reforms would have made the elite economic losers, by undermining the wealth that the slave trade and slave plantations brought them. Second, such reforms would have been possible only if the political power of the king and the elite were curtailed. For instance, if the king continued to command his five hundred musketeers, who would have believed an announcement that slavery had been abolished? What would have stopped the king from changing his mind later on? The only real guarantee would have been a change in political institutions so that citizens gained some countervailing political power, giving them some say over taxation or what the musketeers did. But in this case it is dubious that sustaining the consumption and lifestyle of the king and the elite would have been high on their list of priorities. In this scenario, changes that would have created better economic institutions in society would have made the king and aristocracy political as well as economic losers.

The interaction of economic and political institutions five hundred years ago is still relevant for understanding why the modern state of Congo is still miserably poor today. The advent of European rule in this area, and deeper into the basin of the River Congo at the time of the "scramble for Africa" in the late nineteenth century, led to an insecurity of human and property rights even more egregious than that which characterized the precolonial Kongo. In addition, it reproduced the pattern of extractive institutions and political absolutism that empowered and enriched a few at the expense of the masses, though the few now were Belgian colonialists, most notably King Leopold II.

When Congo became independent in 1960, the same pattern of economic institutions, incentives, and performance reproduced itself. These Congolese extractive economic institutions were again supported by highly extractive political institutions. The situation was worsened because European colonialism created a polity, Congo, made up of many different precolonial states and societies that the national state, run from Kinshasa, had little control over. Though President Mobutu used the state to enrich himself and his cronies—for example, through the Zairianization program of 1973, which involved the mass expropriation of foreign economic interests—he presided over a noncentralized state with little authority over much of the country, and had to appeal to foreign assistance to stop the provinces of Katanga and Kasai from seceding in the 1960s. This lack of political centralization, almost to the point of total collapse of the state, is a feature that Congo shares with much of sub-Saharan Africa.

The modern Democratic Republic of Congo remains poor because its citizens still lack the economic institutions that create the basic incentives that make a society prosperous. It is not geography, culture, or the ignorance of its citizens or politicians that keep the Congo poor, but its extractive economic institutions. These are still in place after all these centuries because political power continues to be narrowly concentrated in the hands of an elite who have little incentive to enforce secure property rights for the people, to provide the basic public services that would improve the quality of life, or to encourage economic progress. Rather, their interests are to extract income and sustain their power. They have not used this power to build a centralized state, for to do so would create the same problems of opposition and political challenges that promoting economic growth would. Moreover, as in much of the rest of sub-Saharan Africa, infighting triggered by rival groups attempting to take control of extractive institutions destroyed any tendency for state centralization that might have existed.

The history of the Kingdom of Kongo, and the more recent history of the Congo, vividly illustrates how political institutions determine economic institutions and, through these, the economic incentives and the scope for economic growth. It also illustrates the symbiotic relationship between political absolutism and economic institutions that empower and enrich a few at the expense of many.

GROWTH UNDER EXTRACTIVE POLITICAL INSTITUTIONS

Congo today is an extreme example, with lawlessness and highly insecure property rights. However, in most cases such extremism would not serve the interest of the elite, since it would destroy all economic incentives and generate few resources to be extracted. The central thesis of this book is that economic growth and prosperity are associated with inclusive economic and political institutions, while extractive institutions typically lead to stagnation and poverty. But this implies neither that extractive institutions can never generate growth nor that all extractive institutions are created equal.

There are two distinct but complementary ways in which growth under extractive political institutions can emerge. First, even if economic institutions are extractive, growth is possible when elites can directly allocate resources to high-productivity activities that they themselves control. A prominent example of this type of growth under

extractive institutions was the Caribbean Islands between the sixteenth and eighteenth centuries. Most people were slaves, working
under gruesome conditions in plantations, living barely above subsistence level. Many died from malnutrition and exhaustion. In Barbados, Cuba, Haiti, and Jamaica in the seventeenth and eighteenth
centuries, a small minority, the planter elite, controlled all political
power and owned all the assets, including all the slaves. While the
majority had no rights, the planter elite's property and assets were
well protected. Despite the extractive economic institutions that savagely exploited the majority of the population, these islands were
among the richest places in the world, because they could produce
sugar and sell it in world markets. The economy of the islands stagnated only when there was a need to shift to new economic activities,
which threatened both the incomes and the political power of the
planter elite.

Another example is the economic growth and industrialization of
the Soviet Union from the first Five-Year Plan in 1928 until the 1970s.
Political and economic institutions were highly extractive, and markets were heavily constrained. Nevertheless, the Soviet Union was
able to achieve rapid economic growth because it could use the
power of the state to move resources from agriculture, where they
were very inefficiently used, into industry.

The second type of growth under extractive political institutions
arises when the institutions permit the development of somewhat,
even if not completely, inclusive economic institutions. Many societies with extractive political institutions will shy away from inclusive
economic institutions because of fear of creative destruction. But the
degree to which the elite manage to monopolize power varies across
societies. In some, the position of the elite could be sufficiently secure
that they may permit some moves toward inclusive economic institutions when they are fairly certain that this will not threaten their political power. Alternatively, the historical situation could be such as to
endow an extractive political regime with rather inclusive economic
institutions, which they decide not to block. These provide the second way in which growth can take place under extractive political
institutions.

The rapid industrialization of South Korea under General Park is an example. Park came to power via a military coup in 1961, but he did so in a society heavily supported by the United States and with an economy where economic institutions were essentially inclusive. Though Park's regime was authoritarian, it felt secure enough to promote economic growth, and in fact did so very actively—perhaps partly because the regime was not directly supported by extractive economic institutions. Differently from the Soviet Union and most other cases of growth under extractive institutions, South Korea transitioned from extractive political institutions toward inclusive political institutions in the 1980s. This successful transition was due to a confluence of factors.

By the 1970s, economic institutions in South Korea had become sufficiently inclusive that they reduced one of the strong rationales for extractive political institutions—the economic elite had little to gain from their own or the military's dominance of politics. The relative equality of income in South Korea also meant that the elite had less to fear from pluralism and democracy. The key influence of the United States, particularly given the threat from North Korea, also meant that the strong democracy movement that challenged the military dictatorship could not be repressed for long. Though General Park's assassination in 1979 was followed by another military coup, led by Chun Doo-hwan, Chun's chosen successor, Roh Tae-woo, initiated a process of political reforms that led to the consolidation of a pluralistic democracy after 1992. Of course, no transition of this sort took place in the Soviet Union. In consequence, Soviet growth ran out of steam, and the economy began to collapse in the 1980s and then totally fell apart in the 1990s.

Chinese economic growth today also has several commonalities with both the Soviet and South Korean experiences. While the early stages of Chinese growth were spearheaded by radical market reforms in the agricultural sector, reforms in the industrial sector have been more muted. Even today, the state and the Communist Party play a central role in deciding which sectors and which companies will receive additional capital and will expand—in the process, making and breaking fortunes. As in the Soviet Union in its heyday, China is growing rapidly, but this is still growth under extractive institutions, under the control of the state, with little sign of a transition to inclusive political institutions. The fact that Chinese economic institutions are still far from fully inclusive also suggests that a South Korean–style transition is less likely, though of course not impossible.

It is worth noting that political centralization is key to both ways in which growth under extractive political institutions can occur. Without some degree of political centralization, the planter elite in Barbados, Cuba, Haiti, and Jamaica would not have been able to keep law and order and defend their own assets and property. Without significant political centralization and a firm grip on political power, neither the South Korean military elites nor the Chinese Communist Party would have felt secure enough to manufacture significant economic reforms and still manage to cling to power. And without such centralization, the state in the Soviet Union or China could not have been able to coordinate economic activity to channel resources toward high productivity areas. A major dividing line between extractive political institutions is therefore their degree of political centralization. Those without it, such as many in sub-Saharan Africa, will find it difficult to achieve even limited growth.

Even though extractive institutions can generate some growth, they will usually not generate sustained economic growth, and certainly not the type of growth that is accompanied by creative destruction. When both political and economic institutions are extractive, the incentives will not be there for creative destruction and technological change. For a while the state may be able to create rapid economic growth by allocating resources and people by fiat, but this process is intrinsically limited. When the limits are hit, growth stops, as it did in the Soviet Union in the 1970s. Even when the Soviets achieved rapid economic growth, there was little technological change in most of the economy, though by pouring massive resources into the military they were able to develop military technologies and even pull ahead of the United States in the space and nuclear race for a short while. But this growth without creative destruction and without broad-based technological innovation was not sustainable and came to an abrupt end.

In addition, the arrangements that support economic growth under extractive political institutions are, by their nature, fragile—they can collapse or can be easily destroyed by the infighting that the extractive institutions themselves generate. In fact, extractive political and economic institutions create a general tendency for infighting, because they lead to the concentration of wealth and power in the hands of a narrow elite. If another group can overwhelm and outmaneuver this elite and take control of the state, they will be the ones enjoying this wealth and power. Consequently, as our discussion of the collapse of the later Roman Empire and the Maya cities will illustrate (pages 166–172 and 143–149), fighting to control the all-powerful state is always latent, and it will periodically intensify and bring the undoing of these regimes, as it turns into civil war and sometimes into total breakdown and collapse of the state. One implication of this is that even if a society under extractive institutions initially achieves some degree of state centralization, it will not last. In fact, the infighting to take control of extractive institutions often leads to civil wars and widespread lawlessness, enshrining a persistent absence of state centralization as in many nations in sub-Saharan Africa and some in Latin America and South Asia.

Finally, when growth comes under extractive political institutions but where economic institutions have inclusive aspects, as they did in South Korea, there is always the danger that economic institutions become more extractive and growth stops. Those controlling political power will eventually find it more beneficial to use their power to limit competition, to increase their share of the pie, or even to steal and loot from others rather than support economic progress. The distribution and ability to exercise power will ultimately undermine the very foundations of economic prosperity, unless political institutions are transformed from extractive to inclusive.

4.

Small Differences and Critical

Junctures: The Weight of History

The World the Plague Created

IN 1346 THE BUBONIC plague, the Black Death, reached the port city of Tana at the mouth of the River Don on the Black Sea. Transmitted by fleas living on rats, the plague was brought from China by traders traveling along the Silk Road, the great trans-Asian commercial artery. Thanks to Genoese traders, the rats were soon spreading the fleas and the plague from Tana to the entire Mediterranean. By early 1347, the plague had reached Constantinople. In the spring of 1348, it was spreading through France and North Africa and up the boot of Italy. The plague wiped out about half of the population of any area it hit. Its arrival in the Italian city of Florence was witnessed firsthand by the Italian writer Giovanni Boccaccio. He later recalled:

> In the face of its onrush, all the wisdom and ingenuity of man were unavailing . . . the plague began, in a terrifying and extraordinary manner, to make its disastrous effects apparent. It did not take the form it had assumed in the East, where if anyone bled from the nose it was an obvious portent of certain death. On the contrary, its earliest symptom was the appearance of certain swellings in the groin or armpit, some of which were egg-shaped whilst others were roughly the size of a common apple . . . Later on the symptoms

of the disease changed, and many people began to find dark blotches and bruises on their arms, thighs and other parts of their bodies . . . Against these maladies . . . All the advice of physicians and all the power of medicine were profitless and unavailing . . . And in most cases death occurred within three days from the appearance of the symptoms we have described.

People in England knew the plague was coming their way and were well aware of impending doom. In mid-August 1348, King Edward III asked the Archbishop of Canterbury to organize prayers, and many bishops wrote letters for priests to read out in church to help people cope with what was about to hit them. Ralph of Shrewsbury, Bishop of Bath, wrote to his priests:

Almighty God uses thunder, lightening [*sic*], and other blows which issue from his throne to scourge the sons whom he wishes to redeem. Accordingly, since a catastrophic pestilence from the East has arrived in a neighboring kingdom, it is to be very much feared that, unless we pray devoutly and incessantly, a similar pestilence will stretch its poisonous branches into this realm, and strike down and consume the inhabitants. Therefore we must all come before the presence of the Lord in confession, reciting psalms.

It didn't do any good. The plague hit and quickly wiped out about half the English population. Such catastrophes can have a huge effect on the institutions of society. Perhaps understandably, scores of people went mad. Boccaccio noted that "some maintained that an infallible way of warding off this appalling evil was to drink heavily, enjoy life to the full, go round singing and merrymaking, gratify all one's cravings whenever the opportunity offered, and shrug the thing off as an enormous joke . . . and this explains why those women who recovered were possibly less chaste in the period that followed." Yet the

plague also had a socially, economically, and politically transformative impact on medieval European societies.

At the turn of the fourteenth century, Europe had a feudal order,
an organization of society that first emerged in Western Europe after
the collapse of the Roman Empire. It was based on a hierarchical relationship between the king and the lords beneath him, with the peasants at the bottom. The king owned the land and he granted it to the
lords in exchange for military services. The lords then allocated land
to peasants, in exchange for which peasants had to perform extensive
unpaid labor and were subject to many fines and taxes. Peasants, who
because of their "servile" status were thus called serfs, were tied to the
land, unable to move elsewhere without the permission of their lord,
who was not just the landlord, but also the judge, jury, and police
force. It was a highly extractive system, with wealth flowing upward
from the many peasants to the few lords.

The massive scarcity of labor created by the plague shook the
foundations of the feudal order. It encouraged peasants to demand
that things change. At Eynsham Abbey, for example, the peasants
demanded that many of the fines and unpaid labor be reduced. They
got what they wanted, and their new contract began with the asser-
tion "At the time of the mortality or pestilence, which occurred in
1349, scarcely two tenants remained in the manor, and they expressed
their intention of leaving unless Brother Nicholas of Upton, then
abbot and lord of the manor, made a new agreement with them."
He did.

What happened at Eynsham happened everywhere. Peasants
started to free themselves from compulsory labor services and many
obligations to their lords. Wages started to rise. The government tried
to put a stop to this and, in 1351, passed the Statute of Laborers,
which commenced:

> Because a great part of the people and especially of
> the workmen and servants has now died in that pesti-
> lence, some, seeing the straights of the masters and
> the scarcity of servants, are not willing to serve unless

they receive excessive wages . . . We, considering the
grave inconveniences which might come from the lack
especially of ploughmen and such labourers, have . . .
seen fit to ordain: that every man and woman of our
kingdom of England . . . shall be bound to serve him
who has seen fit so to seek after him; and he shall take
only the wages liveries, meed or salary which, in the
places where he sought to serve, were accustomed to
be paid in the twentieth year of our reign of England
[King Edward III came to the throne on January 25,
1327, so the reference here is to 1347] or the five or six
common years next preceding.

The statute in effect tried to fix wages at the levels paid before the
Black Death. Particularly concerning for the English elite was "enticement," the attempt by one lord to attract the scarce peasants of another. The solution was to make prison the punishment for leaving
employment without permission of the employer:

And if a reaper or mower, or other workman or ser-
vant, of whatever standing or condition he be, who is
retained in the service of any one, do depart from the
said service before the end of the term agreed, without permission or reasonable cause, he shall undergo
the penalty of imprisonment, and let no one . . . moreover, pay or permit to be paid to any one more wages,
livery, meed or salary than was customary as has been
said.

The attempt by the English state to stop the changes of institutions
and wages that came in the wake of the Black Death didn't work. In
1381 the Peasants' Revolt broke out, and the rebels, under the leadership of Wat Tyler, even captured most of London. Though they were
ultimately defeated, and Tyler was executed, there were no more
attempts to enforce the Statute of Laborers. Feudal labor services

dwindled away, an inclusive labor market began to emerge in England, and wages rose.

The plague seems to have hit most of the world, and everywhere a similar fraction of the population perished. Thus the demographic impact in Eastern Europe was the same as in England and Western Europe. The social and economic forces at play were also the same. Labor was scarce and people demanded greater freedoms. But in the East, a more powerful contradictory logic was at work. Fewer people meant higher wages in an inclusive labor market. But this gave lords a greater incentive to keep the labor market extractive and the peasants servile. In England this motivation had been in play, too, as reflected in the Statute of Laborers. But workers had sufficient power that they got their way. Not so in Eastern Europe. After the plague, Eastern landlords started to take over large tracts of land and expand their holdings, which were already larger than those in Western Europe. Towns were weaker and less populous, and rather than becoming freer, workers began to see their already existing freedoms encroached on.

The effects became especially clear after 1500, when Western Europe began to demand the agricultural goods, such as wheat, rye, and livestock, produced in the East. Eighty percent of the imports of rye into Amsterdam came from the Elbe, Vistula, and Oder river valleys. Soon half of the Netherlands' booming trade was with Eastern Europe. As Western demand expanded, Eastern landlords ratcheted up their control over the labor force to expand their supply. It was to be called the Second Serfdom, distinct and more intense than its original form of the early Middle Ages. Lords increased the taxes they levied on their tenants' own plots and took half of the gross output. In Korczyn, Poland, all work for the lord in 1533 was paid. But by 1600 nearly half was unpaid forced labor. In 1500, workers in Mecklenburg, in eastern Germany, owed only a few days' unpaid labor services a year. By 1550 it was one day a week, and by 1600, three days per week. Workers' children had to work for the lord for free for several years. In Hungary, landlords took complete control of the land in 1514, legislating one day a week of unpaid labor services for each worker. In 1550 this was raised to two days per week. By the end of the century, it was three days. Serfs subject to these rules made up 90 percent of the rural population by this time.

Though in 1346 there were few differences between Western and Eastern Europe in terms of political and economic institutions, by 1600 they were worlds apart. In the West, workers were free of feudal dues, fines, and regulations and were becoming a key part of a booming market economy. In the East, they were also involved in such an economy, but as coerced serfs growing the food and agricultural goods demanded in the West. It was a market economy, but not an inclusive one. This institutional divergence was the result of a situation where the differences between these areas initially seemed very small: in the East, lords were a little better organized; they had slightly more rights and more consolidated landholdings. Towns were weaker and smaller, peasants less organized. In the grand scheme of history, these were small differences. Yet these small differences between the East and the West became very consequential for the lives of their populations and for the future path of institutional development when the feudal order was shaken up by the Black Death.

The Black Death is a vivid example of a critical juncture, a major event or confluence of factors disrupting the existing economic or political balance in society. A critical juncture is a double-edged sword that can cause a sharp turn in the trajectory of a nation. On the one hand it can open the way for breaking the cycle of extractive institutions and enable more inclusive ones to emerge, as in England. Or it can intensify the emergence of extractive institutions, as was the case with the Second Serfdom in Eastern Europe.

Understanding how history and critical junctures shape the path of economic and political institutions enables us to have a more complete theory of the origins of differences in poverty and prosperity. In addition, it enables us to account for the lay of the land today and why some nations make the transition to inclusive economic and political institutions while others do not.

THE MAKING OF INCLUSIVE INSTITUTIONS

England was unique among nations when it made the breakthrough to sustained economic growth in the seventeenth century. Major economic changes were preceded by a political revolution that brought a distinct set of economic and political institutions, much more inclusive than those of any previous society. These institutions would have profound implications not only for economic incentives and prosperity, but also for who would reap the benefits of prosperity. They were based not on consensus but, rather, were the result of intense conflict as different groups competed for power, contesting the authority of others and attempting to structure institutions in their own favor. The culmination of the institutional struggles of the sixteenth and seventeenth centuries were two landmark events: the English Civil War between 1642 and 1651, and particularly the Glorious Revolution of 1688.

The Glorious Revolution limited the power of the king and the executive, and relocated to Parliament the power to determine economic institutions. At the same time, it opened up the political system to a broad cross section of society, who were able to exert considerable influence over the way the state functioned. The Glorious Revolution was the foundation for creating a pluralistic society, and it built on and accelerated a process of political centralization. It created the world's first set of inclusive political institutions.

As a consequence, economic institutions also started becoming more inclusive. Neither slavery nor the severe economic restrictions of the feudal medieval period, such as serfdom, existed in England at the beginning of the seventeenth century. Nevertheless, there were many restrictions on economic activities people could engage in. Both the domestic and international economy were choked by monopolies. The state engaged in arbitrary taxation and manipulated the legal system. Most land was caught in archaic forms of property rights that made it impossible to sell and risky to invest in.

This changed after the Glorious Revolution. The government adopted a set of economic institutions that provided incentives for investment, trade, and innovation. It steadfastly enforced property rights, including patents granting property rights for ideas, thereby providing a major stimulus to innovation. It protected law and order. Historically unprecedented was the application of English law to all citizens. Arbitrary taxation ceased, and monopolies were abolished almost completely. The English state aggressively promoted mercantile activities and worked to promote domestic industry, not only by removing barriers to the expansion of industrial activity but also by lending the full power of the English navy to defend mercantile interests. By rationalizing property rights, it facilitated the construction of infrastructure, particularly roads, canals, and later railways, that would prove to be crucial for industrial growth.

These foundations decisively changed incentives for people and impelled the engines of prosperity, paving the way for the Industrial Revolution. First and foremost, the Industrial Revolution depended on major technological advances exploiting the knowledge base that had accumulated in Europe during the past centuries. It was a radical break from the past, made possible by scientific inquiry and the talents of a number of unique individuals. The full force of this revolution came from the market that created profitable opportunities for technologies to be developed and applied. It was the inclusive nature of markets that allowed people to allocate their talents to the right lines of business. It also relied on education and skills, for it was the relatively high levels of education, at least by the standards of the time, that enabled the emergence of entrepreneurs with the vision to employ new technologies for their businesses and to find workers with the skills to use them.

It is not a coincidence that the Industrial Revolution started in England a few decades following the Glorious Revolution. The great inventors such as James Watt (perfecter of the steam engine), Richard Trevithick (the builder of the first steam locomotive), Richard Arkwright (the inventor of the spinning frame), and Isambard Kingdom Brunel (the creator of several revolutionary steamships) were able to take up the economic opportunities generated by their ideas, were confident that their property rights would be respected, and had access to markets where their innovations could be profitably sold and used. In 1775, just after he had the patent renewed on his steam engine, which he called his "Fire engine," James Watt wrote to his father:

> Dear Father,
> After a series of various and violent Oppositions I have at last got an Act of Parliament vesting the property of my new Fire engines in me and my Assigns, throughout Great Britain & the plantations for twenty five years to come, which I hope will be very beneficial to me, as there is already considerable demand for them.

This letter reveals two things. First, Watt was motivated by the market opportunities he anticipated, by the "considerable demand" in Great Britain and its plantations, the English overseas colonies. Second, it shows how he was able to influence Parliament to get what he wanted since it was responsive to the appeals of individuals and innovators.

The technological advances, the drive of businesses to expand and invest, and the efficient use of skills and talent were all made possible by the inclusive economic institutions that England developed. These in turn were founded on her inclusive political institutions.

England developed these inclusive political institutions because of two factors. First were political institutions, including a centralized state, that enabled her to take the next radical—in fact, unprecedented—step toward inclusive institutions with the onset of the Glorious Revolution. While this factor distinguished England from much of the world, it did not significantly differentiate it from Western European countries such as France and Spain. More important was the second factor. The events leading up to the Glorious Revolution forged a broad and powerful coalition able to place durable constraints on the power of the monarchy and the executive, which were forced to be open to the demands of this coalition. This laid the foundations for pluralistic political institutions, which then enabled the development of economic institutions that would underpin the first Industrial Revolution.

SMALL DIFFERENCES THAT MATTER

World inequality dramatically increased with the British, or English, Industrial Revolution because only some parts of the world adopted the innovations and new technologies that men such as Arkwright and Watt, and the many who followed, developed. The response of different nations to this wave of technologies, which determined whether they would languish in poverty or achieve sustained economic growth, was largely shaped by the different historical paths of their institutions. By the middle of the eighteenth century, there were already notable differences in political and economic institutions around the world. But where did these differences come from?

English political institutions were on their way to much greater pluralism by 1688, compared with those in France and Spain, but if we go back in time one hundred years, to 1588, the differences shrink to almost nothing. All three countries were ruled by relatively absolutist monarchs: Elizabeth I in England, Philip II in Spain, and Henry III in France. All were battling with assemblies of citizens—such as the Parliament in England, the Cortes in Spain, and the Estates-General in France—that were demanding more rights and control over the monarchy. These assemblies all had somewhat different powers and scopes. For instance, the English Parliament and the Spanish Cortes had power over taxation, while the Estates-General did not. In Spain this mattered little, because after 1492 the Spanish Crown had a vast American empire and benefited massively from the gold and silver found there. In England the situation was different. Elizabeth I was far less financially independent, so she had to beg Parliament for more taxes. In exchange, Parliament demanded concessions, in particular restrictions on the right of Elizabeth to create monopolies. It was a conflict Parliament gradually won. In Spain the Cortes lost a similar conflict. Trade wasn't just monopolized; it was monopolized by the Spanish monarchy.

These distinctions, which initially appeared small, started to matter a great deal in the seventeenth century. Though the Americas had been discovered by 1492 and Vasco da Gama had reached India by rounding the Cape of Good Hope, at the southern tip of Africa, in

1498, it was only after 1600 that a huge expansion of world trade, particularly in the Atlantic, started to take place. In 1585 the first English colonization of North America began at Roanoke, in what is now North Carolina. In 1600 the English East India Company was formed. In 1602 it was followed by the Dutch equivalent. In 1607 the colony of Jamestown was founded by the Virginia Company. By the 1620s the Caribbean was being colonized, with Barbados occupied in 1627. France was also expanding in the Atlantic, founding Quebec City in 1608 as the capital of New France in what is now Canada. The consequences of this economic expansion for institutions were very different for England than for Spain and France because of small initial differences.

Elizabeth I and her successors could not monopolize the trade with the Americas. Other European monarchs could. So while in England, Atlantic trade and colonization started creating a large group of wealthy traders with few links to the Crown, this was not the case in Spain or France. The English traders resented royal control and demanded changes in political institutions and the restriction of royal prerogatives. They played a critical role in the English Civil War and the Glorious Revolution. Similar conflicts took place everywhere. French kings, for example, faced the Fronde Rebellion between 1648 and 1652. The difference was that in England it was far more likely that the opponents to absolutism would prevail because they were relatively wealthy and more numerous than the opponents to absolutism in Spain and France.

The divergent paths of English, French, and Spanish societies in the seventeenth century illustrate the importance of the interplay of small institutional differences with critical junctures. During critical junctures, a major event or confluence of factors disrupts the existing balance of political or economic power in a nation. These can affect only a single country, such as the death of Chairman Mao Zedong in 1976, which at first created a critical juncture only for Communist China. Often, however, critical junctures affect a whole set of societies, in the way that, for example, colonization and then decolonization affected most of the globe.

Such critical junctures are important because there are formidable barriers against gradual improvements, resulting from the synergy between extractive political and economic institutions and the support they give each other. The persistence of this feedback loop creates a vicious circle. Those who benefit from the status quo are wealthy and well organized, and can effectively fight major changes that will take away their economic privileges and political power.

Once a critical juncture happens, the small differences that matter are the initial institutional differences that put in motion very different responses. This is the reason why the relatively small institutional differences in England, France, and Spain led to fundamentally different development paths. The paths resulted from the critical juncture created by the economic opportunities presented to Europeans by Atlantic trade.

Even if small institutional differences matter greatly during critical junctures, not all institutional differences are small, and naturally, larger institutional differences lead to even more divergent patterns during such junctures. While the institutional differences between England and France were small in 1588, the differences between Western and Eastern Europe were much greater. In the West, strong centralized states such as England, France, and Spain had latent constitutional institutions (Parliament, the Estates-General, and the Cortes). There were also underlying similarities in economic institutions, such as the lack of serfdom.

Eastern Europe was a different matter. The kingdom of Poland-Lithuania, for example, was ruled by an elite class called the Szlachta, who were so powerful they had even introduced elections for kings. This was not absolute rule as in France under Louis XIV, the Sun King, but absolutism of an elite, extractive political institutions all the same. The Szlachta ruled over a mostly rural society dominated by serfs, who had no freedom of movement or economic opportunities. Farther east, the Russian emperor Peter the Great was also consolidating an absolutism far more intense and extractive than even Louis XIV could manage. Map 8 (page 109) provides one simple way of seeing the extent of the divergence between Western and Eastern Europe at the beginning of the nineteenth century. It plots whether or not a country still had serfdom in 1800. Countries that appear dark did;

those that are light did not. Eastern Europe is dark; Western Europe is light.

Yet the institutions of Western Europe had not always been so different from those in the East. They began, as we saw earlier, to diverge in the fourteenth century when the Black Death hit in 1346. There were small differences between political and economic institutions in Western and Eastern Europe. England and Hungary were even ruled by members of the same family, the Angevins. The more important institutional differences that emerged after the Black Death then created the background upon which the more significant divergence between the East and the West would play out during the seventeenth, eighteenth, and nineteenth centuries.

But where do the small institutional differences that start this process of divergence arise in the first place? Why did Eastern Europe have different political and economic institutions than the West in the fourteenth century? Why was the balance of power between Crown and Parliament different in England than in France and Spain? As we will see in the next chapter, even societies that are far less complex than our modern society create political and economic institutions that have powerful effects on the lives of their members. This is true even for hunter-gatherers, as we know from surviving societies such as the San people of modern Botswana, who do not farm or even live in permanent settlements.

No two societies create the same institutions; they will have distinct customs, different systems of property rights, and different ways of dividing a killed animal or loot stolen from another group. Some will recognize the authority of elders, others will not; some will achieve some degree of political centralization early on, but not others. Societies are constantly subject to economic and political conflict that is resolved in different ways because of specific historical differences, the role of individuals, or just random factors.

These differences are often small to start with, but they cumulate, creating a process of institutional drift. Just as two isolated populations of organisms will drift apart slowly in a process of genetic drift, because random genetic mutations cumulate, two otherwise similar societies will also slowly drift apart institutionally. Though, just like

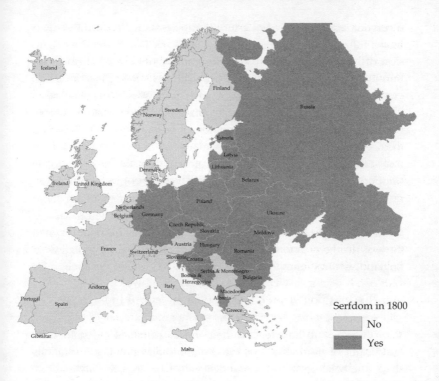

Map 8: Serfdom in Europe in 1800

genetic drift, institutional drift has no predetermined path and does not even need to be cumulative; over centuries it can lead to perceptible, sometimes important differences. The differences created by institutional drift become especially consequential, because they influence how society reacts to changes in economic or political circumstances during critical junctures.

The richly divergent patterns of economic development around the world hinge on the interplay of critical junctures and institutional drift. Existing political and economic institutions—sometimes shaped by a long process of institutional drift and sometimes resulting from divergent responses to prior critical junctures—create the anvil upon which future change will be forged. The Black Death and the expansion of world trade after 1600 were both major critical junctures for European powers and interacted with different initial institutions to create a major divergence. Because in 1346 in Western Europe peasants had more power and autonomy than they did in Eastern Europe, the Black Death led to the dissolution of feudalism in the West and the Second Serfdom in the East. Because Eastern and Western Europe had started to diverge in the fourteenth century, the new economic opportunities of the seventeenth, eighteenth, and nineteenth centuries would also have fundamentally different implications for these different parts of Europe. Because in 1600 the grip of the Crown was weaker in England than in France and Spain, Atlantic trade opened the way to the creation of new institutions with greater pluralism in England, while strengthening the French and Spanish monarchs.

THE CONTINGENT PATH OF HISTORY

The outcomes of the events during critical junctures are shaped by the weight of history, as existing economic and political institutions shape the balance of power and delineate what is politically feasible. The outcome, however, is not historically predetermined but contingent. The exact path of institutional development during these periods depends on which one of the opposing forces will succeed, which groups will be able to form effective coalitions, and which leaders will be able to structure events to their advantage.

The role of contingency can be illustrated by the origins of inclusive political institutions in England. Not only was there nothing preordained in the victory of the groups vying for limiting the power of the Crown and for more pluralistic institutions in the Glorious Revolution of 1688, but the entire path leading up to this political revolution was at the mercy of contingent events. The victory of the winning groups was inexorably linked to the critical juncture created by the rise of Atlantic trade that enriched and emboldened merchants opposing the Crown. But a century earlier it was far from obvious that England would have any ability to dominate the seas, colonize many parts of the Caribbean and North America, or capture so much of the lucrative trade with the Americas and the East. Neither Elizabeth I nor other Tudor monarchs before her had built a powerful, unified navy. The English navy relied on privateers and independent merchant ships and was much less powerful than the Spanish fleet. The profits of the Atlantic nonetheless attracted these privateers, challenging the Spanish monopoly of the ocean. In 1588 the Spanish decided to put an end to these challenges to their monopoly, as well as to English meddling in the Spanish Netherlands, at the time fighting against Spain for independence.

The Spanish monarch Philip II sent a powerful fleet, the Armada, commanded by the Duke of Medina Sidonia. It appeared a foregone conclusion to many that the Spanish would conclusively defeat the English, solidify their monopoly of the Atlantic, and probably over-throw Elizabeth I, perhaps ultimately gaining control of the British Isles. Yet something very different transpired. Bad weather and strate-gic mistakes by Sidonia, who had been put in charge at the last min-ute after a more experienced commander died, made the Spanish Armada lose their advantage. Against all odds, the English destroyed much of the fleet of their more powerful opponents. The Atlantic seas were now open to the English on more equal terms. Without this un-likely victory for the English, the events that would create the trans-formative critical juncture and spawn the distinctively pluralistic political institutions of post-1688 England would never have got mov-ing. Map 9 (page 112) shows the trail of Spanish shipwrecks as the Armada was chased right around the British Isles.

Of course, nobody in 1588 could foresee the consequences of the fortunate English victory. Few probably understood at the time that this would create a critical juncture leading up to a major political revolution a century later.

There should be no presumption that any critical juncture will lead to a successful political revolution or to change for the better. History is full of examples of revolutions and radical movements replacing one tyranny with another, in a pattern that the German sociologist Robert Michels dubbed the iron law of oligarchy, a particularly perni-cious form of the vicious circle. The end of colonialism in the decades

Map 9: The Spanish Armada, shipwrecks, and key places
that made the Turning Point

following the Second World War created critical junctures for many former colonies. However, in most cases in sub-Saharan Africa and many in Asia, the postindependence governments simply took a page out of Robert Michels's book and repeated and intensified the abuses of their predecessors, often severely narrowing the distribution of political power, dismantling constraints, and undermining the already meager incentives that economic institutions provided for investment and economic progress. It was only in a few cases, societies such as Botswana (see pages 404–414), that critical junctures were used to launch a process of political and economic change that paved the way for economic growth.

Critical junctures can also result in major change toward rather than away from extractive institutions. Inclusive institutions, even though they have their own feedback loop, the virtuous circle, can also reverse course and become gradually more extractive because of challenges during critical junctures—and whether this happens is, again, contingent. The Venetian Republic, as we will see in chapter 6, made major strides toward inclusive political and economic institutions in the medieval period. But while such institutions became gradually stronger in England after the Glorious Revolution of 1688, in Venice they ultimately transformed themselves into extractive institutions under the control of a narrow elite that monopolized both economic opportunities and political power.

UNDERSTANDING THE LAY OF THE LAND

The emergence of a market economy based on inclusive institutions and sustained economic growth in eighteenth-century England sent ripples all around the world, not least because it allowed England to colonize a large part of it. But if the influence of English economic growth certainly spread around the globe, the economic and political institutions that created it did not automatically do so. The diffusion of the Industrial Revolution had different effects on the world in the same way that the Black Death had different effects on Western and Eastern Europe, and in the same way that the expansion of Atlantic trade had different effects in England and Spain. It was the institutions in place in different parts of the world that determined the impact, and these institutions were indeed different—small differences had been amplified over time by prior critical junctures. These institutional differences and their implications have tended to persist to the present due to the vicious and virtuous circles, albeit imperfectly, and are the key to understanding both how world inequality emerged and the nature of the lay of the land around us.

Some parts of the world developed institutions that were very close to those in England, though by a very different route. This was particularly true of some European "settler colonies" such as Australia, Canada, and the United States, though their institutions were just forming as the Industrial Revolution was getting under way. As we saw in chapter 1, a process starting with the foundation of the Jamestown colony in 1607 and culminating in the War of Independence and the enactment of the U.S. Constitution shares many of the same characteristics as the long struggle in England of Parliament against the monarchy, for it also led to a centralized state with pluralistic political institutions. The Industrial Revolution then spread rapidly to such countries.

Western Europe, experiencing many of the same historical processes, had institutions similar to England at the time of the Industrial Revolution. There were small but consequential differences between England and the rest, which is why the Industrial Revolution happened in England and not France. This revolution then created an entirely new situation and considerably different sets of challenges to European regimes, which in turn spawned a new set of conflicts culminating in the French Revolution. The French Revolution was another critical juncture that led the institutions of Western Europe to converge with those of England, while Eastern Europe diverged further.

The rest of the world followed different institutional trajectories. European colonization set the stage for institutional divergence in the Americas, where in contrast to the inclusive institutions developed in the United States and Canada extractive ones emerged in Latin America, which explains the patterns of inequality we see in the Americas. The extractive political and economic institutions of the Spanish conquistadors in Latin America have endured, condemning much of the region to poverty. Argentina and Chile have, however, fared better than most other countries in the region. They had few indigenous people or mineral riches and were "neglected" while the Spanish focused on the lands occupied by the Aztec, Maya, and Incan civilizations. Not coincidentally, the poorest part of Argentina is the northwest, the only section of the country integrated into the Spanish colonial economy. Its persistent poverty, the legacy of extractive institutions, is similar to that created by the Potosí *mita* in Bolivia and Peru (pages 16–18).

Africa was the part of the world with the institutions least able to take advantage of the opportunities made available by the Industrial Revolution. For at least the last one thousand years, outside of small pockets and during limited periods of time, Africa has lagged behind the rest of the world in terms of technology, political development, and prosperity. It is the part of the world where centralized states formed very late and very tenuously. Where they did form, they were likely as highly absolutist as the Kongo and often short lived, usually collapsing. Africa shares this trajectory of lack of state centralization with countries such as Afghanistan, Haiti, and Nepal, which have also failed to impose order over their territories and create anything resembling stability to achieve even a modicum of economic progress. Though located in very different parts of the world, Afghanistan, Haiti, and Nepal have much in common institutionally with most nations in sub-Saharan Africa, and are thus some of the poorest countries in the world today.

How African institutions evolved into their present-day extractive form again illustrates the process of institutional drift punctuated by critical junctures, but this time often with highly perverse outcomes, particularly during the expansion of the Atlantic slave trade. There were new economic opportunities for the Kingdom of Kongo when European traders arrived. The long-distance trade that transformed Europe also transformed the Kingdom of Kongo, but again, initial institutional differences mattered. Kongolese absolutism transmogrified from completely dominating society, with extractive economic institutions that merely captured all the agricultural output of its citizens, to enslaving people en masse and selling them to the Portuguese in exchange for guns and luxury goods for the Kongolese elite.

The initial differences between England and Kongo meant that while new long-distance trade opportunities created a critical juncture toward pluralistic political institutions in the former, they also extinguished any hope of absolutism being defeated in the Kongo. In much of Africa the substantial profits to be had from slaving led not only to its intensification and even more insecure property rights for the people but also to intense warfare and the destruction of many existing institutions; within a few centuries, any process of state centralization was totally reversed, and many of the African states had largely collapsed. Though some new, and sometimes powerful, states did form to exploit the slave trade, they were based on warfare and plunder. The critical juncture of the discovery of the Americas may have helped England develop inclusive institutions but it made institutions in Africa even more extractive.

Though the slave trade mostly ended after 1807, subsequent European colonialism not only threw into reverse nascent economic modernization in parts of southern and western Africa but also cut off any possibility of indigenous institutional reform. This meant that even outside of areas such as Congo, Madagascar, Namibia, and Tanzania, the areas where plunder, mass disruption, and even whole-scale murder were the rule, there was little chance for Africa to change its institutional path.

Even worse, the structures of colonial rule left Africa with a more complex and pernicious institutional legacy in the 1960s than at the start of the colonial period. The development of the political and economic institutions in many African colonies meant that rather than creating a critical juncture for improvements in their institutions, independence created an opening for unscrupulous leaders to take over and intensify the extraction that European colonialists presided over. The political incentives these structures created led to a style of politics that reproduced the historical patterns of insecure and inefficient property rights under states with strong absolutist tendencies but nonetheless lacking any centralized authority over their territories.

The Industrial Revolution has still not spread to Africa because that continent has experienced a long vicious circle of the persistence and re-creation of extractive political and economic institutions. Botswana is the exception. As we will see (pages 404–414), in the nineteenth century, King Khama, the grandfather of Botswana's first prime minister at independence, Seretse Khama, initiated institutional changes to modernize the political and economic institutions of his tribe. Quite uniquely, these changes were not destroyed in the colonial period, partly as a consequence of Khama's and other chiefs' clever challenges to colonial authority. Their interplay with the critical juncture that independence from colonial rule created laid the foundations for Botswana's economic and political success. It was another case of small historical differences mattering.

There is a tendency to see historical events as the inevitable consequences of deep-rooted forces. While we place great emphasis on how the history of economic and political institutions creates vicious and virtuous circles, contingency, as we have emphasized in the context of the development of English institutions, can always be a factor. Seretse Khama, studying in England in the 1940s, fell in love with Ruth Williams, a white woman. As a result, the racist apartheid regime in South Africa persuaded the English government to ban him from the protectorate, then called Bechuanaland (whose administration was under the High Commissioner of South Africa), and he resigned his kingship. When he returned to lead the anticolonial struggle, he did so with the intention not of entrenching the traditional institutions but of adapting them to the modern world. Khama was an extraordinary man, uninterested in personal wealth and dedicated to building his country. Most other African countries have not been so fortunate. Both things mattered, the historical development of institutions in Botswana and contingent factors that led these to be built on rather than overthrown or distorted as they were elsewhere in Africa.

IN THE NINETEENTH CENTURY, absolutism not so different from that in Africa or Eastern Europe was blocking the path of industrialization in much of Asia. In China, the state was strongly absolutist, and independent cities, merchants, and industrialists were either nonexistent or much weaker politically. China was a major naval power and heavily involved in long-distance trade centuries before the Europeans. But it had turned away from the oceans just at the wrong time, when Ming emperors decided in the late fourteenth and early fifteenth centuries that increased long-distance trade and the creative destruction that it might bring would be likely to threaten their rule.

In India, institutional drift worked differently and led to the development of a uniquely rigid hereditary caste system that limited the functioning of markets and the allocation of labor across occupations much more severely than the feudal order in medieval Europe. It also underpinned another strong form of absolutism under the Mughal rulers. Most European countries had similar systems in the Middle Ages. Modern Anglo-Saxon surnames such as Baker, Cooper, and Smith are direct descendants of hereditary occupational categories. Bakers baked, coopers made barrels, and smiths forged metals. But these categories were never as rigid as Indian caste distinctions and gradually became meaningless as predictors of a person's occupation. Though Indian merchants did trade throughout the Indian Ocean, and a major textile industry developed, the caste system and Mughal absolutism were serious impediments to the development of inclusive economic institutions in India. By the nineteenth century, things were even less hospitable for industrialization as India became an extractive colony of the English. China was never formally colonized by a European power, but after the English successfully defeated the Chinese in the Opium Wars between 1839 and 1842, and then again between 1856 and 1860, China had to sign a series of humiliating treaties and allow European exports to enter. As China, India, and others failed to take advantage of commercial and industrial opportunities, Asia, except for Japan, lagged behind as Western Europe was forging ahead.

THE COURSE OF institutional development that Japan charted in the nineteenth century again illustrates the interaction between critical junctures and small differences created by institutional drift. Japan, like China, was under absolutist rule. The Tokugawa family took over in 1600 and ruled over a feudal system that also banned international trade. Japan, too, faced a critical juncture created by Western intervention as four U.S. warships, commanded by Matthew C. Perry, entered Edo Bay in July 1853, demanding trade concessions similar to those

England obtained from the Chinese in the Opium Wars. But this critical juncture played out very differently in Japan. Despite their proximity and frequent interactions, by the nineteenth century China and Japan had already drifted apart institutionally.

While Tokugawa rule in Japan was absolutist and extractive, it had only a tenuous hold on the leaders of the other major feudal domains and was susceptible to challenge. Even though there were peasant rebellions and civil strife, absolutism in China was stronger, and the opposition less organized and autonomous. There were no equivalents of the leaders of the other domains in China who could challenge the absolutist rule of the emperor and trace an alternative institutional path. This institutional difference, in many ways small relative to the differences separating China and Japan from Western Europe, had decisive consequences during the critical juncture created by the forceful arrival of the English and Americans. China continued in its absolutist path after the Opium Wars, while the U.S. threat cemented the opposition to Tokugawa rule in Japan and led to a political revolution, the Meiji Restoration, as we will see in chapter 10. This Japanese political revolution enabled more inclusive political institutions and much more inclusive economic institutions to develop, and laid the foundations for subsequent rapid Japanese growth, while China languished under absolutism.

How Japan reacted to the threat posed by U.S. warships, by starting a process of fundamental institutional transformation, helps us understand another aspect of the lay of the land around us: transitions from stagnation to rapid growth. South Korea, Taiwan, and finally China achieved breakneck rates of economic growth since the Second World War through a path similar to the one that Japan took. In each of these cases, growth was preceded by historic changes in the countries' economic institutions—though not always in their political institutions, as the Chinese case highlights.

The logic of how episodes of rapid growth come to an abrupt end and are reversed is also related. In the same way that decisive steps toward inclusive economic institutions can ignite rapid economic growth, a sharp turn away from inclusive institutions can lead to economic stagnation. But more often, collapses of rapid growth, such as in Argentina or the Soviet Union, are a consequence of growth under extractive institutions coming to an end. As we have seen, this can happen either because of infighting over the spoils of extraction, leading to the collapse of the regime, or because the inherent lack of innovation and creative destruction under extractive institutions puts a limit on sustained growth. How the Soviets ran hard into these limits will be discussed in greater detail in the next chapter.

IF THE POLITICAL and economic institutions of Latin America over the past five hundred years were shaped by Spanish colonialism, those of the Middle East were shaped by Ottoman colonialism. In 1453 the Ottomans under Sultan Mehmet II captured Constantinople, making it their capital. During the rest of the century, the Ottomans conquered large parts of the Balkans and most of the rest of Turkey. In the first half of the sixteenth century, Ottoman rule spread throughout the Middle East and North Africa. By 1566, at the death of Sultan Süleyman I, known as the Magnificent, their empire stretched from Tunisia in the West, through Egypt, all the way to Mecca in the Arabian Peninsula, and on to what is now modern Iraq. The Ottoman state was absolutist, with the sultan accountable to few and sharing power with none. The economic institutions the Ottomans imposed were highly extractive. There was no private property in land, which all formally belonged to the state. Taxation of land and agricultural output, together with loot from war, was the main source of government revenues. However, the Ottoman state did not dominate the Middle East in the same way that it could dominate its heartland in Anatolia or even to the extent that the Spanish state dominated Latin American society. The Ottoman state was continuously challenged by Bedouins and other tribal powers in the Arabian Peninsula. It lacked not only the ability to impose a stable order in much of the Middle East but also the administrative capacity to collect taxes. So it "farmed" them out to individuals, selling off the right to others to collect taxes in whatever way they could. These tax farmers became autonomous and powerful. Rates of taxation in the Middle Eastern territories were very high, varying between one-half or two-thirds of what farmers produced. Much of this revenue was kept by the tax farmers. Because the Ottoman state failed to establish a stable order in these areas, property rights were far from secure, and there was a great deal of lawlessness and banditry as armed groups vied for local control. In Palestine, for example, the situation was so dire that starting in the late sixteenth century, peasants left the most fertile land and moved up to mountainous areas, which gave them greater protection against banditry.

Extractive economic institutions in the urban areas of the Ottoman Empire were no less stifling. Commerce was under state control, and occupations were strictly regulated by guilds and monopolies. The consequence was that at the time of the Industrial Revolution the economic institutions of the Middle East were extractive. The region stagnated economically.

By the 1840s, the Ottomans were trying to reform institutions—for example, by reversing tax farming and getting locally autonomous groups under control. But absolutism persisted until the First World War, and reform efforts were thwarted by the usual fear of creative destruction and the anxiety among elite groups that they would lose economically or politically. While Ottoman reformers talked of introducing private property rights to land in order to increase agricultural productivity, the status quo persisted because of the desire for political control and taxation. Ottoman colonization was followed by European colonization after 1918. When European control ended, the same dynamics we have seen in sub-Saharan Africa took hold, with extractive colonial institutions taken over by independent elites. In some cases, such as the monarchy of Jordan, these elites were direct creations of the colonial powers, but this, too, happened frequently in Africa, as we will see. Middle Eastern countries without oil today have income levels similar to poor Latin American nations. They did not suffer from such immiserizing forces as the slave trade, and they benefited for a longer period from flows of technology from Europe. In the Middle Ages, the Middle East itself was also a relatively advanced part of the world economically. So today it is not as poor as Africa, but the majority of its people still live in poverty.

❖   ❖   ❖

WE HAVE SEEN that neither geographic- nor cultural- nor ignorance-based theories are helpful for explaining the lay of the land around us. They do not provide a satisfactory account for the prominent patterns of world inequality: the fact that the process of economic divergence started with the Industrial Revolution in England during the eighteenth and nineteenth centuries and then spread to Western Europe and to European settler colonies; the persistent divergence between different parts of the Americas; the poverty of Africa or the Middle East; the divergence between Eastern and Western Europe; and the transitions from stagnation to growth and the sometimes abrupt end to growth spurts. Our institutional theory does.

In the remaining chapters, we will discuss in greater detail how this institutional theory works and illustrate the wide range of phenomena it can account for. These range from the origins of the Neolithic Revolution to the collapse of several civilizations, either because of the intrinsic limits to growth under extractive institutions or because of limited steps toward inclusiveness being reversed.

We will see how and why decisive steps toward inclusive political institutions were taken during the Glorious Revolution in England. We will look more specifically at the following:

- How inclusive institutions emerged from the interplay of the critical juncture created by Atlantic trade and the nature of preexisting English institutions.

- How these institutions persisted and became strengthened to lay the foundations for the Industrial Revolution, thanks in part to the virtuous circle and in part to fortunate turns of contingency.

- How many regimes reigning over absolutist and extractive institutions steadfastly resisted the spread of new technologies unleashed by the Industrial Revolution.

- How Europeans themselves stamped out the possibility of economic growth in many parts of the world that they conquered.

- How the vicious circle and the iron law of oligarchy have created a powerful tendency for extractive institutions to persist, and thus the lands where the Industrial Revolution originally did not spread remain relatively poor.

- Why the Industrial Revolution and other new technologies have not spread and are unlikely to spread to places around the world today where a minimum degree of centralization of the state hasn't been achieved.

Our discussion will also show that certain areas that managed to transform institutions in a more inclusive direction, such as France or Japan, or that prevented the establishment of extractive institutions, such as the United States or Australia, were more receptive to the spread of the Industrial Revolution and pulled ahead of the rest. As in England, this was not always a smooth process, and along the way, many challenges to inclusive institutions were overcome, sometimes because of the dynamics of the virtuous circle, sometimes thanks to the contingent path of history.

Finally, we will also discuss how the failure of nations today is heavily influenced by their institutional histories, how much policy advice is informed by incorrect hypotheses and is potentially misleading, and how nations are still able to seize critical junctures and break the mold to reform their institutions and embark upon a path to greater prosperity.

5.

"I'VE SEEN THE FUTURE, AND IT WORKS": GROWTH UNDER EXTRACTIVE INSTITUTIONS

I'VE SEEN THE FUTURE

INSTITUTIONAL DIFFERENCES PLAY the critical role in explaining economic growth throughout the ages. But if most societies in history are based on extractive political and economic institutions, does this imply that growth never takes place? Obviously not. Extractive institutions, by their very logic, must create wealth so that it can be extracted. A ruler monopolizing political power and in control of a centralized state can introduce some degree of law and order and a system of rules, and stimulate economic activity.

But growth under extractive institutions differs in nature from growth brought forth by inclusive institutions. Most important, it will be not sustained growth that requires technological change, but rather growth based on existing technologies. The economic trajectory of the Soviet Union provides a vivid illustration of how the authority and incentives provided by the state can spearhead rapid economic growth under extractive institutions and how this type of growth ultimately comes to an end and collapses.

THE FIRST WORLD WAR had ended and the victorious and the vanquished powers met in the great palace of Versailles, outside Paris, to decide on the parameters of the peace. Prominent among the attendees was Woodrow Wilson, president of the United States. Notice-able by its absence was any representation from Russia. The old tsarist regime had been overthrown by the Bolsheviks in October 1917. A civil war then raged between the Reds (the Bolsheviks) and the Whites. The English, French, and Americans sent an expeditionary force to fight against the Bolsheviks. A mission led by a young diplo-mat, William Bullitt, and the veteran intellectual and journalist Lincoln Steffens was sent to Moscow to meet with Lenin to try to understand the intentions of the Bolsheviks and how to come to terms with them. Steffens had made his name as an iconoclast, a muckraker journalist who had persistently denounced the evils of capitalism in the United States. He had been in Russia at the time of the revolution. His pres-ence was intended to make the mission look credible and not too hostile. The mission returned with the outlines of an offer from Lenin about what it would take for peace with the newly created Soviet Union. Steffens was bowled over by what he saw as the great poten-tial of the Soviet regime.

"Soviet Russia," he recalled in his 1931 autobiography, "was a rev-olutionary government with an evolutionary plan. Their plan was not to end evils such as poverty and riches, graft, privilege, tyranny, and war by direct action, but to seek out and remove their causes. They had set up a dictatorship, supported by a small, trained minority, to make and maintain for a few generations a scientific rearrangement of economic forces which would result in economic democracy first and political democracy last."

When Steffens returned from his diplomatic mission he went to see his old friend the sculptor Jo Davidson and found him making a portrait bust of the wealthy financier Bernard Baruch. "So you've been over in Russia," Baruch remarked. Steffens answered, "I have been over into the future, and it works." He would perfect this adage into a form that went down in history: "I've seen the future, and it works."

Right up until the early 1980s, many Westerners were still seeing the future in the Soviet Union, and they kept on believing that it was working. In a sense it was, or at least it did for a time. Lenin had died in 1924, and by 1927 Joseph Stalin had consolidated his grip on the country. He purged his opponents and launched a drive to rapidly industrialize the country. He did it via energizing the State Planning Committee, Gosplan, which had been founded in 1921. Gosplan wrote the first Five-Year Plan, which ran between 1928 and 1933. Economic growth Stalin style was simple: develop industry by government command and obtain the necessary resources for this by taxing agriculture at very high rates. The communist state did not have an effective tax system, so instead Stalin "collectivized" agriculture. This process entailed the abolition of private property rights to land and the herding of all people in the countryside into giant collective farms run by the Communist Party. This made it much easier for Stalin to grab agricultural output and use it to feed all the people who were building and manning the new factories. The consequences of this for the rural folk were calamitous. The collective farms completely lacked incentives for people to work hard, so production fell sharply. So much of what was produced was extracted that there was not enough to eat. People began to starve to death. In the end, probably six million people died of famine, while hundreds of thousands of others were murdered or banished to Siberia during the forcible collectivization.

Neither the newly created industry nor the collectivized farms were economically efficient in the sense that they made the best use of what resources the Soviet Union possessed. It sounds like a recipe for economic disaster and stagnation, if not outright collapse. But the Soviet Union grew rapidly. The reason for this is not difficult to understand. Allowing people to make their own decisions via markets is the best way for a society to efficiently use its resources. When the state or a narrow elite controls all these resources instead, neither the right incentives will be created nor will there be an efficient allocation of the skills and talents of people. But in some instances the productivity of labor and capital may be so much higher in one sector or activity, such as heavy industry in the Soviet Union, that even a top-down process under extractive institutions that allocates resources toward that sector can generate growth. As we saw in chapter 3, extractive institutions in Caribbean islands such as Barbados, Cuba, Haiti, and Jamaica could generate relatively high levels of incomes because they allocated resources to the production of sugar, a commodity coveted worldwide. The production of sugar based on gangs of slaves was certainly not "efficient," and there was no technological change or creative destruction in these societies, but this did not prevent them from achieving some amount of growth under extractive institutions. The situation was similar in the Soviet Union, with industry playing the role of sugar in the Caribbean. Industrial growth in the Soviet Union was further facilitated because its technology was so backward relative to what was available in Europe and the United States, so large gains could be reaped by reallocating resources to the industrial sector, even if all this was done inefficiently and by force.

Before 1928 most Russians lived in the countryside. The technology used by peasants was primitive, and there were few incentives to be productive. Indeed, the last vestiges of Russian feudalism were eradicated only shortly before the First World War. There was thus huge unrealized economic potential from reallocating this labor from agriculture to industry. Stalinist industrialization was one brutal way of unlocking this potential. By fiat, Stalin moved these very poorly used resources into industry, where they could be employed more productively, even if industry itself was very inefficiently organized relative to what could have been achieved. In fact, between 1928 and 1960 national income grew at 6 percent a year, probably the most rapid spurt of economic growth in history up until then. This quick economic growth was not created by technological change, but by reallocating labor and by capital accumulation through the creation of new tools and factories.

Growth was so rapid that it took in generations of Westerners, not just Lincoln Steffens. It took in the Central Intelligence Agency of the United States. It even took in the Soviet Union's own leaders, such as Nikita Khrushchev, who famously boasted in a speech to Western diplomats in 1956 that "we will bury you [the West]." As late as 1977, a leading academic textbook by an English economist argued that Soviet-style economies were superior to capitalist ones in terms of economic growth, providing full employment and price stability and even in producing people with altruistic motivation. Poor old Western capitalism did better only at providing political freedom. Indeed, the most widely used university textbook in economics, written by Nobel Prize–winner Paul Samuelson, repeatedly predicted the coming economic dominance of the Soviet Union. In the 1961 edition, Samuelson predicted that Soviet national income would overtake that of the United States possibly by 1984, but probably by 1997. In the 1980 edition there was little change in the analysis, though the two dates were delayed to 2002 and 2012.

Though the policies of Stalin and subsequent Soviet leaders could produce rapid economic growth, they could not do so in a sustained way. By the 1970s, economic growth had all but stopped. The most important lesson is that extractive institutions cannot generate sustained technological change for two reasons: the lack of economic incentives and resistance by the elites. In addition, once all the very inefficiently used resources had been reallocated to industry, there were few economic gains to be had by fiat. Then the Soviet system hit a roadblock, with lack of innovation and poor economic incentives preventing any further progress. The only area in which the Soviets did manage to sustain some innovation was through enormous efforts in military and aerospace technology. As a result they managed to put the first dog, Leika, and the first man, Yuri Gagarin, in space. They also left the world the AK-47 as one of their legacies.

Gosplan was the supposedly all-powerful planning agency in charge of the central planning of the Soviet economy. One of the benefits of the sequence of five-year plans written and administered by Gosplan was supposed to have been the long time horizon necessary for rational investment and innovation. In reality, what got implemented in Soviet industry had little to do with the five-year plans, which were frequently revised and rewritten or simply ignored. The development of industry took place on the basis of commands by Stalin and the Politburo, who changed their minds frequently and often completely revised their previous decisions. All plans were labeled "draft" or "preliminary." Only one copy of a plan labeled "final"—that for light industry in 1939—has ever come to light. Stalin himself said in 1937 that "only bureaucrats can think that planning work ends with the creation of the plan. The creation of the plan is just the beginning. The real direction of the plan develops only after the putting together of the plan." Stalin wanted to maximize his discretion to reward people or groups who were politically loyal, and punish those who were not. As for Gosplan, its main role was to provide Stalin with information so he could better monitor his friends and enemies. It actually tried to avoid making decisions. If you made a decision that turned out badly, you might get shot. Better to avoid all responsibility.

An example of what could happen if you took your job too seriously, rather than successfully second-guessing what the Communist Party wanted, is provided by the Soviet census of 1937. As the returns came in, it became clear that they would show a population of about 162 million, far less than the 180 million Stalin had anticipated and indeed below the figure of 168 million that Stalin himself announced in 1934. The 1937 census was the first conducted since 1926, and therefore the first one that followed the mass famines and purges of the early 1930s. The accurate population numbers reflected this. Stalin's response was to have those who organized the census arrested and sent to Siberia or shot. He ordered another census, which took place in 1939. This time the organizers got it right; they found that the population was actually 171 million.

Stalin understood that in the Soviet economy, people had few incentives to work hard. A natural response would have been to introduce such incentives, and sometimes he did—for example, by directing food supplies to areas where productivity had fallen—to reward improvements. Moreover, as early as 1931 he gave up on the idea of creating "socialist men and women" who would work without monetary incentives. In a famous speech he criticized "equality mongering," and thereafter not only did different jobs get paid different wages but also a bonus system was introduced. It is instructive to understand how this worked. Typically a firm under central planning had to meet an output target set under the plan, though such plans were often renegotiated and changed. From the 1930s, workers were paid bonuses if the output levels were attained. These could be quite high—for instance, as much as 37 percent of the wage for management or senior engineers. But paying such bonuses created all sorts of disincentives to technological change. For one thing, innovation, which took resources away from current production, risked the output targets not being met and the bonuses not being paid. For another, output targets were usually based on previous production levels. This created a huge incentive never to expand output, since this only meant having to produce more in the future, since future targets would be "ratcheted up." Underachievement was always the best way to meet targets and get the bonus. The fact that bonuses were paid monthly also kept everyone focused on the present, while innovation is about making sacrifices today in order to have more tomorrow.

Even when bonuses and incentives were effective in changing behavior, they often created other problems. Central planning was just not good at replacing what the great eighteenth-century economist Adam Smith called the "invisible hand" of the market. When the plan was formulated in tons of steel sheet, the sheet was made too heavy. When it was formulated in terms of area of steel sheet, the sheet was made too thin. When the plan for chandeliers was made in tons, they were so heavy, they could hardly hang from ceilings.

By the 1940s, the leaders of the Soviet Union, even if not their admirers in the West, were well aware of these perverse incentives. The Soviet leaders acted as if they were due to technical problems, which could be fixed. For example, they moved away from paying bonuses based on output targets to allowing firms to set aside portions of profits to pay bonuses. But a "profit motive" was no more encouraging to innovation than one based on output targets. The system of prices used to calculate profits was almost completely unconnected to the value of new innovations or technology. Unlike in a market economy, prices in the Soviet Union were set by the government, and thus bore little relation to value. To more specifically create incentives for innovation, the Soviet Union introduced explicit innovation bonuses in 1946. As early as 1918, the principle had been recognized that an innovator should receive monetary rewards for his innovation, but the rewards set were small and unrelated to the value of the new technology. This changed only in 1956, when it was stipulated that the bonus should be proportional to the productivity of the innovation. However, since productivity was calculated in terms of economic benefits measured using the existing system of prices, this was again not much of an incentive to innovate. One could fill many pages with examples of the perverse incentives these schemes generated. For example, because the size of the innovation bonus fund was limited by the wage bill of a firm, this immediately reduced the incentive to produce or adopt any innovation that might have economized on labor.

Focusing on the different rules and bonus schemes tends to mask the inherent problems of the system. As long as political authority and power rested with the Communist Party, it was impossible to fundamentally change the basic incentives that people faced, bonuses or no bonuses. Since its inception, the Communist Party had used not just carrots but also sticks, big sticks, to get its way. Productivity in the economy was no different. A whole set of laws created criminal offenses for workers who were perceived to be shirking. In June 1940, for example, a law made absenteeism, defined as any twenty minutes unauthorized absence or even idling on the job, a criminal offense that could be punished by six months' hard labor and a 25 percent cut in pay. All sorts of similar punishments were introduced, and were implemented with astonishing frequency. Between 1940 and 1955, 36 million people, about one-third of the adult population, were found guilty of such offenses. Of these, 15 million were sent to prison and 250,000 were shot. In any year, there would be 1 million adults in prison for labor violations; this is not to mention the 2.5 million people Stalin exiled to the gulags of Siberia. Still, it didn't work. Though you can move someone to a factory, you cannot force people to think and have good ideas by threatening to shoot them. Coercion like this might have generated a high output of sugar in Barbados or Jamaica, but it could not compensate for the lack of incentives in a modern industrial economy.

The fact that truly effective incentives could not be introduced in the centrally planned economy was not due to technical mistakes in the design of the bonus schemes. It was intrinsic to the whole method by which extractive growth had been achieved. It had been done by government command, which could solve some basic economic problems. But stimulating sustained economic growth required that individuals use their talent and ideas, and this could never be done with a Soviet-style economic system. The rulers of the Soviet Union would have had to abandon extractive economic institutions, but such a move would have jeopardized their political power. Indeed, when Mikhail Gorbachev started to move away from extractive economic institutions after 1987, the power of the Communist Party crumbled, and with it, the Soviet Union.

THE SOVIET UNION was able to generate rapid growth even under extractive institutions because the Bolsheviks built a powerful centralized state and used it to allocate resources toward industry. But as in all instances of growth under extractive institutions, this experience did not feature technological change and was not sustained. Growth first slowed down and then totally collapsed. Though ephemeral, this type of growth still illustrates how extractive institutions can stimulate economic activity.

Throughout history most societies have been ruled by extractive institutions, and those that have managed to impose some extent of order over the countries have been able to generate some limited growth—even if none of these extractive societies have managed to achieve sustained growth. In fact, some of the major turning points in history are characterized by institutional innovations that cemented extractive institutions and increased the authority of one group to impose law and order and benefit from extraction. In the rest of this chapter, we will first discuss the nature of institutional innovations that establish some degree of state centralization and enable growth under extractive institutions. We shall then show how these ideas help us understand the Neolithic Revolution, the momentous transition to agriculture, which underpins many aspects of our current civilization. We will conclude by illustrating, with the example of the Maya city-states, how growth under extractive institutions is limited not only because of lack of technological progress but also because it will encourage infighting from rival groups wishing to take control of the state and the extraction it generates.

On the Banks of the Kasai

One of the great tributaries of the River Congo is the Kasai. Rising in Angola, it heads north and merges with the Congo northeast of Kinshasa, the capital of the modern Democratic Republic of Congo. Though the Democratic Republic of Congo is poor compared with the rest of the world, there have always been significant differences in the prosperity of various groups within Congo. The Kasai is the boundary between two of these. Soon after passing into Congo along the western bank, you'll find the Lele people; on the eastern bank are the Bushong (Map 6, page 59). On the face of it there ought to be few differences between these two groups with regard to their prosperity. They are separated only by a river, which either can cross by boat. The two different tribes have a common origin and related languages. In addition, many of the things they build are similar in style, including their houses, clothes, and crafts.

Yet when the anthropologist Mary Douglas and the historian Jan Vansina studied these groups in the 1950s, they discovered some startling differences between them. As Douglas put it: "The Lele are poor, while the Bushong are rich . . . Everything that the Lele have or can do, the Bushong have more and can do better." Simple explanations for this inequality are easy to come by. One difference, reminiscent of that between places in Peru that were or were not subject to the Potosí *mita,* is that the Lele produced for subsistence while the Bushong produced for exchange in the market. Douglas and Vansina also noted that the Lele used inferior technology. For instance, they did not use nets for hunting, even though these greatly improve productivity. Douglas argued, "[T]he absence of nets is consistent with a general Lele tendency not to invest time and labor in long-term equipment."

There were also important distinctions in agricultural technologies and organization. The Bushong practiced a sophisticated form of mixed farming where five crops were planted in succession in a two-year system of rotation. They grew yams, sweet potatoes, manioc (cassava), and beans and gathered two and sometimes three maize harvests a year. The Lele had no such system and managed to reap only one annual harvest of maize.

There were also striking differences in law and order. The Lele were dispersed into fortified villages, which were constantly in conflict. Anyone traveling between two or even venturing into the forest to collect food was liable to be attacked or kidnapped. In the Bushong country, this rarely, if ever, happened.

What lay behind these differences in the patterns of production, agricultural technology, and prevalence of order? Obviously it was not geography that induced the Lele to use inferior hunting and agricultural technology. It was certainly not ignorance, because they knew about the tools used by the Bushong. An alternative explanation might be culture; could it be that the Lele had a culture that did not encourage them to invest in hunting nets and sturdier and better-built houses? But this does not seem to have been true, either. As with the people of Kongo, the Lele were very interested in purchasing guns, and Douglas even remarked that "their eager purchase of firearms . . . shows their culture does not restrict them to inferior techniques when these do not require long-term collaboration and effort." So neither a cultural aversion to technology nor ignorance nor geography does a good job of explaining the greater prosperity of the Bushong relative to the Lele.

The reason for differences between these two peoples lies in the different political institutions that emerged in the lands of the Bushong and the Lele. We noted earlier that the Lele lived in fortified villages that were not part of a unified political structure. It was different on the other side of the Kasai. Around 1620 a political revolution took place led by a man called Shyaam, who forged the Kuba Kingdom, which we saw on Map 6 (page 59), with the Bushong at its heart and with himself as king. Prior to this period, there were probably few differences between the Bushong and the Lele; the differences emerged as a consequence of the way Shyaam reorganized society to the east of the river. He built a state and a pyramid of political institutions. These were not just significantly more centralized than what came before but also involved highly elaborate structures. Shyaam and his successors created a bureaucracy to raise taxes and a legal system and police force to administer the law. Leaders were checked by councils, which they had to consult with before making decisions. There was even trial by jury, an apparently unique event in sub-Saharan Africa prior to European colonialism. Nevertheless, the centralized state that Shyaam constructed was a tool of extraction and highly absolutist. Nobody voted for him, and state policy was dictated from the top, not by popular participation.

This political revolution introducing state centralization and law and order in the Kuba country in turn led to an economic revolution. Agriculture was reorganized and new technologies were adopted to increase productivity. The crops that had previously been the staples were replaced by new, higher-yield ones from the Americas (in particular, maize, cassava, and chili peppers). The intense mixed-farming cycle was introduced at this time, and the amount of food produced per capita doubled. To adopt these crops and reorganize the agricultural cycle, more hands were needed in the fields. So the age of marriage was lowered to twenty, which brought men into the agricultural labor force at a younger age. The contrast with the Lele is stark. Their men tended to marry at thirty-five and only then worked in the fields. Until then, they dedicated their lives to fighting and raiding.

The connection between the political and economic revolution was simple. King Shyaam and those who supported him wanted to extract taxes and wealth from the Kuba, who had to produce a surplus above what they consumed themselves. While Shyaam and his men did not introduce inclusive institutions to the eastern bank of the Kasai, some amount of economic prosperity is intrinsic to extractive institutions that achieve some degree of state centralization and impose law and order. Encouraging economic activity was of course in the interest of Shyaam and his men, as otherwise there would have been nothing to extract. Just like Stalin, Shyaam created by command a set of institutions that would generate the wealth necessary to support this system. Compared to the utter absence of law and order that reigned on the other bank of the Kasai, this generated significant economic prosperity—even if much of it was likely extracted by Shyaam and his elites. But it was necessarily limited. Just as in the Soviet Union, there was no creative destruction in the Kuba Kingdom and no technological innovation after this initial change. This situation was more or less unaltered by the time the kingdom was first encountered by Belgian colonial officials in the late nineteenth century.

KING SHYAAM'S ACHIEVEMENT illustrates how some limited degree of economic success can be achieved through extractive institutions. Creating such growth requires a centralized state. To centralize the state, a political revolution is often necessary. Once Shyaam created this state, he could use its power to reorganize the economy and boost agricultural productivity, which he could then tax.

Why was it that the Bushong, and not the Lele, had a political revolution? Couldn't the Lele have had their own King Shyaam? What Shyaam accomplished was an institutional innovation not tied in any deterministic way to geography, culture, or ignorance. The Lele could have had such a revolution and similarly transformed their institutions, but they didn't. Perhaps this is for reasons that we do not understand, because of our limited knowledge of their society today. Most likely it is because of the contingent nature of history. The same contingency was probably at work when some of the societies in the Middle East twelve thousand years ago embarked upon an even more radical set of institutional innovations leading to settled societies and then to the domestication of plants and animals, as we discuss next.

THE LONG SUMMER

About 15,000 BC, the Ice Age came to an end as the Earth's climate warmed up. Evidence from the Greenland ice cores suggests that average temperatures rose by as much as fifteen degrees Celsius in a short span of time. This warming seems to have coincided with rapid increases in human populations as the global warming led to expanding animal populations and much greater availability of wild plants and foods. This process was put into rapid reverse at about 14,000 BC, by a period of cooling known as the Younger Dryas, but after 9600 BC, global temperatures rose again, by seven degrees Celsius in less than a decade, and have since stayed high. Archaeologist Brian Fagan calls it the Long Summer. The warming-up of the climate was a huge critical juncture that formed the background to the Neolithic Revolution, where human societies made the transition to sedentary life, farming, and herding. This and the rest of subsequent human history have played out basking in this Long Summer.

There is a fundamental difference between farming and herding and hunting-gathering. The former is based on the domestication of plant and animal species, with active intervention in their life cycles to change genetics to make those species more useful to humans. Domestication is a technological change that enables humans to produce a lot more food from the available plants and animals. The domestication of maize, for example, began when humans gathered teosinte, the wild crop that was maize's ancestor. Teosinte cobs are very small, barely a few centimeters long. They are dwarfed by a cob of modern maize. Yet gradually, by selecting the larger ears of teosinte, and plants whose ears did not break but stayed on the stalk to be harvested, humans created modern maize, a crop that provides far more nourishment from the same piece of land.

The earliest evidence of farming, herding, and the domestication of plants and animals comes from the Middle East, in particular from the area known as the Hilly Flanks, which stretches from the south of modern-day Israel, up through Palestine and the west bank of the River Jordan, via Syria and into southeastern Turkey, northern Iraq, and western Iran. Around 9500 BC the first domestic plants, emmer and two-row barley, were found in Jericho on the west bank of the River Jordan in Palestine; and emmer, peas, and lentils, at Tell Aswad, farther north in Syria. Both were sites of the so-called Natufian culture and both supported large villages; the village of Jericho had a population of possibly five hundred people by this time.

Why did the first farming villages happen here and not elsewhere? Why was it the Natufians, and not other peoples, who domesticated peas and lentils? Were they lucky and just happened to be living where there were many potential candidates for domestication? While this is true, many other people were living among these species, but they did not domesticate them. As we saw in chapter 2 in Maps 4 and 5, research by geneticists and archaeologists to pin down the distribution of the wild ancestors of modern domesticated animals and plants reveals that many of these ancestors were spread over very large areas, millions of square kilometers. The wild ancestors of domesticated animal species were spread throughout Eurasia. Though the Hilly Flanks were particularly well endowed in terms of wild crop species, even they were very far from unique. It was not that the Natufians lived in an area uniquely endowed with wild species that made them special. It was that they were sedentary before they started domesticating plants or animals. One piece of evidence comes from gazelle teeth, which are composed of cementum, a bony connective tissue that grows in layers. During the spring and summer, when cementum's growth is most rapid, the layers are a different color from the layers that form in the winter. By taking a slice through a tooth you can see the color of the last layer created before the gazelle died. Using this technique, you can determine if the gazelle was killed in summer or winter. At Natufian sites, one finds gazelles killed in all seasons, suggesting year-round residence. The village of Abu Hureyra, on the river Euphrates, is one of the most intensively researched Natufian settlements. For almost forty years archaeologists have examined the layers of the village, which provides one of the best documented examples of sedentary life before and after the transition to farming. The settlement probably began around 9500 BC, and the inhabitants continued their hunter-gatherer lifestyle for another five hundred years before switching to agriculture. Archaeologists estimate that the population of the village prior to farming was between one hundred and three hundred.

You can think of all sorts of reasons why a society might find it advantageous to become sedentary. Moving about is costly; children and old people have to be carried, and it is impossible to store food for lean times when you are on the move. Moreover, tools such as grinding stones and sickles were useful for processing wild foods, but are heavy to carry. There is evidence that even mobile hunter-gatherers stored food in select locations such as caves. One attraction of maize is that it stores very well, and this is a key reason why it became so intensively cultivated throughout the Americas. The ability to deal more effectively with storage and accumulate food stocks must have been a key incentive for adopting a sedentary way of life.

While it might be collectively desirable to become sedentary, this doesn't mean that it will necessarily happen. A mobile group of hunter-gatherers would have to agree to do this, or someone would have to force them. Some archaeologists have suggested that increasing population density and declining living standards were key factors in the emergence of sedentary life, forcing mobile people to stay in one place. Yet the density of Natufian sites is no greater than that of previous groups, so there does not appear to be evidence of increasing population density. Skeletal and dental evidence does not suggest deteriorating health, either. For instance, food shortage tends to create thin lines in people's tooth enamel, a condition called hypoplasia. These lines are in fact less prevalent in Natufian people than in later farming people.

More important is that while sedentary life had pluses, it also had minuses. Conflict resolution was probably much harder for sedentary groups, since disagreements could be resolved less easily by people or groups merely moving away. Once people had built permanent buildings and had more assets than they could carry, moving away was a much less attractive option. So villages needed more effective ways of resolving conflict and more elaborate notions of property. Decisions would have to be made about who had access to which piece of land close to the village, or who got to pick fruit from which stand of trees and fish in which part of the stream. Rules had to be developed, and the institutions that made and enforced rules had to be elaborated.

In order for sedentary life to emerge, it therefore seems plausible that hunter-gatherers would have had to be forced to settle down, and this would have to have been preceded by an institutional innovation concentrating power in the hands of a group that would become the political elite, enforce property rights, maintain order, and also benefit from their status by extracting resources from the rest of society. In fact, a political revolution similar to that initiated by King Shyaam, even if on a smaller scale, is likely to have been the breakthrough that led to sedentary life.

The archaeological evidence indeed suggests that the Natufians developed a complex society characterized by hierarchy, order, and inequality—beginnings of what we would recognize as extractive institutions—a long time before they became farmers. One compelling piece of evidence for such hierarchy and inequality comes from Natufian graves. Some people were buried with large amounts of obsidian and dentalium shells, which came from the Mediterranean coast near Mount Carmel. Other types of ornamentation include necklaces, garters, and bracelets, which were made out of canine teeth and deer phalanges as well as shells. Other people were buried without any of these things. Shells and also obsidian were traded, and control of this trade was quite likely a source of power accumulation and inequality. Further evidence of economic and political inequality comes from the Natufian site of Ain Mallaha, just north of the Sea of Galilee. Amid a group of about fifty round huts and many pits, clearly used for storage, there is a large, intensively plastered building close to a cleared central place. This building was almost certainly the house of a chief. Among the burials at the site, some are much more elaborate, and there is also evidence of a skull cult, possibly indicating ancestor worship. Such cults are widespread in Natufian sites, particularly Jericho. The preponderance of evidence from Natufian sites suggests that these were probably already societies with elaborate institutions determining inheritance of elite status. They engaged in trade with distant places and had nascent forms of religion and political hierarchies.

The emergence of political elites most likely created the transition first to sedentary life and then to farming. As the Natufian sites show, sedentary life did not necessarily mean farming and herding. People could settle down but still make their living by hunting and gathering. After all, the Long Summer made wild crops more bountiful, and hunting and gathering was likely to have been more attractive. Most people may have been quite satisfied with a subsistence life based on hunting and gathering that did not require a lot of effort. Even technological innovation doesn't necessarily lead to increased agricultural production. In fact, it is known that a major technological innovation, the introduction of the steel axe among the group of Australian Aboriginal peoples known as Yir Yoront, led not to more intense production but to more sleeping, because it allowed subsistence requirements to be met more easily, with little incentive to work for more.

The traditional, geography-based explanation for the Neolithic Revolution—the centerpiece of Jared Diamond's argument, which we discussed in chapter 2—is that it was driven by the fortuitous availability of many plant and animal species that could easily be domesticated. This made farming and herding attractive and induced sedentary life. After societies became sedentary and started farming, they began to develop political hierarchy, religion, and significantly more complex institutions. Though widely accepted, the evidence from the Natufians suggests that this traditional explanation puts the cart before the horse. Institutional changes occurred in societies quite a while before they made the transition to farming and were probably the cause both of the move to sedentarism, which reinforced the institutional changes, and subsequently of the Neolithic Revolution. This pattern is suggested not only by the evidence from the Hilly Flanks, which is the area most intensively studied, but also by the preponderance of evidence from the Americas, sub-Saharan Africa, and East Asia.

Certainly the transition to farming led to greater agricultural productivity and enabled a significant expansion of population. For instance, in sites such as Jericho and Abu Hureyra, one sees that the early farming village was much larger than the prefarming one. In general, villages grew by between two and six times when the transition took place. Moreover, many of the consequences that people have traditionally argued as having flowed from this transition undoubtedly happened. There was greater occupational specialization and more rapid technological progress, and probably the development of more complex and possibly less egalitarian political institutions. But whether this happened in a particular place was not determined by the availability of plant and animal species. Instead, it was a consequence of the society's having experienced the types of institutional, social, and political innovations that would have allowed sedentary life and then farming to emerge.

Though the Long Summer and the presence of crop and animal species allowed this to happen, it did not determine where or when exactly, after the climate had warmed up, it would happen. Rather, this was determined by the interaction of a critical juncture, the Long Summer, with small but important institutional differences that mattered. As the climate warmed up, some societies, such as the Natufians, developed elements of centralized institutions and hierarchy, though these were on a very small scale relative to those of modern nation-states. Like the Bushong under Shyaam, societies reorganized to take advantage of the greater opportunities created by the glut of wild plants and animals, and it was no doubt the political elites who were the main beneficiaries of these new opportunities and of the political centralization process. Other places that had only slightly different institutions did not permit their political elites to take similar advantage of this juncture and lagged behind the process of political centralization and the creation of settled, agricultural, and more complex societies. This paved the way to a subsequent divergence of exactly the type we have seen before. Once these differences emerged, they spread to some places but not to others. For example, farming spread into Europe from the Middle East starting around 6500 BC, mostly as a consequence of the migration of farmers. In Europe, institutions drifted away from parts of the world, such as Africa, where initial institutions had been different and where the innovations set in motion by the Long Summer in the Middle East happened only much later, and even then in a different form.

THE INSTITUTIONAL INNOVATIONS of the Natufians, though they did most likely underpin the Neolithic Revolution, did not leave a simple legacy in world history and did not lead inexorably to the long-run prosperity of their homelands in modern Israel, Palestine, and Syria. Syria and Palestine are relatively poor parts of the modern world, and the prosperity of Israel was largely imported by the settlement of Jewish people after the Second World War and their high levels of education and easy access to advanced technologies. The early growth of the Natufians did not become sustained for the same reason that Soviet growth fizzled out. Though highly significant, even revolutionary for its time, this was growth under extractive institutions. For the Natufian society it was also likely that this type of growth created deep conflicts over who would control institutions and the extraction they enabled. For every elite benefiting from extraction there is a non-elite who would love to replace him. Sometimes infighting simply replaces one elite with another. Sometimes it destroys the whole extractive society, unleashing a process of state and societal collapse, as the spectacular civilization that Maya city-states built more than one thousand years ago experienced.

THE UNSTABLE EXTRACTION

Farming emerged independently in several places around the world. In what is now modern Mexico, societies formed that established states and settlements, and transitioned to agriculture. As with the Natufians in the Middle East, they also achieved some degree of economic growth. The Maya city-states in the area of southern Mexico, Belize, Guatemala, and Western Honduras in fact built a fairly sophisticated civilization under their own brand of extractive institutions. The Maya experience illustrates not only the possibility of growth under extractive institutions but also another fundamental limit to this type of growth: the political instability that emerges and ultimately leads to collapse of both society and state as different groups and people fight to become the extractors.

Maya cities first began to develop around 500 BC. These early cities eventually failed, sometime in the first century AD. A new political model then emerged, creating the foundation for the Classic Era, between AD 250 and 900. This period marked the full flowering of Maya culture and civilization. But this more sophisticated civilization would also collapse in the course of the next six hundred years. By the time the Spanish conquistadors arrived in the early sixteenth century, the great temples and palaces of such Maya sites as Tikal, Palenque, and

Calakmul had receded into the forest, not to be rediscovered until the nineteenth century.

The Maya cities never unified into an empire, though some cities were subservient to others, and they often appear to have cooperated, particularly in warfare. The main connection between the region's city-states, fifty of which we can recognize by their own glyphs, is that their people spoke around thirty-one different but closely related Mayan languages. The Mayas developed a writing system, and there are at least fifteen thousand remaining inscriptions describing many aspects of elite life, culture, and religion. They also had a sophisticated calendar for recording dates known as the Long Count. It was very much like our own calendar in that it counted the unfolding of years from a fixed date and was used by all Maya cities. The Long Count began in 3114 BC, though we do not know what significance the Mayas attached to this date, which long precedes the emergence of anything resembling Maya society.

The Mayas were skilled builders who independently invented cement. Their buildings and their inscriptions provide vital information on the trajectories of the Maya cities, as they often recorded events dated according to the Long Count. Looking across all the Maya cities, archaeologists can thus count how many buildings were finished in particular years. Around AD 500 there are few dated monuments. For example, the Long Count date corresponding to AD 514 recorded just ten. There was then a steady increase, reaching twenty by AD 672 and forty by the middle of the eighth century. After this the number of dated monuments collapses. By the ninth century, it is down to ten per year, and by the tenth century, to zero. These dated inscriptions give us a clear picture of the expansion of Maya cities and their subsequent contraction from the late eighth century.

This analysis of dates can be complemented by examining the lists of kings the Mayas recorded. At the Maya city of Copán, now in western Honduras, there is a famous monument known as Altar Q. Altar Q records the names of all the kings, starting from the founder of the dynasty K'inich Yax K'uk' Mo', or "King Green-Sun First Quetzal Macaw," named after not just the sun but also two of the exotic birds of the Central American forest whose feathers were greatly valued by the Mayas. K'inich Yax K'uk' Mo' came to power in Copán in AD 426, which we know from the Long Count date on Altar Q. He founded a dynasty that would reign for four hundred years. Some of K'inich Yax's successors had equally graphic names. The thirteenth ruler's glyph translates as "18 Rabbit," who was followed by "Smoke Monkey" and then "Smoke Shell," who died in AD 763. The last name on the altar is King Yax Pasaj Chan Yoaat, or "First Dawned Sky Lightening God," who was the sixteenth ruler of this line and assumed the throne at the death of Smoke Shell. After him we know of only one more king, Ukit Took ("Patron of Flint"), from a fragment of an altar. After Yax Pasaj, the buildings and inscriptions stopped, and it seems that the dynasty was shortly overthrown. Ukit Took was probably not even the real claimant to the throne but a pretender.

There is a final way of looking at this evidence at Copán, one developed by the archaeologists AnnCorinne Freter, Nancy Gonlin, and David Webster. These researchers mapped the rise and fall of Copán by examining the spread of the settlement in the Copán Valley over a period of 850 years, from AD 400 to AD 1250, using a technique called obsidian hydration, which calculates the water content of obsidian on the date it was mined. Once mined, the water content increases at a known rate, allowing archaeologists to calculate the date a piece of obsidian was mined. Freter, Gonlin, and Webster were then able to map where pieces of dated obsidian were found in the Copán Valley and trace how the city expanded and then contracted. Since it is possible to make a reasonable guess about the number of houses and buildings in a particular area, the total population of the city can be estimated. In the period AD 400–449, the population was negligible, estimated at about six hundred people. It rose steadily to a peak of twenty-eight thousand in AD 750–799. Though this does not appear large by contemporary urban standards, it was massive for that period; these numbers imply that in this period, Copán had a larger population than London or Paris. Other Maya cities, such as Tikal and Calakmul, were undoubtedly much larger. In line with the evidence from the Long Count dates, AD 800 was the population peak for Copán. After this it began to decline, and by AD 900 it had fallen to around fifteen thousand people. From there the fall continued, and by AD 1200 the population had returned to what it was eight hundred years previously.

The basis for the economic development of the Maya Classical Era was the same as that for the Bushong and the Natufians: the creation of extractive institutions with some degree of state centralization. These institutions had several key elements. Around AD 100, in the city of Tikal in Guatemala, there emerged a new type of dynastic kingdom. A ruling class based on the *ajaw* (lord or ruler) took root with a king called the *k'uhul ajaw* (divine lord) and, underneath him, a hierarchy of aristocrats. The divine lord organized the society with the cooperation of these elites and also communicated with the gods. As far as we know, this new set of political institutions did not allow for any sort of popular participation, but it did bring stability. The *k'uhul ajaw* raised tribute from farmers and organized labor to build the great monuments, and the coalescence of these institutions created the basis for an impressive economic expansion. The Maya's economy was based on extensive occupational specialization, with skilled potters, weavers, woodworkers, and tool and ornament makers. They also traded obsidian, jaguar pelts, marine shells, cacao, salt, and feathers among themselves and other polities over long distances in Mexico. They probably had money, too, and like the Aztecs, used cacao beans for currency.

The way in which the Maya Classical Era was founded on the creation of extractive political institutions was very similar to the situation among the Bushong, with Yax Ehb' Xook at Tikal playing a role similar to that of King Shyaam. The new political institutions led to a significant increase in economic prosperity, much of which was then extracted by the new elite based around the *k'uhul ajaw*. Once this system had consolidated, by around AD 300, there was little further technological change, however. Though there is some evidence of improved irrigation and water management techniques, agricultural technology was rudimentary and appears not to have changed. Building and artistic techniques became much more sophisticated over time, but in total there was little innovation.

There was no creative destruction. But there were other forms of destruction as the wealth that the extractive institutions created for the *k'uhul ajaw* and the Maya elite led to constant warfare, which worsened over time. The sequence of conflicts is recorded in the Maya inscriptions, with special glyphs indicating that a war took place at a particular date in the Long Count. The planet Venus was the celestial patron of war, and the Mayas regarded some phases of the planet's orbit as particularly auspicious for waging war. The glyph that indicated warfare, known as "star wars" by archaeologists, shows a star showering the earth with a liquid that could be water or blood. The inscriptions also reveal patterns of alliance and competition. There were long contests for power between the larger states, such as Tikal, Calakmul, Copán, and Palenque, and these subjugated smaller states into a vassal status. Evidence for this comes from glyphs marking royal accessions. During this period, they start indicating that the smaller states were now being dominated by another, outside ruler.

Map 10 (page 148) shows the main Maya cities and the various patterns of contact between them as reconstructed by the archaeologists Nikolai Grube and Simon Martin. These patterns indicate that though the large cities such as Calakmul, Dos Pilas, Piedras Negras, and Yaxchilan had extensive diplomatic contacts, some were often dominated by others and they also fought each other.

The overwhelming fact about the Maya collapse is that it coincides with the overthrow of the political model based on the *k'uhul ajaw*. We saw in Copán that after Yax Pasaj's death in AD 810 there were no more kings. At around this time the royal palaces were abandoned. Twenty miles to the north of Copán, in the city of Quiriguá, the last king, Jade Sky, ascended to the throne between AD 795 and 800. The last dated monument is from AD 810 by the Long Count, the same year that Yax Pasaj died. The city was abandoned soon after. Throughout the Maya area the story is the same; the political institutions that had provided the context for the expansion of trade, agriculture, and population vanished. Royal courts did not function, monuments and temples were not carved, and palaces were emptied. As political and social institutions unraveled, reversing the process of state centralization, the economy contracted and the population fell.

In some cases the major centers collapsed from widespread vio-

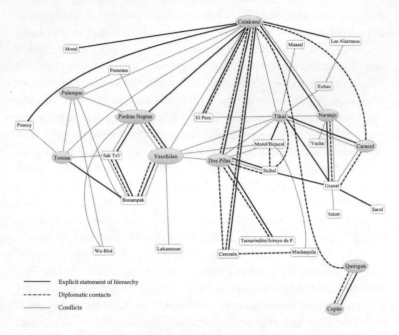

Map 10: The Maya city-states, and inter-city contacts and conflicts

lence. The Petexbatun region of Guatemala—where the great temples were subsequently pulled down and the stone used to build extensive defensive walls—provides one vivid example. As we'll see in the next chapter, it was very similar to what happened in the later Roman Empire. Later, even in places such as Copán, where there are fewer signs of violence at the time of the collapse, many monuments were defaced or destroyed. In some places the elite remained even after the initial overthrow of the *k'uhul ajaw*. In Copán there is evidence of the elite continuing to erect new buildings for at least another two hundred years before they also disappeared. Elsewhere elites seem to have gone at the same time as the divine lord.

Existing archaeological evidence does not allow us to reach a definitive conclusion about why the *k'uhul ajaw* and elites surrounding him were overthrown and the institutions that had created the Maya

Classical Era collapsed. We know this took place in the context of intensified inter-city warfare, and it seems likely that opposition and rebellion within the cities, perhaps led by different factions of the elite, overthrew the institution.

Though the extractive institutions that the Mayas created produced sufficient wealth for the cities to flourish and the elite to become wealthy and generate great art and monumental buildings, the system was not stable. The extractive institutions upon which this narrow elite ruled created extensive inequality, and thus the potential for in-fighting between those who could benefit from the wealth extracted from the people. This conflict ultimately led to the undoing of the Maya civilization.

WHAT GOES WRONG?

Extractive institutions are so common in history because they have a powerful logic: they can generate some limited prosperity while at the same time distributing it into the hands of a small elite. For this growth to happen, there must be political centralization. Once this is in place, the state—or the elite controlling the state—typically has incentives to invest and generate wealth, encourage others to invest so that the state can extract resources from them, and even mimic some of the processes that would normally be set in motion by inclusive eco-nomic institutions and markets. In the Caribbean plantation econo-mies, extractive institutions took the form of the elite using coercion to force slaves to produce sugar. In the Soviet Union, they took the form of the Communist Party reallocating resources from agriculture to industry and structuring some sort of incentives for managers and workers. As we have seen, such incentives were undermined by the nature of the system.

The potential for creating extractive growth gives an impetus to political centralization and is the reason why King Shyaam wished to create the Kuba Kingdom, and likely accounts for why the Natufians in the Middle East set up a primitive form of law and order, hierarchy, and extractive institutions that would ultimately lead to the Neolithic Revolution. Similar processes also likely underpinned the emergence of settled societies and the transition to agriculture in the Americas, and can be seen in the sophisticated civilization that the Mayas built on foundations laid by highly extractive institutions coercing many for the benefit of their narrow elites.

The growth generated by extractive institutions is very different in nature from growth created under inclusive institutions, however. Most important, it is not sustainable. By their very nature, extractive institutions do not foster creative destruction and generate at best only a limited amount of technological progress. The growth they engender thus lasts for only so long. The Soviet experience gives a vivid illustration of this limit. Soviet Russia generated rapid growth as it caught up rapidly with some of the advanced technologies in the world, and resources were allocated out of the highly inefficient agricultural sector and into industry. But ultimately the incentives faced in every sector, from agriculture to industry, could not stimulate technological progress. This took place in only a few pockets where resources were being poured and where innovation was strongly rewarded because of its role in the competition with the West. Soviet growth, however rapid it was, was bound to be relatively short lived, and it was already running out of steam by the 1970s.

Lack of creative destruction and innovation is not the only reason why there are severe limits to growth under extractive institutions. The history of the Maya city-states illustrates a more ominous and, alas, more common end, again implied by the internal logic of extractive institutions. As these institutions create significant gains for the elite, there will be strong incentives for others to fight to replace the current elite. Infighting and instability are thus inherent features of extractive institutions, and they not only create further inefficiencies but also often reverse any political centralization, sometimes even leading to the total breakdown of law and order and descent into chaos, as the Maya city-states experienced following their relative success during their Classical Era.

Though inherently limited, growth under extractive institutions may nonetheless appear spectacular when it's in motion. Many in the Soviet Union and many more in the Western world were awestruck by Soviet growth in the 1920s, '30s, '40s, '50s, '60s, and even as late as the '70s, in the same way that they are mesmerized by the break-neck pace of economic growth in China today. But as we will discuss in greater detail in chapter 15, China under the rule of the Communist Party is another example of society experiencing growth under extractive institutions and is similarly unlikely to generate sustained growth unless it undergoes a fundamental political transformation toward inclusive political institutions.

6.

DRIFTING APART

HOW VENICE BECAME A MUSEUM

THE GROUP OF ISLANDS that form Venice lie at the far north of the Adriatic Sea. In the Middle Ages, Venice was possibly the richest place in the world, with the most advanced set of inclusive economic institutions underpinned by nascent political inclusiveness. It gained its independence in AD 810, at what turned out to be a fortuitous time. The economy of Europe was recovering from the decline it had suffered as the Roman Empire collapsed, and kings such as Charlemagne were reconstituting strong central political power. This led to stability, greater security, and an expansion of trade, which Venice was in a unique position to take advantage of. It was a nation of seafarers, placed right in the middle of the Mediterranean. From the East came spices, Byzantine-manufactured goods, and slaves. Venice became rich. By 1050, when Venice had already been expanding economically for at least a century, it had a population of 45,000 people. This increased by more than 50 percent, to 70,000, by 1200. By 1330 the population had again increased by another 50 percent, to 110,000; Venice was then as big as Paris, and probably three times the size of London.

One of the key bases for the economic expansion of Venice was a series of contractual innovations making economic institutions much more inclusive. The most famous was the *commenda*, a rudimentary type of joint stock company, which formed only for the duration of a single trading mission. A *commenda* involved two partners, a "sedentary" one who stayed in Venice and one who traveled. The sedentary partner put capital into the venture, while the traveling partner accompanied the cargo. Typically, the sedentary partner put in the lion's share of the capital. Young entrepreneurs who did not have wealth themselves could then get into the trading business by traveling with the merchandise. It was a key channel of upward social mobility. Any losses in the voyage were shared according to the amount of capital the partners had put in. If the voyage made money, profits were based on two types of *commenda* contracts. If the *commenda* was unilateral, then the sedentary merchant provided 100 percent of the capital and received 75 percent of the profits. If it was bilateral, the sedentary merchant provided 67 percent of the capital and received 50 percent of the profits. Studying official documents, one sees how powerful a force the *commenda* was in fostering upward social mobility: these documents are full of new names, people who had previously not been among the Venetian elite. In government documents of AD 960, 971, and 982, the number of new names comprise 69 percent, 81 percent, and 65 percent, respectively, of those recorded.

This economic inclusiveness and the rise of new families through trade forced the political system to become even more open. The doge, who governed Venice, was selected for life by the General Assembly. Though a general gathering of all citizens, in practice the General Assembly was dominated by a core group of powerful families. Though the doge was very powerful, his power was gradually reduced over time by changes in political institutions. After 1032 the doge was elected along with a newly created Ducal Council, whose job was also to ensure that the doge did not acquire absolute power. The first doge hemmed in by this council, Domenico Flabianico, was a wealthy silk merchant from a family that had not previously held high office. This institutional change was followed by a huge expansion of Venetian mercantile and naval power. In 1082 Venice was granted extensive trade privileges in Constantinople, and a Venetian Quarter was created in that city. It soon housed ten thousand Venetians. Here we see inclusive economic and political institutions beginning to work in tandem.

The economic expansion of Venice, which created more pressure for political change, exploded after the changes in political and economic institutions that followed the murder of the doge in 1171. The first important innovation was the creation of a Great Council, which was to be the ultimate source of political power in Venice from this point on. The council was made up of officeholders of the Venetian state, such as judges, and was dominated by aristocrats. In addition to these officeholders, each year a hundred new members were nominated to the council by a nominating committee whose four members were chosen by lot from the existing council. The council also subsequently chose the members for two subcouncils, the Senate and the Council of Forty, which had various legislative and executive tasks. The Great Council also chose the Ducal Council, which was expanded from two to six members. The second innovation was the creation of yet another council, chosen by the Great Council by lot, to nominate the doge. Though the choice had to be ratified by the General Assembly, since they nominated only one person, this effectively gave the choice of doge to the council. The third innovation was that a new doge had to swear an oath of office that circumscribed ducal power. Over time these constraints were continually expanded so that subsequent doges had to obey magistrates, then have all their decisions approved by the Ducal Council. The Ducal Council also took on the role of ensuring that the doge obeyed all decisions of the Great Council.

These political reforms led to a further series of institutional innovations: in law, the creation of independent magistrates, courts, a court of appeals, and new private contract and bankruptcy laws. These new Venetian economic institutions allowed the creation of new legal business forms and new types of contracts. There was rapid financial innovation, and we see the beginnings of modern banking around this time in Venice. The dynamic moving Venice toward fully inclusive institutions looked unstoppable.

But there was a tension in all this. Economic growth supported by the inclusive Venetian institutions was accompanied by creative destruction. Each new wave of enterprising young men who became rich via the *commenda* or other similar economic institutions tended to reduce the profits and economic success of established elites. And they did not just reduce their profits; they also challenged their political power. Thus there was always a temptation, if they could get away with it, for the existing elites sitting in the Great Council to close down the system to these new people.

At the Great Council's inception, membership was determined each year. As we saw, at the end of the year, four electors were randomly chosen to nominate a hundred members for the next year, who were automatically selected. On October 3, 1286, a proposal was made to the Great Council that the rules be amended so that nominations had to be confirmed by a majority in the Council of Forty, which was tightly controlled by elite families. This would have given this elite veto power over new nominations to the council, something they previously had not had. The proposal was defeated. On October 5, 1286, another proposal was put forth; this time it passed. From then on there was to be automatic confirmation of a person if his father and grandfathers had served on the council. Otherwise, confirmation was required by the Ducal Council. On October 17 another change in the rules was passed stipulating that an appointment to the Great Council must be approved by the Council of Forty, the doge, and the Ducal Council.

The debates and constitutional amendments of 1286 presaged *La Serrata* ("The Closure") of Venice. In February 1297, it was decided that if you had been a member of the Great Council in the previous four years, you received automatic nomination and approval. New nominations now had to be approved by the Council of Forty, but with only twelve votes. After September 11, 1298, current members and their families no longer needed confirmation. The Great Council was now effectively sealed to outsiders, and the initial incumbents had become a hereditary aristocracy. The seal on this came in 1315, with the *Libro d'Oro,* or "Gold Book," which was an official registry of the Venetian nobility.

Those outside this nascent nobility did not let their powers erode without a struggle. Political tensions mounted steadily in Venice between 1297 and 1315. The Great Council partially responded by making itself bigger. In an attempt to co-opt its most vocal opponents, it grew from 450 to 1,500. This expansion was complemented by repression. A police force was introduced for the first time in 1310, and there was a steady growth in domestic coercion, undoubtedly as a way of solidifying the new political order.

Having implemented a political *Serrata,* the Great Council then moved to adopt an economic *Serrata.* The switch toward extractive political institutions was now being followed by a move toward extractive economic institutions. Most important, they banned the use of *commenda* contracts, one of the great institutional innovations that had made Venice rich. This shouldn't be a surprise: the *commenda* benefited new merchants, and now the established elite was trying to exclude them. This was just one step toward more extractive economic institutions. Another step came when, starting in 1314, the Venetian state began to take over and nationalize trade. It organized state galleys to engage in trade and, from 1324 on, began to charge individuals high levels of taxes if they wanted to engage in trade. Long-distance trade became the preserve of the nobility. This was the beginning of the end of Venetian prosperity. With the main lines of business monopolized by the increasingly narrow elite, the decline was under way. Venice appeared to have been on the brink of becoming the world's first inclusive society, but it fell to a coup. Political and economic institutions became more extractive, and Venice began to experience economic decline. By 1500 the population had shrunk to one hundred thousand. Between 1650 and 1800, when the population of Europe rapidly expanded, that of Venice contracted.

Today the only economy Venice has, apart from a bit of fishing, is tourism. Instead of pioneering trade routes and economic institutions, Venetians make pizza and ice cream and blow colored glass for hordes of foreigners. The tourists come to see the pre-*Serrata* wonders of Venice, such as the Doge's Palace and the horses of St. Mark's Cathedral, which were looted from Byzantium when Venice ruled the Mediterranean. Venice went from economic powerhouse to museum.

IN THIS CHAPTER we focus on the historical development of institutions in different parts of the world and explain why they evolved in different ways. We saw in chapter 4 how the institutions of Western

Europe diverged from those in Eastern Europe and then how those of England diverged from those in the rest of Western Europe. This was a consequence of small institutional differences, mostly resulting from institutional drift interacting with critical junctures. It might then be tempting to think that these institutional differences are the tip of a deep historical iceberg where under the waterline we find English and European institutions inexorably drifting away from those elsewhere, based on historical events dating back millennia. The rest, as they say, is history.

Except that it isn't, for two reasons. First, moves toward inclusive institutions, as our account of Venice shows, can be reversed. Venice became prosperous. But its political and economic institutions were overthrown, and that prosperity went into reverse. Today Venice is rich only because people who make their income elsewhere choose to spend it there admiring the glory of its past. The fact that inclusive institutions can go into reverse shows that there is no simple cumulative process of institutional improvement.

Second, small institutional differences that play a crucial role during critical junctures are by their nature ephemeral. Because they are small, they can be reversed, then can reemerge and be reversed again. We will see in this chapter that, in contrast with what one would expect from the geography or culture theories, England, where the decisive step toward inclusive institutions would take place in the seventeenth century, was a backwater, not only in the millennia following the Neolithic Revolution in the Middle East but also at the beginning of the Middle Ages, following the fall of the Western Roman Empire. The British Isles were marginal to the Roman Empire, certainly of less importance than continental Western Europe, North Africa, the Balkans, Constantinople, or the Middle East. When the Western Roman Empire collapsed in the fifth century AD, Britain suffered the most complete decline. But the political revolutions that would ultimately bring the Industrial Revolution would take place not in Italy, Turkey, or even western continental Europe, but in the British Isles.

In understanding the path to England's Industrial Revolution and the countries that followed it, Rome's legacy is nonetheless important for several reasons. First, Rome, like Venice, underwent major early institutional innovations. As in Venice, Rome's initial economic success was based on inclusive institutions—at least by the standards of their time. As in Venice, these institutions became decidedly more extractive over time. With Rome, this was a consequence of the change from the Republic (510 BC–49 BC) to the Empire (49 BC–AD 476). Even though during the Republican period Rome built an impressive empire, and long-distance trade and transport flourished, much of the Roman economy was based on extraction. The transition from republic to empire increased extraction and ultimately led to the kind of infighting, instability, and collapse that we saw with the Maya city-states.

Second and more important, we will see that Western Europe's subsequent institutional development, though it was not a direct inheritance of Rome, was a consequence of critical junctures that were common across the region in the wake of the collapse of the Western Roman Empire. These critical junctures had little parallel in other parts of the world, such as Africa, Asia, or the Americas, though we will also show via the history of Ethiopia that when other places did experience similar critical junctures, they sometimes reacted in ways that were remarkably similar. Roman decline led to feudalism, which, as a by-product, caused slavery to wither away, brought into existence cities that were outside the sphere of influence of monarchs and aristocrats, and in the process created a set of institutions where the political powers of rulers were weakened. It was upon this feudal foundation that the Black Death would create havoc and further strengthen independent cities and peasants at the expense of monarchs, aristocrats, and large landowners. And it was on this canvas that the opportunities created by the Atlantic trade would play out. Many parts of the world did not undergo these changes, and in consequence drifted apart.

ROMAN VIRTUES . . .

Roman plebeian tribune Tiberius Gracchus was clubbed to death in 133 BC by Roman senators and his body was thrown unceremoniously into the Tiber. His murderers were aristocrats like Tiberius himself, and the assassination was masterminded by his cousin Publius Cornelius Scipio Nasica. Tiberius Gracchus had an impeccable aristocratic pedigree as a descendant of some of the more illustrious leaders of the Roman Republic, including Lucius Aemilius Paullus, hero of the Illyrian and Second Punic wars, and Scipio Africanus, the general who defeated Hannibal in the Second Punic War. Why had the powerful senators of his day, even his cousin, turned against him?

The answer tells us much about the tensions in the Roman Republic and the causes of its subsequent decline. What pitted Tiberius against these powerful senators was his willingness to stand against them in a crucial question of the day: the allocation of land and the rights of plebeians, common Roman citizens.

By the time of Tiberius Gracchus, Rome was a well-established republic. Its political institutions and the virtues of Roman citizen-soldiers—as captured by Jacques-Louis David's famous painting *Oath of the Horatii,* which shows the sons swearing to their fathers that they will defend the Roman Republic to their death—are still seen by many historians as the foundation of the republic's success. Roman citizens created the republic by overthrowing their king, Lucius Tarquinius Superbus, known as Tarquin the Proud, around 510 BC. The republic cleverly designed political institutions with many inclusive elements. It was governed by magistrates elected for a year. That the office of magistrate was elected, annually, and held by multiple people at the same time reduced the ability of any one person to consolidate or exploit his power. The republic's institutions contained a system of checks and balances that distributed power fairly widely. This was so even if not all citizens had equal representation, as voting was indirect. There was also a large number of slaves crucial for production in much of Italy, making up perhaps one-third of the population. Slaves of course had no rights, let alone political representation.

All the same, as in Venice, Roman political institutions had pluralistic elements. The plebeians had their own assembly, which could elect the plebeian tribunes, who had the power to veto actions by the magistrates, call the Plebeian Assembly, and propose legislation. It was the plebeians who put Tiberius Gracchus in power in 133 BC.

Their power had been forged by "secession," a form of strike by plebeians, particularly soldiers, who would withdraw to a hill outside the city and refuse to cooperate with the magistrates until their complaints were dealt with. This threat was of course particularly important during a time of war. It was supposedly during such a secession in the fifth century BC that citizens gained the right to elect their tribunes and enact laws that would govern their community. Their political and legal protection, even if limited by our current standards, created economic opportunities for citizens and some degree of inclusivity in economic institutions. As a result, trade throughout the Mediterranean flourished under the Roman Republic. Archaeological evidence suggests that while the majority of both citizens and slaves lived not much above subsistence level, many Romans, including some common citizens, achieved high incomes, with access to public services such as a city sewage system and street lighting.

Moreover, there is evidence that there was also some economic growth under the Roman Republic. We can track the economic fortunes of the Romans from shipwrecks. The empire the Romans built was in a sense a web of port cities—from Athens, Antioch, and Alexandria in the east; via Rome, Carthage, and Cadiz; all the way to London in the far west. As Roman territories expanded, so did trade and shipping, which can be traced from shipwrecks found by archaeologists on the floor of the Mediterranean. These wrecks can be dated in many ways. Often the ships carried amphorae full of wine or olive oil, being transported from Italy to Gaul, or Spanish olive oil to be sold or distributed for free in Rome. Amphorae, sealed vessels made of clay, often contained information on who had made them and when. Just near the river Tiber in Rome is a small hill, Monte Testaccio, also known as Monte dei Cocci ("Pottery Mountain"), made up of approximately fifty-three million amphorae. When the amphorae were unloaded from ships, they were discarded, over the centuries creating a huge hill.

Other goods on the ships and the ship itself can sometimes be dated using radiocarbon dating, a powerful technique used by archaeologists to date the age of organic remains. Plants create energy by photosynthesis, which uses the energy from the sun to convert carbon dioxide into sugars. As they do this, plants incorporate a quantity of a naturally occurring radioisotope, carbon-14. After plants die, the carbon-14 deteriorates due to radioactive decay. When archaeologists find a shipwreck, they can date the ship's wood by comparing the remaining carbon-14 fraction in it to that expected from atmospheric carbon-14. This gives an estimate of when the tree was cut down. Only about 20 shipwrecks have been dated to as long ago as 500 BC. These were probably not Roman ships, and could well have been Carthaginian, for example. But then the number of Roman shipwrecks increases rapidly. Around the time of the birth of Christ, they reached a peak of 180.

Shipwrecks are a powerful way of tracing the economic contours of the Roman Republic, and they do show evidence of some economic growth, but they have to be kept in perspective. Probably two-thirds of the contents of the ships were the property of the Roman state, taxes and tribute being brought back from the provinces to Rome, or grain and olive oil from North Africa to be handed out free to the citizens of the city. It is these fruits of extraction that mostly constructed Monte Testaccio.

Another fascinating way to find evidence of economic growth is from the Greenland Ice Core Project. As snowflakes fall, they pick up small quantities of pollution in the atmosphere, particularly the metals lead, silver, and copper. The snow freezes and piles up on top of the snow that fell in previous years. This process has been going on for millennia, and provides an unrivaled opportunity for scientists to understand the extent of atmospheric pollution thousands of years ago. In 1990–1992 the Greenland Ice Core Project drilled down through 3,030 meters of ice covering about 250,000 years of human history. One of the major findings of this project, and others preceding it, was that there was a distinct increase in atmospheric pollutants starting around 500 BC. Atmospheric quantities of lead, silver, and copper then increased steadily, reaching a peak in the first century AD. Remarkably, this atmospheric quantity of lead is reached again only in the thirteenth century. These findings show how intense, compared with what came before and after, Roman mining was. This upsurge in mining clearly indicates economic expansion.

But Roman growth was unsustainable, occurring under institutions that were partially inclusive and partially extractive. Though Roman citizens had political and economic rights, slavery was widespread and very extractive, and the elite, the senatorial class, dominated both the economy and politics. Despite the presence of the Plebeian Assembly and plebeian tribune, for example, real power rested with the Senate, whose members came from the large landowners constituting the senatorial class. According to the Roman historian Livy, the Senate was created by Rome's first king, Romulus, and consisted of one hundred men. Their descendants made up the senatorial class, though new blood was also added. The distribution of land was very unequal and most likely became more so by the second century BC. This was at the root of the problems that Tiberius Gracchus brought to the fore as tribune.

As its expansion throughout the Mediterranean continued, Rome experienced an influx of great riches. But this bounty was captured mostly by a few wealthy families of senatorial rank, and inequality between rich and poor increased. Senators owed their wealth not only to their control of the lucrative provinces but also to their very large estates throughout Italy. These estates were manned by gangs of slaves, often captured in the wars that Rome fought. But where the land for these estates came from was equally significant. Rome's armies during the Republic consisted of citizen-soldiers who were small landowners, first in Rome and later in other parts of Italy. Traditionally they fought in the army when necessary and then returned to their plots. As Rome expanded and the campaigns got longer, this model ceased to work. Soldiers were away from their plots for years at a time, and many landholdings fell into disuse. The soldiers' families sometimes found themselves under mountains of debt and on the brink of starvation. Many of the plots were therefore gradually abandoned, and absorbed by the estates of the senators. As the senatorial class got richer and richer, the large mass of landless citizens gathered in Rome, often after being decommissioned from the army. With no land to return to, they sought work in Rome. By the late second century BC, the situation had reached a dangerous boiling point, both because the gap between rich and poor had widened to unprecedented levels and because there were hordes of discontented citizens in Rome ready to rebel in response to these injustices and turn against the Roman aristocracy. But political power rested with the rich land-owners of the senatorial class, who were the beneficiaries of the changes that had gone on over the last two centuries. Most had no intention of changing the system that had served them so well.

According to the Roman historian Plutarch, Tiberius Gracchus, when traveling through Etruria, a region in what is now central Italy, became aware of the hardship that families of citizen-soldiers were suffering. Whether because of this experience or because of other frictions with the powerful senators of his time, he would soon em-bark upon a daring plan to change land allocation in Italy. He stood for plebeian tribune in 133 BC, then used his office to propose land reform: a commission would investigate whether public lands were being illegally occupied and would redistribute land in excess of the legal limit of three hundred acres to landless Roman citizens. The three-hundred-acre limit was in fact part of an old law, though ig-nored and not implemented for centuries. Tiberius Gracchus's pro-posal sent shockwaves through the senatorial class, who were able to block implementation of his reforms for a while. When Tiberius man-aged to use the power of the mob supporting him to remove another tribune who threatened to veto his land reform, his proposed com-mission was finally founded. The Senate, though, prevented imple-mentation by starving the commission of funds.

Things came to a head when Tiberius Gracchus claimed for his land reform commission the funds left by the king of the Greek city Pergamum to the Roman people. He also attempted to stand for tri-bune a second time, partly because he was afraid of persecution by the Senate after he stepped down. This gave the senators the pretext to charge that Tiberius was trying to declare himself king. He and his supporters were attacked, and many were killed. Tiberius Gracchus himself was one of the first to fall, though his death would not solve the problem, and others would attempt to reform the distribution of land and other aspects of Roman economy and society. Many would meet a similar fate. Tiberius Gracchus's brother Gaius, for example, was also murdered by landowners, after he took the mantle from his brother.

These tensions would surface again periodically during the next century—for example, leading to the "Social War" between 91 BC and 87 BC. The aggressive defender of the senatorial interests, Lucius Cornelius Sulla, not only viciously suppressed the demands for change but also severely curtailed the powers of the plebeian tribunes. The same issues would also be a central factor in the support that Julius Caesar received from the people of Rome in his fight against the Senate.

The political institutions forming the core of the Roman Republic were overthrown by Julius Caesar in 49 BC when he moved his legion across the Rubicon, the river separating the Roman provinces of Cisalpine Gaul from Italy. Rome fell to Caesar, and another civil war broke out. Though Caesar was victorious, he was murdered by disgruntled senators, led by Brutus and Cassius, in 44 BC. The Roman Republic would never be re-created. A new civil war broke out between Caesar's supporters, particularly Mark Anthony and Octavian, and his foes. After Anthony and Octavian won, they fought each other, until Octavian emerged triumphant in the battle of Actium in 31 BC. By the following year, and for the next forty-five years, Octavian, known after 28 BC as Augustus Caesar, ruled Rome alone. Augustus created the Roman Empire, though he preferred the title princeps, a sort of "first among equals," and called the regime the Principate. Map 11 shows the Roman Empire at its greatest extent in 117 AD. It also includes the river Rubicon, which Caesar so fatefully crossed.

It was this transition from republic to principate, and later naked empire, that laid the seeds of the decline of Rome. The partially inclusive political institutions, which had formed the basis for the economic success, were gradually undermined. Even if the Roman Republic created a tilted playing field in favor of the senatorial class and other wealthy Romans, it was not an absolutist regime and had never before concentrated so much power in one position. The changes unleashed by Augustus, as with the Venetian *Serrata,* were at first political but then would have significant economic consequences. As a result of these changes, by the fifth century AD the Western Roman Empire, as the West was called after it split from the East, had declined economically and militarily, and was on the brink of collapse.

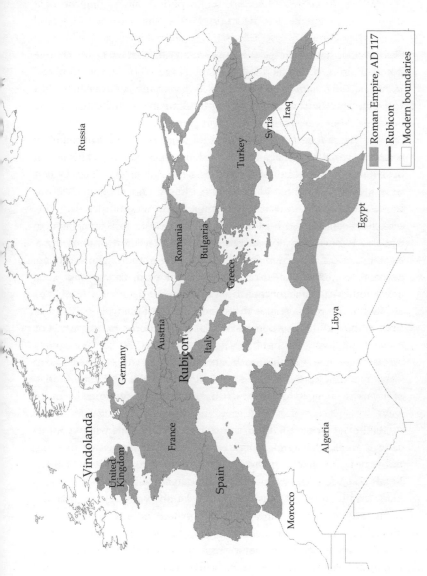

Map 11: The Roman Empire in AD 117

. . . ROMAN VICES

Flavius Aetius was one of the larger-than-life characters of the late Roman Empire, hailed as "the last of the Romans" by Edward Gibbon, author of *The Decline and Fall of the Roman Empire*. Between AD 433 and 454, until he was murdered by the emperor Valentinian III, Aetius, a general, was probably the most powerful person in the Roman Empire. He shaped both domestic and foreign policy, and fought a series of crucial battles against the barbarians, and also other Romans in civil wars. He was unique among powerful generals fighting in civil wars in not seeking the emperorship himself. Since the end of the second century, civil war had become a fact of life in the Roman Empire. Between the death of Marcus Aurelius in AD 180 until the collapse of the Western Roman Empire in AD 476, there was hardly a decade that did not see a civil war or a palace coup against an emperor. Few emperors died of natural causes or in battle. Most were murdered by usurpers or their own troops.

Aetius's career illustrates the changes from Roman Republic and early Empire to the late Roman Empire. Not only did his involvement in incessant civil wars and his power in every aspect of the empire's business contrast with the much more limited power of generals and senators during earlier periods, but it also highlights how the fortunes of Romans changed radically in the intervening centuries in other ways.

By the late Roman Empire, the so-called barbarians who were initially dominated and incorporated into Roman armies or used as slaves now dominated many parts of the empire. As a young man, Aetius had been held hostage by barbarians, first by the Goths under Alaric and then by the Huns. Roman relations with these barbarians are indicative of how things had changed since the Republic. Alaric was both a ferocious enemy and an ally, so much so that in 405 he was appointed one of the senior-most generals of the Roman army. The arrangement was temporary, however. By 408, Alaric was fighting against the Romans, invading Italy and sacking Rome.

The Huns were also both powerful foes and frequent allies of the Romans. Though they, too, held Aetius hostage, they later fought alongside him in a civil war. But the Huns did not stay long on one side, and under Attila they fought a major battle against the Romans in 451, just across the Rhine. This time defending the Romans were the Goths, under Theodoric.

All of this did not stop Roman elites from trying to appease barbarian commanders, often not to protect Roman territories but to gain the upper hand in internal power struggles. For example, the Vandals, under their king, Geiseric, ravaged large parts of the Iberian Peninsula and then conquered the Roman bread baskets in North Africa from 429 onward. The Roman response to this was to offer Geiseric the emperor Valentinian III's child daughter as a bride. Geiseric was at the time married to the daughter of one of the leaders of the Goths, but this does not seem to have stopped him. He annulled his marriage under the pretext that his wife was trying to murder him and sent her back to her family after mutilating her by cutting off both her ears and her nose. Fortunately for the bride-to-be, because of her young age she was kept in Italy and never consummated her marriage to Geiseric. Later she would marry another powerful general, Petronius Maximus, the mastermind of the murder of Aetius by the emperor Valentinian III, who would himself shortly be murdered in a plot hatched by Maximus. Maximus later declared himself emperor, but his reign would be very short, ended by his death during the major offensive by the Vandals under Geiseric against Italy, which saw Rome fall and savagely plundered.

BY THE EARLY fifth century, the barbarians were literally at the gate. Some historians argue that it was a consequence of the more formidable opponents the Romans faced during the late Empire. But the success of the Goths, Huns, and Vandals against Rome was a symptom, not the cause, of Rome's decline. During the Republic, Rome had dealt with much more organized and threatening opponents, such as the Carthaginians. The decline of Rome had causes very similar to those of the Maya city-states. Rome's increasingly extractive political and economic institutions generated its demise because they caused infighting and civil war.

The origins of the decline go back at least to Augustus's seizure of power, which set in motion changes that made political institutions much more extractive. These included changes in the structure of the army, which made secession impossible, thus removing a crucial element that ensured political representation for common Romans. The emperor Tiberius, who followed Augustus in AD 14, abolished the Plebeian Assembly and transferred its powers to the Senate. Instead of a political voice, Roman citizens now had free handouts of wheat and, subsequently, olive oil, wine, and pork, and were kept entertained by circuses and gladiatorial contests. With Augustus's reforms, emperors began to rely not so much on the army made up of citizen-soldiers, but on the Praetorian Guard, the elite group of professional soldiers created by Augustus. The Guard itself would soon become an important independent broker of who would become emperor, often through not peaceful means but civil wars and intrigue. Augustus also strengthened the aristocracy against common Roman citizens, and the growing inequality that had underpinned the conflict between Tiberius Gracchus and the aristocrats continued, perhaps even strengthened.

The accumulation of power at the center made the property rights of common Romans less secure. State lands also expanded with the empire as a consequence of confiscation, and grew to as much as half of the land in many parts of the empire. Property rights became particularly unstable because of the concentration of power in the hands of the emperor and his entourage. In a pattern not too different from what happened in the Maya city-states, infighting to take control of this powerful position increased. Civil wars became a regular occurrence, even before the chaotic fifth century, when the barbarians ruled supreme. For example, Septimius Severus seized power from Didius Julianus, who had made himself emperor after the murder of Pertinax in AD 193. Severus, the third emperor in the so-called Year of the Five Emperors, then waged war against his rival claimants, the generals Pescennius Niger and Clodius Albinus, who were finally defeated in AD 194 and 197, respectively. Severus confiscated all the property of his losing opponents in the ensuing civil war. Though able rulers, such as Trajan (AD 98 to 117), Hadrian, and Marcus Aurelius in the next century, could stanch decline, they could not, or did not want to, address the fundamental institutional problems. None of these men proposed abandoning the empire or re-creating effective political institutions along the lines of the Roman Republic. Marcus Aurelius, for all his successes, was followed by his son Commodus, who was more like Caligula or Nero than his father.

The rising instability was evident from the layout and location of towns and cities in the empire. By the third century AD every sizeable city in the empire had a defensive wall. In many cases monuments were plundered for stone, which was used in fortifications. In Gaul before the Romans had arrived in 125 BC, it was usual to build settlements on hilltops, since these were more easily defended. With the initial arrival of Rome, settlements moved down to the plains. In the third century, this trend was reversed.

Along with mounting political instability came changes in society that moved economic institutions toward greater extraction. Though citizenship was expanded to the extent that by AD 212 nearly all the inhabitants of the empire were citizens, this change went along with changes in status between citizens. Any sense that there might have been of equality before the law deteriorated. For example, by the reign of Hadrian (AD 117 to 138), there were clear differences in the types of laws applied to different categories of Roman citizen. Just as important, the role of citizens was completely different from how it had been in the days of the Roman Republic, when they were able to exercise some power over political and economic decisions through the assemblies in Rome.

Slavery remained a constant throughout Rome, though there is some controversy over whether the fraction of slaves in the population actually declined over the centuries. Equally important, as the empire developed, more and more agricultural workers were reduced to semi-servile status and tied to the land. The status of these servile "*coloni*" is extensively discussed in legal documents such as the *Codex Theodosianus* and *Codex Justinianus,* and probably originated during the reign of Diocletian (AD 284 to 305). The rights of landlords over the *coloni* were progressively increased. The emperor Constantine in 332 allowed landlords to chain a *colonus* whom they suspected was trying to escape, and from AD 365, *coloni* were not allowed to sell their own property without their landlord's permission.

Just as we can use shipwrecks and the Greenland ice cores to track the economic expansion of Rome during earlier periods, we can use them also to trace its decline. By AD 500 the peak of 180 ships was reduced to 20. As Rome declined, Mediterranean trade collapsed, and some scholars have even argued that it did not return to its Roman height until the nineteenth century. The Greenland ice tells a similar story. The Romans used silver for coins, and lead had many uses, including for pipes and tableware. After peaking in the first century AD, the deposits of lead, silver, and copper in the ice cores declined.

The experience of economic growth during the Roman Republic was impressive, as were other examples of growth under extractive institutions, such as the Soviet Union. But that growth was limited and was not sustained, even when it is taken into account that it occurred under partially inclusive institutions. Growth was based on relatively high agricultural productivity, significant tribute from the provinces, and long-distance trade, but it was not underpinned by technological progress or creative destruction. The Romans inherited some basic technologies, iron tools and weapons, literacy, plow agriculture, and building techniques. Early on in the Republic, they created others: cement masonry, pumps, and the water wheel. But thereafter, technology was stagnant throughout the period of the Roman Empire. In shipping, for instance, there was little change in ship design or rigging, and the Romans never developed the stern rudder, instead steering ships with oars. Water wheels spread very slowly, so that water power never revolutionized the Roman economy. Even such great achievements as aqueducts and city sewers used existing technology, though the Romans perfected it. There could be some economic growth without innovation, relying on existing technology, but it was growth without creative destruction. And it did not last. As property rights became more insecure and the economic rights of citizens followed the decline of their political rights, economic growth likewise declined.

A remarkable thing about new technologies in the Roman period is that their creation and spread seem to have been driven by the state. This is good news, until the government decides that it is not interested in technological development—an all-too-common occurrence due to the fear of creative destruction. The great Roman writer Pliny the Elder relates the following story. During the reign of the emperor Tiberius, a man invented unbreakable glass and went to the emperor anticipating that he would get a great reward. He demonstrated his invention, and Tiberius asked him if he had told anyone else about it. When the man replied no, Tiberius had the man dragged away and killed, "lest gold be reduced to the value of mud." There are two interesting things about this story. First, the man went to Tiberius in the first place for a reward, rather than setting himself up in business and making a profit by selling the glass. This shows the role of the Roman government in controlling technology. Second, Tiberius was happy to destroy the innovation because of the adverse economic effects it would have had. This is the fear of the economic effects of creative destruction.

There is also direct evidence from the period of the Empire of the fear of the political consequences of creative destruction. Suetonius tells how the emperor Vespasian, who ruled between AD 69 and 79, was approached by a man who had invented a device for transporting columns to the Capitol, the citadel of Rome, at a relatively small cost. Columns were large, heavy, and very difficult to transport. Moving them to Rome from the mines where they were made involved the labor of thousands of people, at great expense to the government. Vespasian did not kill the man, but he also refused to use the innovation, declaring, "How will it be possible for me to feed the populace?" Again an inventor came to the government. Perhaps this was more natural than with the unbreakable glass, as the Roman government was most heavily involved with column mining and transportation. Again the innovation was turned down because of the threat of creative destruction, not so much because of its economic impact, but because of fear of political creative destruction. Vespasian was concerned that unless he kept the people happy and under control it would be politically destabilizing. The Roman plebeians had to be kept busy and pliant, so it was good to have jobs to give them, such as moving columns about. This complemented the bread and circuses, which were also dispensed for free to keep the population content. It is perhaps telling that both of these examples came soon after the collapse of the Republic. The Roman emperors had far more power to block change than the Roman rulers during the Republic.

Another important reason for the lack of technological innovation was the prevalence of slavery. As the territories Romans controlled expanded, vast numbers were enslaved, often being brought back to Italy to work on large estates. Many citizens in Rome did not need to work: they lived off the handouts from the government. Where was innovation to come from? We have argued that innovation comes from new people with new ideas, developing new solutions to old problems. In Rome the people doing the producing were slaves and, later, semi-servile *coloni* with few incentives to innovate, since it was their masters, not they, who stood to benefit from any innovation. As we will see many times in this book, economies based on the repression of labor and systems such as slavery and serfdom are notoriously noninnovative. This is true from the ancient world to the modern era. In the United States, for example, the northern states took part in the Industrial Revolution, not the South. Of course slavery and serfdom created huge wealth for those who owned the slaves and controlled the serfs, but it did not create technological innovation or prosperity for society.

No One Writes from Vindolanda

By AD 43 the Roman emperor Claudius had conquered England, but not Scotland. A last, futile attempt was made by the Roman governor Agricola, who gave up and, in AD 85, built a series of forts to protect England's northern border. One of the biggest of these was at Vindolanda, thirty-five miles west of Newcastle and depicted on Map 11 (page 165) at the far northwest of the Roman Empire. Later, Vindolanda was incorporated into the eighty-five-mile defensive wall that the emperor Hadrian constructed, but in AD 103, when a Roman centurion, Candidus, was stationed there, it was an isolated fort. Candidus was engaged with his friend Octavius in supplying the Roman garrison and received a reply from Octavius to a letter he had sent:

> Octavius to his brother Candidus, greetings.
> I have several times written to you that I have bought about five thousand modii of ears of grain, on account of which I need cash. Unless you send me some cash, at least five hundred denarii, the result will be that I shall lose what I have laid out as a deposit, about three hundred denarii, and I shall be embarrassed. So, I ask you, send me some cash as soon as possible. The hides which you write are at Cataractonium—write that they be given to me and the wagon about which you write. I would have already been to collect them except that I did not care to injure the animals while the roads are bad. See with Tertius about the 8½ denarii which he received from Fatalis. He has not credited them to my account. Make sure that you send me cash so that I may have ears of grain on the threshing-floor. Greet Spectatus and Firmus. Farewell.

The correspondence between Candidus and Octavius illustrates some significant facets of the economic prosperity of Roman England: It reveals an advanced monetary economy with financial services. It reveals the presence of constructed roads, even if sometimes in bad condition. It reveals the presence of a fiscal system that raised taxes to pay Candidus's wages. Most obviously it reveals that both men were literate and were able to take advantage of a postal service of sorts. Roman England also benefited from the mass manufacture of high-quality pottery, particularly in Oxfordshire; urban centers with baths and public buildings; and house construction techniques using mortar and tiles for roofs.

By the fourth century, all were in decline, and after AD 411 the Roman Empire gave up on England. Troops were withdrawn; those left were not paid, and as the Roman state crumbled, administrators were expelled by the local population. By AD 450 all these trappings of economic prosperity were gone. Money vanished from circulation. Urban areas were abandoned, and buildings stripped of stone. The roads were overgrown with weeds. The only type of pottery fabricated was crude and handmade, not manufactured. People forgot how to use mortar, and literacy declined substantially. Roofs were made of branches, not tiles. Nobody wrote from Vindolanda anymore.

After AD 411, England experienced an economic collapse and became a poor backwater—and not for the first time. In the previous chapter we saw how the Neolithic Revolution started in the Middle East around 9500 BC. While the inhabitants of Jericho and Abu Hureyra were living in small towns and farming, the inhabitants of England were still hunting and gathering, and would do so for at least another 5,500 years. Even then the English didn't invent farming or herding; these were brought from the outside by migrants who had been spreading across Europe from the Middle East for thousands of years. As the inhabitants of England caught up with these major innovations, those in the Middle East were inventing cities, writing, and pottery. By 3500 BC, large cities such as Uruk and Ur emerged in Mesopotamia, modern Iraq. Uruk may have had a population of fourteen thousand in 3500 BC, and forty thousand soon afterward. The potter's wheel was invented in Mesopotamia at about the same time as was wheeled transportation. The Egyptian capital of Memphis emerged as a large city soon thereafter. Writing appeared independently in both regions. While the Egyptians were building the great pyramids of Giza around 2500 BC, the English constructed their most famous ancient monument, the stone circle at Stonehenge. Not bad by English standards, but not even large enough to have housed one of the ceremonial boats buried at the foot of King Khufu's pyramid. England continued to lag behind and to borrow from the Middle East and the rest of Europe up to and including the Roman period.

Despite such an inauspicious history, it was in England that the first truly inclusive society emerged and where the Industrial Revolution got under way. We argued earlier (pages 102–113) that this was the result of a series of interactions between small institutional differences and critical junctures—for example, the Black Death and the discovery of the Americas. English divergence had historical roots, but the view from Vindolanda suggests that these roots were not that deep and certainly not historically predetermined. They were not planted in the Neolithic Revolution, or even during the centuries of Roman hegemony. By AD 450, at the start of what historians used to call the Dark Ages, England had slipped back into poverty and political chaos. There would be no effective centralized state in England for hundreds of years.

DIVERGING PATHS

The rise of inclusive institutions and the subsequent industrial growth in England did not follow as a direct legacy of Roman (or earlier) institutions. This does not mean that nothing significant happened with the fall of the Western Roman Empire, a major event affecting most of Europe. Since different parts of Europe shared the same critical junctures, their institutions would drift in a similar fashion, perhaps in a distinctively European way. The fall of the Roman Empire was a crucial part of these common critical junctures. This European path contrasts with paths in other parts of the world, including sub-Saharan Africa, Asia, and the Americas, which developed differently partly because they did not face the same critical junctures.

Roman England collapsed with a bang. This was less true in Italy, or Roman Gaul (modern France), or even North Africa, where many of the old institutions lived on in some form. Yet there is no doubt that the change from the dominance of a single Roman state to a plethora of states run by Franks, Visigoths, Ostrogoths, Vandals, and Burgundians was significant. The power of these states was far weaker, and they were buffeted by a long series of incursions from their peripheries. From the north came the Vikings and Danes in their longboats. From the east came the Hunnic horsemen. Finally, the emergence of Islam as a religion and political force in the century after the death of Mohammed in AD 632 led to the creation of new Islamic states in most of the Byzantine Empire, North Africa, and

Spain. These common processes rocked Europe, and in their wake a particular type of society, commonly referred to as feudal, emerged. Feudal society was decentralized because strong central states had atrophied, even if some rulers such as Charlemagne attempted to reconstruct them.

Feudal institutions, which relied on unfree, coerced labor (the serfs), were obviously extractive, and they formed the basis for a long period of extractive and slow growth in Europe during the Middle Ages. But they also were consequential for later developments. For instance, during the reduction of the rural population to the status of serfs, slavery disappeared from Europe. At a time when it was possible for elites to reduce the entire rural population to serfdom, it did not seem necessary to have a separate class of slaves as every previous society had had. Feudalism also created a power vacuum in which independent cities specializing in production and trade could flourish. But when the balance of power changed after the Black Death, and serfdom began to crumble in Western Europe, the stage was set for a much more pluralistic society without the presence of any slaves.

The critical junctures that gave rise to feudal society were distinct, but they were not completely restricted to Europe. A relevant comparison is with the modern African country of Ethiopia, which developed from the Kingdom of Aksum, founded in the north of the country around 400 BC. Aksum was a relatively developed kingdom for its time and engaged in international trade with India, Arabia, Greece, and the Roman Empire. It was in many ways comparable to the Eastern Roman Empire in this period. It used money, built monumental public buildings and roads, and had very similar technology, for example, in agriculture and shipping. There are also interesting ideological parallels between Aksum and Rome. In AD 312, the Roman emperor Constantine converted to Christianity, as did King Ezana of Aksum about the same time. Map 12 (opposite) shows the location of the historical state of Aksum in modern-day Ethiopia and Eritrea, with outposts across the Red Sea in Saudi Arabia and Yemen.

Just as Rome declined, so did Aksum, and its historical decline followed a pattern close to that of the Western Roman Empire. The role played by the Huns and Vandals in the decline of Rome was taken by the Arabs, who, in the seventh century, expanded into the Red Sea and down the Arabian Peninsula. Aksum lost its colonies in Arabia and its trade routes. This precipitated economic decline: money stopped being coined, the urban population fell, and there was a refocusing of the state into the interior of the country and up into the highlands of modern Ethiopia.

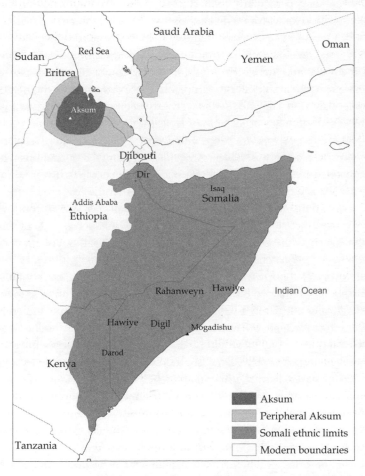

Map 12: The Aksum Empire and the Somali clan families

In Europe, feudal institutions emerged following the collapse of central state authority. The same thing happened in Ethiopia, based on a system called *gult,* which involved a grant of land by the emperor. The institution is mentioned in thirteenth-century manuscripts, though it may have originated much earlier. The term *gult* is derived from an Amharic word meaning "he assigned a fief." It signified that in exchange for the land, the *gult* holder had to provide services to the emperor, particularly military ones. In turn, the *gult* holder had the right to extract tribute from those who farmed the land. A variety of historical sources suggest that *gult* holders extracted between one-half and three-quarters of the agricultural output of peasants. This system was an independent development with notable similarities to European feudalism, but probably even more extractive. At the height of feudalism in England, serfs faced less onerous extraction and lost about half of their output to their lords in one form or another.

But Ethiopia was not representative of Africa. Elsewhere, slavery was not replaced by serfdom; African slavery and the institutions that supported it were to continue for many more centuries. Even Ethiopia's ultimate path would be very different. After the seventh century, Ethiopia remained isolated in the mountains of East Africa from the processes that subsequently influenced the institutional path of Europe, such as the emergence of independent cities, the nascent constraints on monarchs and the expansion of Atlantic trade after the discovery of the Americas. In consequence, its version of absolutist institutions remained largely unchallenged. The African continent would later interact in a very different capacity with Europe and Asia. East Africa became a major supplier of slaves to the Arab world, and West and Central Africa would be drawn into the world economy during the European expansion associated with the Atlantic trade as suppliers of slaves: How the Atlantic trade led to sharply divergent paths between Western Europe and Africa is yet another example of institutional divergence resulting from the interaction between critical junctures and existing institutional differences. While in England the profits of the slave trade helped to enrich those who opposed absolutism, in Africa they helped to create and strengthen absolutism.

Farther away from Europe, the processes of institutional drift were obviously even freer to go their own way. In the Americas, for example, which had been cut off from Europe around 15,000 BC by the melting of the ice that linked Alaska to Russia, there were similar institutional innovations as those of the Natufians, leading to sedentary life, hierarchy, and inequality—in short, extractive institutions. These took place first in Mexico and in Andean Peru and Bolivia, and led to the American Neolithic Revolution, with the domestication of maize. It was in these places that early forms of extractive growth took place, as we have seen in the Maya city-states. But in the same way that big breakthroughs toward inclusive institutions and industrial growth in Europe did not come in places where the Roman world had the strongest hold, inclusive institutions in the Americas did not develop in the lands of these early civilizations. In fact, as we saw in chapter 1, these densely settled civilizations interacted in a perverse way with European colonialism to create a "reversal of fortune," making the places that were previously relatively wealthy in the Americas relatively poor. Today it is the United States and Canada, which were then far behind the complex civilizations in Mexico, Peru, and Bolivia, that are much richer than the rest of the Americas.

CONSEQUENCES OF EARLY GROWTH

The long period between the Neolithic Revolution, which started in 9500 BC, and the British Industrial Revolution of the late eighteenth century is littered with spurts of economic growth. These spurts were triggered by institutional innovations that ultimately faltered. In Ancient Rome the institutions of the Republic, which created some degree of economic vitality and allowed for the construction of a massive empire, unraveled after the coup of Julius Caesar and the construction of the empire under Augustus. It took centuries for the Roman Empire finally to vanish, and the decline was drawn out; but once the relatively inclusive republican institutions gave way to the more extractive institutions of the empire, economic regress became all but inevitable.

The Venetian dynamics were similar. The economic prosperity of Venice was forged by institutions that had important inclusive elements, but these were undermined when the existing elite closed the system to new entrants and even banned the economic institutions that had created the prosperity of the republic.

However notable the experience of Rome, it was not Rome's inheritance that led directly to the rise of inclusive institutions in England and to the British Industrial Revolution. Historical factors shape how institutions develop, but this is not a simple, predetermined, cumulative process. Rome and Venice illustrate how early steps toward inclusivity were reversed. The economic and institutional landscape that Rome created throughout Europe and the Middle East did not inexorably lead to the more firmly rooted inclusive institutions of later centuries. In fact, these would emerge first and most strongly in England, where the Roman hold was weakest and where it disappeared most decisively, almost without a trace, during the fifth century AD. Instead, as we discussed in chapter 4, history plays a major role through institutional drift that creates institutional differences, albeit sometimes small, which then get amplified when they interact with critical junctures. It is because these differences are often small that they can be reversed easily and are not necessarily the consequence of a simple cumulative process.

Of course, Rome had long-lasting effects on Europe. Roman law and institutions influenced the laws and institutions that the kingdoms of the barbarians set up after the collapse of the Western Roman Empire. It was also Rome's fall that created the decentralized political landscape that developed into the feudal order. The disappearance of slavery and the emergence of independent cities were long, drawn out (and, of course, historically contingent) by-products of this process. These would become particularly consequential when the Black Death shook feudal society deeply. Out of the ashes of the Black Death emerged stronger towns and cities, and a peasantry no longer tied to the land and newly free of feudal obligations. It was precisely these critical junctures unleashed by the fall of the Roman Empire that led to a strong institutional drift affecting all of Europe in a way that has no parallel in sub-Saharan Africa, Asia, or the Americas.

By the sixteenth century, Europe was institutionally very distinct from sub-Saharan Africa and the Americas. Though not much richer than the most spectacular Asian civilizations in India or China, Europe differed from these polities in some key ways. For example, it had developed representative institutions of a sort unseen there. These were to play a critical role in the development of inclusive institutions. As we will see in the next two chapters, small institutional differences would be the ones that would really matter within Europe; and these favored England, because it was there that the feudal order had made way most comprehensively for commercially minded farmers and independent urban centers where merchants and industrialists could flourish. These groups were already demanding more secure property rights, different economic institutions, and political voice from their monarchs. This whole process would come to a head in the seventeenth century.

7.

THE TURNING POINT

TROUBLE WITH STOCKINGS

IN 1583 WILLIAM LEE returned from his studies at the University of Cambridge to become the local priest in Calverton, England. Elizabeth I (1558–1603) had recently issued a ruling that her people should always wear a knitted cap. Lee recorded that "knitters were the only means of producing such garments but it took so long to finish the article. I began to think. I watched my mother and my sisters sitting in the evening twilight plying their needles. If garments were made by two needles and one line of thread, why not several needles to take up the thread."

This momentous thought was the beginning of the mechanization of textile production. Lee became obsessed with making a machine that would free people from endless hand-knitting. He recalled, "My duties to Church and family I began to neglect. The idea of my machine and the creating of it ate into my heart and brain."

Finally, in 1589, his "stocking frame" knitting machine was ready. He traveled to London with excitement to seek an interview with Elizabeth I to show her how useful the machine would be and to ask her for a patent that would stop other people from copying the design. He rented a building to set the machine up and, with the help of his local member of Parliament Richard Parkyns, met Henry Carey, Lord Hunsdon, a member of the Queen's Privy Council. Carey arranged for Queen Elizabeth to come see the machine, but her reaction was devastating. She refused to grant Lee a patent, instead observing, "Thou aimest high, Master Lee. Consider thou what the invention could do to my poor subjects. It would assuredly bring to them ruin by depriving them of employment, thus making them beggars." Crushed, Lee moved to France to try his luck there; when he failed there, too, he returned to England, where he asked James I (1603–1625), Elizabeth's successor, for a patent. James I also refused, on the same grounds as Elizabeth. Both feared that the mechanization of stocking production would be politically destabilizing. It would throw people out of work, create unemployment and political instability, and threaten royal power. The stocking frame was an innovation that promised huge productivity increases, but it also promised creative destruction.

THE REACTION TO LEE'S brilliant invention illustrates a key idea of this book. The fear of creative destruction is the main reason why there was no sustained increase in living standards between the Neolithic and Industrial revolutions. Technological innovation makes human societies prosperous, but also involves the replacement of the old with the new, and the destruction of the economic privileges and political power of certain people. For sustained economic growth we need new technologies, new ways of doing things, and more often than not they will come from newcomers such as Lee. It may make society prosperous, but the process of creative destruction that it initiates threatens the livelihood of those who work with old technologies, such as the hand-knitters who would have found themselves unemployed by Lee's technology. More important, major innovations such as Lee's stocking frame machine also threaten to reshape political power. Ultimately it was not concern about the fate of those who might become unemployed as a result of Lee's machine that led Elizabeth I and James I to oppose his patent; it was their fear that they would become political losers—their concern that those displaced by the invention would create political instability and threaten their own power. As we saw with the Luddites (pages 85–86), it is often possible to bypass the resistance of workers such as hand-knitters. But the elite, especially when their political power is threatened, form a more formidable barrier to innovation. The fact that they have much to lose from creative destruction means not only that they will not be the

ones introducing new innovations but also that they will often resist
and try to stop such innovations. Thus society needs newcomers to
introduce the most radical innovations, and these newcomers and the
creative destruction they wreak must often overcome several sources
of resistance, including that from powerful rulers and elites.

Prior to seventeenth-century England, extractive institutions were
the norm throughout history. They have at times been able to generate economic growth, as shown in the last two chapters, especially
when they've contained inclusive elements, as in Venice and Rome.
But they did not permit creative destruction. The growth they generated was not sustained, and came to an end because of the absence
of new innovations, because of political infighting generated by the
desire to benefit from extraction, or because the nascent inclusive
elements were conclusively reversed, as in Venice.

The life expectancy of a resident of the Natufian village of Abu
Hureyra was probably not that much different from that of a citizen
of Ancient Rome. The life expectancy of a typical Roman was fairly
similar to that of an average inhabitant of England in the seventeenth
century. In terms of incomes, in 301 AD the Roman emperor Diocletian
issued the Edict on Maximum Prices, which set out a schedule of
wages that various types of workers would be paid. We don't know
exactly how well Diocletian's wages and prices were enforced, but
when the economic historian Robert Allen used his edict to calculate
the living standards of a typical unskilled worker, he found them to
be almost exactly the same as those of an unskilled worker in
seventeenth-century Italy. Farther north, in England, wages were
higher and increasing, and things were changing. How this came to
be is the topic of this chapter.

EVER-PRESENT POLITICAL CONFLICT

Conflict over institutions and the distribution of resources has been
pervasive throughout history. We saw, for example, how political
conflict shaped the evolution of Ancient Rome and Venice, where it
was ultimately resolved in favor of the elites, who were able to increase their hold on power.

English history is also full of conflict between the monarchy and its subjects, between different factions fighting for power, and between elites and citizens. The outcome, though, has not always been to strengthen the power of those who held it. In 1215 the barons, the layer of the elite beneath the king, stood up to King John and made him sign the Magna Carta ("the Great Charter") at Runnymede (see Map 9, page 112). This document enacted some basic principles that were significant challenges to the authority of the king. Most important, it established that the king had to consult with the barons in order to raise taxes. The most contentious clause was number 61, which stated that "the barons shall choose any twenty-five barons of the realm they wish, who with all their might are to observe, maintain and cause to be observed the peace and liberties which we have granted and confirmed to them by this our present charter." In essence, the barons created a council to make sure that the king implemented the charter, and if he didn't, these twenty-five barons had the right to seize castles, lands, and possessions ". . . until, in their judgement, amends have been made." King John didn't like the Magna Carta, and as soon as the barons dispersed, he got the pope to annul it. But both the political power of the barons and the influence of the Magna Carta remained. England had taken its first hesitant step toward pluralism.

Conflict over political institutions continued, and the power of the monarchy was further constrained by the first elected Parliament in 1265. Unlike the Plebeian Assembly in Rome or the elected legislatures of today, its members had originally been feudal nobles, and subsequently were knights and the wealthiest aristocrats of the nation. Despite consisting of elites, the English Parliament developed two distinguishing characteristics. First, it represented not only elites closely allied to the king but also a broad set of interests, including minor aristocrats involved in different walks of life, such as commerce and industry, and later the "gentry," a new class of commercial and upwardly mobile farmers. Thus the Parliament empowered a quite broad section of society—especially by the standards of the time. Second, and largely as a result of the first characteristic, many members of Parliament were consistently opposed to the monarchy's attempts to increase its power and would become the mainstay of those fighting against the monarchy in the English Civil War and then in the Glorious Revolution.

The Magna Carta and the first elected Parliament notwithstanding, political conflict continued over the powers of the monarchy and who was to be king. This intra-elite conflict ended with the War of the Roses, a long duel between the Houses of Lancaster and York, two families with contenders to be king. The winners were the Lancastrians, whose candidate for king, Henry Tudor, became Henry VII in 1485.

Two other interrelated processes took place. The first was increasing political centralization, put into motion by the Tudors. After 1485 Henry VII disarmed the aristocracy, in effect demilitarizing them and thereby massively expanding the power of the central state. His son, Henry VIII, then implemented through his chief minister, Thomas Cromwell, a revolution in government. In the 1530s, Cromwell introduced a nascent bureaucratic state. Instead of the government being just the private household of the king, it could become a separate set of enduring institutions. This was complemented by Henry VIII's break with the Roman Catholic Church and the "Dissolution of the Monasteries," in which Henry expropriated all the Church lands. The removal of the power of the Church was part of making the state more centralized. This centralization of state institutions meant that for the first time, inclusive political institutions became possible. This process initiated by Henry VII and Henry VIII not only centralized state institutions but also increased the demand for broader-based political representation. The process of political centralization can actually lead to a form of absolutism, as the king and his associates can crush other powerful groups in society. This is indeed one of the reasons why there will be opposition against state centralization, as we saw in chapter 3. However, in opposition to this force, the centralization of state institutions can also mobilize demand for a nascent form of pluralism, as it did in Tudor England. When the barons and local elites recognize that political power will be increasingly more centralized and that this process is hard to stop, they will make demands to have a say in how this centralized power is used. In England during the late fifteenth and sixteenth centuries, this meant greater efforts by these groups to have Parliament as a counterweight against the Crown and to partially control the way the state functioned. Thus the Tudor project not only initiated political centralization, one pillar of inclusive institutions, but also indirectly contributed to pluralism, the other pillar of inclusive institutions.

These developments in political institutions took place in the context of other major changes in the nature of society. Particularly significant was the widening of political conflict which was broadening the set of groups with the ability to make demands on the monarchy and the political elites. The Peasants' Revolt of 1381 (page 99) was pivotal, after which the English elite were rocked by a long sequence of popular insurrections. Political power was being redistributed not simply from the king to the lords, but also from the elite to the people. These changes, together with the increasing constraints on the king's power, made the emergence of a broad coalition opposed to absolutism possible and thus laid the foundations for pluralistic political institutions.

Though contested, the political and economic institutions the Tudors inherited and sustained were clearly extractive. In 1603 Elizabeth I, Henry VIII's daughter who had acceded to the throne of England in 1558, died without children, and the Tudors were replaced by the Stuart dynasty. The first Stuart king, James I, inherited not only the institutions but the conflicts over them. He desired to be an absolutist ruler. Though the state had become more centralized and social change was redistributing power in society, political institutions were not yet pluralistic. In the economy, extractive institutions manifested themselves not just in the opposition to Lee's invention, but in the form of monopolies, monopolies, and more monopolies. In 1601 a list of these was read out in Parliament, with one member ironically asking, "Is not bread there?" By 1621 there were seven hundred of them. As the English historian Christopher Hill put it, a man lived

> in a house built with monopoly bricks, with windows ... of monopoly glass; heated by monopoly coal (in Ireland monopoly timber), burning in a grate

made of monopoly iron . . . He washed himself in monopoly soap, his clothes in monopoly starch. He
dressed in monopoly lace, monopoly linen, monopoly
leather, monopoly gold thread . . . His clothes were
held up by monopoly belts, monopoly buttons, monopoly pins. They were dyed with monopoly dyes. He
ate monopoly butter, monopoly currants, monopoly
red herrings, monopoly salmon, and monopoly lob-
sters. His food was seasoned with monopoly salt, monopoly pepper, monopoly vinegar . . . He wrote with
monopoly pens, on monopoly writing paper; read
(through monopoly spectacles, by the light of monopoly candles) monopoly printed books.

These monopolies, and many more, gave individuals or groups
the sole right to control the production of many goods. They impeded
the type of allocation of talent, which is so crucial to economic prosperity.

Both James I and his son and successor Charles I aspired to
strengthen the monarchy, reduce the influence of Parliament, and
establish absolutist institutions similar to those being constructed in
Spain and France to further their and the elite's control of the economy, making institutions more extractive. The conflict between James
I and Parliament came to a head in the 1620s. Central in this conflict
was the control of trade both overseas and within the British Isles.
The Crown's ability to grant monopolies was a key source of revenue
for the state, and was used frequently as a way of granting exclusive
rights to supporters of the king. Not surprisingly, this extractive institution blocking entry and inhibiting the functioning of the market was
also highly damaging to economic activity and to the interests of
many members of Parliament. In 1623 Parliament scored a notable
victory by managing to pass the Statute of Monopolies, which prohibited James I from creating new domestic monopolies. He would still
be able to grant monopolies on international trade, however, since
the authority of Parliament did not extend to international affairs. Existing monopolies, international or otherwise, stood untouched.

Parliament did not sit regularly and had to be called into session by the king. The convention that emerged after the Magna Carta was that the king was required to convene Parliament to get assent for new taxes. Charles I came to the throne in 1625, declined to call Parliament after 1629, and intensified James I's efforts to build a more solidly absolutist regime. He induced forced loans, meaning that people had to "lend" him money, and he unilaterally changed the terms of loans and refused to repay his debts. He created and sold monopolies in the one dimension that the Statute of Monopolies had left to him: overseas trading ventures. He also undermined the independence of the judiciary and attempted to intervene to influence the outcome of legal cases. He levied many fines and charges, the most contentious of which was "ship money"—in 1634 taxing the coastal counties to pay for the support of the Royal Navy and, in 1635, extending the levy to the inland counties. Ship money was levied each year until 1640.

Charles's increasingly absolutist behavior and extractive policies created resentment and resistance throughout the country. In 1640 he faced conflict with Scotland and, without enough money to put a proper army into the field, was forced to call Parliament to ask for more taxes. The so-called Short Parliament sat for only three weeks. The parliamentarians who came to London refused to talk about taxes, but aired many grievances, until Charles dismissed them. The Scots realized that Charles did not have the support of the nation and invaded England, occupying the city of Newcastle. Charles opened negotiations, and the Scots demanded that Parliament be involved. This induced Charles to call what then became known as the Long Parliament, because it continued to sit until 1648, refusing to dissolve even when Charles demanded it do so.

In 1642 the Civil War broke out between Charles and Parliament, even though there were many in Parliament who sided with the Crown. The pattern of conflicts reflected the struggle over economic and political institutions. Parliament wanted an end to absolutist political institutions; the king wanted them strengthened. These conflicts were rooted in economics. Many supported the Crown because they had been granted lucrative monopolies. For example, the local monopolies controlled by the rich and powerful merchants of Shrewsbury and Oswestry were protected by the Crown from competition by London merchants. These merchants sided with Charles I. On the other side, the metallurgical industry had flourished around Birmingham because monopolies were weak there and newcomers to the industry did not have to serve a seven-year apprenticeship, as they did in other parts of the country. During the Civil War, they made swords and produced volunteers for the parliamentary side. Similarly, the lack of guild regulation in the county of Lancashire allowed for the development before 1640 of the "New Draperies," a new style of lighter cloth. The area where the production of these cloths was concentrated was the only part of Lancashire to support Parliament.

Under the leadership of Oliver Cromwell, the Parliamentarians—known as the Roundheads after the style in which their hair was cropped—defeated the royalists, known as Cavaliers. Charles was tried and executed in 1649. His defeat and the abolition of the monarchy did not, however, result in inclusive institutions. Instead, monarchy was replaced by the dictatorship of Oliver Cromwell. Following Cromwell's death, the monarchy was restored in 1660 and clawed back many of the privileges that had been stripped from it in 1649. Charles's son, Charles II, then set about the same program of creating absolutism in England. These attempts were only intensified by his brother James II, who ascended to the throne after Charles's death in 1685. In 1688 James's attempt to reestablish absolutism created another crisis and another civil war. Parliament this time was more united and organized. They invited the Dutch *Statholder,* William of Orange, and his wife, Mary, James's Protestant daughter, to replace James. William would bring an army and claim the throne, to rule not as an absolutist monarch but under a constitutional monarchy forged by Parliament. Two months after William's landing in the British Isles at Brixham in Devon (see Map 9, page 112), James's army disintegrated and he fled to France.

THE GLORIOUS REVOLUTION

After victory in the Glorious Revolution, Parliament and William negotiated a new constitution. The changes were foreshadowed by William's "Declaration," made shortly prior to his invasion. They were further enshrined in the Declaration of Rights, produced by Parliament in February 1689. The Declaration was read out to William at the same session where he was offered the crown. In many ways the Declaration, which would be called the Bill of Rights after its signing into law, was vague. Crucially, however, it did establish some central constitutional principles. It determined the succession to the throne, and did so in a way that departed significantly from the then-received hereditary principles. If Parliament could remove a monarch and replace him with one more to their liking once, then why not again? The Declaration of Rights also asserted that the monarch could not suspend or dispense with laws, and it reiterated the illegality of taxation without parliamentary consent. In addition, it stated that there could be no standing army in England without parliamentary consent. Vagueness entered into such clauses as number 8, which stated, "The election of members of Parliament ought to be free," but did not specify how "free" was to be determined. Even vaguer was clause 13, whose main point was that Parliaments ought to be held frequently. Since when and whether Parliament would be held had been such a contentious issue for the entire century, one might have expected much more specificity in this clause. Nevertheless, the reason for this vague wording is clear. Clauses have to be enforced. During the reign of Charles II, a Triennial Act had been in place that asserted that Parliaments had to be called at least once every three years. But Charles ignored it, and nothing happened, because there was no method of enforcing it. After 1688, Parliament could have tried to introduce a method for enforcing this clause, as the barons had done with their council after King John signed the Magna Carta. They did not do so because they did not need to. This was because authority and decision-making power switched to Parliament after 1688. Even without specific constitutional rules or laws, William simply gave up on many of the practices of previous kings. He stopped interfering in legal decisions and gave up previous "rights," such as getting the customs revenues for life. Taken together, these changes in political institutions represented the triumph of Parliament over the king, and thus the end of absolutism in England and subsequently Great Britain—as England and Scotland were united by the Act of Union in 1707. From then on Parliament was firmly in control of state policy. This made a huge difference, because the interests of Parliament were very different from those of the Stuart kings. Since many of those in Parliament had important investments in trade and industry, they had a strong stake in enforcing property rights. The Stuarts had frequently infringed on property rights; now they would be upheld. Moreover, when the Stuarts controlled how the government spent money, Parliament opposed greater taxes and balked at strengthening the power of the state. Now that Parliament itself controlled spending, it was happy to raise taxes and spend the money on activities that it deemed valuable. Chief among them was the strengthening of the navy, which would protect the overseas mercantile interests of many of the members of Parliament.

Even more important than the interest of parliamentarians was the emerging pluralistic nature of political institutions. The English people now had access to Parliament, and the policy and economic institutions made in Parliament, in a way they never had when policy was driven by the king. This was partially, of course, because members of Parliament were elected. But since England was far from being a democracy in this period, this access provided only a modest amount of responsiveness. Among its many inequities was that less than 2 percent of the population could vote in the eighteenth century, and these had to be men. The cities where the Industrial Revolution took place, Birmingham, Leeds, Manchester, and Sheffield, had no independent representation in Parliament. Instead, rural areas were overrepresented. Just as bad, the right to vote in the rural areas, the "counties," was based on ownership of land, and many urban areas, the "boroughs," were controlled by a small elite who did not allow the new industrialists to vote or run for office. In the borough of Buckingham, for instance, thirteen burgesses had the exclusive right to vote. On top of this there were the "rotten boroughs," which had historically had the right to vote but had "rotted away," either because their population had moved over time or, in the case on Dunwich on the east coast of England, had actually fallen into the ocean as a result of coastal erosion. In each of these rotten boroughs, a small number of voters elected two members of Parliament. Old Sarum had seven voters, Dunwich thirty-two, and each elected two members of Parliament.

But there were other ways to influence Parliament and thus economic institutions. The most important was via petitioning, and this was much more significant than the limited extent of democracy for the emergence of pluralism after the Glorious Revolution. Anybody could petition Parliament, and petition they did. Significantly, when people petitioned, Parliament listened. It is this more than anything that reflects the defeat of absolutism, the empowerment of a fairly broad segment of society, and the rise of pluralism in England after 1688. The frantic petitioning activity shows that it was indeed such a broad group in society, far beyond those sitting or even being represented in Parliament, that had the power to influence the way the state worked. And they used it.

The case of monopolies best illustrates this. We saw above how monopolies were at the heart of extractive economic institutions in the seventeenth century. They came under attack in 1623 with the Statute of Monopolies, and were a serious bone of contention during the English Civil War. The Long Parliament abolished all the domestic monopolies that so impinged on people's lives. Though Charles II and James II could not bring these back, they managed to maintain the ability to grant overseas monopolies. One was the Royal African Company, whose monopoly charter was issued by Charles II in 1660. This company held a monopoly on the lucrative African slave trade, and its governor and major shareholder was Charles's brother James, soon to become James II. After 1688 the Company lost not just its governor, but its main supporter. James had assiduously protected the monopoly of the company against "interlopers," the independent traders who tried to buy slaves in West Africa and sell them in the Americas. This was a very profitable trade, and the Royal African

Company faced a lot of challenges, since all other English trade in the Atlantic was free. In 1689 the Company seized the cargo of an interloper, one Nightingale. Nightingale sued the Company for illegal seizure of goods, and Chief Justice Holt ruled that the Company's seizure was unlawful because it was exercising a monopoly right created by royal prerogative. Holt reasoned that monopoly privileges could be created only by statute, and this had to be done by Parliament. So Holt pushed all future monopolies, not just of the Royal Africa Company, into the hands of Parliament. Before 1688 James II would quickly have removed any judge who made such a ruling. After 1688 things were different.

Parliament now had to decide what to do with the monopoly, and the petitions began to fly. One hundred and thirty-five came from interlopers demanding free access to trade in the Atlantic. Though the Royal African Company responded in kind, it could not hope to match the number or scope of the petitions demanding its demise. The interlopers succeeded in framing their opposition in terms not just of narrow self-interest, but of national interest, which indeed it was. As a result, only 5 of the 135 petitions were signed by the interlopers themselves, and 73 of the interlopers' petitions came from the provinces outside London, as against 8 for the Company. From the colonies, where petitioning was also allowed, the interlopers gathered 27 petitions, the Company 11. The interlopers also gathered far more signatures for their petitions, in total 8,000, as opposed to 2,500 for the Company. The struggle continued until 1698, when the Royal African Company monopoly was abolished.

Along with this new locus for the determination of economic institutions and the new responsiveness after 1688, parliamentarians started making a series of key changes in economic institutions and government policy that would ultimately pave the way for the Industrial Revolution. Property rights eroded under the Stuarts were strengthened. Parliament began a process of reform in economic institutions to promote manufacturing, rather than taxing and impeding it. The "hearth tax"—an annual tax for each fireplace or stove, which fell most heavily on manufacturers, who were bitterly opposed to it—was abolished in 1689, soon after William and Mary ascended the throne. Instead of taxing hearths, Parliament moved to start taxing land.

Redistributing the tax burden was not the only pro-manufacturing policy that Parliament supported. A whole series of acts and legislations that would expand the market and the profitability of woolen textiles was passed. This all made political sense, since many of the parliamentarians who opposed James were heavily invested in these nascent manufacturing enterprises. Parliament also passed legislation that allowed for a complete reorganization of property rights in land, permitting the consolidation and elimination of many archaic forms of property and user rights.

Another priority of Parliament was reforming finance. Though there had been an expansion of banking and finance in the period leading up to the Glorious Revolution, this process was further cemented by the creation of the Bank of England in 1694, as a source of funds for industry. It was another direct consequence of the Glorious Revolution. The foundation of the Bank of England paved the way for a much more extensive "financial revolution," which led to a great expansion of financial markets and banking. By the early eighteenth century, loans would be available to everyone who could put up the necessary collateral. The records of a relatively small bank, C. Hoare & Co. in London, which have survived intact from the period 1702–1724, illustrate this point. Though the bank did lend money to aristocrats and lords, fully two-thirds of the biggest borrowers from Hoare's over this period were not from the privileged social classes. Instead they were merchants and businessmen, including one John Smith, a man with the name of the eponymous average Englishman, who was loaned £2,600 by the bank during the period 1715–1719.

So far we have emphasized how the Glorious Revolution transformed English political institutions, making them more pluralistic, and also started laying the foundations for inclusive economic institutions. There is one more significant change in institutions that emerged from the Glorious Revolution: Parliament continued the process of political centralization that was initiated by the Tudors. It was not just that constraints increased, or that the state regulated the economy in a different way, or that the English state spent money on different things; but also the capability and capacity of the state increased in all directions. This again illustrates the linkages between political centralization and pluralism: Parliament had opposed making the state more effective and better resourced prior to 1688 because it could not control it. After 1688 it was a different story.

The state started expanding, with expenditures soon reaching around 10 percent of national income. This was underpinned by an expansion of the tax base, particularly with respect to the excise tax, which was levied on the production of a long list of domestically produced commodities. This was a very large state budget for the period, and is in fact larger than what we see today in many parts of the world. The state budgets in Colombia, for example, reached this relative size only in the 1980s. In many parts of sub-Saharan Africa—for example, in Sierra Leone—the state budget even today would be far smaller relative to the size of the economy without the large inflows of foreign aid.

But the expansion of the size of the state is only part of the process of political centralization. More important than this was the qualitative way the state functioned and the way those who controlled it and those who worked in it behaved. The construction of state institutions in England reached back into the Middle Ages, but as we've seen (page 186), steps toward political centralization and the development of modern administration were decisively taken by Henry VII and Henry VIII. Yet the state was still far from the modern form that would emerge after 1688. For example, many appointees were made on political grounds, not because of merit or talent, and the state still had a very limited capacity to raise taxes.

After 1688 Parliament began to improve the ability to raise revenue through taxation, a development well illustrated by the excise tax bureaucracy, which expanded rapidly from 1,211 people in 1690 to 4,800 by 1780. Excise tax inspectors were stationed throughout the country, supervised by collectors who engaged in tours of inspection to measure and check the amount of bread, beer, and other goods subject to the excise tax. The extent of this operation is illustrated by the reconstruction of the excise rounds of Supervisor George Cowperthwaite by the historian John Brewer. Between June 12 and July 5,

1710, Supervisor Cowperthwaite traveled 290 miles in the Richmond district of Yorkshire. During this period he visited 263 victualers, 71 maltsters, 20 chandlers, and one common brewer. In all, he took 81 different measurements of production and checked the work of 9 different excisemen who worked for him. Eight years later we find him working just as hard, but now in the Wakefield district, in a different part of Yorkshire. In Wakefield, he traveled more than nineteen miles a day on average and worked six days a week, normally inspecting four or five premises. On his day off, Sunday, he made up his books, so we have a complete record of his activities. Indeed, the excise tax system had very elaborate record keeping. Officers kept three different types of records, all of which were supposed to match one another, and any tampering with these records was a serious offense. This remarkable level of state supervision of society exceeds what the governments of most poor countries can achieve today, and this in 1710. Also significantly, after 1688 the state began to rely more on talent and less on political appointees, and developed a powerful infrastructure to run the country.

THE INDUSTRIAL REVOLUTION

The Industrial Revolution was manifested in every aspect of the English economy. There were major improvements in transportation, metallurgy, and steam power. But the most significant area of innovation was the mechanization of textile production and the development of factories to produce these manufactured textiles. This dynamic process was unleashed by the institutional changes that flowed from the Glorious Revolution. This was not just about the abolition of domestic monopolies, which had been achieved by 1640, or about different taxes or access to finance. It was about a fundamental reorganization of economic institutions in favor of innovators and entrepreneurs, based on the emergence of more secure and efficient property rights.

Improvements in the security and efficiency of property rights, for example, played a central role in the "transportation revolution," paving the way for the Industrial Revolution. Investment in canals and roads, the so-called turnpikes, massively increased after 1688. These investments, by reducing the costs of transportation, helped to create an important prerequisite for the Industrial Revolution. Prior to 1688, investment in such infrastructure had been impeded by arbitrary acts by the Stuart kings. The change in the situation after 1688 is vividly illustrated by the case of the river Salwerpe, in Worcestershire, England. In 1662 Parliament passed an act to encourage investment to make the Salwerpe navigable, and the Baldwyn family invested £6,000 to this end. In return they got the right to charge people for navigation on the river. In 1693 a bill was introduced to Parliament to transfer the rights to charge for navigation to the Earl of Shrewsbury and Lord Coventry. This act was challenged by Sir Timothy Baldwyn, who immediately submitted a petition to Parliament claiming that the proposed bill was essentially expropriating his father, who had already heavily invested in the river in anticipation of the charges he could then levy. Baldwyn argued that "the new act tends to make void the said act, and to take away all the works and materials done in pursuance thereof." Reallocation of rights such as this was exactly the sort of thing done by Stuart monarchs. Baldwyn noted, "[I]t is of dangerous consequence to take away any person's right, purchased under an act of Parliament, without their consent." In the event, the new act failed, and Baldwyn's rights were upheld. Property rights were much more secure after 1688, partly because securing them was consistent with the interests of Parliament and partly because pluralistic institutions could be influenced by petitioning. We see here that after 1688 the political system became significantly more pluralistic and created a relatively level playing field within England.

Underlying the transportation revolution and, more generally, the reorganization of land that took place in the eighteenth century were parliamentary acts that changed the nature of property ownership. Until 1688 there was even the legal fiction that all the land in England was ultimately owned by the Crown, a direct legacy from the feudal organization of society. Many pieces of land were encumbered by numerous archaic forms of property rights and many cross-cutting claims. Much land was held in so-called equitable estates, which meant that the landowner could not mortgage, lease, or sell the land. Common land could often be used only for traditional uses. There were enormous impediments to using land in ways that would be economically desirable. Parliament began to change this, allowing groups of people to petition Parliament to simplify and reorganize property rights, alterations that were subsequently embodied into hundreds of acts of Parliament.

This reorganization of economic institutions also manifested itself in the emergence of an agenda to protect domestic textile production against foreign imports. Not surprisingly, parliamentarians and their constituents were not opposed to all entry barriers and monopolies. Those that would increase their own market and profits would be welcome. However, crucially, the pluralistic political institutions—the fact that Parliament represented, empowered, and listened to a broad segment of society—meant that these entry barriers would not choke other industrialists or completely shut out newcomers, as the *Serrata* did in Venice (pages 155–156). The powerful woolen manufacturers soon made this discovery.

In 1688 some of the most significant imports into England were textiles from India, calicoes and muslins, which comprised about one-quarter of all textile imports. Also important were silks from China. Calicoes and silks were imported by the East India Company, which prior to 1688 enjoyed a government-sanctioned monopoly over the trade with Asia. But the monopoly and the political power of the East India Company was sustained through heavy bribes to James II. After 1688 the company was in a vulnerable position and soon under attack. This took the form of an intense war of petitions with traders hoping to trade in the Far East and India demanding that Parliament sanction competition for the East India Company, while the company responded with counterpetitions and offers to lend Parliament money. The company lost, and a new East India Company to compete with it was founded. But textile producers did not just want more competition in the trade to India. They wanted imports of cheap Indian textiles (calicoes) taxed or even banned. These producers faced strong competition from these cheap Indian imports. At this point the most important domestic manufacturers produced woolen textiles, but the producers of cotton cloths were becoming both more important economically and more powerful politically.

The wool industry mounted attempts to protect itself as early as the 1660s. It promoted the "Sumptuary Laws," which, among other things, prohibited the wearing of lighter cloth. It also lobbied Parliament to pass legislation in 1666 and 1678 that would make it illegal for someone to be buried in anything other than a woolen shroud. Both measures protected the market for woolen goods and reduced the competition that English manufacturers faced from Asia. Nevertheless, in this period the East India Company was too strong to restrict imports of Asian textiles. The tide changed after 1688. Between 1696 and 1698, woolen manufacturers from East Anglia and the West Country allied with silk weavers from London, Canterbury, and the Levant Company to restrict imports. The silk importers from the Levant, even if they had recently lost their monopoly, wished to exclude Asian silks to create a niche for silks from the Ottoman Empire. This coalition started to present bills to Parliament to place restrictions on the wearing of Asian cottons and silks, and also restrictions on the dyeing and printing of Asian textiles in England. In response, in 1701, Parliament finally passed "an Act for the more effectual imploying the poor, by incouraging the manufactures of this kingdom." From September 1701, it decreed: "All wrought silks, bengals and stuffs, mixed with silk or herba, of the manufacture of Persia, China, or East-India, all Calicoes painted, dyed, printed, or stained there, which are or shall be imported into this kingdom, shall not be worn."

It was now illegal to wear Asian silks and calicoes in England. But it was still possible to import them for reexport to Europe or elsewhere, in particular to the American colonies. Moreover, plain calicoes could be imported and finished in England, and muslins were exempt from the ban. After a long struggle, these loopholes, as the domestic woolen textile manufacturers viewed them, were closed by the Calico Act of 1721: "After December 25, 1722, it shall not be lawful for any person or persons whatsoever to use or wear in Great Britain, in any garment or apparel whatsoever, any printed, painted, stained or dyed Calicoe." Though this act removed competition from

Asia for English woolens, it still left an active domestic cotton and linen industry competing against the woolens: cotton and linen were mixed to produce a popular cloth called fustian. Having excluded Asian competition, the wool industry now turned to clamp down on linen. Linen was primarily made in Scotland and Ireland, which gave some scope to an English coalition to demand those countries' exclusion from English markets. However, there were limits to the power of the woolen manufacturers. Their new attempts encountered strong opposition from fustian producers in the burgeoning industrial centers of Manchester, Lancaster, and Liverpool. The pluralistic political institutions implied that all these different groups now had access to the policy process in Parliament via voting and, more important, petitioning. Though the petitions flew from the pens of both sides, amassing signatures for and against, the outcome of this conflict was a victory for the new interests against those of the wool industry. The Manchester Act of 1736 agreed that "great quantities of stuffs made from linen yarn and cotton wool have for several years past been manufactured, and have been printed and painted within this kingdom of Great Britain." It then went on to assert that "nothing in the said recited Act [of 1721] shall extend or be construed to prohibit the wearing or using in apparel, household stuff, furniture or otherwise, any sort of stuff made out of linen yarn and cotton wool, manufactured and printed or painted with any colour or colours within the kingdom of Great Britain."

The Manchester Act was a significant victory for the nascent cotton manufacturers. But its historical and economic significance was in fact much greater. First, it demonstrated the limits of entry barriers that the pluralistic political institutions of parliamentary England would permit. Second, over the next half century, technological innovations in the manufacture of cotton cloth would play a central role in the Industrial Revolution and fundamentally transform society by introducing the factory system.

After 1688, though domestically a level playing field emerged, internationally Parliament strove to tilt it. This was evident not only from the Calicoe Acts but also from the Navigation Acts, the first of which was passed in 1651, and they remained in force with alternations for the next two hundred years. The aim of these acts was to facilitate England's monopolization of international trade—though crucially this was monopolization not by the state but by the private sector. The basic principle was that English trade should be carried in English ships. The acts made it illegal for foreign ships to transport goods from outside Europe to England or its colonies, and it was similarly illegal for third-party countries' ships to ship goods from a country elsewhere in Europe to England. This advantage for English traders and manufacturers naturally increased their profits and may have further encouraged innovation in these new and highly profitable activities.

By 1760 the combination of all these factors—improved and new property rights, improved infrastructure, a changed fiscal regime, greater access to finance, and aggressive protection of traders and manufacturers—was beginning to have an effect. After this date, there was a jump in the number of patented inventions, and the great flowering of technological change that was to be at the heart of the Industrial Revolution began to be evident. Innovations took place on many fronts, reflecting the improved institutional environment. One crucial area was power, most famously the transformations in the use of the steam engine that were a result of James Watt's ideas in the 1760s.

Watt's initial breakthrough was to introduce a separate condensing chamber for the steam so that the cylinder that housed the piston could be kept continually hot, instead of having to be warmed up and cooled down. He subsequently developed many other ideas, including much more efficient methods of converting the motion of the steam engine into useful power, notably his "sun and planets" gear system. In all these areas technological innovations built on earlier work by others. In the context of the steam engine, this included early work by English inventor Thomas Newcomen and also by Dionysius Papin, a French physicist and inventor.

The story of Papin's invention is another example of how, under extractive institutions, the threat of creative destruction impeded technological change. Papin developed a design for a "steam digester" in 1679, and in 1690 he extended this into a piston engine. In 1705 he used this rudimentary engine to build the world's first steamboat. Papin was by this time a professor of mathematics at the University of Marburg, in the German state of Kassel. He decided to steam the boat down the river Fulda to the river Weser. Any boat making this trip was forced to stop at the city of Münden. At that time, river traffic on the Fulda and Weser was the monopoly of a guild of boatmen. Papin must have sensed that there might be trouble. His friend and mentor, the famous German physicist Gottfried Leibniz, wrote to the Elector of Kassel, the head of state, petitioning that Papin should be allowed to ". . . pass unmolested . . ." through Kassel. Yet Leibniz's petition was rebuffed and he received the curt answer that "the Electoral Councillors have found serious obstacles in the way of granting the above petition, and, without giving their reasons, have directed me to inform you of their decision, and that in consequence the request is not granted by his Electoral Highness." Undeterred, Papin decided to make the journey anyway. When his steamer arrived at Münden, the boatmen's guild first tried to get a local judge to impound the ship, but was unsuccessful. The boatmen then set upon Papin's boat and smashed it and the steam engine to pieces. Papin died a pauper and was buried in an unmarked grave. In Tudor or Stuart England, Papin might have received similar hostile treatment, but this all changed after 1688. Indeed, Papin was intending to sail his boat to London before it was destroyed.

In metallurgy, key contributions were made in the 1780s by Henry Cort, who introduced new techniques for dealing with impurities in iron, allowing for a much better quality wrought iron to be produced. This was critical for the manufacture of machine parts, nails, and tools. The production of vast quantities of wrought iron using Cort's techniques was facilitated by the innovations of Abraham Darby and his sons, who pioneered the use of coal to smelt iron beginning in 1709. This process was enhanced in 1762 by the adaptation, by John Smeaton, of water power to operate blowing cylinders in making coke. After this, charcoal vanished from the production of iron, to be replaced by coal, which was much cheaper and more readily available.

Even though innovation is obviously cumulative, there was a

distinct acceleration in the middle of the eighteenth century. In no place was this more visible than in textile production. The most basic operation in the production of textiles is spinning, which involves taking plant or animal fibers, such as cotton or wool, and twisting them together to form yarn. This yarn is then woven to make up textiles. One of the great technological innovations of the medieval period was the spinning wheel, which replaced hand spinning. This invention appeared around 1280 in Europe, probably disseminating from the Middle East. The methods of spinning did not change until the eighteenth century. Significant innovations began in 1738, when Lewis Paul patented a new method of spinning using rollers to replace human hands to draw out the fibers being spun. The machine did not work well, however, and it was the innovations of Richard Arkwright and James Hargreaves that truly revolutionized spinning.

In 1769 Arkwright, one of the dominant figures of the Industrial Revolution, patented his "water frame," which was a huge improvement over Lewis's machine. He formed a partnership with Jedediah Strutt and Samuel Need, who were hosiery manufacturers. In 1771 they built one of the world's first factories, at Cromford. The new machines were powered by water, but Arkwright later made the crucial transition to steam power. By 1774 his firm employed six hundred workers, and he expanded aggressively, eventually setting up factories in Manchester, Matlock, Bath, and New Lanark in Scotland. Arkwright's innovations were complemented by Hargreaves's invention in 1764 of the spinning jenny, which was further developed by Samuel Crompton in 1779 into the "mule," and later by Richard Roberts into the "self-acting mule." The effects of these innovations were truly revolutionary: earlier in the century, it took 50,000 hours for hand spinners to spin one hundred pounds of cotton. Arkwright's water frame could do it in 300 hours, and the self-acting mule in 135.

Along with the mechanization of spinning came the mechanization of weaving. An important first step was the invention of the flying shuttle by John Kay in 1733. Though it initially simply increased the productivity of hand weavers, its most enduring impact would be in opening the way to mechanized weaving. Building on the flying shuttle, Edmund Cartwright introduced the power loom in 1785, a first step in a series of innovations that would lead to machines replacing manual skills in weaving as they were also doing in spinning.

The English textile industry not only was the driving force behind the Industrial Revolution but also revolutionized the world economy. English exports, led by cotton textiles, doubled between 1780 and 1800. It was the growth in this sector that pulled ahead the whole economy. The combination of technological and organizational innovation provides the model for economic progress that transformed the economies of the world that became rich.

New people with new ideas were crucial to this transformation. Consider innovation in transportation. In England there were several waves of such innovations: first canals, then roads, and finally railways. In each of these waves the innovators were new men. Canals started to develop in England after 1770, and by 1810 they had linked up many of the most important manufacturing areas. As the Industrial Revolution unfolded, canals played an important role in reducing transportation costs for moving around the bulky new finished industrial goods, such as cotton textiles, and the inputs that went into them, particularly raw cotton and coal for the steam engines. Early innovators in building canals were men such as James Brindley, who was employed by the Duke of Bridgewater to build the Bridgewater Canal, which ended up linking the key industrial city of Manchester to the port of Liverpool. Born in rural Derbyshire, Brindley was a millwright by profession. His reputation for finding creative solutions to engineering problems came to the attention of the duke. He had no previous experience with transportation problems, which also was true of other great canal engineers such as Thomas Telford, who started life as a stonemason, or John Smeaton, an instrument maker and engineer.

Just as the great canal engineers had no previous connection to transportation, neither did the great road and railway engineers. John McAdam, who invented tarmac around 1816, was the second son of a minor aristocrat. The first steam train was built by Richard Trevithick in 1804. Trevithick's father was involved in mining in Cornwall, and

Richard entered the same business at an early age, becoming fascinated by steam engines used for pumping out the mines. More significant were the innovations of George Stephenson, the son of illiterate parents and the inventor of the famous train "The Rocket," who began work as an engineman at a coal mine.

New men also drove the critical cotton textile industry. Some of the pioneers of this new industry were people who had previously been heavily involved in the production and trade of woolen cloths. John Foster, for example, employed seven hundred handloom weavers in the woolen industry at the time he switched to cotton and opened Black Dyke Mills in 1835. But men such as Foster were a minority. Only about one-fifth of the leading industrialists at this time had previously been involved in anything like manufacturing activities. This is not surprising. For one, the cotton industry developed in new towns in the north of England. Factories were a completely new way of organizing production. The woolen industry had been organized in a very different way, by "putting out" materials to individuals in their homes, who spun and wove on their own. Most of those in the woolen industry were therefore ill equipped to switch to cotton, as Foster did. Newcomers were needed to develop and use the new technologies. The rapid expansion of cotton decimated the wool industry—creative destruction in action.

Creative destruction redistributes not simply income and wealth, but also political power, as William Lee learned when he found the authorities so unreceptive to his invention because they feared its political consequences. As the industrial economy expanded in Manchester and Birmingham, the new factory owners and middle-class groups that emerged around them began to protest their disenfranchisement and the government policies opposed to their interests. Their prime candidate was the Corn Laws, which banned the import of "corn"—all grains and cereals, but principally wheat—if the price got too low, thus ensuring that the profits of large landowners were kept high. This policy was very good for big landowners who produced wheat, but bad for manufacturers, because they had to pay higher wages to compensate for the high price of bread.

With workers concentrated into new factories and industrial centers, it became easier to organize and riot. By the 1820s, the political exclusion of the new manufacturers and manufacturing centers was becoming untenable. On August 16, 1819, a meeting to protest the political system and the policies of the government was planned to be held in St. Peter's Fields, Manchester. The organizer was Joseph Johnson, a local brush manufacturer and one of the founders of the radical newspaper the *Manchester Observer*. Other organizers included John Knight, a cotton manufacturer and reformer, and John Thacker Saxton, editor of the *Manchester Observer*. Sixty thousand protestors gathered, many holding banners such as "No Corn Laws," "Universal Suffrage," and "Vote by Ballot" (meaning voting should take place secretly, not openly, as it did in 1819). The authorities were very nervous about the meeting, and a force of six hundred cavalry of the Fifteenth Hussars had been assembled. As the speeches began, a local magistrate decided to issue a warrant for the arrest of the speakers. As police tried to enforce the warrant, they met with the opposition of the crowd, and fighting broke out. At this point the Hussars charged the crowd. Within a few chaotic minutes, eleven people were dead and probably six hundred wounded. The *Manchester Observer* called it the Peterloo Massacre.

But given the changes that had already taken place in economic and political institutions, long-run repression was not a solution in England. The Peterloo Massacre would remain an isolated incident. Following the riot, the political institutions in England gave way to the pressure, and the destabilizing threat of much wider social unrest, particularly after the 1830 revolution in France against Charles X, who had tried to restore the absolutism destroyed by the French Revolution of 1789. In 1832 the government passed the First Reform Act. It enfranchised Birmingham, Leeds, Manchester, and Sheffield, and broadened the base of voting so that manufacturers could be represented in Parliament. The consequent shift in political power moved policy in the direction favored by these newly represented interests; in 1846 they managed to get the hated Corn Laws repealed, demonstrating again that creative destruction meant a redistribution not just of income, but also of political power. And naturally, changes in the distribution of political power in time would lead to a further redistribution of income.

It was the inclusive nature of English institutions that allowed this process to take place. Those who suffered from and feared creative destruction were no longer able to stop it.

WHY IN ENGLAND?

The Industrial Revolution started and made its biggest strides in England because of her uniquely inclusive economic institutions. These in turn were built on foundations laid by the inclusive political institutions brought about by the Glorious Revolution. It was the Glorious Revolution that strengthened and rationalized property rights, improved financial markets, undermined state-sanctioned monopolies in foreign trade, and removed the barriers to the expansion of industry. It was the Glorious Revolution that made the political system open and responsive to the economic needs and aspirations of society. These inclusive economic institutions gave men of talent and vision such as James Watt the opportunity and incentive to develop their skills and ideas and influence the system in ways that benefited them and the nation. Naturally these men, once they had become successful, had the same urges as any other person. They wanted to block others from entering their businesses and competing against them and feared the process of creative destruction that might put them out of business, as they had previously bankrupted others. But after 1688 this became harder to accomplish. In 1775 Richard Arkwright took out an encompassing patent that he hoped would give him a monopoly on the rapidly expanding cotton spinning industry in the future. He could not get the courts to enforce it.

Why did this unique process start in England and why in the seventeenth century? Why did England develop pluralistic political institutions and break away from extractive institutions? As we have seen, the political developments leading up to the Glorious Revolution were shaped by several interlinked processes. Central was the political conflict between absolutism and its opponents. The outcome of this conflict not only put a stop to the attempts to create a renewed and stronger absolutism in England, but also empowered those wishing to fundamentally change the institutions of society. The opponents of absolutism did not simply attempt to build a different type of absolutism. This was not simply the House of Lancaster defeating the House of York in the War of the Roses. Instead, the Glorious Revolution involved the emergence of a new regime based on constitutional rule and pluralism.

This outcome was a consequence of the drift in English institutions and the way they interacted with critical junctures. We saw in the previous chapter how feudal institutions were created in Western Europe after the collapse of the Western Roman Empire. Feudalism spread throughout most of Europe, West and East. But as chapter 4 showed, Western and Eastern Europe began to diverge radically after the Black Death. Small differences in political and economic institutions meant that in the West the balance of power led to institutional improvement; in the East, to institutional deterioration. But this was not a path that would necessarily and inexorably lead to inclusive institutions. Many more crucial turns would have to be taken on the way. Though the Magna Carta had attempted to establish some basic institutional foundations for constitutional rule, many other parts of Europe, even Eastern Europe, saw similar struggles with similar documents. Yet, after the Black Death, Western Europe significantly drifted away from the East. Documents such as the Magna Carta started to have more bite in the West. In the East, they came to mean little. In England, even before the conflicts of the seventeenth century, the norm was established that the king could not raise new taxes without the consent of Parliament. No less important was the slow, incremental drift of power away from elites to citizens more generally, as exemplified by the political mobilization of rural communities, seen in England with such moments as the Peasants' Revolt of 1381.

This drift of institutions now interacted with another critical juncture caused by the massive expansion of trade into the Atlantic. As we saw in chapter 4, one crucial way in which this influenced future institutional dynamics depended on whether or not the Crown was able to monopolize this trade. In England the somewhat greater power of Parliament meant that the Tudor and Stuart monarchs could not do so. This created a new class of merchants and businessmen, who aggressively opposed the plan to create absolutism in England. By 1686 in London, for example, there were 702 merchants exporting to the Caribbean and 1,283 importing. North America had 691 exporting and 626 importing merchants. They employed warehousemen, sailors, captains, dockworkers, clerks—all of whom broadly shared their interests. Other vibrant ports, such as Bristol, Liverpool, and Portsmouth, were similarly full of such merchants. These new men wanted and demanded different economic institutions, and as they got wealthier through trade, they became more powerful. The same forces were at work in France, Spain, and Portugal. But there the kings were much more able to control trade and its profits. The type of new group that was to transform England did emerge in those countries, but was considerably smaller and weaker.

When the Long Parliament sat and the Civil War broke out in 1642, these merchants primarily sided with the parliamentary cause. In the 1670s they were heavily involved in the formation of the Whig Party, to oppose Stuart absolutism, and in 1688 they would be pivotal in deposing James II. So the expanding trade opportunities presented by the Americas, the mass entry of English merchants into this trade and the economic development of the colonies, and the fortunes they made in the process, tipped the balance of power in the struggle between the monarchy and those opposed to absolutism.

Perhaps most critically, the emergence and empowerment of diverse interests—ranging from the gentry, a class of commercial farmers that had emerged in the Tudor period, to different types of manufacturers to Atlantic traders—meant that the coalition against Stuart absolutism was not only strong but also broad. This coalition was strengthened even more by the formation of the Whig Party in the 1670s, which provided an organization to further its interests. Its empowerment was what underpinned pluralism following the Glorious Revolution. If all those fighting against the Stuarts had the same interests and the same background, the overthrow of the Stuart monarchy would have been much more likely to be a replay of the House of Lancaster versus the House of York, pitting one group against another narrow set of interests, and ultimately replacing and re-creating the same or a different form of extractive institutions. A broad coalition meant that there would be greater demands for the creation of pluralist political institutions. Without some sort of pluralism, there would be a danger that one of the diverse interests would usurp power at the expense of the rest. The fact that Parliament after 1688 represented such a broad coalition was a crucial factor in making members of Parliament listen to petitions, even when they came from people outside of Parliament and even from those without a vote. This was a crucial factor in preventing attempts by one group to create a monopoly at the expense of the rest, as wool interests tried to do before the Manchester Act.

The Glorious Revolution was a momentous event precisely because it was led by an emboldened broad coalition and further empowered this coalition, which managed to forge a constitutional regime with constraints on the power of both the executive and, equally crucially, any one of its members. It was, for example, these constraints that prevented the wool manufacturers from being able to crush the potential competition from the cotton and fustian manufacturers. Thus this broad coalition was essential in the lead-up to a strong Parliament after 1688, but it also meant that there were checks within Parliament against any single group becoming too powerful and abusing its power. It was the critical factor in the emergence of pluralistic political institutions. The empowerment of such a broad coalition also played an important role in the persistence and strengthening of these inclusive economic and political institutions, as we will see in chapter 11.

Still none of this made a truly pluralistic regime inevitable, and its emergence was in part a consequence of the contingent path of history. A coalition that was not too different was able to emerge victorious from the English Civil War against the Stuarts, but this only led to Oliver Cromwell's dictatorship. The strength of this coalition was also no guarantee that absolutism would be defeated. James II could have defeated William of Orange. The path of major institutional change was, as usual, no less contingent than the outcome of other political conflicts. This was so even if the specific path of institutional drift that created the broad coalition opposed to absolutism and the critical juncture of Atlantic trading opportunities stacked the cards against the Stuarts. In this instance, therefore, contingency and a broad coalition were deciding factors underpinning the emergence of pluralism and inclusive institutions.

8.

NOT ON OUR TURF:
BARRIERS TO DEVELOPMENT

NO PRINTING ALLOWED

IN 1445 IN THE GERMAN city of Mainz, Johannes Gutenberg unveiled an innovation with profound consequences for subsequent economic history: a printing press based on movable type. Until then, books either had to be hand-copied by scribes, a very slow and laborious process, or they were block-printed with specific pieces of wood cut for printing each page. Books were few and far between, and very expensive. After Gutenberg's invention, things began to change. Books were printed and became more readily available. Without this innovation, mass literacy and education would have been impossible.

In Western Europe, the importance of the printing press was quickly recognized. In 1460 there was already a printing press across the border, in Strasbourg, France. By the late 1460s the technology had spread throughout Italy, with presses in Rome and Venice, soon followed by Florence, Milan, and Turin. By 1476 William Caxton had set up a printing press in London, and two years later there was one in Oxford. During the same period, printing spread throughout the Low Countries, into Spain, and even into Eastern Europe, with a press opening in Budapest in 1473 and in Cracow a year later.

Not everyone saw printing as a desirable innovation. As early as 1485 the Ottoman sultan Bayezid II issued an edict that Muslims were expressly forbidden from printing in Arabic. This rule was further reinforced by Sultan Selim I in 1515. It was not until 1727 that the first printing press was allowed in the Ottoman lands. Then Sultan Ahmed III issued a decree granting İbrahim Müteferrika permission to set up a press. Even this belated step was hedged with restraints. Though the decree noted "the fortunate day this Western technique will be unveiled like a bride and will not again be hidden," Müteferrika's printing was going to be closely monitored. The decree stated:

> so that the printed books will be free from printing mistakes, the wise, respected and meritorious religious scholars specializing in Islamic Law, the excellent Kadi of Istanbul, Mevlana İshak, and Selaniki's Kadi, Mevlana Sahib, and Galata's Kadi, Mevlana Asad, may their merits be increased, and from the illustrious religious orders, the pillar of the righteous religious scholars, the Sheykh of the Kasim Paşa Mevlevihane, Mevlana Musa, may his wisdom and knowledge increase, will oversee the proofreading.

Müteferrika was allowed to set up a printing press, but whatever he printed had to be vetted by a panel of three religious and legal scholars, the Kadis. Maybe the wisdom and knowledge of the Kadis, like everybody else's, would have increased much faster had the printing press been more readily available. But that was not to be, even after Müteferrika was given permission to set up his press.

Not surprisingly Müteferrika printed few books in the end, only seventeen between 1729, when the press began to operate, and 1743, when he stopped working. His family tried to continue the tradition, but they managed to print only another seven books by the time they finally gave up in 1797. Outside of the core of the Ottoman Empire in Turkey, printing lagged even further behind. In Egypt, for instance, the first printing press was set up only in 1798, by Frenchmen who were part of the abortive attempt by Napoleon Bonaparte to capture the country. Until well into the second half of the nineteenth century, book production in the Ottoman Empire was still primarily undertaken by scribes hand-copying existing books. In the early eighteenth century, there were reputed to be eighty thousand such scribes active in Istanbul.

This opposition to the printing press had the obvious consequences for literacy, education, and economic success. In 1800 probably only 2 to 3 percent of the citizens of the Ottoman Empire were literate, compared with 60 percent of adult males and 40 percent of adult females in England. In the Netherlands and Germany, literacy rates were even higher. The Ottoman lands lagged far behind the European countries with the lowest educational attainment in this period, such as Portugal, where probably only around 20 percent of adults could read and write.

Given the highly absolutist and extractive Ottoman institutions, the sultan's hostility to the printing press is easy to understand. Books spread ideas and make the population much harder to control. Some of these ideas may be valuable new ways to increase economic growth, but others may be subversive and challenge the existing political and social status quo. Books also undermine the power of those who control oral knowledge, since they make that knowledge readily available to anyone who can master literacy. This threatened to undermine the existing status quo, where knowledge was controlled by elites. The Ottoman sultans and religious establishment feared the creative destruction that would result. Their solution was to forbid printing.

THE INDUSTRIAL REVOLUTION created a critical juncture that affected almost every country. Some nations, such as England, not only allowed, but actively encouraged, commerce, industrialization, and entrepreneurship, and grew rapidly. Many, such as the Ottoman Empire, China, and other absolutist regimes, lagged behind as they blocked or at the very least did nothing to encourage the spread of industry. Political and economic institutions shaped the response to technological innovation, creating once again the familiar pattern of interaction between existing institutions and critical junctures leading to divergence in institutions and economic outcomes.

The Ottoman Empire remained absolutist until it collapsed at the end of the First World War, and was thus able to successfully oppose or impede innovations such as the printing press and the creative destruction that would have resulted. The reason that the economic changes that took place in England did not happen in the Ottoman Empire is the natural connection between extractive, absolutist political institutions and extractive economic institutions. Absolutism is rule unconstrained by law or the wishes of others, though in reality absolutists rule with the support of some small group or elite. In nineteenth-century Russia, for example, the tsars were absolutist rulers supported by a nobility that represented about 1 percent of the total population. This narrow group organized political institutions to perpetuate their power. There was no Parliament or political representation of other groups in Russian society until 1905, when the tsar created the Duma, though he quickly undermined what few powers he had given to it. Unsurprisingly, economic institutions were extractive, organized to make the tsar and nobility as wealthy as possible. The basis of this, as of many extractive economic systems, was a mass system of labor coercion and control, in the particularly pernicious form of Russian serfdom.

Absolutism was not the only type of political institution preventing industrialization. Though absolutist regimes were not pluralistic and feared creative destruction, many had centralized states, or at least states that were centralized enough to impose bans on innovations such as the printing press. Even today, countries such as Afghanistan, Haiti, and Nepal have national states that lack political centralization. In sub-Saharan Africa the situation is even worse. As we argued earlier, without a centralized state to provide order and enforce rules and property rights, inclusive institutions could not emerge. We will see in this chapter that in many parts of sub-Saharan Africa (for example, Somalia and southern Sudan) a major barrier to industrialization was the lack of any form of political centralization. Without these natural prerequisites, industrialization had no chance of getting off the ground.

Absolutism and a lack of, or weak, political centralization are two different barriers to the spread of industry. But they are also connected; both are kept in place by fear of creative destruction and because the process of political centralization often creates a tendency toward absolutism. Resistance to political centralization is motivated by reasons similar to resistance to inclusive political institutions: fear of losing political power, this time to the newly centralizing state and those who control it. We saw in the previous chapter how the process of political centralization under the Tudor monarchy in England increased demands for voice and representation by different local elites in national political institutions as a way of staving off this loss of political power. A stronger Parliament was created, ultimately enabling the emergence of inclusive political institutions.

But in many other cases, just the opposite takes place, and the process of political centralization also ushers in an era of greater absolutism. This is illustrated by the origins of Russian absolutism, which was forged by Peter the Great between 1682 and his death in 1725. Peter built a new capital at Saint Petersburg, stripping away power from the old aristocracy, the Boyars, in order to create a modern bureaucratic state and modern army. He even abolished the Boyar Duma that had made him tsar. Peter introduced the Table of Ranks, a completely new social hierarchy whose essence was service to the tsar. He also took control over the Church, just as Henry VIII did when centralizing the state in England. With this process of political centralization, Peter was taking power away from others and redirecting it toward himself. His military reforms led the traditional royal guards, the Streltsy, to rebel. Their revolt was followed by others, such as the Bashkirs in Central Asia and the Bulavin Rebellion. None succeeded.

Though Peter the Great's project of political centralization was a success and the opposition was overcome, the type of forces that opposed state centralization, such as the Streltsy, who saw their power being challenged, won out in many parts of the world, and the resulting lack of state centralization meant the persistence of a different type of extractive political institutions.

In this chapter, we will see how during the critical juncture created by the Industrial Revolution, many nations missed the boat and failed to take advantage of the spread of industry. Either they had absolutist political and extractive economic institutions, as in the Ottoman Empire, or they lacked political centralization, as in Somalia.

A SMALL DIFFERENCE THAT MATTERED

Absolutism crumbled in England during the seventeenth century but got stronger in Spain. The Spanish equivalent of the English Parliament, the Cortes, existed in name only. Spain was forged in 1492 with the merger of the kingdoms of Castile and Aragon via the marriage of Queen Isabella and King Ferdinand. That date coincided with the end of the Reconquest, the long process of ousting the Arabs who had occupied the south of Spain, and built the great cities of Granada, Cordova, and Seville, since the eighth century. The last Arab state on the Iberian Peninsula, Granada, fell to Spain at the same time Christopher Columbus arrived in the Americas and started claiming lands for Queen Isabella and King Ferdinand, who had funded his voyage.

The merger of the crowns of Castile and Aragon and subsequent dynastic marriages and inheritances created a European superstate. Isabella died in 1504, and her daughter Joanna was crowned queen of Castile. Joanna was married to Philip of the House of Habsburg, the son of the emperor of the Holy Roman Empire, Maximilian I. In 1516 Charles, Joanna and Philip's son, was crowned Charles I of Castile and Aragon. When his father died, Charles inherited the Netherlands and Franche-Comté, which he added to his territories in Iberia and the Americas. In 1519, when Maximilian I died, Charles also inherited the Habsburg territories in Germany and became Emperor Charles V of the Holy Roman Empire. What had been a merger of two Spanish kingdoms in 1492 became a multicontinental empire, and Charles continued the project of strengthening the absolutist state that Isabella and Ferdinand had begun.

The effort to build and consolidate absolutism in Spain was massively aided by the discovery of precious metals in the Americas. Silver had already been discovered in large quantities in Guanajuato, in Mexico, by the 1520s, and soon thereafter in Zacatecas, Mexico. The conquest of Peru after 1532 created even more wealth for the monarchy. This came in the form of a share, the "royal fifth," in any loot from conquest and also from mines. As we saw in chapter 1, a mountain of silver was discovered in Potosí by the 1540s, pouring more wealth into the coffers of the Spanish king.

At the time of the merger of Castile and Aragon, Spain was among the most economically successful parts of Europe. After its absolutist political system solidified, it went into relative and then, after 1600, absolute economic decline. Almost the first acts of Isabella and Ferdinand after the Reconquest was the expropriation of the Jews. The approximately two hundred thousand Jews in Spain were given four months to leave. They had to sell off all their land and assets at very low prices and were not allowed to take any gold or silver out of the country. A similar human tragedy was played out just over one hundred years later. Between 1609 and 1614, Philip III expelled the Moriscos, the descendants of the citizens of the former Arab states in the south of Spain. Just as with the Jews, the Moriscos had to leave with only what they could carry and were not allowed to take with them any gold, silver, or other precious metals.

Property rights were insecure in other dimensions under Habsburg rule in Spain. Philip II, who succeeded his father, Charles V, in 1556, defaulted on his debts in 1557 and again in 1560, ruining the Fugger and Welser banking families. The role of the German banking families was then assumed by Genoese banking families, who were in turn ruined by subsequent Spanish defaults during the reign of the Habsburgs in 1575, 1596, 1607, 1627, 1647, 1652, 1660, and 1662.

Just as crucial as the instability of property rights in absolutist Spain was the impact of absolutism on the economic institutions of trade and the development of the Spanish colonial empire. As we saw in the previous chapter, the economic success of England was based on rapid mercantile expansion. Though, compared with Spain and Portugal, England was a latecomer to Atlantic trade, she allowed for relatively broad-based participation in trading and colonial opportunities. What filled the Crown's coffers in Spain enriched the newly emerging merchant class in England. It was this merchant class that would form the basis of early England economic dynamism and become the bulwark of the anti-absolutist political coalition.

In Spain these processes that led to economic progress and institutional change did not take place. After the Americas had been discovered, Isabella and Ferdinand organized trade between their new colonies and Spain via a guild of merchants in Seville. These merchants controlled all trade and made sure that the monarchy got its share of the wealth of the Americas. There was no free trade with any of the colonies, and each year a large flotilla of ships would return from the Americas bringing precious metals and valuable goods to Seville. The narrow, monopolized base of this trade meant that no broad class of merchants could emerge via trading opportunities with the colonies. Even trade within the Americas was heavily regulated. For example, a merchant in a colony such as New Spain, roughly modern Mexico, could not trade directly with anyone in New Granada, modern Colombia. These restrictions on trade within the Spanish Empire reduced its economic prosperity and also, indirectly, the potential benefits that Spain could have gained by trading with another, more prosperous empire. Nevertheless, they were attractive because they guaranteed that the silver and gold would keep flowing to Spain.

The extractive economic institutions of Spain were a direct result of the construction of absolutism and the different path, compared with England, taken by political institutions. Both the Kingdom of Castile and the Kingdom of Aragon had their Cortes, a parliament representing the different groups, or "estates," of the kingdom. As with the English Parliament, the Castilian Cortes needed to be summoned to assent to new taxes. Nevertheless, the Cortes in Castile and Aragon primarily represented the major cities, rather than both the urban and rural areas, as the English Parliament did. By the fifteenth century, it represented only eighteen cities, each of whom sent two deputies. In consequence, the Cortes did not represent as broad a set of groups as the English Parliament did, and it never developed as a nexus of diverse interests vying to place constraints on absolutism. It could not legislate, and even the scope of its powers with respect to taxation was limited. This all made it easier for the Spanish monarchy to sideline the Cortes in the process of consolidating its own absolutism. Even with silver coming from the Americas, Charles V and Philip II required ever-increasing tax revenues to finance a series of expensive wars. In 1520 Charles V decided to present the Cortes with demands for increased taxation. Urban elites used the moment to call for much wider change in the Cortes and its powers. This opposition turned violent and quickly became known as the Comunero Rebellion. Charles was able to crush the rebellion with loyal troops. Throughout the rest of the sixteenth century, though, there was a continuous battle as the Crown tried to wrest away from the Cortes what rights to levy new taxes and increase old ones that it had. Though this battle ebbed and flowed, it was ultimately won by the monarchy. After 1664 the Cortes did not meet again until it would be reconstructed during the Napoleonic invasions almost 150 years later.

In England the defeat of absolutism in 1688 led not only to pluralistic political institutions but also to the further development of a much more effective centralized state. In Spain the opposite happened as absolutism triumphed. Though the monarchy emasculated the Cortes and removed any potential constraints on its behavior, it became increasingly difficult to raise taxes, even when attempted by direct negotiations with individual cities. While the English state was creating a modern, efficient tax bureaucracy, the Spanish state was again moving in the opposite direction. The monarchy was not only failing to create secure property rights for entrepreneurs and monopolizing trade, but it was also selling offices, often making them hereditary, indulging in tax farming, and even selling immunity from justice.

The consequences of these extractive political and economic institutions in Spain were predictable. During the seventeenth century, while England was moving toward commercial growth and then rapid industrialization, Spain was tailspinning toward widespread economic decline. At the start of the century, one in five people in Spain was living in urban areas. By the end, this figure had halved to one in ten, in a process that corresponded to increasing impoverishment of the Spanish population. Spanish incomes fell, while England grew rich.

The persistence and the strengthening of absolutism in Spain, while it was being uprooted in England, is another example of small differences mattering during critical junctures. The small differences were in the strengths and nature of representative institutions; the critical juncture was the discovery of the Americas. The interaction of these sent Spain off on a very different institutional path from England. The relatively inclusive economic institutions that resulted in England created unprecedented economic dynamism, culminating in the Industrial Revolution, while industrialization did not stand a chance in Spain. By the time industrial technology was spreading in many parts of the world, the Spanish economy had declined so much that there was not even a need for the Crown or the land-owning elites in Spain to block industrialization.

Fear of Industry

Without the changes in political institutions and political power similar to those that emerged in England after 1688, there was little chance for absolutist countries to benefit from the innovations and new technologies of the Industrial Revolution. In Spain, for example, the lack of secure property rights and the widespread economic decline meant that people simply did not have the incentive to make the necessary investments and sacrifices. In Russia and Austria-Hungary, it wasn't simply the neglect and mismanagement of the elites and the insidious economic slide under extractive institutions that prevented industrialization; instead, the rulers actively blocked any attempt to introduce these technologies and basic investments in infrastructure such as railroads that could have acted as their conduits.

At the time of the Industrial Revolution, in the eighteenth and early nineteenth centuries, the political map of Europe was quite different from how it is today. The Holy Roman Empire, a patchwork quilt of more than four hundred polities, most of which would eventually coalesce into Germany, occupied most of Central Europe. The House of Habsburg was still a major political force, and its empire, known as the Habsburg or Austro-Hungarian Empire, spread over a vast area of around 250,000 square miles, even if it no longer included Spain, after the Bourbons had taken over the Spanish throne in 1700. In terms of population, it was the third-largest state in Europe and comprised one-seventh of the population of Europe. In the late eighteenth century the Habsburg lands included, in the west, what is today Belgium, then known as the Austrian Netherlands. The largest part, however, was the contiguous block of lands based around Austria and Hungary, including the Czech Republic and Slovakia to the north, and Slovenia, Croatia, and large parts of Italy and Serbia to the south. To the east it also incorporated much of what is today Romania and Poland.

Merchants in the Habsburg domains were much less important than in England, and serfdom prevailed in the lands in Eastern Europe. As we saw in chapter 4, Hungary and Poland were at the heart of the Second Serfdom of Eastern Europe. The Habsburgs, unlike the Stuarts, were successful in sustaining strongly absolutist rule. Francis I, who ruled as the last emperor of the Holy Roman Empire, between 1792 and 1806, and then emperor of Austria-Hungary until his death in 1835, was a consummate absolutist. He did not recognize any limitations on his power and, above all, he wished to preserve the political status quo. His basic strategy was opposing change, any sort of change. In 1821 he made this clear in a speech, characteristic of Habsburg rulers, he gave to the teachers at a school in Laibach, asserting, "I do not need savants, but good, honest citizens. Your task is to bring young men up to be this. He who serves me must teach what I order him. If anyone can't do this, or comes with new ideas, he can go, or I will remove him."

The empress Maria Theresa, who reigned between 1740 and 1780, frequently responded to suggestions about how to improve or change institutions by remarking. "Leave everything as it is." Nevertheless, she and her son Joseph II, who was emperor between 1780 and 1790, were responsible for an attempt to construct a more powerful central state and more effective administrative system. Yet they did this in the context of a political system with no real constraints on their actions and with few elements of pluralism. There was no national parliament that would exert even a modicum of control on the monarch, only a system of regional estates and diets, which historically had some powers with respect to taxation and military recruitment. There were even fewer controls on what the Austro-Hungarian Habsburgs could do than there were on Spanish monarchs, and political power was narrowly concentrated.

As Habsburg absolutism strengthened in the eighteenth century, the power of all non-monarchical institutions weakened further. When a deputation of citizens from the Austrian province of the Tyrol petitioned Francis for a constitution, he responded, "So, you want a constitution! . . . Now look, I don't care for it, I will give you a constitution but you must know that the soldiers obey me, and I will not ask you twice if I need money . . . In any case I advise you to be careful what you are going to say." Given this response, the Tyrolese leaders replied, "If thou thinkest thus, it is better to have no constitution," to which Francis answered, "That is also my opinion."

Francis dissolved the State Council that Maria Theresa had used as a forum for consultation with her ministers. From then on there would be no consultation or public discussion of the Crown's decisions. Francis created a police state and ruthlessly censored anything that could be regarded as mildly radical. His philosophy of rule was characterized by Count Hartig, a long-standing aide, as the "unabated maintenance of the sovereign's authority, and a denial of all claims on the part of the people to a participation in that authority." He was helped in all this by Prince von Metternich, appointed as his foreign minister in 1809. Metternich's power and influence actually outlasted that of Francis, and he remained foreign minister for almost forty years.

At the center of Habsburg economic institutions stood the feudal order and serfdom. As one moved east within the empire, feudalism became more intense, a reflection of the more general gradient in economic institutions we saw in chapter 4, as one moved from Western to Eastern Europe. Labor mobility was highly circumscribed, and emigration was illegal. When the English philanthropist Robert Owen tried to convince the Austrian government to adopt some social reforms in order to ameliorate the conditions of poor people, one of Metternich's assistants, Friedrich von Gentz, replied, "We do not desire at all that the great masses shall become well off and independent . . . How could we otherwise rule over them?"

In addition to serfdom, which completely blocked the emergence of a labor market and removed the economic incentives or initiative from the mass of the rural population, Habsburg absolutism thrived on monopolies and other restrictions on trade. The urban economy was dominated by guilds, which restricted entry into professions. Until 1775 there were internal tariffs within Austria itself and in Hungary until 1784. There were very high tariffs on imported goods, with many explicit prohibitions on the import and export of goods.

The suppression of markets and the creation of extractive economic institutions are of course quite characteristic of absolutism, but Francis went further. It was not simply that extractive economic institutions removed the incentive for individuals to innovate or adopt new technology. We saw in chapter 2 how in the Kingdom of Kongo attempts to promote the use of plows were unsuccessful because people lacked any incentive, given the extractive nature of the economic institutions. The king of Kongo realized that if he could induce people to use plows, agricultural productivity would be higher, generating more wealth, which he could benefit from. This is a potential incentive for all governments, even absolutist ones. The problem in Kongo was that people understood that whatever they produced could be confiscated by an absolutist monarch, and therefore they had no incentive to invest or use better technology. In the Habsburg lands, Francis did not encourage his citizens to adopt better technology; on the contrary, he actually opposed it, and blocked the dissemination of technologies that people would have been otherwise willing to adopt with the existing economic institutions.

Opposition to innovation was manifested in two ways. First, Francis I was opposed to the development of industry. Industry led to factories, and factories would concentrate poor workers in cities, particularly in the capital city of Vienna. Those workers might then become supporters for opponents of absolutism. His policies were aimed at locking into place the traditional elites and the political and economic status quo. He wanted to keep society primarily agrarian. The best way to do this, Francis believed, was to stop the factories being built in the first place. This he did directly—for instance, in 1802, banning the creation of new factories in Vienna. Instead of encouraging the importation and adoption of new machinery, the basis of industrialization, he banned it until 1811.

Second, he opposed the construction of railways, one of the key new technologies that came with the Industrial Revolution. When a plan to build a northern railway was put before Francis I, he replied, "No, no, I will have nothing to do with it, lest the revolution might come into the country."

Since the government would not grant a concession to build a steam railway, the first railway built in the empire had to use horse-drawn carriages. The line, which ran between the city of Linz, on the Danube, to the Bohemian city of Budweis, on the Moldau River, was built with gradients and corners, which meant that it was impossible subsequently to convert it to steam engines. So it continued with horse power until the 1860s. The economic potential for railway development in the empire had been sensed early by the banker Salomon Rothschild, the representative in Vienna of the great banking family. Salomon's brother Nathan, who was based in England, was very impressed by George Stephenson's engine "The Rocket" and the potential for steam locomotion. He contacted his brother to encourage him to look for opportunities to develop railways in Austria, since he believed that the family could make large profits by financing railway development. Nathan agreed, but the scheme went nowhere because Emperor Francis again simply said no.

The opposition to industry and steam railways stemmed from Francis's concern about the creative destruction that accompanied the development of a modern economy. His main priorities were ensuring the stability of the extractive institutions over which he ruled and protecting the advantages of the traditional elites who supported him. Not only was there little to gain from industrialization, which would undermine the feudal order by attracting labor from the countryside to the cities, but Francis also recognized the threat that major economic changes would pose to his political power. As a consequence, he blocked industry and economic progress, locking in economic backwardness, which manifested itself in many ways. For instance, as late as 1883, when 90 percent of world iron output was produced using coal, more than half of the output in the Habsburg territories still used much less efficient charcoal. Similarly, right up to the First World War, when the empire collapsed, textile weaving was never fully mechanized but still undertaken by hand.

Austria-Hungary was not alone in fearing industry. Farther east, Russia had an equally absolutist set of political institutions, forged by Peter the Great, as we saw earlier in this chapter. Like Austria-Hungary, Russia's economic institutions were highly extractive, based on serf-dom, keeping at least half of the population tied to the land. Serfs had to work for nothing three days a week on the lands of their lords. They could not move, they lacked freedom of occupation, and they could be sold at will by their lord to another lord. The radical phi-losopher Peter Kropotkin, one of the founders of modern anarchism, left a vivid depiction of the way serfdom worked during the reign of Tsar Nicholas I, who ruled Russia from 1825 until 1855. He recalled from his childhood

> stories of men and women torn from their families and their villages and sold, lost in gambling, or exchanged for a couple of hunting dogs, and transported to some remote part of Russia . . . of children taken from their parents and sold to cruel or dissolute masters; of flog-ging "in the stables," which occurred every day with unheard of cruelty; of a girl who found her only salva-tion in drowning herself; of an old man who had grown grey-haired in his master's service and at last hanged himself under his master's window; and of re-volts of serfs, which were suppressed by Nicholas I's generals by flogging to death each tenth or fifth man taken out of the ranks, and by laying waste the vil-lage . . . As to the poverty which I saw during our jour-neys in certain villages, especially in those which

> belonged to the imperial family, no words would be
> adequate to describe the misery to readers who have
> not seen it.

Exactly as in Austria-Hungary, absolutism didn't just create a set of economic institutions that impeded the prosperity of the society. There was a similar fear of creative destruction and a fear of industry and the railways. At the heart of this during the reign of Nicholas I was Count Egor Kankrin, who served as finance minister between 1823 and 1844 and played a key role in opposing the changes in society necessary for promoting economic prosperity.

Kankrin's policies were aimed at strengthening the traditional political pillars of the regime, particularly the landed aristocracy, and keeping the society rural and agrarian. Upon becoming minister of finance, Kankrin quickly opposed and reversed a proposal by the previous finance minister, Gurev, to develop a government-owned Commercial Bank to lend to industry. Instead, Kankrin reopened the State Loan Bank, which had been closed during the Napoleonic Wars. This bank was originally created to lend to large landowners at subsidized rates, a policy Kankrin approved of. The loans required the applicants to put up serfs as "security," or collateral, so that only feudal landowners could get such loans. To finance the State Loan Bank, Kankrin transferred assets from the Commercial Bank, killing two birds with one stone: there would now be little money left for industry.

Kankrin's attitudes were presciently shaped by the fear that economic change would bring political change, and so were those of Tsar Nicholas. Nicholas's assumption of power in December 1825 had been almost aborted by an attempted coup by military officers, the so-called Decembrists, who had a radical program of social change. Nicholas wrote to Grand Duke Mikhail: "Revolution is on Russia's doorstep, but I swear that it will not penetrate the country while there is breath in my body."

Nicholas feared the social changes that creating a modern economy would bring. As he put it in a speech he made to a meeting of manufacturers at an industrial exhibit in Moscow:

both the state and manufacturers must turn their attention to a subject, without which the very factories
would become an evil rather than a blessing; this is
the care of the workers who increase in number annually. They need energetic and paternal supervision of
their morals; without it this mass of people will gradually be corrupted and eventually turn into a class as
miserable as they are dangerous for their masters.

Just as with Francis I, Nicholas feared that the creative destruction
unleashed by a modern industrial economy would undermine the
political status quo in Russia. Urged on by Nicholas, Kankrin took
specific steps to slow the potential for industry. He banned several
industrial exhibitions, which had previously been held periodically to
showcase new technology and facilitate technology adoption.

In 1848 Europe was rocked by a series of revolutionary outbursts.
In response, A. A. Zakrevskii, the military governor of Moscow, who
was in charge of maintaining public order, wrote to Nicholas: "For the
preservation of calm and prosperity, which at present time only Russia enjoys, the government must not permit the gathering of homeless
and dissolute people, who will easily join every movement, destroying social or private peace." His advice was brought before Nicholas's
ministers, and in 1849 a new law was enacted that put severe limits
on the number of factories that could be opened in any part of Moscow. It specifically forbade the opening of any new cotton or woolen
spinning mills and iron foundries. Other industries, such as weaving
and dyeing, had to petition the military governor if they wanted to
open new factories. Eventually cotton spinning was explicitly banned.
The law was intended to stop any further concentration of potentially
rebellious workers in the city.

Opposition to railways accompanied opposition to industry, exactly as in Austria-Hungary. Before 1842 there was only one railway
in Russia. This was the Tsarskoe Selo Railway, which ran seventeen
miles from Saint Petersburg to the imperial residences of Tsarskoe
Selo and Pavlovsk. Just as Kankrin opposed industry, he saw no

reason to promote railways, which he argued would bring a socially dangerous mobility, noting that "railways do not always result from natural necessity, but are more an object of artificial need or luxury. They encourage unnecessary travel from place to place, which is entirely typical of our time."

Kankrin turned down numerous bids to build railways, and it was only in 1851 that a line was built linking Moscow and Saint Petersburg. Kankrin's policy was continued by Count Kleinmichel, who was made head of the main administration of Transport and Public Buildings. This institution became the main arbiter of railway construction, and Kleinmichel used it as a platform to discourage their construction. After 1849 he even used his power to censor discussion in the newspapers of railway development.

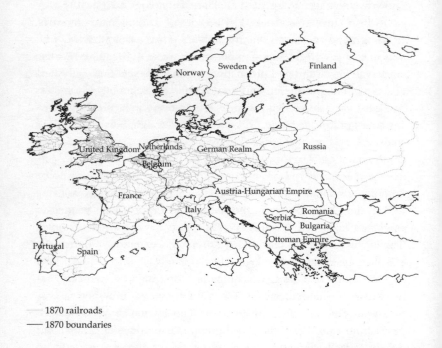

Map 13: Railroads in Europe in 1870

Map 13 (opposite) shows the consequences of this logic. While Britain and most of northwest Europe was crisscrossed with railways in 1870, very few penetrated the vast territory of Russia. The policy against railways was only reversed after Russia's conclusive defeat by British, French, and Ottoman forces in the Crimean War, 1853–1856, when the backwardness of its transportation network was understood to be a serious liability for Russian security. There was also little railway development in Austria-Hungary outside of Austria and the western parts of the empire, though the 1848 Revolutions had brought change to these territories, particularly the abolition of serfdom.

NO SHIPPING ALLOWED

Absolutism reigned not just in much of Europe but also in Asia, and similarly prevented industrialization during the critical juncture created by the Industrial Revolution. The Ming and Qing dynasties of China and the absolutism of the Ottoman Empire illustrate this pattern. Under the Song dynasty, between 960 and 1279, China led the world in many technological innovations. The Chinese invented clocks, the compass, gunpowder, paper and paper money, porcelain, and blast furnaces to make cast iron before Europe did. They independently developed spinning wheels and waterpower at more or less the same time that these emerged at the other end of Eurasia. In consequence, in 1500 standards of living were probably at least as high in China as they were in Europe. For centuries China also had a centralized state with a meritocratically recruited civil service.

Yet China was absolutist, and the growth under the Song dynasty was under extractive institutions. There was no political representation for groups other than the monarchy in society, nothing resembling a Parliament or a Cortes. Merchants always had a precarious status in China, and the great inventions of the Song were not spurred by market incentives but were brought into existence under the auspices, or even the orders, of the government. Little of this was commercialized. The grip of the state tightened during the Ming and Qing dynasties that followed the Song. At the root of all this was the usual logic of extractive institutions. As most rulers presiding over extractive institutions, the absolutist emperors of China opposed change, sought stability, and in essence feared creative destruction.

This is best illustrated by the history of international trade. As we have seen, the discovery of the Americas and the way international trade was organized played a key role in the political conflicts and institutional changes of early modern Europe. In China, while private merchants were commonly involved in trade within the country, the state monopolized overseas trade. When the Ming dynasty came to power in 1368, it was Emperor Hongwu who first ruled, for thirty years. Hongwu was concerned that overseas trade would be politically and socially destabilizing and he allowed international trade to take place only if it were organized by the government and only if it involved tribute giving, and not commercial activity. Hongwu even executed hundreds of people accused of trying to turn tribute missions into commercial ventures. Between 1377 and 1397, no oceangoing tribute missions were allowed. He banned private individuals from trading with foreigners and would not allow Chinese to sail overseas.

In 1402 Emperor Yongle came to the throne and initiated one of the most famous periods of Chinese history by restarting government-sponsored foreign trade on a big scale. Yongle sponsored Admiral Zheng He to undertake six huge missions to Southeast and South Asia, Arabia, and Africa. The Chinese knew about these places from a long history of trading relations, but nothing had ever happened on this scale before. The first fleet included 27,800 men and 62 large treasure ships, accompanied by 190 smaller ships, including ones specifically for carrying freshwater, others for supplies, and others for troops. Yet Emperor Yongle put a temporary stop on the missions after the sixth one in 1422. This was made permanent by his successor, Hongxi, who ruled from 1424 to 1425. Hongxi's premature death brought to the throne Emperor Xuande, who at first allowed Zheng He a final mission, in 1433. But after this, all overseas trade was banned. By 1436 the construction of seagoing ships was even made illegal. The ban on overseas trade was not lifted until 1567.

These events, though only the tip of the extractive iceberg that prevented many economic activities deemed to be potentially destabilizing, were to have a fundamental impact on Chinese economic development. Just at the time when international trade and the discovery of the Americas were fundamentally transforming the institutions of England, China was cutting itself off from this critical juncture and turning inward. This inward turn did not end in 1567. The Ming dynasty was overrun in 1644 by the Jurchen people, the Manchus of inner Asia, who created the Qing dynasty. A period of intense political instability then ensued. The Qings engaged in mass expropriation of property and assets. In the 1690s, T'ang Chen, a retired Chinese scholar and failed merchant, wrote:

> More than fifty years have passed since the founding
> of the Ch'ing [Qing] dynasty, and the empire grows
> poorer each day. Farmers are destitute, artisans are
> destitute, merchants are destitute, and officials too are
> destitute. Grain is cheap, yet it is hard to eat one's fill.
> Cloth is cheap, yet it is hard to cover one's skin. Boat-
> loads of goods travel from one marketplace to another,
> but the cargoes must be sold at a loss. Officials upon
> leaving their posts discover they have no wherewithal
> to support their households. Indeed the four occupa-
> tions are all impoverished.

In 1661 the emperor Kangxi ordered that all people living along the coast from Vietnam to Chekiang—essentially the entire southern coast, once the most commercially active part of China—should move seventeen miles inland. The coast was patrolled by troops to enforce the measure, and until 1693 there was a ban on shipping everywhere on the coast. This ban was periodically reimposed in the eighteenth century, effectively stunting the emergence of Chinese overseas trade. Though some did develop, few were willing to invest when the emperor could suddenly change his mind and ban trade, making investments in ships, equipment, and trading relations worthless or even worse.

The reasoning of the Ming and Qing states for opposing international trade is by now familiar: the fear of creative destruction. The leaders' primary aim was political stability. International trade was potentially destabilizing as merchants were enriched and embold-ened, as they were in England during the era of Atlantic expansion. This was not just what the rulers believed during the Ming and Qing dynasties, but also the attitude of the rulers of the Song dynasty, even if they were willing to sponsor technological innovations and permit greater commercial freedom, provided that this was under their con-trol. Things got worse under the Ming and Qing dynasties as the con-trol of the state on economic activity tightened and overseas trade was banned. There were certainly markets and trade in Ming and Qing China, and the government taxed the domestic economy quite lightly. However, it did little to support innovation, and it exchanged the development of mercantile or industrial prosperity for political stability. The consequence of all this absolutist control of the econ-omy was predictable: the Chinese economy was stagnant throughout the nineteenth and early twentieth centuries while other economies were industrializing. By the time Mao set up his communist regime in 1949, China had become one of the poorest countries in the world.

THE ABSOLUTISM OF PRESTER JOHN

Absolutism as a set of political institutions and the economic conse-quences that flowed from it were not restricted to Europe and Asia. It was present in Africa, for example, with the Kingdom of Kongo, as we saw in chapter 2. An even more durable example of African abso-lutism is Ethiopia, or Abyssinia, whose roots we came across in chap-ter 6, when we discussed the emergence of feudalism after the decline of Aksum. Abyssinian absolutism was even more long-lived than its European counterparts, because it was faced with very different chal-lenges and critical junctures.

After the conversion of the Aksumite king Ezana to Christianity, the Ethiopians remained Christian, and by the fourteenth century they had become the focus of the myth of King Prester John. Prester John was a Christian king who had been cut off from Europe by the rise of Islam in the Middle East. Initially his kingdom was thought to be lo-cated in India. However, as European knowledge of India increased, people realized that this was not true. The king of Ethiopia, since he was a Christian, then became a natural target for the myth. Ethiopian kings in fact tried hard to forge alliances with European monarchs against Arab invasions, sending diplomatic missions to Europe from at least 1300 onward, even persuading the Portuguese king to send soldiers.

These soldiers, along with diplomats, Jesuits, and travelers wishing to meet Prester John, left many accounts of Ethiopia. Some of the most interesting from an economic point of view are by Francisco Álvares, a chaplain accompanying a Portuguese diplomatic mission, who was in Ethiopia from 1520 to 1527. In addition, there are accounts by Jesuit Manoel de Almeida, who lived in Ethiopia from 1624, and by John Bruce, a traveler who was in the country between 1768 and 1773. The writings of these people give a rich account of political and economic institutions at the time in Ethiopia and leave no doubt that Ethiopia was a perfect specimen of absolutism. There were no pluralistic institutions of any kind, nor any checks and constraints on the power of the emperor, who claimed the right to rule on the basis of supposed descent from the legendary King Solomon and the Queen of Sheba.

The consequence of absolutism was great insecurity of property rights driven by the political strategy of the emperor. Bruce, for example, noted that

> all the land is the king's; he gives it to whom he pleases
> during pleasure, and resumes it when it is his will. As
> soon as he dies the whole land in the kingdom is at
> the disposal of the Crown; and not only so, but, by
> death of the present owner, his possessions however
> long enjoyed, revert to the king, and do not fall to the
> eldest son.

Álvares claimed there would be much more "fruit and tillage if the great men did not ill-treat the people." Almeida's account of how the society worked is very consistent. He observed:

It is so usual for the emperor to exchange, alter and take away the lands each man holds every two or three years, sometimes every year and even many times in the course of a year, that it causes no surprise. Often one man plows the soil, another sows it and another reaps. Hence it arises that there is no one who takes care of the land he enjoys; there is not even anyone to plant a tree because he knows that he who plants it very rarely gathers the fruit. For the king, however, it is useful that they should be so dependent upon him.

These descriptions suggest major similarities between the political and economic structures of Ethiopia and those of European absolutism, though they also make it clear that absolutism was more intense in Ethiopia, and economic institutions even more extractive. Moreover, as we emphasized in chapter 6, Ethiopia was not subject to the same critical junctures that helped undermine the absolutist regime in England. It was cut off from many of the processes that shaped the modern world. Even if this had not been the case, the intensity of its absolutism would probably have led the absolutism to strengthen even more. For example, as in Spain, international trade in Ethiopia, including the lucrative slave trade, was controlled by the monarch. Ethiopia was not completely isolated: Europeans did search for Prester John, and it did have to fight wars against surrounding Islamic polities. Nevertheless, the historian Edward Gibbon noted with some accuracy that "encompassed on all sides by the enemies of their religion, the Aethiopians slept near a thousand years, forgetful of the world by whom they were forgotten."

As the European colonization of Africa began in the nineteenth century, Ethiopia was an independent kingdom under Ras (Duke) Kassa, who was crowned Emperor Tewodros II in 1855. Tewodros embarked on a modernization of the state, creating a more centralized bureaucracy and judiciary, and a military capable of controlling the country and possibly fighting the Europeans. He placed military governors, responsible for collecting taxes and remitting them to him, in charge of all the provinces. His negotiations with European powers were difficult, and in exasperation he imprisoned the English consul. In 1868 the English sent an expeditionary force, which sacked his capital. Tewodros committed suicide.

All the same, Tewodros's reconstructed government did manage to pull off one of the great anticolonial triumphs of the nineteenth century, against the Italians. In 1889 the throne went to Menelik II, who was immediately faced with the interest of Italy in establishing a colony there. In 1885 the German chancellor Bismarck had convened a conference in Berlin where the European powers hatched the "Scramble for Africa"—that is, they decided how to divide up Africa into different spheres of interest. At the conference, Italy secured its rights to colonies in Eritrea, along the coast of Ethiopia, and Somalia. Ethiopia, though not represented at the conference, somehow managed to survive intact. But the Italians still kept designs, and in 1896 they marched an army south from Eritrea. Menelik's response was similar to that of a European medieval king; he formed an army by getting the nobility to call up their armed men. This approach could not put an army in the field for long, but it could put a huge one together for a short time. This short time was just enough to defeat the Italians, whose fifteen thousand men were overwhelmed by Menelik's one hundred thousand in the Battle of Adowa in 1896. It was the most serious military defeat a precolonial African country was able to inflict on a European power, and secured Ethiopia's independence for another forty years.

The last emperor of Ethiopia, Ras Tafari, was crowned Haile Selassie in 1930. Haile Selassie ruled until he was overthrown by a second Italian invasion, which began in 1935, but he returned from exile with the help of the English in 1941. He then ruled until he was overthrown in a 1974 coup by the Derg, "the Committee," a group of Marxist army officers, who then proceeded to further impoverish and ravage the country. The basic extractive economic institutions of the absolutist Ethiopian empire, such as *gult* (page 178), and the feudalism created after the decline of Aksum, lasted until they were abolished after the 1974 revolution.

Today Ethiopia is one of the poorest countries in the world. The income of an average Ethiopian is about one-fortieth that of an average citizen of England. Most people live in rural areas and practice subsistence agriculture. They lack clean water, electricity, and access to proper schools or health care. Life expectancy is about fifty-five years and only one-third of adults are literate. A comparison between England and Ethiopia spans world inequality. The reason Ethiopia is where it is today is that, unlike in England, in Ethiopia absolutism persisted until the recent past. With absolutism came extractive economic institutions and poverty for the mass of Ethiopians, though of course the emperors and nobility benefited hugely. But the most enduring implication of the absolutism was that Ethiopian society failed to take advantage of industrialization opportunities during the nineteenth and early twentieth centuries, underpinning the abject poverty of its citizens today.

THE CHILDREN OF SAMAALE

Absolutist political institutions around the world impeded industrialization either indirectly, in the way they organized the economy, or directly, as we have seen in Austria-Hungary and Russia. But absolutism was not the only barrier to the emergence of inclusive economic institutions. At the dawn of the nineteenth century, many parts of the world, especially in Africa, lacked a state that could provide even a minimal degree of law and order, which is a prerequisite for having a modern economy. There was not the equivalent of Peter the Great in Russia starting the process of political centralization and then forging Russian absolutism, let alone that of the Tudors in England centralizing the state without fully destroying—or, more appropriately, without fully being able to destroy—the Parliament and other constraints on their power. Without some degree of political centralization, even if the elites of these African polities had wished to greet industrialization with open arms, there wouldn't have been much they could have done.

Somalia, situated in the Horn of Africa, illustrates the devastating effects of lack of political centralization. Somalia has been dominated historically by people organized into six clan families. The four largest of these, the Dir, Darod, Isaq, and Hawiye, all trace their ancestry back to a mythical ancestor, Samaale. These clan families originated in the north of Somalia and gradually spread south and east, and are even today primarily pastoral people who migrate with their flocks of goats, sheep, and camels. In the south, the Digil and the Rahanweyn, sedentary agriculturalists, make up the last two of the clan families. The territories of these clans are depicted on Map 12 (page 177).

Somalis identify first with their clan family, but these are very large and contain many subgroups. First among these are clans that trace their descent back to one of the larger clan families. More significant are the groupings within clans called *diya*-paying groups, which consist of closely related kinspeople who pay and collect *diya,* or "blood wealth," compensation against the murder of one of their members. Somali clans and *diya*-paying groups were historically locked in to almost continual conflict over the scarce resources at their disposal, particularly water sources and good grazing land for their animals. They also constantly raided the herds of neighboring clans and *diya*-paying groups. Though clans had leaders called sultans, and also elders, these people had no real power. Political power was very widely dispersed, with every Somali adult man being able to have his say on decisions that might affect the clan or group. This was achieved through an informal council made up of all adult males. There was no written law, no police, and no legal system to speak of, except that Sharia law was used as a framework within which informal laws were embedded. These informal laws for a *diya*-paying group would be encoded in what was called a *heer,* a body of explicitly formulated obligations, rights, and duties the group demanded others obey in their interactions with the group. With the advent of colonial rule, these *heers* began to be written down. For example, the Hassan Ugaas lineage formed a *diya*-paying group of about fifteen hundred men and was a subclan of the Dir clan family in British Somaliland. On March 8, 1950, their *heer* was recorded by the British district commissioner, the first three clauses of which read

1. When a man of the Hassan Ugaas is murdered by an external group twenty camels of his blood wealth (100) will be

taken by his next of kin and the remaining eighty camels shared amongst all the Hassan Ugaas.

2. If a man of the Hassan Ugaas is wounded by an outsider and his injuries are valued at thirty-three-and-a-third camels, ten camels must be given to him and the remained to his jiffo-group (a sub-group of the *diya* group).

3. Homicide amongst members of the Hassan Ugaas is subject to compensation at the rate of thirty-three-and-a-third camels, payable only to the deceased's next of kin. If the culprit is unable to pay all or part, he will be assisted by his lineage.

The heavy focus of the *heer* on killing and wounding reflects the almost constant state of warfare between *diya*-paying groups and clans. Central to this was blood wealth and blood feuding. A crime against a particular person was a crime against the whole *diya*-paying group, and necessitated collective compensation, blood wealth. If such blood wealth was not paid, the *diya*-paying group of the person who had committed the crime faced the collective retribution of the victim. When modern transportation reached Somalia, blood wealth was extended to people who were killed or injured in motor accidents. The Hassan Ugaas's *heer* didn't refer only to murder; clause 6 was "If one man of the Hassan Ugaas insults another at a Hassan Ugaas council he shall pay 150 shillings to the offended party."

In early 1955, the flocks of two clans, the Habar Tol Ja'lo and the Habar Yuunis, were grazing close to each other in the region of Domberelly. A man from the Yuunis was wounded after a dispute with a member of the Tol Ja'lo over camel herding. The Yuunis clan immediately retaliated, attacking the Tol Ja'lo clan and killing a man. This death led, following the code of blood wealth, to the Yuunis clan offering compensation to the Tol Ja'lo clan, which was accepted. The blood wealth was to be handed over in person, as usual in the form of camels. At the handing-over ceremony, one of the Tol Ja'lo killed a member of the Yuunis, mistaking him for a member of the *diya*-

paying group of the murderer. This led to all-out warfare, and within the next forty-eight hours thirteen Yuunis and twenty-six Tol Ja'lo had been killed. Warfare continued for another year before elders from both clans, brought together by the English colonial administration, managed to broker a deal (the exchange of blood wealth) that satisfied both sides and was paid over the next three years.

The paying of blood wealth took place in the shadow of the threat of force and feuding, and even when it was paid, it did not necessarily stop conflict. Usually conflict died down and then flared up again.

Political power was thus widely dispersed in Somali society, almost pluralistically. But without the authority of a centralized state to enforce order, let alone property rights, this led not to inclusive institutions. Nobody respected the authority of another, and nobody, including the British colonial state when it eventually arrived, was able to impose order. The lack of political centralization made it impossible for Somalia to benefit from the Industrial Revolution. In such a climate it would have been unimaginable to invest in or adopt the new technologies emanating from Britain, or indeed to create the types of organizations necessary to do so.

The complex politics of Somalia had even more subtle implications for economic progress. We mentioned earlier some of the great technological puzzles of African history. Prior to the expansion of colonial rule in the late nineteenth century, African societies did not use wheeled transportation or plow agriculture and few had writing. Ethiopia did, as we have seen. The Somalis also had a written script, but unlike the Ethiopians, they did not use it. We have already seen instances of this in African history. African societies may not have used wheels or plows, but they certainly knew about them. In the case of the Kingdom of Kongo, as we have seen, this was fundamentally due to the fact that the economic institutions created no incentives for people to adopt these technologies. Could the same issues arise with the adoption of writing?

We can get some sense of this from the Kingdom of Taqali, situated to the northwest of Somalia, in the Nuba Hills of southern Sudan. The Kingdom of Taqali was formed in the late eighteenth century by a band of warriors led by a man called Isma'il, and it stayed independent until amalgamated into the British Empire in 1884. The Taqali kings and people had access to writing in Arabic, but it was not used—except by the kings, for external communication with other polities and diplomatic correspondence. At first this situation seems very puzzling. The traditional account of the origin of writing in Mesopotamia is that it was developed by states in order to record information, control people, and levy taxes. Wasn't the Taqali state interested in this?

These questions were investigated by the historian Janet Ewald in the late 1970s as she tried to reconstruct the history of the Taqali state. Part of the story is that the citizens resisted the use of writing because they feared that it would be used to control resources, such as valuable land, by allowing the state to claim ownership. They also feared that it would lead to more systematic taxation. The dynasty that Isma'il started did not gel into a powerful state. Even if it had wanted to, the state was not strong enough to impose its will over the objections of the citizens. But there were other, more subtle factors at work. Various elites also opposed political centralization, for example, preferring oral to written interaction with citizens, because this allowed them maximum discretion. Written laws or orders could not be taken back or denied and were harder to change; they set benchmarks that governing elites might want to reverse. So neither the ruled nor the rulers of Taqali saw the introduction of writing to be to their advantage. The ruled feared how the rulers would use it, and the rulers themselves saw the absence of writing as aiding their quite precarious grip on power. It was the politics of Taqali that kept writing from being introduced. Though the Somalis had even less of a well-defined elite compared with the Taqali kingdom, it is quite plausible that the same forces inhibited their use of writing and their adoption of other basic technologies.

The Somali case shows the consequences of the lack of political centralization for economic growth. The historical literature does not record instances of attempts to create such centralization in Somalia. However, it is clear why this would have been very difficult. To politically centralize would have meant that some clans would have been subject to the control of others. But they rejected any such dominance, and the surrender of their power that this would have entailed; the balance of military power in the society would also have made it difficult to create such centralized institutions. In fact, it is likely that any group or clan attempting to centralize power would not only have faced stiff resistance but would have lost its existing power and privileges. As a consequence of this lack of political centralization and the implied absence of even the most basic security of property rights, Somali society never generated incentives to invest in productivity-enhancing technologies. As the process of industrialization was under way in other parts of the world in the nineteenth and early twentieth centuries, Somalis were feuding and fending for their lives, and their economic backwardness became more ingrained.

ENDURING BACKWARDNESS

The Industrial Revolution created a transformative critical juncture for the whole world during the nineteenth century and beyond: those societies that allowed and incentivized their citizens to invest in new technologies could grow rapidly. But many around the world failed to do so—or explicitly chose not to do so. Nations under the grip of extractive political and economic institutions did not generate such incentives. Spain and Ethiopia provide examples where the absolutist control of political institutions and the implied extractive economic institutions choked economic incentives long before the dawn of the nineteenth century. The outcome was similar in other absolutist regimes—for example, in Austria-Hungary, Russia, the Ottoman Empire, and China, though in these cases the rulers, because of fear of creative destruction, not only neglected to encourage economic progress but also took explicit steps to block the spread of industry and the introduction of new technologies that would bring industrialization.

Absolutism is not the only form of extractive political institutions and was not the only factor preventing industrialization. Inclusive political and economic institutions necessitate some degree of political centralization so that the state can enforce law and order, uphold property rights, and encourage economic activity when necessary by investing in public services. Yet even today, many nations, such as Afghanistan, Haiti, Nepal, and Somalia, have states that are unable to maintain the most rudimentary order, and economic incentives are all but destroyed. The case of Somalia illustrates how the process of industrialization also passed by such societies. Political centralization is resisted for the same reason that absolutist regimes resist change: the often well-placed fear that change will reallocate political power from those that dominate today to new individuals and groups. Thus, as absolutism blocks moves toward pluralism and economic change, so do the traditional elites and clans dominating the scene in societies without state centralization. As a consequence, societies that still lacked such centralization in the eighteenth and nineteenth centuries were particularly disadvantaged in the age of industry.

While the variety of extractive institutions ranging from absolutism to states with little centralization failed to take advantage of the spread of industry, the critical juncture of the Industrial Revolution had very different effects in other parts of the world. As we will see in chapter 10, societies that had already taken steps toward inclusive political and economic institutions, such as the United States and Australia, and those where absolutism was more seriously challenged, such as France and Japan, took advantage of these new economic opportunities and started a process of rapid economic growth. As such, the usual pattern of interaction between a critical juncture and existing institutional differences leading to further institutional and economic divergence played out again in the nineteenth century, and this time with an even bigger bang and more fundamental effects on the prosperity and poverty of nations.

9.

REVERSING DEVELOPMENT

SPICE AND GENOCIDE

THE MOLUCCAN ARCHIPELAGO in modern Indonesia is made up of three groups of islands. In the early seventeenth century, the northern Moluccas housed the independent kingdoms of Tidore, Ternate, and Bacan. The middle Moluccas were home to the island kingdom of Ambon. In the south were the Banda Islands, a small archipelago that was not yet politically unified. Though they seem remote to us today, the Moluccas were then central to world trade as the only producers of the valuable spices cloves, mace, and nutmeg. Of these, nutmeg and mace grew only in the Banda Islands. Inhabitants of these islands produced and exported these rare spices in exchange for food and manufactured goods coming from the island of Java, from the entrepôt of Melaka on the Malaysian Peninsula, and from India, China, and Arabia.

The first contact the inhabitants had with Europeans was in the sixteenth century, with Portuguese mariners who came to buy spices. Before then spices had to be shipped through the Middle East, via trade routes controlled by the Ottoman Empire. Europeans searched for a passage around Africa or across the Atlantic to gain direct access to the Spice Islands and the spice trade. The Cape of Good Hope was rounded by the Portuguese mariner Bartolomeu Dias in 1488, and India was reached via the same route by Vasco da Gama in 1498. For the first time the Europeans now had their own independent route to the Spice Islands.

The Portuguese immediately set about the task of trying to control the trade in spices. They captured Melaka in 1511. Strategically situated on the western side of the Malaysian Peninsula, merchants from all over Southeast Asia came there to sell their spices to other merchants, Indian, Chinese, and Arabs, who then shipped them to the West. As the Portuguese traveler Tomé Pires put it in 1515: "The trade and commerce between the different nations for a thousand leagues on every hand must come to Melaka . . . Whoever is lord of Melaka has his hands at the throat of Venice."

With Melaka in their hands, the Portuguese systematically tried to gain a monopoly of the valuable spice trade. They failed.

The opponents they faced were not negligible. Between the fourteenth and sixteenth centuries, there was a great deal of economic development in Southeast Asia based on trade in spices. City-states such as Aceh, Banten, Melaka, Makassar, Pegu, and Brunei expanded

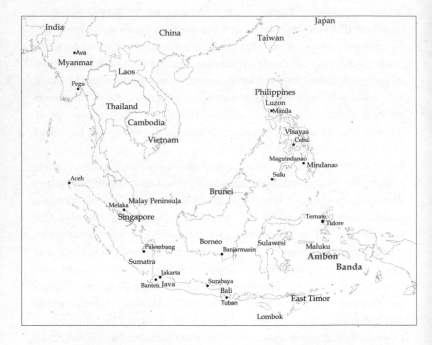

Map 14: Southeast Asia, the Spice Islands, Ambon, and Banda in 1600

rapidly, producing and exporting spices along with other products such as hardwoods.

These states had absolutist forms of government similar to those in Europe in the same period. The development of political institutions was spurred by similar processes, including technological change in methods of warfare and international trade. State institutions became more centralized, with a king at the center claiming absolute power. Like absolutist rulers in Europe, Southeast Asian kings relied heavily on revenues from trade, both engaging in it themselves and granting monopolies to local and foreign elites. As in absolutist Europe, this generated some economic growth but was a far-from-ideal set of economic institutions for economic prosperity, with significant entry barriers and insecure property rights for most. But the process of commercialization was under way even as the Portuguese were trying to establish their dominance in the Indian Ocean.

The presence of Europeans swelled and had a much greater impact with the arrival of the Dutch. The Dutch quickly realized that monopolizing the supply of the valuable spices of the Moluccas would be much more profitable than competing against local or other European traders. In 1600 they persuaded the ruler of Ambon to sign an exclusive agreement that gave them the monopoly on the clove trade in Ambon. With the founding of the Dutch East India Company in 1602, the Dutch attempts to capture the entire spice trade and eliminate their competitors, by hook or by crook, took a turn for the better for the Dutch and for the worse for Southeast Asia. The Dutch East India Company was the second European joint stock company, following the English East India Company, major landmarks in the development of the modern corporation, which would subsequently play a major role in European industrial growth. It was also the second company that had its own army and the power to wage war and colonize foreign lands. With the military power of the company now brought to bear, the Dutch proceeded to eliminate all potential interlopers to enforce their treaty with the ruler of Ambon. They captured a key fort held by the Portuguese in 1605 and forcibly removed all other traders. They then expanded to the northern Moluccas, forcing the rulers of Tidore, Ternate, and Bacan to agree that no cloves could be grown or traded in their territories. The treaty they imposed on Ternate even allowed the Dutch to come and destroy any clove trees they found there.

Ambon was ruled in a manner similar to much of Europe and the Americas during that time. The citizens of Ambon owed tribute to the ruler and were subject to forced labor. The Dutch took over and intensified these systems to extract more labor and more cloves from the island. Prior to the arrival of the Dutch, extended families paid tribute in cloves to the Ambonese elite. The Dutch now stipulated that each household was tied to the soil and should cultivate a certain number of clove trees. Households were also obligated to deliver forced labor to the Dutch.

The Dutch also took control of the Banda Islands, intending this time to monopolize mace and nutmeg. But the Banda Islands were organized very differently from Ambon. They were made up of many small autonomous city-states, and there was no hierarchical social or political structure. These small states, in reality no more than small towns, were run by village meetings of citizens. There was no central authority whom the Dutch could coerce into signing a monopoly treaty and no system of tribute that they could take over to capture the entire supply of nutmeg and mace. At first this meant that the Dutch had to compete with English, Portuguese, Indian, and Chinese merchants, losing the spices to their competitors when they did not pay high prices. Their initial plans of setting up a monopoly of mace and nutmeg dashed, the Dutch governor of Batavia, Jan Pieterszoon Coen, came up with an alternative plan. Coen founded Batavia, on the island of Java, as the Dutch East India Company's new capital in 1618. In 1621 he sailed to Banda with a fleet and proceeded to massacre almost the entire population of the islands, probably about fifteen thousand people. All their leaders were executed along with the rest, and only a few were left alive, enough to preserve the know-how necessary for mace and nutmeg production. After this genocide was complete, Coen then proceeded to create the political and economic structure necessary for his plan: a plantation society. The islands were divided into sixty-eight parcels, which were given to sixty-eight Dutchmen, mostly former and current employees of the Dutch East

REVERSING DEVELOPMENT • 249

India Company. These new plantation owners were taught how to produce the spices by the few surviving Bandanese and could buy slaves from the East India Company to populate the now-empty islands and to produce spices, which would have to be sold at fixed prices back to the company.

The extractive institutions created by the Dutch in the Spice Islands had the desired effects, though, in Banda this was at the cost of fifteen thousand innocent lives and the establishment of a set of economic and political institutions that would condemn the islands to underdevelopment. By the end of the seventeenth century, the Dutch had reduced the world supply of these spices by about 60 percent and the price of nutmeg had doubled.

The Dutch spread the strategy they perfected in the Moluccas to the entire region, with profound implications for the economic and political institutions of the rest of Southeast Asia. The long commercial expansion of several states in the area that had started in the fourteenth century went into reverse. Even the polities which were not directly colonized and crushed by the Dutch East India Company turned inward and abandoned trade. The nascent economic and political change in Southeast Asia was halted in its tracks.

To avoid the threat of the Dutch East India Company, several states abandoned producing crops for export and ceased commercial activity. Autarky was safer than facing the Dutch. In 1620 the state of Banten, on the island of Java, cut down its pepper trees in the hope that this would induce the Dutch to leave it in peace. When a Dutch merchant visited Maguindanao, in the southern Philippines, in 1686, he was told, "Nutmeg and cloves can be grown here, just as in Malaku. They are not there now because the old Raja had all of them ruined before his death. He was afraid the Dutch Company would come to fight with them about it." What a trader heard about the ruler of Maguindanao in 1699 was similar: "He had forbidden the continued planting of pepper so that he could not thereby get involved in war whether with the [Dutch] company or with other potentates." There was de-urbanization and even population decline. In 1635 the Burmese moved their capital from Pegu, on the coast, to Ava, far inland up the Irrawaddy River.

We do not know what the path of economic and political development of Southeast Asian states would have been without Dutch aggression. They may have developed their own brand of absolutism, they may have remained in the same state they were in at the end of the sixteenth century, or they may have continued their commercialization by gradually adopting more and more inclusive institutions. But as in the Moluccas, Dutch colonialism fundamentally changed their economic and political development. The people in Southeast Asia stopped trading, turned inward, and became more absolutist. In the next two centuries, they would be in no position to take advantage of the innovations that would spring up in the Industrial Revolution. And ultimately their retreat from trade would not save them from Europeans; by the end of the eighteenth century, nearly all were part of European colonial empires.

WE SAW IN CHAPTER 7 how European expansion into the Atlantic fueled the rise of inclusive institutions in Britain. But as illustrated by the experience of the Moluccas under the Dutch, this expansion sowed the seeds of underdevelopment in many diverse corners of the world by imposing, or further strengthening existing, extractive institutions. These either directly or indirectly destroyed nascent commercial and industrial activity throughout the globe or they perpetuated institutions that stopped industrialization. As a result, as industrialization was spreading in some parts of the world, places that were part of European colonial empires stood no chance of benefiting from these new technologies.

THE ALL-TOO-USUAL INSTITUTION

In Southeast Asia the spread of European naval and commercial power in the early modern period curtailed a promising period of economic expansion and institutional change. In the same period as the Dutch East India Company was expanding, a very different sort of trade was intensifying in Africa: the slave trade.

In the United States, southern slavery was often referred to as the "peculiar institution." But historically, as the great classical scholar Moses Finlay pointed out, slavery was anything but peculiar, it was present in almost every society. It was, as we saw earlier, endemic in Ancient Rome and in Africa, long a source of slaves for Europe, though not the only one.

In the Roman period slaves came from Slavic peoples around the Black Sea, from the Middle East, and also from Northern Europe. But by 1400, Europeans had stopped enslaving each other. Africa, however, as we saw in chapter 6, did not undergo the transition from slavery to serfdom as did medieval Europe. Before the early modern period, there was a vibrant slave trade in East Africa, and large numbers of slaves were transported across the Sahara to the Arabian Peninsula. Moreover, the large medieval West African states of Mali, Ghana, and Songhai made heavy use of slaves in the government, the army, and agriculture, adopting organizational models from the Muslim North African states with whom they traded.

It was the development of the sugar plantation colonies of the Caribbean beginning in the early seventeenth century that led to a dramatic escalation of the international slave trade and to an unprecedented increase in the importance of slavery within Africa itself. In the sixteenth century, probably about 300,000 slaves were traded in the Atlantic. They came mostly from Central Africa, with heavy involvement of Kongo and the Portuguese based farther south in Luanda, now the capital of Angola. During this time, the trans-Saharan slave trade was still larger, with probably about 550,000 Africans moving north as slaves. In the seventeenth century, the situation reversed. About 1,350,000 Africans were sold as slaves in the Atlantic trade, the majority now being shipped to the Americas. The numbers involved in the Saharan trade were relatively unchanged. The eighteenth century saw another dramatic increase, with about 6,000,000 slaves being shipped across the Atlantic and maybe 700,000 across the Sahara. Adding the figures up over periods and parts of Africa, well over 10,000,000 Africans were shipped out of the continent as slaves.

Map 15 (page 252) gives some sense of the scale of the slave trade. Using modern country boundaries, it depicts estimates of the cumulative extent of slavery between 1400 and 1900 as a percent of population in 1400. Darker colors show more intense slavery. For example, in Angola, Benin, Ghana, and Togo, total cumulative slave exports amounted to more than the entire population of the country in 1400.

The sudden appearance of Europeans all around the coast of Western and Central Africa eager to buy slaves could not but have a transformative impact on African societies. Most slaves who were shipped to the Americas were war captives subsequently transported to the coast. The increase in warfare was fueled by huge imports of guns and ammunition, which the Europeans exchanged for slaves. By 1730 about 180,000 guns were being imported every year just along the West African coast, and between 1750 and the early nine-

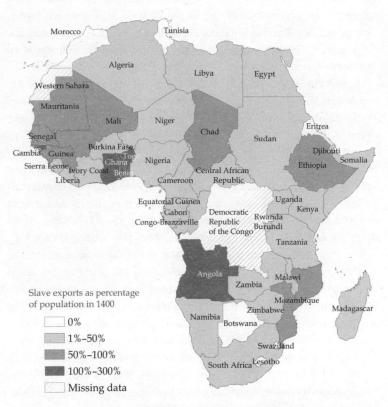

Map 15: Slave exports from Africa

teenth century, the British alone sold between 283,000 and 394,000 guns a year. Between 1750 and 1807, the British sold an extraordinary 22,000 tons of gunpowder, making an average of about 384,000 kilograms annually, along with 91,000 kilograms of lead per year. Farther to the south, the trade was just as vigorous. On the Loango coast, north of the Kingdom of Kongo, Europeans sold about 50,000 guns a year.

All this warfare and conflict not only caused major loss of life and human suffering but also put in motion a particular path of institutional development in Africa. Before the early modern era, African societies were less centralized politically than those of Eurasia. Most polities were small scale, with tribal chiefs and perhaps kings controlling land and resources. Many, as we showed with Somalia, had no structure of hierarchical political authority at all. The slave trade initiated two adverse political processes. First, many polities initially became more absolutist, organized around a single objective: to enslave and sell others to European slavers. Second, as a consequence but, paradoxically, in opposition to the first process, warring and slaving ultimately destroyed whatever order and legitimate state authority existed in sub-Saharan Africa. Apart from warfare, slaves were also kidnapped and captured by small-scale raiding. The law also became a tool of enslavement. No matter what crime you committed, the penalty was slavery. The English merchant Francis Moore observed the consequences of this along the Senegambia coast of West Africa in the 1730s:

> Since this slave trade has been us'd, all punishments are changed into slavery; there being an advantage on such condemnations, they strain for crimes very hard, in order to get the benefit of selling the criminal. Not only murder, theft and adultery, are punished by selling the criminal for slave, but every trifling case is punished in the same manner.

Institutions, even religious ones, became perverted by the desire to capture and sell slaves. One example is the famous oracle at

Arochukwu, in eastern Nigeria. The oracle was widely believed to speak for a prominent deity in the region respected by the major local ethnic groups, the Ijaw, the Ibibio, and the Igbo. The oracle was approached to settle disputes and adjudicate on disagreements. Plaintiffs who traveled to Arochukwu to face the oracle had to descend from the town into a gorge of the Cross River, where the oracle was housed in a tall cave, the front of which was lined with human skulls. The priests of the oracle, in league with the Aro slavers and merchants, would dispense the decision of the oracle. Often this involved people being "swallowed" by the oracle, which actually meant that once they had passed through the cave, they were led away down the Cross River and to the waiting ships of the Europeans. This process in which all laws and customs were distorted and broken to capture slaves and more slaves had devastating effects on political centralization, though in some places it did lead to the rise of powerful states whose main raison d'être was raiding and slaving. The Kingdom of Kongo itself was probably the first African state to experience a metamorphosis into a slaving state, until it was destroyed by civil war. Other slaving states arose most prominently in West Africa and included Oyo in Nigeria, Dahomey in Benin, and subsequently Asante in Ghana.

The expansion of the state of Oyo in the middle of the seventeenth century, for example, is directly related to the increase of slave exports on the coast. The state's power was the result of a military revolution that involved the import of horses from the north and the formation of a powerful cavalry that could decimate opposing armies. As Oyo expanded south toward the coast, it crushed the intervening polities and sold many of their inhabitants for slaves. In the period between 1690 and 1740, Oyo established its monopoly in the interior of what came to be known as the Slave Coast. It is estimated that 80 to 90 percent of the slaves sold on the coast were the result of these conquests. A similar dramatic connection between warfare and slave supply came farther west in the eighteenth century, on the Gold Coast, the area that is now Ghana. After 1700 the state of Asante expanded from the interior, in much the same way as Oyo had previously. During the first half of the eighteenth century, this expansion triggered the so-called Akan Wars, as Asante defeated one independent state after another. The last, Gyaman, was conquered in 1747. The preponderance of the 375,000 slaves exported from the Gold Coast between 1700 and 1750 were captives taken in these wars.

Probably the most obvious impact of this massive extraction of human beings was demographic. It is difficult to know with any certitude what the population of Africa was before the modern period, but scholars have made various plausible estimates of the impact of the slave trade on the population. The historian Patrick Manning estimates that the population of those areas of West and West-Central Africa that provided slaves for export was around twenty-two to twenty-five million in the early eighteenth century. On the conservative assumption that during the eighteenth and early nineteenth centuries these areas would have experienced a rate of population growth of about half a percent a year without the slave trade, Manning estimated that the population of this region in 1850 ought to have been at least forty-six to fifty-three million. In fact, it was about one-half of this.

This massive difference was not only due to about eight million people being exported as slaves from this region between 1700 and 1850, but the millions likely killed by continual internal warfare aimed at capturing slaves. Slavery and the slave trade in Africa further disrupted family and marriage structures and may also have reduced fertility.

Beginning in the late eighteenth century, a strong movement to abolish the slave trade began to gain momentum in Britain, led by the charismatic figure of William Wilberforce. After repeated failures, in 1807 the abolitionists persuaded the British Parliament to pass a bill making the slave trade illegal. The United States followed with a similar measure the next year. The British government went further, though: it actively sought to implement this measure by stationing naval squadrons in the Atlantic to try to stamp out the slave trade. Though it took some time for these measures to be truly effective, and it was not until 1834 that slavery itself was abolished in the British Empire, the days of the Atlantic slave trade, by far the largest part of the trade, were numbered.

Though the end of the slave trade after 1807 did reduce the external demand for slaves from Africa, this did not mean that slavery's impact on African societies and institutions would magically melt away. Many African states had become organized around slaving, and the British putting an end to the trade did not change this reality. Moreover, slavery had become much more prevalent within Africa itself. These factors would ultimately shape the path of development in Africa not only before but also after 1807.

In the place of slavery came "legitimate commerce," a phrase coined for the export from Africa of new commodities not tied to the slave trade. These goods included palm oil and kernels, peanuts, ivory, rubber, and gum arabic. As European and North American incomes expanded with the spread of the Industrial Revolution, demand for many of these tropical products rose sharply. Just as African societies took aggressive advantage of the economic opportunities presented by the slave trade, they did the same with legitimate commerce. But they did so in a peculiar context, one in which slavery was a way of life but the external demand for slaves had suddenly dried up. What were all these slaves to do now that they could not be sold to Europeans? The answer was simple: they could be profitably put to work, under coercion, in Africa, producing the new items of legitimate commerce.

One of the best documented examples was in Asante, in modern Ghana. Prior to 1807, the Asante Empire had been heavily involved in the capturing and export of slaves, bringing them down to the coast to be sold at the great slaving castles of Cape Coast and Elmina. After 1807, with this option closed off, the Asante political elite reorganized their economy. However, slaving and slavery did not end. Rather, slaves were settled on large plantations, initially around the capital city of Kumase, but later spread throughout the empire (corresponding to most of the interior of Ghana). They were employed in the production of gold and kola nuts for export, but also grew large quantities of food and were intensively used as porters, since Asante did not use wheeled transportation. Farther east, similar adaptations took place. In Dahomey, for example, the king had large palm oil plantations near the coastal ports of Whydah and Porto Novo, all based on slave labor.

So the abolition of the slave trade, rather than making slavery in Africa wither away, simply led to a redeployment of the slaves, who were now used within Africa rather than in the Americas. Moreover, many of the political institutions the slave trade had wrought in the previous two centuries were unaltered and patterns of behavior persisted. For example, in Nigeria in the 1820s and '30s the once-great Oyo Kingdom collapsed. It was undermined by civil wars and the rise of the Yoruba city-states, such as Illorin and Ibadan, that were directly involved in the slave trade, to its south. In the 1830s, the capital of Oyo was sacked, and after that the Yoruba cities contested power with Dahomey for regional dominance. They fought an almost continuous series of wars in the first half of the century, which generated a massive supply of slaves. Along with this went the normal rounds of kidnapping and condemnation by oracles and smaller-scale raiding. Kidnapping was such a problem in some parts of Nigeria that parents would not let their children play outside for fear they would be taken and sold into slavery.

As a result slavery, rather than contracting, appears to have expanded in Africa throughout the nineteenth century. Though accurate figures are hard to come by, a number of existing accounts written by travelers and merchants during this time suggest that in the West African kingdoms of Asante and Dahomey and in the Yoruba city-states well over half of the population were slaves. More accurate data exist from early French colonial records for the western Sudan, a large swath of western Africa, stretching from Senegal, via Mali and Burkina Faso, to Niger and Chad. In this region 30 percent of the population was enslaved in 1900.

Just as with the emergence of legitimate commerce, the advent of formal colonization after the Scramble for Africa failed to destroy slavery in Africa. Though much of European penetration into Africa was justified on the grounds that slavery had to be combated and abolished, the reality was different. In most parts of colonial Africa, slavery continued well into the twentieth century. In Sierra Leone, for example, it was only in 1928 that slavery was finally abolished, even though the capital city of Freetown was originally established in the late eighteenth century as a haven for slaves repatriated from the

Americas. It then became an important base for the British antislavery squadron and a new home for freed slaves rescued from slave ships captured by the British navy. Even with this symbolism slavery lingered in Sierra Leone for 130 years. Liberia, just south of Sierra Leone, was likewise founded for freed American slaves in the 1840s. Yet there, too, slavery lingered into the twentieth century; as late as the 1960s, it was estimated that one-quarter of the labor force were coerced, living and working in conditions close to slavery. Given the extractive economic and political institutions based on the slave trade, industrialization did not spread to sub-Saharan Africa, which stagnated or even experienced economic retardation as other parts of the world were transforming their economies.

MAKING A DUAL ECONOMY

The "dual economy" paradigm, originally proposed in 1955 by Sir Arthur Lewis, still shapes the way that most social scientists think about the economic problems of less-developed countries. According to Lewis, many less-developed or underdeveloped economies have a dual structure and are divided into a modern sector and a traditional sector. The modern sector, which corresponds to the more developed part of the economy, is associated with urban life, modern industry, and the use of advanced technologies. The traditional sector is associated with rural life, agriculture, and "backward" institutions and technologies. Backward agricultural institutions include the communal ownership of land, which implies the absence of private property rights on land. Labor was used so inefficiently in the traditional sector, according to Lewis, that it could be reallocated to the modern sector without reducing the amount the rural sector could produce. For generations of development economists building on Lewis's insights, the "problem of development" has come to mean moving people and resources out of the traditional sector, agriculture and the countryside, and into the modern sector, industry and cities. In 1979 Lewis received the Nobel Prize for his work on economic development.

Lewis and development economists building on his work were certainly right in identifying dual economies. South Africa was one of the clearest examples, split into a traditional sector that was backward and poor and a modern one that was vibrant and prosperous. Even today the dual economy Lewis identified is everywhere in South Africa. One of the most dramatic ways to see this is by driving across the border between the state of KwaZulu-Natal, formerly Natal, and the state of the Transkei. The border follows the Great Kei River. To the east of the river in Natal, along the coast, are wealthy beachfront properties on wide expanses of glorious sandy beaches. The interior is covered with lush green sugarcane plantations. The roads are beautiful; the whole area reeks of prosperity. Across the river, it is as if it were a different time and a different country. The area is largely devastated. The land is not green, but brown and heavily deforested. Instead of affluent modern houses with running water, toilets, and all the modern conveniences, people live in makeshift huts and cook on open fires. Life is certainly traditional, far from the modern existence to the east of the river. By now you will not be surprised that these differences are linked with major differences in economic institutions between the two sides of the river.

To the east, in Natal, we have private property rights, functioning legal systems, markets, commercial agriculture, and industry. To the west, the Transkei had communal property in land and all-powerful traditional chiefs until recently. Looked at through the lens of Lewis's theory of dual economy, the contrast between the Transkei and Natal illustrates the problems of African development. In fact, we can go further, and note that, historically, all of Africa was like the Transkei, poor with premodern economic institutions, backward technology, and rule by chiefs. According to this perspective, then, economic development should simply be about ensuring that the Transkei eventually turns into Natal.

This perspective has much truth to it but misses the entire logic of how the dual economy came into existence and its relationship to the modern economy. The backwardness of the Transkei is not just a historic remnant of the natural backwardness of Africa. The dual economy between the Transkei and Natal is in fact quite recent, and is anything but natural. It was created by the South African white elites in order to produce a reservoir of cheap labor for their businesses and reduce competition from black Africans. The dual economy is another example of underdevelopment created, not of underdevelopment as it naturally emerged and persisted over centuries.

South Africa and Botswana, as we will see later, did avoid most of the adverse effects of the slave trade and the wars it wrought. South Africans' first major interaction with Europeans came when the Dutch East India Company founded a base in Table Bay, now the harbor of Cape Town, in 1652. At this time the western part of South Africa was sparsely settled, mostly by hunter-gatherers called the Khoikhoi people. Farther east, in what is now the Ciskei and Transkei, there were densely populated African societies specializing in agriculture. They did not initially interact heavily with the new colony of the Dutch, nor did they become involved in slaving. The South African coast was far removed from slave markets, and the inhabitants of the Ciskei and Transkei, known as the Xhosa, were just far enough inland not to attract anyone's attention. As a consequence, these societies did not feel the brunt of many of the adverse currents that hit West and Central Africa.

The isolation of these places changed in the nineteenth century. For the Europeans there was something very attractive about the climate and the disease environment of South Africa. Unlike West Africa, for example, South Africa had a temperate climate that was free of the tropical diseases such as malaria and yellow fever that had turned much of Africa into the "white man's graveyard" and prevented Europeans from settling or even setting up permanent outposts. South Africa was a much better prospect for European settlement. European expansion into the interior began soon after the British took over Cape Town from the Dutch during the Napoleonic Wars. This precipitated a long series of Xhosa wars as the settlement frontier expanded further inland. The penetration into the South African interior was intensified in 1835, when the remaining Europeans of Dutch descent, who would become known as Afrikaners or Boers, started their famous mass migration known as the Great Trek away from the British control of the coast and the Cape Town area. The Afrikaners subsequently founded two independent states in the interior of Africa, the Orange Free State and the Transvaal.

North of the fence:
Nogales, Arizona

Jim West/imagebroker.net/Photolibrary

South of the fence:
Nogales, Sonora

Jim West/age fotostock/Photolibrary

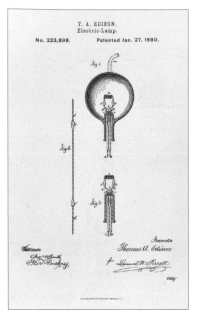

Consequences of a level playing field:
Thomas Edison's 1880 patent for the lightbulb

Records of the Patent and Trademark Office; Record
Group 241; National Archives

Economic losers from creative destruction: machine-breaking
Luddites in early-nineteenth-century Britain

Mary Evans Picture Library/Tom Morgan

Consequences of a complete lack of political centralization in Somalia

REUTERS/Mohamed Guled /Landov

Successive beneficiaries of extractive institutions in Congo:

King of Kongo

King Leopold II

Joseph-Désiré Mobutu

© Richard Melloul/Sygma/CORBIS

Laurent Kabila

© Reuters/CORBIS

The Glorious Revolution: William III of Orange is read the Bill of
Rights before being offered the crown of England by parliament

After Edgar Melville Ward/The Bridgeman Art Library/Getty Images

The bubonic plague of the fourteenth century creates a critical juncture (*The Triumph of
Death* painting of the Black Death by Brueghel the Elder) The Granger Collection, NY

Beneficiary of institutional innovation: the King of Kuba

The emergence of hierarchy and inequality before farming: the grave goods of the Natufian elite http://en.wikipedia.org/wiki/File:Natufian-Burial-ElWad.jpg

Extractive growth: Soviet Gulag labor builds the White Sea canal SOVFOTO

Britain falls far behind: the ruins of the Roman empire at Vindolanda

Innovation, essence of inclusive economic growth: James Watt's steam engine

ARKWRIGHT'S FIRST COTTON FACTORY AT CROMFORD.

Organizational change, a consequence of inclusive institutions: the factory of Richard Arkwright at Cromford The Granger Collection, NY

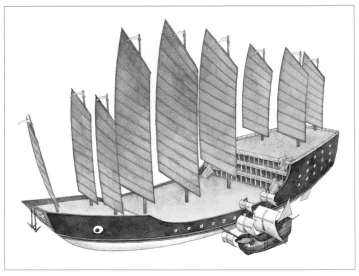

Fruits of unsustainable extractive growth: Zheng He's ship alongside Columbus's *Santa Maria* Gregory A. Harlin/National Geographic Stock

Bird's-eye view of the dual economy in South Africa: poverty in Transkei, prosperity in Natal Roger de la Harpe/Africa Imagery

Consequences of the Industrial Revolution: the storming of the Bastille

Bridgeman-Giraudon/Art Resource, NY

Challenges to inclusive institutions: the Standard Oil Company

Library of Congress Prints and Photographs Division Washington, D.C.

Noncreative destruction: abandoned Hastings railway station on the way to
Bo in Sierra Leone © Matt Stephenson: www.itsayshere.org

Extractive institutions today: children working in an Uzbek cotton field

Breaking a mold: three Tswana chiefs on their way to London

Photograph by Willoughby, courtesy of Botswana National Archives & Records Services

Breaking another mold: Rosa Parks challenges extractive institutions in the U.S. south The Granger Collection, NY

Extractive institutions devour their children: the Chinese Cultural Revolution vs. "degenerate intellectuals" Weng Rulan, 1967, IISH Collection, International Institute of Social History (Amsterdam)

The next stage in the development of South Africa came with the discovery of vast diamond reserves in Kimberly in 1867 and of rich gold mines in Johannesburg in 1886. This huge mineral wealth in the interior immediately convinced the British to extend their control over all of South Africa. The resistance of the Orange Free State and the Transvaal led to the famous Boer Wars in 1880–1881 and 1899–1902. After initial unexpected defeat, the British managed to merge the Afrikaner states with the Cape Province and Natal, to found the Union of South Africa in 1910. Beyond the fighting between Afrikaners and the British, the development of the mining economy and the expansion of European settlement had other implications for the development of the area. Most notably, they generated demand for food and other agricultural products and created new economic opportunities for native Africans both in agriculture and trade.

The Xhosa, in the Ciskei and Transkei, reacted quickly to these economic opportunities, as the historian Colin Bundy documented. As early as 1832, even before the mining boom, a Moravian missionary in the Transkei observed the new economic dynamism in these areas and noted the demand from the Africans for the new consumer goods that the spread of Europeans had begun to reveal to them. He wrote, "To obtain these objects, they look . . . to get money by the labour of their hands, and purchase clothes, spades, ploughs, wagons and other useful articles."

The civil commissioner John Hemming's description of his visit to Fingoland in the Ciskei in 1876 is equally revealing. He wrote that he was

> struck with the very great advancement made by the
> Fingoes in a few years . . . Wherever I went I found
> substantial huts and brick or stone tenements. In many
> cases, substantial brick houses had been erected . . .
> and fruit trees had been planted; wherever a stream of
> water could be made available it had been led out and
> the soil cultivated as far as it could be irrigated; the
> slopes of the hills and even the summits of the moun-
> tains were cultivated wherever a plough could be in-

troduced. The extent of the land turned over surprised me; I have not seen such a large area of cultivated land for years.

As in other parts of sub-Saharan Africa, the use of the plow was new in agriculture, but when given the opportunity, African farmers seemed to have been quite ready to adopt the technology. They were also prepared to invest in wagons and irrigation works.

As the agricultural economy developed, the rigid tribal institutions started to give way. There is a great deal of evidence that changes in property rights to land took place. In 1879 the magistrate in Umzim-kulu of Griqualand East, in the Transkei, noted "the growing desire of the part of natives to become proprietors of land—they have pur-chased 38,000 acres." Three years later he recorded that around eight thousand African farmers in the district had bought and started to work on ninety thousand acres of land.

Africa was certainly not on the verge of an Industrial Revolution, but real change was under way. Private property in land had weak-ened the chiefs and enabled new men to buy land and make their wealth, something that was unthinkable just decades earlier. This also illustrates how quickly the weakening of extractive institutions and absolutist control systems can lead to newfound economic dynamism. One of the success stories was Stephen Sonjica in the Ciskei, a self-made farmer from a poor background. In an address in 1911, Sonjica noted how when he first expressed to his father his desire to buy land, his father had responded: "Buy land? How can you want to buy land? Don't you know that all land is God's, and he gave it to the chiefs only?" Sonjica's father's reaction was understandable. But Sonjica was not deterred. He got a job in King William's Town and noted:

> I cunningly opened a private bank account into which
> I diverted a portion of my savings . . . This went only
> until I had saved eighty pounds . . . [I bought] a span
> of oxen with yokes, gear, plough and the rest of agri-

cultural paraphernalia . . . I now purchased a small
farm . . . I cannot too strongly recommend [farming] as
a profession to my fellow man . . . They should however adopt modern methods of profit making.

An extraordinary piece of evidence supporting the economic dynamism and prosperity of African farmers in this period is revealed in
a letter sent in 1869 by a Methodist missionary, W. J. Davis. Writing to
England, he recorded with pleasure that he had collected forty-six
pounds in cash "for the Lancashire Cotton Relief Fund." In this period
the prosperous African farmers were donating money for relief of the
poor English textile workers!

This new economic dynamism, not surprisingly, did not please the
traditional chiefs, who, in a pattern that is by now familiar to us, saw
this as eroding their wealth and power. In 1879 Matthew Blyth, the
chief magistrate of the Transkei, observed that there was opposition
to surveying the land so that it could be divided into private property.
He recorded that "some of the chiefs . . . objected, but most of the
people were pleased . . . the chiefs see that the granting of individual
titles will destroy their influence among the headmen."

Chiefs also resisted improvements made on the lands, such as the
digging of irrigation ditches or the building of fences. They recognized that these improvements were just a prelude to individual property rights to the land, the beginning of the end for them. European
observers even noted that chiefs and other traditional authorities,
such as witch doctors, attempted to prohibit all "European ways,"
which included new crops, tools such as plows, and items of trade.
But the integration of the Ciskei and the Transkei into the British colonial state weakened the power of the traditional chiefs and authorities, and their resistance would not be enough to stop the new
economic dynamism in South Africa. In Fingoland in 1884, a European observer noted that the people had

transferred their allegiance to us. Their chiefs have
been changed to a sort of titled landowner . . . without

political power. No longer afraid of the jealousy of the chief or of the deadly weapon . . . the witchdoctor, which strikes down the wealthy cattle owner, the able counsellor, the introduction of novel customs, the skilful agriculturalist, reducing them all to the uniform level of mediocrity—no longer apprehensive of this, the Fingo clansman . . . is a progressive man. Still remaining a peasant farmer . . . he owns wagons and ploughs; he opens water furroughs for irrigation; he is the owner of a flock of sheep.

Even a modicum of inclusive institutions and the erosion of the powers of the chiefs and their restrictions were sufficient to start a vigorous African economic boom. Alas, it would be short lived. Between 1890 and 1913 it would come to an abrupt end and go into reverse. During this period two forces worked to destroy the rural prosperity and dynamism that Africans had created in the previous fifty years. The first was antagonism by European farmers who were competing with Africans. Successful African farmers drove down the price of crops that Europeans also produced. The response of Europeans was to drive the Africans out of business. The second force was even more sinister. The Europeans wanted a cheap labor force to employ in the burgeoning mining economy, and they could ensure this cheap supply only by impoverishing the Africans. This they went about methodically over the next several decades.

The 1897 testimony of George Albu, the chairman of the Association of Mines, given to a Commission of Inquiry pithily describes the logic of impoverishing Africans so as to obtain cheap labor. He explained how he proposed to cheapen labor by "simply telling the boys that their wages are reduced." His testimony goes as follows:

> **Commission:** Suppose the kaffirs [black Africans] retire back to their kraal [cattle pen]? Would you be in favor of asking the Government to enforce labour?
> **Albu:** Certainly . . . I would make it compulsory . . . Why should a nigger be allowed to do nothing? I think

a kaffir should be compelled to work in order to earn his living.

Commission: If a man can live without work, how can you force him to work?

Albu: Tax him, then . . .

Commission: Then you would not allow the kaffir to hold land in the country, but he must work for the white man to enrich him?

Albu: He must do his part of the work of helping his neighbours.

Both of the goals of removing competition with white farmers and developing a large low-wage labor force were simultaneously accomplished by the Natives Land Act of 1913. The act, anticipating Lewis's notion of dual economy, divided South Africa into two parts, a modern prosperous part and a traditional poor part. Except that the prosperity and poverty were actually being created by the act itself. It stated that 87 percent of the land was to be given to the Europeans, who represented about 20 percent of the population. The remaining 13 percent was to go to the Africans. The Land Act had many predecessors, of course, because gradually Europeans had been confining Africans onto smaller and smaller reserves. But it was the act of 1913 that definitively institutionalized the situation and set the stage for the formation of the South African Apartheid regime, with the white minority having both the political and economic rights and the black majority being excluded from both. The act specified that several land reserves, including the Transkei and the Ciskei, were to become the African "Homelands." Later these would become known as the Bantustans, another part of the rhetoric of the Apartheid regime in South Africa, since it claimed that the African peoples of Southern Africa were not natives of the area but were descended from the Bantu people who had migrated out of Eastern Nigeria about a thousand years before. They thus had no more—and of course, in practice, less—entitlement to the land than the European settlers.

Map 16 (page 266) shows the derisory amount of land allocated to Africans by the 1913 Land Act and its successor in 1936. It also records information from 1970 on the extent of a similar land allocation that took place during the construction of another dual economy in Zimbabwe, which we discuss in chapter 13.

The 1913 legislation also included provisions intended to stop black sharecroppers and squatters from farming on white-owned land in any capacity other than as labor tenants. As the secretary for native affairs explained, "The effect of the act was to put a stop, for the future, to all transactions involving anything in the nature of partnership between Europeans and natives in respect of land or the fruits of land. All new contracts with natives must be contracts of service. Provided there is a bona fide contract of this nature there is nothing to prevent an employer from paying a native in kind, or by the privilege of cultivating a defined piece of ground . . . But the native cannot pay the master anything for his right to occupy the land."

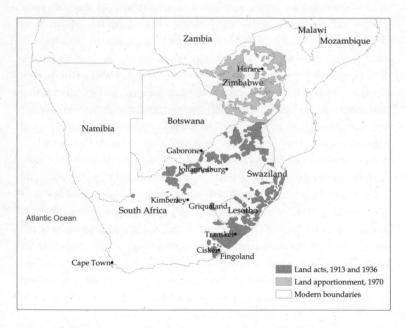

Map 16: The amounts of land allocated to Africans by the minority white regimes in South Africa and Zimbabwe

To the development economists who visited South Africa in the 1950s and '60s, when the academic discipline was taking shape and the ideas of Arthur Lewis were spreading, the contrast between these Homelands and the prosperous modern white European economy seemed to be exactly what the dual economy theory was about. The European part of the economy was urban and educated, and used modern technology. The Homelands were poor, rural, and backward; labor there was very unproductive; people, uneducated. It seemed to be the essence of timeless, backward Africa.

Except that the dual economy was not natural or inevitable. It had been created by European colonialism. Yes, the Homelands were poor and technologically backward, and the people were uneducated. But all this was an outcome of government policy, which had forcibly stamped out African economic growth and created the reservoir of cheap, uneducated African labor to be employed in European-controlled mines and lands. After 1913 vast numbers of Africans were evicted from their lands, which were taken over by whites, and crowded into the Homelands, which were too small for them to earn an independent living from. As intended, therefore, they would be forced to look for a living in the white economy, supplying their labor cheaply. As their economic incentives collapsed, the advances that had taken place in the preceding fifty years were all reversed. People gave up their plows and reverted to farming with hoes—that is, if they farmed at all. More often they were just available as cheap labor, which the Homelands had been structured to ensure.

It was not only the economic incentives that were destroyed. The political changes that had started to take place also went into reverse. The power of chiefs and traditional rulers, which had previously been in decline, was strengthened, because part of the project of creating a cheap labor force was to remove private property in land. So the chiefs' control over land was reaffirmed. These measures reached their apogee in 1951, when the government passed the Bantu Authorities Act. As early as 1940, G. Findlay put his finger right on the issue:

> Tribal tenure is a guarantee that the land will never
> properly be worked and will never really belong to

the natives. Cheap labour must have a cheap breeding
place, and so it is furnished to the Africans at their
own expense.

The dispossession of the African farmers led to their mass impoverishment. It created not only the institutional foundations of a backward economy, but the poor people to stock it.

The available evidence demonstrates the reversal in living standards in the Homelands after the Natives Land Act of 1913. The Transkei and the Ciskei went into a prolonged economic decline. The
employment records from the gold mining companies collected by
the historian Francis Wilson show that this decline was widespread in
the South African economy as a whole. Following the Natives Land
Act and other legislation, miners' wages fell by 30 percent between
1911 and 1921. In 1961, despite relatively steady growth in the South
African economy, these wages were still 12 percent lower than they
had been in 1911. No wonder that over this period South Africa became the most unequal country in the world.

But even in these circumstances, couldn't black Africans have
made their way in the European, modern economy, started a business, or have become educated and begun a career? The government
made sure these things could not happen. No African was allowed to
own property or start a business in the European part of the economy—the 87 percent of the land. The Apartheid regime also realized
that educated Africans competed with whites rather than supplying
cheap labor to the mines and to white-owned agriculture. As early as
1904 a system of job reservation for Europeans was introduced in the
mining economy. No African was allowed to be an amalgamator, an
assayer, a banksman, a blacksmith, a boiler maker, a brass finisher, a
brassmolder, a bricklayer . . . and the list went on and on, all the way
to woodworking machinist. At a stroke, Africans were banned from
occupying any skilled job in the mining sector. This was the first in-
carnation of the famous "colour bar," one of the several racist inventions of South Africa's regime. The colour bar was extended to the
entire economy in 1926, and lasted until the 1980s. It is not surprising
that black Africans were uneducated; the South African state not only

removed the possibility of Africans benefiting economically from an education but also refused to invest in black schools and discouraged black education. This policy reached its peak in the 1950s, when, under the leadership of Hendrik Verwoerd, one of the architects of the Apartheid regime that would last until 1994, the government passed the Bantu Education Act. The philosophy behind this act was bluntly spelled out by Verwoerd himself in a speech in 1954:

> The Bantu must be guided to serve his own commu-
> nity in all respects. There is no place for him in the
> European community above the level of certain forms
> of labour . . . For that reason it is to no avail to him to
> receive a training which has as its aim absorption in
> the European community while he cannot and will not
> be absorbed there.

Naturally, the type of dual economy articulated in Verwoerd's speech is rather different from Lewis's dual economy theory. In South Africa the dual economy was not an inevitable outcome of the process of development. It was created by the state. In South Africa there was to be no seamless movement of poor people from the backward to the modern sector as the economy developed. On the contrary, the success of the modern sector relied on the existence of the backward sector, which enabled white employers to make huge profits by paying very low wages to black unskilled workers. In South Africa there would not be a process of the unskilled workers from the traditional sector gradually becoming educated and skilled, as Lewis's approach envisaged. In fact, the black workers were purposefully kept unskilled and were barred from high-skill occupations so that skilled white workers would not face competition and could enjoy high wages. In South Africa black Africans were indeed "trapped" in the traditional economy, in the Homelands. But this was not the problem of development that growth would make good. The Homelands were what enabled the development of the white economy.

It should also be no surprise that the type of economic development that white South Africa was achieving was ultimately limited, being based on extractive institutions the whites had built to exploit the blacks. South African whites had property rights, they invested in education, and they were able to extract gold and diamonds and sell them profitably in the world market. But over 80 percent of the South African population was marginalized and excluded from the great majority of desirable economic activities. Blacks could not use their talents; they could not become skilled workers, businessmen, entrepreneurs, engineers, or scientists. Economic institutions were extractive; whites became rich by extracting from blacks. Indeed, white South Africans shared the living standards of people of Western European countries, while black South Africans were scarcely richer than those in the rest of sub-Saharan Africa. This economic growth without creative destruction, from which only the whites benefited, continued as long as revenues from gold and diamonds increased. By the 1970s, however, the economy had stopped growing.

And it will again be no surprise that this set of extractive economic institutions was built on foundations laid by a set of highly extractive political institutions. Before its overthrow in 1994, the South African political system vested all power in whites, who were the only ones allowed to vote and run for office. Whites dominated the police force, the military, and all political institutions. These institutions were structured under the military domination of white settlers. At the time of the foundation of the Union of South Africa in 1910, the Afrikaner polities of the Orange Free State and the Transvaal had explicit racial franchises, barring blacks completely from political participation. Natal and the Cape Colony allowed blacks to vote if they had sufficient property, which typically they did not. The status quo of Natal and the Cape Colony was kept in 1910, but by the 1930s, blacks had been explicitly disenfranchised everywhere in South Africa.

The dual economy of South Africa did come to an end in 1994. But not because of the reasons that Sir Arthur Lewis theorized about. It was not the natural course of economic development that ended the color bar and the Homelands. Black South Africans protested and rose up against the regime that did not recognize their basic rights and did not share the gains of economic growth with them. After the Soweto uprising of 1976, the protests became more organized and stronger, ultimately bringing down the Apartheid state. It was the empowerment of blacks who managed to organize and rise up that ultimately ended South Africa's dual economy in the same way that South African whites' political force had created it in the first place.

DEVELOPMENT REVERSED

World inequality today exists because during the nineteenth and twentieth centuries some nations were able to take advantage of the Industrial Revolution and the technologies and methods of organization that it brought while others were unable to do so. Technological change is only one of the engines of prosperity, but it is perhaps the most critical one. The countries that did not take advantage of new technologies did not benefit from the other engines of prosperity, either. As we have shown in this and the previous chapter, this failure was due to their extractive institutions, either a consequence of the persistence of their absolutist regimes or because they lacked centralized states. But this chapter has also shown that in several instances the extractive institutions that underpinned the poverty of these nations were imposed, or at the very least further strengthened, by the very same process that fueled European growth: European commercial and colonial expansion. In fact, the profitability of European colonial empires was often built on the destruction of independent polities and indigenous economies around the world, or on the creation of extractive institutions essentially from the ground up, as in the Caribbean islands, where, following the almost total collapse of the native populations, Europeans imported African slaves and set up plantation systems.

We will never know what the trajectories of independent city-states such as those in the Banda Islands, in Aceh, or in Burma (Myanmar) would have been without the European intervention. They may have had their own indigenous Glorious Revolution or slowly moved toward more inclusive political and economic institutions based on growing trade in spices and other valuable commodities. But this possibility was removed by the expansion of the Dutch East India Company. The company stamped out any hope of indigenous development in the Banda Islands by carrying out its genocide. Its threat also made the city-states in many other parts of Southeast Asia pull back from commerce.

The story of one of the oldest civilizations in Asia, India, is similar, though the reversing of development was done not by the Dutch but by the British. India was the largest producer and exporter of textiles in the world in the eighteenth century. Indian calicoes and muslins flooded the European markets and were traded throughout Asia and even eastern Africa. The main agent that carried them to the British Isles was the English East India Company. Founded in 1600, two years before its Dutch version, the English East India Company spent the seventeenth century trying to establish a monopoly on the valuable exports from India. It had to compete with the Portuguese, who had bases in Goa, Chittagong, and Bombay, and the French with bases at Pondicherry, Chandernagore, Yanam, and Karaikal. Worse still for the East India Company was the Glorious Revolution, as we saw in chapter 7. The monopoly of the East India Company had been granted by the Stuart kings and was immediately challenged after 1688, and even abolished for over a decade. The loss of power was significant, as we saw earlier (pages 199–200), because British textile producers were able to induce Parliament to ban the import of calicoes, the East India Company's most profitable item of trade. In the eighteenth century, under the leadership of Robert Clive, the East India Company switched strategies and began to develop a continental empire. At the time, India was split into many competing polities, though many were still nominally under the control of the Mughal emperor in Delhi. The East India Company first expanded in Bengal in the east, vanquishing the local powers at the battles of Plassey in 1757 and Buxar in 1764. The East India Company looted local wealth and took over, and perhaps even intensified, the extractive taxation institutions of the Mughal rulers of India. This expansion coincided with the massive contraction of the Indian textile industry, since, after all, there was no longer a market for these goods in Britain. The contraction went along with de-urbanization and increased poverty. It initiated a long period of reversed development in India. Soon, instead of producing textiles, Indians were buying them from Britain and growing opium for the East India Company to sell in China.

The Atlantic slave trade repeated the same pattern in Africa, even if starting from less developed conditions than in Southeast Asia and India. Many African states were turned into war machines intent on capturing and selling slaves to Europeans. As conflict between different polities and states grew into continuous warfare, state institutions, which in many cases had not yet achieved much political centralization in any case, crumbled in large parts of Africa, paving the way for persistent extractive institutions and the failed states of today that we will study later. In a few parts of Africa that escaped the slave trade, such as South Africa, Europeans imposed a different set of institutions, this time designed to create a reservoir of cheap labor for their mines and farms. The South African state created a dual economy, preventing 80 percent of the population from taking part in skilled occupations, commercial farming, and entrepreneurship. All this not only explains why industrialization passed by large parts of the world but also encapsulates how economic development may sometimes feed on, and even create, the underdevelopment in some other part of the domestic or the world economy.

10.

THE DIFFUSION OF PROSPERITY

HONOR AMONG THIEVES

EIGHTEENTH-CENTURY ENGLAND—or more appropriately, Great Britain after the 1707 union of England, Wales, and Scotland—had a simple solution for dealing with criminals: out of sight, out of mind, or at least out of trouble. They transported many to penal colonies in the empire. Before the War of Independence, the convicted criminals, convicts, were primarily sent to the American colonies. After 1783 the independent United States of America was no longer so welcoming to British convicts, and the authorities in Britain had to find another home for them. They first thought about West Africa. But the climate, with endemic diseases such as malaria and yellow fever, against which Europeans had no immunity, was so deadly that the authorities decided it was unacceptable to send even convicts to the "white man's graveyard." Their next option was Australia. Its eastern seaboard had been explored by the great seafarer Captain James Cook. On April 29, 1770, Cook landed in a wonderful inlet, which he called Botany Bay in honor of the rich species found there by the naturalists traveling with him. This seemed like an ideal location to British government officials. The climate was temperate, and the place was as far out of sight and mind as could be imagined.

A fleet of eleven ships packed with convicts was on its way to Botany Bay in January 1788 under the command of Captain Arthur Phillip. On January 26, now celebrated as Australia Day, they set up camp in Sydney Cove, the heart of the modern city of Sydney. They called the colony New South Wales. On board one of the ships, the

Alexander, captained by Duncan Sinclair, were a married couple of convicts, Henry and Susannah Cable. Susannah had been found guilty of stealing and was initially sentenced to death. This sentence was later commuted to fourteen years and transportation to the American colonies. That plan fell through with the independence of the United States. In the meantime, in Norwich Castle Jail, Susannah met and fell in love with Henry, a fellow convict. In 1787 she was picked to be transported to the new convict colony in Australia with the first fleet heading there. But Henry was not. By this time Susannah and Henry had a young son, also called Henry. This decision meant the family was to be separated. Susannah was moved to a prison boat moored on the Thames, but the word got out about this wrenching event and reached the ears of a philanthropist, Lady Cadogan. Lady Cadogan organized a successful campaign to reunite the Cables. Now they were both to be transported with young Henry to Australia. Lady Cadogan also raised £20 to purchase goods for them, which they would receive in Australia. They sailed on the *Alexander,* but when they arrived in Botany Bay, the parcel of goods had vanished, or at least that is what Captain Sinclair claimed.

What could the Cables do? Not much, according to English or British law. Even though in 1787, Britain had inclusive political and economic institutions, this inclusiveness did not extend to convicts, who had practically no rights. They could not own property. They could certainly not sue anyone in court. In fact, they could not even give evidence in court. Sinclair knew this and probably stole the parcel. Though he would never admit it, he did boast that he could not be sued by the Cables. He was right according to British law. And in Britain the whole affair would have ended there. But not in Australia. A writ was issued to David Collins, the judge advocate there, as follows:

> Whereas Henry Cable and his wife, new settlers of this place, had before they left England a certain parcel shipped on board the Alexander transport Duncan Sinclair Master, consisting of cloaths and several other articles suitable for their present situation, which were collected and bought at the expence of many charita-

ble disposed persons for the use of the said Henry
Cable, his wife and child. Several applications has
been made for the express purpose of obtaining the
said parcel from the Master of the Alexander now
lying at this port, and that without effect (save and
except) a small part of the said parcel containing a few
books, the residue and remainder, which is of a more
considerable value still remains on board the said ship
Alexander, the Master of which, seems to be very ne-
glectfull in not causing the same to be delivered, to its
respective owners as aforesaid.

Henry and Susannah, since they were both illiterate, could not
sign the writ and just put their "crosses" at the bottom. The words
"new settlers of this place" were later crossed out, but were highly
significant. Someone anticipated that if Henry Cable and his wife were
described as convicts, the case would have no hope of proceeding.
Someone had come up instead with the idea of calling them new settlers. This was probably a bit too much for Judge Collins to take, and
most likely he was the one who had these words struck out. But the
writ worked. Collins did not throw out the case, and convened the
court, with a jury entirely made up of soldiers. Sinclair was called
before the court. Though Collins was less than enthusiastic about the
case, and the jury was composed of the people sent to Australia to
guard convicts such as the Cables, the Cables won. Sinclair contested
the whole affair on the grounds that the Cables were criminals. But
the verdict stood, and he had to pay fifteen pounds.

To reach this verdict Judge Collins didn't apply British law; he ignored it. This was the first civil case adjudicated in Australia. The first
criminal case would have appeared equally bizarre to those in Britain.
A convict was found guilty of stealing another convict's bread, which
was worth two pence. At the time, such a case would not have come
to court, since convicts were not allowed to own anything. Australia
was not Britain, and its law would not be just British. And Australia
would soon diverge from Britain in criminal and civil law as well as
in a host of economic and political institutions.

The penal colony of New South Wales initially consisted of the convicts and their guards, mostly soldiers. There were few "free settlers" in Australia until the 1820s, and the transportation of convicts, though it stopped in New South Wales in 1840, continued until 1868 in Western Australia. Convicts had to perform "compulsory work," essentially just another name for forced labor, and the guards intended to make money out of it. Initially the convicts had no pay. They were given only food in return for the labor they performed. The guards kept what they produced. But this system, like the ones with which the Virginia Company experimented in Jamestown, did not work very well, because convicts did not have the incentives to work hard or do good work. They were lashed or banished to Norfolk Island, just thirteen square miles of territory situated more than one thousand miles east of Australia in the Pacific Ocean. But since neither banishing nor lashing worked, the alternative was to give them incentives. This was not a natural idea to the soldiers and guards. Convicts were convicts, and they were not supposed to sell their labor or own property. But in Australia there was nobody else to do the work. There were of course Aboriginals, possibly as many as one million at the time of the founding of New South Wales. But they were spread out over a vast continent, and their density in New South Wales was insufficient for the creation of an economy based on their exploitation. There was no Latin American option in Australia. The guards thus embarked on a path that would ultimately lead to institutions that were even more inclusive than those back in Britain. Convicts were given a set of tasks to do, and if they had extra time, they could work for themselves and sell what they produced.

The guards also benefited from the convicts' new economic freedoms. Production increased, and the guards set up monopolies to sell goods to the convicts. The most lucrative of these was for rum. New South Wales at this time, just like other British colonies, was run by a governor, appointed by the British government. In 1806 Britain appointed William Bligh, the man who seventeen years previously, in 1789, had been captain of the H.M.S. *Bounty,* during the famous "Mutiny on the *Bounty.*" Bligh was a strict disciplinarian, a trait that was probably largely responsible for the mutiny. His ways had not changed, and he immediately challenged the rum monopolists. This would lead to another mutiny, this time by the monopolists, led by a former soldier, John Macarthur. The events, which came to be known as the Rum Rebellion, again led to Bligh's being overpowered by rebels, this time on land rather than aboard the *Bounty*. Macarthur had Bligh locked up. The British authorities subsequently sent more soldiers to deal with the rebellion. Macarthur was arrested and shipped back to Britain. But he was soon released, and he returned to Australia to play a major role in both the politics and economics of the colony.

The roots of the Rum Rebellion were economic. The strategy of giving the convicts incentives was making a lot of money for men such as Macarthur, who arrived in Australia as a soldier in the second group of ships that landed in 1790. In 1796 he resigned from the army to concentrate on business. By that time he already had his first sheep, and realized that there was a lot of money to be made in sheep farming and wool export. Inland from Sydney were the Blue Mountains, which were finally crossed in 1813, revealing vast expanses of open grassland on the other side. It was sheep heaven. Macarthur was soon the richest man in Australia, and he and his fellow sheep magnates became known as the Squatters, since the land on which they grazed their sheep was not theirs. It was owned by the British government. But at first this was a small detail. The Squatters were the elite of Australia, or, more appropriately, the Squattocracy.

Even with a squattocracy, New South Wales did not look anything like the absolutist regimes of Eastern Europe or of the South American colonies. There were no serfs as in Austria-Hungary and Russia, and no large indigenous populations to exploit as in Mexico and Peru. Instead, New South Wales was like Jamestown, Virginia, in many ways: the elite ultimately found it in their interest to create economic institutions that were significantly more inclusive than those in Austria-Hungary, Russia, Mexico, and Peru. Convicts were the only labor force, and the only way to incentivize them was to pay them wages for the work they were doing.

Convicts were soon allowed to become entrepreneurs and hire other convicts. More notably, they were even given land after completing their sentences, and they had all their rights restored. Some of them started to get rich, even the illiterate Henry Cable. By 1798 he owned a hotel called the Ramping Horse, and he also had a shop. He bought a ship and went into the trade of sealskins. By 1809 he owned at least nine farms of about 470 acres and also a number of shops and houses in Sydney.

The next conflict in New South Wales would be between the elite and the rest of the society, made up of convicts, ex-convicts, and their families. The elite, led by former guards and soldiers such as Macarthur, included some of the free settlers who had been attracted to the colony because of the boom in the wool economy. Most of the property was still in the hands of the elite, and the ex-convicts and their descendants wanted an end to transportation, the opportunity of trial by a jury of their peers, and access to free land. The elite wanted none of these. Their main concern was to establish legal title to the lands they squatted on. The situation was again similar to the events that had transpired in North America more than two centuries earlier. As we saw in chapter 1, the victories of the indentured servants against the Virginia Company were followed by the struggles in Maryland and the Carolinas. In New South Wales, the roles of Lord Baltimore and Sir Anthony Ashley-Cooper were played by Macarthur and the Squatters. The British government was again on the side of the elite, though they also feared that one day Macarthur and the Squatters might be tempted to declare independence.

The British government dispatched John Bigge to the colony in 1819 to head a commission of inquiry into the developments there. Bigge was shocked by the rights that the convicts enjoyed and surprised by the fundamentally inclusive nature of the economic institutions of this penal colony. He recommended a radical overhaul: convicts could not own land, nobody should be allowed to pay convicts wages anymore, pardons were to be restricted, ex-convicts were not to be given land, and punishment was to be made much more draconian. Bigge saw the Squatters as the natural aristocracy of Australia and envisioned an autocratic society dominated by them. This wasn't to be.

While Bigge was trying to turn back the clock, ex-convicts and their sons and daughters were demanding greater rights. Most important, they realized, again just as in the United States, that to consolidate their economic and political rights fully they needed political institutions that would include them in the process of decision making. They demanded elections in which they could participate as equals and representative institutions and assemblies in which they could hold office.

The ex-convicts and their sons and daughters were led by the colorful writer, explorer, and journalist William Wentworth. Wentworth was one of the leaders of the first expedition that crossed the Blue Mountains, which opened the vast grasslands to the Squatters; a town on these mountains is still named after him. His sympathies were with the convicts, perhaps because of his father, who was accused of highway robbery and had to accept transportation to Australia to avoid trial and possible conviction. At this time, Wentworth was a strong advocate of more inclusive political institutions, an elected assembly, trial by jury for ex-convicts and their families, and an end to transportation to New South Wales. He started a newspaper, the *Australian,* which would from then on lead the attack on the existing political institutions. Macarthur didn't like Wentworth and certainly not what he was asking for. He went through a list of Wentworth's supporters, characterizing them as follows:

> sentenced to be hung since he came here
> repeatedly flogged at the cart's tail
> a London Jew
> Jew publican lately deprived of his license
> auctioneer transported for trading in slaves
> often flogged here
> son of two convicts
> a swindler—deeply in debt
> an American adventurer
> an attorney with a worthless character
> a stranger lately failed here in a musick shop
> married to the daughter to two convicts
> married to a convict who was formerly a tambourine girl.

Macarthur and the Squatters' vigorous opposition could not stop the tide in Australia, however. The demand for representative institutions was strong and could not be suppressed. Until 1823 the governor had ruled New South Wales more or less on his own. In that year his powers were limited by the creation of a council appointed by the British government. Initially the appointees were from the Squatters and nonconvict elite, Macarthur among them, but this couldn't last. In 1831 the governor Richard Bourke bowed to pressure and for the first time allowed ex-convicts to sit on juries. Ex-convicts and in fact many new free settlers also wanted transportation of convicts from Britain to stop, because it created competition in the labor market and drove down wages. The Squatters liked low wages, but they lost. In 1840 transportation to New South Wales was stopped, and in 1842 a legislative council was created with two-thirds of its members being elected (the rest appointed). Ex-convicts could stand for office and vote if they held enough property, and many did.

By the 1850s, Australia had introduced adult white male suffrage. The demands of the citizens, ex-convicts and their families, were now far ahead of what William Wentworth had first imagined. In fact, by this time he was on the side of conservatives insisting on an unelected Legislative Council. But just like Macarthur before, Wentworth would not be able to halt the tide toward more inclusive political institutions. In 1856 the state of Victoria, which had been carved out of New South Wales in 1851, and the state of Tasmania would become the first places in the world to introduce an effective secret ballot in elections, which stopped vote buying and coercion. Today we still call the standard method of achieving secrecy in voting in elections the Australian ballot.

The initial circumstances in Sydney, New South Wales, were very similar to those in Jamestown, Virginia, 181 years earlier, though the settlers at Jamestown were mostly indentured laborers, rather than convicts. In both cases the initial circumstances did not allow for the creation of extractive colonial institutions. Neither colony had dense populations of indigenous peoples to exploit, ready access to precious metals such as gold or silver, or soil and crops that would make slave plantations economically viable. The slave trade was still vibrant in the 1780s, and New South Wales could have been filled up with slaves had it been profitable. It wasn't. Both the Virginia Company and the soldiers and free settlers who ran New South Wales bowed to the pressures, gradually creating inclusive economic institutions that developed in tandem with inclusive political institutions. This happened with even less of a struggle in New South Wales than it had in Virginia, and subsequent attempts to put this trend into reverse failed.

AUSTRALIA, LIKE THE UNITED STATES, experienced a different path to inclusive institutions than the one taken by England. The same revolutions that shook England during the Civil War and then the Glorious Revolution were not needed in the United States or Australia because of the very different circumstances in which those countries were founded—though this of course does not mean that inclusive institutions were established without any conflict, and, in the process, the United States had to throw off British colonialism. In England there was a long history of absolutist rule that was deeply entrenched and required a revolution to remove it. In the United States and Australia, there was no such thing. Though Lord Baltimore in Maryland and John Macarthur in New South Wales might have aspired to such a role, they could not establish a strong enough grip on society for their plans to bear fruit. The inclusive institutions established in the United States and Australia meant that the Industrial Revolution spread quickly to these lands and they began to get rich. The path these countries took was followed by colonies such as Canada and New Zealand.

There were still other paths to inclusive institutions. Large parts of Western Europe took yet a third path to inclusive institutions under the impetus of the French Revolution, which overthrew absolutism in France and then generated a series of interstate conflicts that spread institutional reform across much of Western Europe. The economic consequence of these reforms was the emergence of inclusive economic institutions in most of Western Europe, the Industrial Revolution, and economic growth.

Breaking the Barriers: The French Revolution

For the three centuries prior to 1789, France was ruled by an absolutist monarchy. French society was divided into three segments, the so-called estates. The aristocrats (the nobility) made up the Second Estate, the clergy the First Estate, and everybody else the Third Estate. Different estates were subject to different laws, and the first two estates had rights that the rest of the population did not. The nobility and the clergy did not pay taxes, while the citizens had to pay several different taxes, as we would expect from a regime that was largely extractive. In fact, not only was the Church exempt from taxes, but it also owned large swaths of land and could impose its own taxes on peasants. The monarch, the nobility, and the clergy enjoyed a luxurious lifestyle, while much of the Third Estate lived in dire poverty. Different laws not only guaranteed a greatly advantageous economic position to the nobility and the clergy, but it also gave them political power.

Life in French cities of the eighteenth century was harsh and unhealthy. Manufacturing was regulated by powerful guilds, which generated good incomes for their members but prevented others from entering these occupations or starting new businesses. The so-called *ancien régime* prided itself on its continuity and stability. Entry by entrepreneurs and talented individuals into new occupations would create instability and was not tolerated. If life in the cities was harsh, life in the villages was probably worse. As we have seen, by this time the most extreme form of serfdom, which tied people to the land and forced them to work for and pay dues to the feudal lords, was long in decline in France. Nevertheless, there were restrictions on mobility and a plethora of feudal dues that the French peasants were required to pay to the monarch, the nobility, and the Church.

Against this background, the French Revolution was a radical affair. On August 4, 1789, the National Constituent Assembly entirely changed French laws by proposing a new constitution. The first article stated:

The National Assembly hereby completely abolishes the feudal system. It decrees that, among the existing rights and dues, both feudal and censuel, all those originating in or representing real or personal serfdom shall be abolished without indemnification.

Its ninth article then continued:

Pecuniary privileges, personal or real, in the payment of taxes are abolished forever. Taxes shall be collected from all the citizens, and from all property, in the same manner and in the same form. Plans shall be considered by which the taxes shall be paid proportionally by all, even for the last six months of the current year.

Thus, in one swoop, the French Revolution abolished the feudal system and all the obligations and dues that it entailed, and it entirely removed the tax exemptions of the nobility and the clergy. But perhaps what was most radical, even unthinkable at the time, was the eleventh article, which stated:

All citizens, without distinction of birth, are eligible to any office or dignity, whether ecclesiastical, civil, or military; and no profession shall imply any derogation.

So there was now equality before the law for all, not only in daily life and business, but also in politics. The reforms of the revolution continued after August 4. It subsequently abolished the Church's authority to levy special taxes and turned the clergy into employees of the state. Together with the removal of the rigid political and social roles, critical barriers against economic activities were stamped out. The guilds and all occupational restrictions were abolished, creating a more level playing field in the cities.

These reforms were a first step toward ending the reign of the absolutist French monarchs. Several decades of instability and war followed the declarations of August 4. But an irreversible step was taken away from absolutism and extractive institutions and toward inclusive political and economic institutions. These changes would be followed by other reforms in the economy and in politics, ultimately culminating in the Third Republic in 1870, which would bring to France the type of parliamentary system that the Glorious Revolution put in motion in England. The French Revolution created much violence, suffering, instability, and war. Nevertheless, thanks to it, the French did not get trapped with extractive institutions blocking economic growth and prosperity, as did absolutist regimes of Eastern Europe such as Austria-Hungary and Russia.

How did the absolutist French monarchy come to the brink of the 1789 revolution? After all, we have seen that many absolutist regimes were able to survive for long periods of time, even in the midst of economic stagnation and social upheaval. As with most instances of revolutions and radical changes, it was a confluence of factors that opened the way to the French Revolution, and these were intimately related to the fact that Britain was industrializing rapidly. And of course the path was, as usual, contingent, as many attempts to stabilize the regime by the monarchy failed and the revolution turned out to be more successful in changing institutions in France and elsewhere in Europe than many could have imagined in 1789.

Many laws and privileges in France were remnants of medieval times. They not only favored the First and Second Estates relative to the majority of the population but also gave them privileges vis-à-vis the Crown. Louis XIV, the Sun King, ruled France for fifty-four years, between 1661 to his death in 1715, though he actually came to the throne in 1643, at the age of five. He consolidated the power of the monarchy, furthering the process toward greater absolutism that had started centuries earlier. Many monarchs often consulted the so-called Assembly of Notables, consisting of key aristocrats handpicked by the Crown. Though largely consultative, the Assembly still acted as a mild constraint on the monarch's power. For this reason, Louis XIV ruled without convening the Assembly. Under his reign, France achieved some economic growth—for example, via participation in Atlantic and colonial trade. Louis's able minister of finance, Jean-Baptiste Colbert, also oversaw the development of government-sponsored and government-controlled industry, a type of extractive growth. This limited amount of growth benefited almost exclusively the First and Second Estates. Louis XIV also wanted to rationalize the French tax system, because the state often had problems financing its frequent wars, its large standing army, and the King's own luxurious retinue, consumption, and palaces. Its inability to tax even the minor nobility put severe limits on its revenues.

Though there had been little economic growth, by the time Louis XVI came to power in 1774, there had nevertheless been large changes in society. Moreover, the earlier fiscal problems had turned into a fiscal crisis, and the Seven Years' War with the British between 1756 and 1763, in which France lost Canada, had been particularly costly. A number of significant figures attempted to balance the royal budget by restructuring the debt and increasing taxes; among them were Anne-Robert-Jacques Turgot, one of the most famous economists of the time; Jacques Necker, who would also play an important role after the revolution; and Charles Alexandre de Calonne. But none succeeded. Calonne, as part of his strategy, persuaded Louis XVI to summon the Assembly of Notables. The king and his advisers expected the Assembly to endorse his reforms much in the same way as Charles I expected the English Parliament to simply agree to pay for an army to fight the Scottish when he called it in 1640. The Assembly took an unexpected step and decreed that only a representative body, the Estates-General, could endorse such reforms.

The Estates-General was a very different body from the Assembly of Notables. While the latter consisted of the nobility and was largely handpicked by the Crown from among major aristocrats, the former included representatives from all three estates. It had last been convened in 1614. When the Estates-General gathered in 1789 in Versailles, it became immediately clear that no agreement could be reached. There were irreconcilable differences, as the Third Estate saw this as its chance to increase its political power and wanted to have more votes in the Estates-General, which the nobility and the clergy steadfastly opposed. The meeting ended on May 5, 1789, without any resolution, except the decision to convene a more powerful body, the National Assembly, deepening the political crisis. The Third Estate, particularly the merchants, businessmen, professionals, and artisans, who all had demands for greater power, saw these developments as evidence of their increasing clout. In the National Assembly, they therefore demanded even more say in the proceedings and greater rights in general. Their support in the streets all over the country by citizens emboldened by these developments led to the reconstitution of the Assembly as the National Constituent Assembly on July 9.

Meanwhile, the mood in the country, and especially in Paris, was becoming more radical. In reaction, the conservative circles around Louis XVI persuaded him to sack Necker, the reformist finance minister. This led to further radicalization in the streets. The outcome was the famous storming of the Bastille on July 14, 1789. From this point onward, the revolution started in earnest. Necker was reinstated, and the revolutionary Marquis de Lafayette was put in charge of the National Guard of Paris.

Even more remarkable than the storming of the Bastille were the dynamics of the National Constituent Assembly, which on August 4, 1789, with its newfound confidence, passed the new constitution, abolishing feudalism and the special privileges of the First and Second Estates. But this radicalization led to fractionalization within the Assembly, since there were many conflicting views about the shape that society should take. The first step was the formation of local clubs, most notably the radical Jacobin Club, which would later take control of the revolution. At the same time, the nobles were fleeing the country in great numbers—the so-called émigrés. Many were also encouraging the king to break with the Assembly and take action, either by himself or with the help of foreign powers, such as Austria, the native country of Queen Marie Antoinette and where most of the émigrés had fled. As many in the streets started to see an imminent threat against the achievements of the revolution over the past two years, radicalization gathered pace. The National Constituent Assembly passed the final version of the constitution on September 29, 1791, turning France into a constitutional monarchy, with equality of rights for all men, no feudal obligations or dues, and an end to all trading restrictions imposed by guilds. France was still a monarchy, but the king now had little role and, in fact, not even his freedom.

But the dynamics of the revolution were then irreversibly altered by the war that broke out in 1792 between France and the "first coalition," led by Austria. The war increased the resolve and radicalism of the revolutionaries and of the masses (the so-called *sans-culottes*, which translates as "without knee breeches," because they could not afford to wear the style of trousers then fashionable). The outcome of this process was the period known as the Terror, under the command of the Jacobin faction led by Robespierre and Saint-Just, unleashed after the executions of Louis XVI and Marie Antoinette. It led to the executions of not only scores of aristocrats and counterrevolutionaries but also several major figures of the revolution, including the former popular leaders Brissot, Danton, and Desmoulins.

But the Terror soon spun out of control and ultimately came to an end in July 1794 with the execution of its own leaders, including Robespierre and Saint-Just. There followed a phase of relative stability, first under the somewhat ineffective Directory, between 1795 and 1799, and then with more concentrated power in the form of a three-person Consulate, consisting of Ducos, Sieyès, and Napoleon Bonaparte. Already during the Directory, the young general Napoleon Bonaparte had become famous for his military successes, and his influence was only to grow after 1799. The Consulate soon became Napoleon's personal rule.

The years between 1799 and the end of Napoleon's reign, 1815, witnessed a series of great military victories for France, including those at Austerlitz, Jena-Auerstadt, and Wagram, bringing continental Europe to its knees. They also allowed Napoleon to impose his will, his reforms, and his legal code across a wide swath of territory. The fall of Napoleon after his final defeat in 1815 would also bring a period of retrenchment, more restricted political rights, and the restoration of the French monarchy under Louis XVIII. But all these were simply slowing the ultimate emergence of inclusive political institutions.

The forces unleashed by the revolution of 1789 ended French absolutism and would inevitably, even if slowly, lead to the emergence of inclusive institutions. France, and those parts of Europe where the revolutionary reforms had been exported, would thus take part in the industrialization process already under way in the nineteenth century.

EXPORTING THE REVOLUTION

On the eve of the French Revolution in 1789, there were severe restrictions placed on Jews throughout Europe. In the German city of Frankfurt, for example, their lives were regulated by orders set out in a statute dating from the Middle Ages. There could be no more than five hundred Jewish families in Frankfurt, and they all had to live in a small, walled part of town, the Judengasse, the Jewish ghetto. They could not leave the ghetto at night, on Sundays, or during any Christian festival.

The Judengasse was incredibly cramped. It was a quarter of a mile long but no more than twelve feet wide and in some places less than ten feet wide. Jews lived under constant repression and regulation. Each year, at most two new families could be admitted to the ghetto, and at most twelve Jewish couples could get married, and only if they were both above the age of twenty-five. Jews could not farm; they could also not trade in weapons, spices, wine, or grain. Until 1726 they had to wear specific markers, two concentric yellow rings for men and a striped veil for women. All Jews had to pay a special poll tax.

As the French Revolution erupted, a successful young businessman, Mayer Amschel Rothschild, lived in the Frankfurt Judengasse. By the early 1780s, Rothschild had established himself as the leading dealer in coins, metals, and antiques in Frankfurt. But like all Jews in the city, he could not open a business outside the ghetto or even live outside it.

This was all to change soon. In 1791 the French National Assembly emancipated French Jewry. The French armies were now also occupying the Rhineland and emancipating the Jews of Western Germany. In Frankfurt their effect would be more abrupt and perhaps somewhat unintentional. In 1796 the French bombarded Frankfurt, demolishing half of the Judengasse in the process. Around two thousand Jews were left homeless and had to move outside the ghetto. The Rothschilds were among them. Once outside the ghetto, and now freed from the myriad regulations barring them from entrepreneurship, they could seize new business opportunities. This included a contract to supply grain to the Austrian army, something they would previously not have been allowed to do.

By the end of the decade, Rothschild was one of the richest Jews in Frankfurt and already a well-established businessman. Full emancipation had to wait until 1811; it was finally implemented by Karl von Dalberg, who had been made Grand Duke of Frankfurt in Napoleon's 1806 reorganization of Germany. Mayer Amschel told his son, "[Y]ou are now a citizen."

Such events did not end the struggle for Jewish emancipation, since there were subsequent reverses, particularly at the Congress of Vienna of 1815, which formed the post-Napoleonic political settlement. But there was no going back to the ghetto for the Rothschilds. Mayer Amschel and his sons would soon have the largest bank in nineteenth-century Europe, with branches in Frankfurt, London, Paris, Naples, and Vienna.

This was not an isolated event. First the French Revolutionary Armies and then Napoleon invaded large parts of continental Europe, and in almost all the areas they invaded, the existing institutions were remnants of medieval times, empowering kings, princes, and nobility and restricting trade both in cities and the countryside. Serfdom and feudalism were much more important in many of these areas than in France itself. In Eastern Europe, including Prussia and the Hungarian part of Austria-Hungary, serfs were tied to the land. In the West this strict form of serfdom had already vanished, but peasants owed to feudal lords various seigneurial fees, taxes, and labor obligations. For example, in the polity of Nassau-Usingen, peasants were subject to 230 different payments, dues, and services. Dues included one that had to be paid after an animal had been slaughtered, called the blood tithe; there was also a bee tithe and a wax tithe. If a piece of property was bought or sold, the lord was owed fees. The guilds regulating all kinds of economic activity in the cities were also typically stronger in these places than in France. In the western German cities of Cologne and Aachen, the adoption of spinning and weaving textile machines was blocked by guilds. Many cities, from Berne in Switzerland to Florence in Italy, were controlled by a few families.

The leaders of the French Revolution and, subsequently, Napoleon exported the revolution to these lands, destroying absolutism, ending feudal land relations, abolishing guilds, and imposing equality before the law—the all-important notion of rule of law, which we will discuss in greater detail in the next chapter. The French Revolution thus prepared not only France but much of the rest of Europe for inclusive institutions and the economic growth that these would spur.

As we have seen, alarmed by the developments in France, several

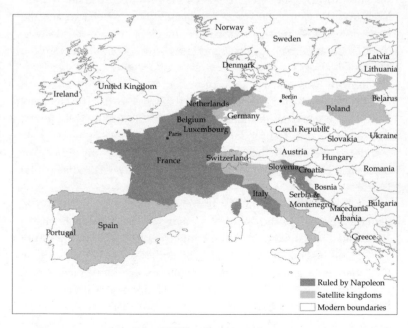

Map 17: Napoleon's empire

European powers organized around Austria in 1792 to attack France, ostensibly to free King Louis XVI, but in reality to crush the French Revolution. The expectation was that the makeshift armies fielded by the revolution would soon crumble. But after some early defeats, the armies of the new French Republic were victorious in an initially defensive war. There were serious organizational problems to overcome. But the French were ahead of other countries in a major innovation: mass conscription. Introduced in August 1793, mass conscription allowed the French to field large armies and develop a military advantage verging on supremacy even before Napoleon's famous military skills came on the scene.

Initial military success encouraged the Republic's leadership to expand France's borders, with an eye toward creating an effective buffer between the new republic and the hostile monarchs of Prussia and Austria. The French quickly seized the Austrian Netherlands and the United Provinces, essentially today's Belgium and the Netherlands. The French also took over much of modern-day Switzerland. In all three places, the French had strong control through the 1790s.

Germany was initially hotly contested. But by 1795, the French had firm control over the Rhineland, the western part of Germany lying on the left bank of the Rhine River. The Prussians were forced to recognize this fact under the Treaty of Basel. Between 1795 and 1802, the French held the Rhineland, but not any other part of Germany. In 1802 the Rhineland was officially incorporated into France.

Italy remained the main seat of war in the second half the 1790s, with the Austrians as the opponents. Savoy was annexed by France in 1792, and a stalemate was reached until Napoleon's invasion in April 1796. In his first major continental campaign, by early 1797, Napoleon had conquered almost all Northern Italy, except for Venice, which was taken by the Austrians. The Treaty of Campo Formio, signed with the Austrians in October 1797, ended the War of the First Coalition and recognized a number of French-controlled republics in Northern Italy. However, the French continued to expand their control over Italy even after this treaty, invading the Papal States and establishing the Roman Republic in March 1798. In January 1799, Naples was conquered and the Parthenopean Republic created. With the exception of Venice, which remained Austrian, the French now controlled the entire Italian peninsula either directly, as in the case of Savoy, or through satellite states, such as the Cisalpine, Ligurian, Roman, and Parthenopean republics.

There was further back-and-forth in the War of the Second Coalition, between 1798 and 1801, but this ended with the French essentially remaining in control. The French revolutionary armies quickly started carrying out a radical process of reform in the lands they'd conquered, abolishing the remaining vestiges of serfdom and feudal land relations and imposing equality before the law. The clergy were stripped of their special status and power, and the guilds in urban areas were stamped out or at the very least much weakened. This happened in the Austrian Netherlands immediately after the French invasion in 1795 and in the United Provinces, where the French founded the Batavian Republic, with political institutions very similar to those in France. In Switzerland the situation was similar, and the guilds as well as feudal landlords and the Church were defeated, feudal privileges removed, and the guilds abolished and expropriated.

What was started by the French Revolutionary Armies was continued, in one form or another, by Napoleon. Napoleon was first and foremost interested in establishing firm control over the territories he conquered. This sometimes involved cutting deals with local elites or putting his family and associates in charge, as during his brief control of Spain and Poland. But Napoleon also had a genuine desire to continue and deepen the reforms of the revolution. Most important, he codified the Roman law and the ideas of equality before the law into a legal system that became known as the Code Napoleon. Napoleon saw this code as his greatest legacy and wished to impose it in every territory he controlled.

Of course, the reforms imposed by the French Revolution and Napoleon were not irreversible. In some places, such as in Hanover, Germany, the old elites were reinstated shortly after Napoleon's fall and much of what the French achieved was lost for good. But in many other places, feudalism, the guilds, and the nobility were permanently destroyed or weakened. For instance, even after the French left, in many cases the Code Napoleon remained in effect.

All in all, French armies wrought much suffering in Europe, but they also radically changed the lay of the land. In much of Europe, gone were feudal relations; the power of the guilds; the absolutist control of monarchs and princes; the grip of the clergy on economic, social, and political power; and the foundation of *ancien régime,* which treated different people unequally based on their birth status. These changes created the type of inclusive economic institutions that would then allow industrialization to take root in these places. By the middle of the nineteenth century, industrialization was rapidly under way in almost all the places that the French controlled, whereas places such as Austria-Hungary and Russia, which the French did not conquer, or Poland and Spain, where French hold was temporary and limited, were still largely stagnant.

SEEKING MODERNITY

In the autumn of 1867, Ōkubo Toshimichi, a leading courtier of the feudal Japanese Satsuma domain, traveled from the capital of Edo, now Tokyo, to the regional city of Yamaguchi. On October 14 he met with leaders of the Chōshū domain. He had a simple proposal: they would join forces, march their armies to Edo, and overthrow the shogun, the ruler of Japan. By this time Ōkubo Toshimichi already had the leaders of the Tosa and Hizen domains on board. Once the leaders of the powerful Chōshū agreed, a secret Satcho Alliance was formed.

In 1868 Japan was an economically underdeveloped country that had been controlled since 1600 by the Tokugawa family, whose ruler had taken the title shogun (commander) in 1603. The Japanese emperor was sidelined and assumed a purely ceremonial role. The Tokugawa shoguns were the dominant members of a class of feudal lords who ruled and taxed their own domains, among them those of Satsuma, ruled by the Shimazu family. These lords, along with their military retainers, the famous samurai, ran a society that was similar to that of medieval Europe, with strict occupational categories, restrictions on trade, and high rates of taxation on farmers. The shogun ruled from Edo, where he monopolized and controlled foreign trade and banned foreigners from the country. Political and economic institutions were extractive, and Japan was poor.

But the domination of the shogun was not complete. Even as the Tokugawa family took over the country in 1600, they could not control everyone. In the south of the country, the Satsuma domain remained quite autonomous and was even allowed to trade independently with the outside world through the Ryūkyū Islands. It was in the Satsuma capital of Kagoshima where Ōkubo Toshimichi was born in 1830. As the son of a samurai, he, too, became a samurai. His talent was spotted early on by Shimazu Nariakira, the lord of Satsuma, who quickly promoted him in the bureaucracy. At the time, Shimazu Nariakira had already formulated a plan to use Satsuma troops to overthrow the shogun. He wanted to expand trade with Asia and Europe, abolish the old feudal economic institutions, and construct a modern state in Japan. His nascent plan was cut short by his death in 1858. His successor, Shimazu Hisamitsu, was more circumspect, at least initially.

Ōkubo Toshimichi had by now become more and more convinced that Japan needed to overthrow the feudal shogunate, and he eventually convinced Shimazu Hisamitsu. To rally support for their cause, they wrapped it in outrage over the sidelining of the emperor. The treaty Ōkubo Toshimichi had already signed with the Tosa domain asserted that "a country does not have two monarchs, a home does not have two masters; government devolves to one ruler." But the real intention was not simply to restore the emperor to power but to change the political and economic institutions completely. On the Tosa side, one of the treaty's signers was Sakamoto Ryōma. As Satsuma and Chōshū mobilized their armies, Sakamoto Ryōma presented the shogun with an eight-point plan, urging him to resign to avoid civil war. The plan was radical, and though clause 1 stated that "political power of the country should be returned to the Imperial Court,

296 · WHY NATIONS FAIL

and all decrees issued by the Court," it included far more than just the restoration of the emperor. Clauses 2, 3, 4, and 5 stated:

2. Two legislative bodies, an Upper and Lower house, should be established, and all government measures should be decided on the basis of general opinion.
3. Men of ability among the lords, nobles and people at large should be employed as councillors, and traditional offices of the past which have lost their purpose should be abolished.
4. Foreign affairs should be carried on according to appropriate regulations worked out on the basis of general opinion.
5. Legislation and regulations of earlier times should be set aside and a new and adequate code should be selected.

Shogun Yoshinobu agreed to resign, and on January 3, 1868, the Meiji Restoration was declared; Emperor Kōmei and, one month later after Kōmei died, his son Meiji were restored to power. Though Satsuma and Chōshū forces now occupied Edo and the imperial capital Kyōto, they feared that the Tokugawas would attempt to regain power and re-create the shogunate. Ōkubo Toshimichi wanted the Tokugawas crushed forever. He persuaded the emperor to abolish the Tokugawa domain and confiscate their lands. On January 27 the former shogun Yoshinobu attacked Satsuma and Chōshū forces, and civil war broke out; it raged until the summer, when finally the Tokugawas were vanquished.

Following the Meiji Restoration there was a process of transformative institutional reforms in Japan. In 1869 feudalism was abolished, and the three hundred fiefs were surrendered to the government and turned into prefectures, under the control of an appointed governor. Taxation was centralized, and a modern bureaucratic state replaced the old feudal one. In 1869 the equality of all social classes before the law was introduced, and restrictions on internal migration and trade were abolished. The samurai class was abolished, though not without having to put down some rebellions. Individual property rights on land were introduced, and people were allowed freedom to enter and practice any trade. The state became heavily involved in the construction of infrastructure. In contrast to the attitudes of absolutist regimes to railways, in 1869 the Japanese regime formed a steamship line between Tokyo and Osaka and built the first railway between Tokyo and Yokohama. It also began to develop a manufacturing industry, and Ōkubo Toshimichi, as minister of finance, oversaw the beginning of a concerted effort of industrialization. The lord of Satsuma domain had been a leader in this, building factories for pottery, cannon, and cotton yarn and importing English textile machinery to create the first modern cotton spinning mill in Japan in 1861. He also built two modern shipyards. By 1890 Japan was the first Asian country to adopt a written constitution, and it created a constitutional monarchy with an elected parliament, the Diet, and an independent judiciary. These changes were decisive factors in enabling Japan to be the primary beneficiary from the Industrial Revolution in Asia.

IN THE MID-NINETEENTH CENTURY both China and Japan were poor nations, languishing under absolutist regimes. The absolutist regime in China had been suspicious of change for centuries. Though there were many similarities between China and Japan—the Tokugawa shogunate had also banned overseas trade in the seventeenth century, as Chinese emperors had done earlier, and were opposed to economic and political change—there were also notable political differences. China was a centralized bureaucratic empire ruled by an absolute emperor. The emperor certainly faced constraints on his power, the most important of which was the threat of rebellion. During the period 1850 to 1864, the whole of southern China was ravaged by the Taiping Rebellion, in which millions died either in conflict or through mass starvation. But opposition to the emperor was not institutionalized.

The structure of Japanese political institutions was different. The shogunate had sidelined the emperor, but as we have seen, the

Tokugawa power was not absolute, and domains such as that of the Satsumas maintained independence, even the ability to conduct foreign trade on their own behalf.

As with France, an important consequence of the British Industrial Revolution for China and Japan was military vulnerability. China was humbled by British sea power during the First Opium War, between 1839 and 1842, and the same threat became all too real for the Japanese as U.S. warships, led by Commodore Matthew Perry, pulled into Edo Bay in 1853. The reality that economic backwardness created military backwardness was part of the impetus behind Shimazu Nariakira's plan to overthrow the shogunate and put in motion the changes that eventually led to the Meiji Restoration. The leaders of the Satsuma domain realized that economic growth—perhaps even Japanese survival—could be achieved only by institutional reforms, but the shogun opposed this because his power was tied to the existing set of institutions. To exact reforms, the shogun had to be overthrown, and he was. The situation was similar in China, but the different initial political institutions made it much harder to overthrow the emperor, something that happened only in 1911. Instead of reforming institutions, the Chinese tried to match the British militarily by importing modern weapons. The Japanese built their own armaments industry.

As a consequence of these initial differences, each country responded differently to the challenges of the nineteenth century, and Japan and China diverged dramatically in the face of the critical juncture created by the Industrial Revolution. While Japanese institutions were being transformed and the economy was embarking on a path of rapid growth, in China forces pushing for institutional change were not strong enough, and extractive institutions persisted largely unabated until they would take a turn for the worse with Mao's communist revolution in 1949.

ROOTS OF WORLD INEQUALITY

This and the previous three chapters have told the story of how inclusive economic and political institutions emerged in England to make the Industrial Revolution possible, and why certain countries benefited from the Industrial Revolution and embarked on the path to growth, while others did not or, in fact, steadfastly refused to allow even the beginning of industrialization. Whether a country did embark on industrialization was largely a function of its institutions. The United States, which underwent a transformation similar to the English Glorious Revolution, had already developed its own brand of inclusive political and economic institutions by the end of the eighteenth century. It would thus become the first nation to exploit the new technologies coming from the British Isles, and would soon surpass Britain and become the forerunner of industrialization and technological change. Australia followed a similar path to inclusive institutions, even if somewhat later and somewhat less noticed. Its citizens, just like those in England and the United States, had to fight to obtain inclusive institutions. Once these were in place, Australia would launch its own process of economic growth. Australia and the United States could industrialize and grow rapidly because their relatively inclusive institutions would not block new technologies, innovation, or creative destruction.

Not so in most of the other European colonies. Their dynamics would be quite the opposite of those in Australia and the United States. Lack of a native population or resources to be extracted made colonialism in Australia and the United States a very different sort of affair, even if their citizens had to fight hard for their political rights and for inclusive institutions. In the Moluccas as in the many other places Europeans colonized in Asia, in the Caribbean, and in South America, citizens had little chance of winning such a fight. In these places, European colonists imposed a new brand of extractive institutions, or took over whatever extractive institutions they found, in order to be able to extract valuable resources, ranging from spices and sugar to silver and gold. In many of these places, they put in motion a set of institutional changes that would make the emergence of inclusive institutions very unlikely. In some of them they explicitly stamped out whatever burgeoning industry or inclusive economic institutions existed. Most of these places would be in no situation to benefit from industrialization in the nineteenth century or even in the twentieth.

The dynamics in the rest of Europe were also quite different from those in Australia and the United States. As the Industrial Revolution in Britain was gathering speed at the end of the eighteenth century, most European countries were ruled by absolutist regimes, controlled by monarchs and by aristocracies whose major source of income was from their landholdings or from trading privileges they enjoyed thanks to prohibitive entry barriers. The creative destruction that would be wrought by the process of industrialization would erode the leaders' trading profits and take resources and labor away from their lands. The aristocracies would be economic losers from industrialization. More important, they would also be political losers, as the process of industrialization would undoubtedly create instability and political challenges to their monopoly of political power.

But the institutional transitions in Britain and the Industrial Revolution created new opportunities and challenges for European states. Though there was absolutism in Western Europe, the region had also shared much of the institutional drift that had impacted Britain in the previous millennium. But the situation was very different in Eastern Europe, the Ottoman Empire, and China. These differences mattered for the dissemination of industrialization. Just like the Black Death or the rise of Atlantic trade, the critical juncture created by industrialization intensified the ever-present conflict over institutions in many European nations. A major factor was the French Revolution of 1789. The end of absolutism in France opened the way for inclusive institutions, and the French ultimately embarked on industrialization and rapid economic growth. The French Revolution in fact did more than that. It exported its institutions by invading and forcibly reforming the extractive institutions of several neighboring countries. It thus opened the way to industrialization not only in France, but in Belgium, the Netherlands, Switzerland, and parts of Germany and Italy. Farther east the reaction was similar to that after the Black Death, when, instead of crumbling, feudalism intensified. Austria-Hungary, Russia, and the Ottoman Empire fell even further behind economically, but their absolutist monarchies managed to stay in place until the First World War.

Elsewhere in the world, absolutism was as resilient as in Eastern Europe. This was particularly true in China, where the Ming-Qing transition led to a state committed to building a stable agrarian society and hostile to international trade. But there were also institutional differences that mattered in Asia. If China reacted to the Industrial Revolution as Eastern Europe did, Japan reacted in the same way as Western Europe. Just as in France, it took a revolution to change the system, this time one led by the renegade lords of the Satsuma, Chōshū, Tosa, and Hizen domains. These lords overthrew the shogun, created the Meiji Restoration, and moved Japan onto the path of institutional reforms and economic growth.

We also saw that absolutism was resilient in isolated Ethiopia. Elsewhere on the continent the very same force of international trade that helped to transform English institutions in the seventeenth century locked large parts of western and central Africa into highly extractive institutions via the slave trade. This destroyed societies in some places and led to the creation of extractive slaving states in others.

The institutional dynamics we have described ultimately determined which countries took advantage of the major opportunities present in the nineteenth century onward and which ones failed to do so. The roots of the world inequality we observe today can be found in this divergence. With a few exceptions, the rich countries of today are those that embarked on the process of industrialization and technological change starting in the nineteenth century, and the poor ones are those that did not.

11.

THE VIRTUOUS CIRCLE

THE BLACK ACT

WINDSOR CASTLE, located just west of London, is one of the great royal residencies of England. In the early eighteenth century, the castle was surrounded by a great forest, full of deer, though little of this remains today. One of the keepers of the forest in 1722, Baptist Nunn, was locked in to a violent conflict. On June 27 he recorded,

> Blacks came in the night shot at me 3 times 2 bullets
> into my chamber window and [I] agreed to pay them
> 5 guineas at Crowthorne on the 30th.

Another entry in Nunn's diary read, "A fresh surprise. One appeared disguised with a message of destruction."

Who were these mysterious "Blacks" making threats, shooting at Nunn, and demanding money? The Blacks were groups of local men who had their faces "blacked" to conceal their appearance at night. They appeared widely across southern England in this period, killing and maiming deer and other animals, burning down haystacks and barns, and destroying fences and fish ponds. On the surface it was sheer lawlessness, but it wasn't. Illegal hunting (poaching) deer in lands owned by the king or other members of the aristocracy had been going on for a long time. In the 1640s, during the Civil War, the entire population of deer at Windsor Castle was killed. After the Restoration in 1660, when Charles II came to the throne, the deer park was restocked. But the Blacks were not just poaching deer to eat; they also engaged in wanton destruction. To what end?

A crucial building block of the Glorious Revolution of 1688 was the pluralistic nature of interests represented in Parliament. None of the merchants, industrialists, gentry, or aristocracy allied with William of Orange and then with the Hanoverian monarchs, who succeeded Queen Anne in 1714, were strong enough to impose their will unilaterally.

Attempts at restoring the Stuart monarchy continued throughout much of the eighteenth century. After James II's death in 1701, his son, James Francis Edward Stuart, the "Old Pretender," was recognized as the lawful heir to the English Crown by France, Spain, the pope, and supporters of the Stuart monarchy in England and Scotland, the so-called Jacobites. In 1708 the Old Pretender attempted to take back the throne with support of French troops, but was unsuccessful. In the ensuing decades there would be several Jacobite revolts, including major ones in 1715 and 1719. In 1745–46, the Old Pretender's son, Charles Edward Stuart, the "Young Pretender," made an attempt to take back the throne, but his forces were defeated by the British army.

The Whig political party, which as we saw (pages 210–211) was founded in the 1670s to represent the new mercantile and economic interests, was the main organization behind the Glorious Revolution, and the Whigs dominated Parliament from 1714 to 1760. Once in power, they were tempted to use their newly found position to prey on the rights of others, to have their cake and eat it, too. They were no different from the Stuart kings, but their power was far from absolute. It was constrained both by competing groups in Parliament, particularly the Tory Party which had formed to oppose the Whigs, and by the very institutions that they had fought to introduce to strengthen Parliament and to prevent the emergence of a new absolutism and the return of the Stuarts. The pluralistic nature of society that emerged from the Glorious Revolution also meant that the population at large, even those without formal representation in Parliament, had been empowered, and "blacking" was precisely a response by the common people to perceptions that the Whigs were exploiting their position.

The case of William Cadogan, a successful general in the War of the Spanish Succession between 1701 and 1714 and in the suppression of the Jacobite revolts, illustrates the sort of encroachment of common people's rights by the Whigs that led to blacking. George I made Cadogan a baron in 1716 and then an earl in 1718. He was also an influential member of the Regency Council of Lords Justices, which presided over major affairs of state, and he served as the acting commander in chief. He bought a large property of about a thousand acres at Caversham, about twenty miles west of Windsor. There he built a grand house and ornate gardens and laid out a 240-acre deer park. Yet this property was consolidated by encroaching on the rights of those around the estate. People were evicted, and their traditional rights to graze animals and collect peat and firewood were abrogated. Cadogan faced the wrath of the Blacks. On January 1, 1722, and again in July, the park was raided by mounted and armed Blacks. The first attack killed sixteen deer. Earl Cadogan was not alone. The estates of many notable landowners and politicians were also raided by the Blacks.

The Whig government was not going to take this lying down. In May 1723, Parliament passed the Black Act, which created an extraordinary fifty new offenses that were punishable by hanging. The Black Act made it a crime not only to carry weapons but to have a blackened face. The law in fact was soon amended to make blacking punishable by hanging. The Whig elites went about implementing the law with gusto. Baptist Nunn set up a network of informers in Windsor Forest to discover the identity of the Blacks. Soon several were arrested. The transition from arrest to hanging ought to have been a straightforward affair. After all, the Black Act had already been enacted, the Whigs were in charge of Parliament, Parliament was in charge of the country, and the Blacks were acting directly contrary to the interests of some powerful Whigs. Even Sir Robert Walpole, secretary of state, then prime minister—and like Cadogan, another influential member of the Regency Council of the Lords Justices—was involved. He had a vested interest in Richmond Park in southwest London, which had been created out of common land by Charles I. This park also encroached upon the traditional rights of local resi-

dents to graze their animals, hunt hares and rabbits, and collect firewood. But the ending of these rights appears to have been rather
laxly enforced, and grazing and hunting continued, until Walpole arranged for his son to become the park ranger. At this time, the park
was closed off, a new wall was constructed, and man traps were in-
stalled. Walpole liked hunting deer, and he had a lodge built for himself at Houghton, within the park. The animosity of local Blacks was
soon ignited.

On November 10, 1724, a local resident outside the park, John
Huntridge, was accused of aiding deer stealers and abetting known
Blacks, both crimes punishable by hanging. The prosecution of Hunt-
ridge came right from the top, initiated by the Regency Council of Lords
Justices, which Walpole and Cadogan dominated. Walpole went so far
as to extract evidence himself as to Huntridge's guilt from an informant,
Richard Blackburn. Conviction ought to have been a foregone conclu-
sion, but it wasn't. After a trial of eight or nine hours, the jury found
Huntridge innocent, partly on procedural grounds, since there were irregularities with the way the evidence had been collected.

Not all Blacks or those who sympathized with them were as lucky
as Huntridge. Though some others were also acquitted or had their
convictions commuted, many were hanged or transported to the
penal colony of choice at the time, North America; the law in fact
stayed on the statute books until it was repealed in 1824. Yet Huntridge's victory is remarkable. The jury was made up not of Huntridge's peers, but of major landowners and gentry, who ought to have
sympathized with Walpole. But this was no longer the seventeenth
century, where the Court of Star Chamber would simply follow the
wishes of Stuart monarchs and act as an open tool of repression
against their opponents, and where kings could remove judges whose
decisions they did not like. Now the Whigs also had to abide by the
rule of law, the principle that laws should not be applied selectively
or arbitrarily and that nobody is above the law.

THE EVENTS SURROUNDING the Black Act would show that the
Glorious Revolution had created the rule of law, and that this notion

was stronger in England and Britain, and the elites were far more constrained by it than they themselves imagined. Notably, the rule of law is not the same as rule by law. Even if the Whigs could pass a harsh, repressive law to quash obstacles from common people, they had to contend with additional constraints because of the rule of law. Their law violated the rights that the Glorious Revolution and the changes in political institutions that followed from it had already established for everybody by tearing down the "divine" rights of kings and the privileges of elites. The rule of law then implied that both elites and nonelites alike would resist its implementation.

The rule of law is a very strange concept when you think about it in historical perspective. Why should laws be applied equally to all? If the king and the aristocracy have political power and the rest don't, it's only natural that whatever is fair game for the king and the aristocracy should be banned and punishable for the rest. Indeed, the rule of law is not imaginable under absolutist political institutions. It is a creation of pluralist political institutions and of the broad coalitions that support such pluralism. It's only when many individuals and groups have a say in decisions, and the political power to have a seat at the table, that the idea that they should all be treated fairly starts making sense. By the early eighteenth century, Britain was becoming sufficiently pluralistic, and the Whig elites would discover that, as enshrined in the notion of the rule of law, laws and institutions would constrain them, too.

But why did the Whigs and parliamentarians abide by such restraints? Why didn't they use their control over Parliament and the state to force an uncompromising implementation of the Black Act and overturn the courts when the decisions didn't go their way? The answer reveals much about the nature of the Glorious Revolution—why it didn't just replace an old absolutism with a new version—the link between pluralism and the rule of law, and the dynamics of virtuous circles. As we saw in chapter 7, the Glorious Revolution was not the overthrow of one elite by another, but a revolution against absolutism by a broad coalition made up of the gentry, merchants, and manufacturers as well as groupings of Whigs and Tories. The emergence of pluralist political institutions was a consequence of this revolution. The rule of law also emerged as a by-product of this process. With many parties at the table sharing power, it was natural to have laws and constraints apply to all of them, lest one party start amassing too much power and ultimately undermine the very foundations of pluralism. Thus the notion that there were limits and restraints on rulers, the essence of the rule of law, was part of the logic of pluralism engendered by the broad coalition that made up the opposition to Stuart absolutism.

In this light, it should be no surprise that the principle of the rule of law, coupled with the notion that monarchs did not have divine rights, was in fact a key argument against Stuart absolutism. As the British historian E. P. Thompson put it, in the struggle against the Stuart monarchs:

> immense efforts were made . . . to project the image of a ruling class which was itself subject to the rule of law, and whose legitimacy rested upon the equity and universality of those legal forms. And the rulers were, in serious senses, whether willingly or unwillingly, the prisoners of their own rhetoric; they played games of power according to rules which suited them, but they could not break those rules or the whole game would be thrown away.

Throwing the game away would destabilize the system and open the way for absolutism by a subset of the broad coalition or even risk the return of the Stuarts. In Thompson's words, what inhibited Parliament from creating a new absolutism was that

> take away law, and the royal prerogative . . . might flood back upon their properties and lives.

Moreover,

> it was inherent in the very nature of the medium which they [those aristocrats, merchants etc. fighting the

Crown] had selected for their own self-defense that it
could not be reserved for the exclusive use only of
their own class. The law, in its forms and traditions,
entailed principles of equity and universality which . . .
had to be extended to all sorts and degrees of men.

Once in place, the notion of the rule of law not only kept absolutism at bay but also created a type of virtuous circle: if the laws applied equally to everybody, then no individual or group, not even
Cadogan or Walpole, could rise above the law, and common people
accused of encroaching on private property still had the right to a fair
trial.

WE SAW HOW INCLUSIVE economic and political institutions emerge.
But why do they persist over time? The history of the Black Act and
the limits to its implementation illustrate the virtuous circle, a powerful process of positive feedback that preserves these institutions in the
face of attempts at undermining them and, in fact, sets in motion
forces that lead to greater inclusiveness. The logic of virtuous circles
stems partly from the fact that inclusive institutions are based on constraints on the exercise of power and on a pluralistic distribution of
political power in society, enshrined in the rule of law. The ability of
a subset to impose its will on others without any constraints, even if
those others are ordinary citizens, as Huntridge was, threatens this
very balance. If it were temporarily suspended in the case of the peasants protesting against elites encroaching on their communal lands,
what was there to guarantee that it would not be suspended again?
And the next time it was suspended, what would prevent the Crown
and aristocracy from taking back what the merchants, businessmen, and the gentry had gained in the intervening half century? In
fact, the next time it was suspended, perhaps the entire project of
pluralism would come crumbling down, because a narrow set of interests would take control at the expense of the broad coalition. The
political system would not risk this. But this made pluralism, and the
rule of law that it implied, persistent features of British political insti-

tutions. And we will see that once pluralism and the rule of law were established, there would be demand for even greater pluralism and greater participation in the political process.

The virtuous circle arises not only from the inherent logic of pluralism and the rule of law, but also because inclusive political institutions tend to support inclusive economic institutions. This then leads to a more equal distribution of income, empowering a broad segment of society and making the political playing field even more level. This limits what one can achieve by usurping political power and reduces the incentives to re-create extractive political institutions. These factors were important in the emergence of truly democratic political institutions in Britain.

Pluralism also creates a more open system and allows independent media to flourish, making it easier for groups that have an interest in the continuation of inclusive institutions to become aware and organize against threats to these institutions. It is highly significant that the English state stopped censoring the media after 1688. The media played a similarly important role in empowering the population at large and in the continuation of the virtuous circle of institutional development in the United States, as we will see in this chapter.

While the virtuous circle creates a tendency for inclusive institutions to persist, it is neither inevitable nor irreversible. Both in Britain and the United States, inclusive economic and political institutions were subject to many challenges. In 1745 the Young Pretender got all the way to Derby, a mere hundred miles from London, with an army to unseat the political institutions forged during the Glorious Revolution. But he was defeated. More important than the challenges from without were potential challenges from within that might also have led to the unraveling of inclusive institutions. As we saw in the context of the Peterloo Massacre in Manchester in 1819 (page 207), and as we will see in more detail next, British political elites thought of using repression to avoid having to further open the political system, but they pulled back from the brink. Similarly, inclusive economic and political institutions in the United States faced serious challenges, which could have conceivably succeeded, but didn't. And of course it was not preordained that these challenges should be defeated. It is due to not only the virtuous circle but also to the realization of the contingent path of history that British and U.S. inclusive institutions survived and became substantially stronger over time.

THE SLOW MARCH OF DEMOCRACY

The response to the Black Act showed ordinary British people that they had more rights than they previously realized. They could defend their traditional rights and economic interests in the courts and in Parliament through the use of petitions and lobbying. But this pluralism had not yet delivered effective democracy. Most adult men could not vote; neither could women; and there were many inequities in the existing democratic structures. All this was to change. The virtuous circle of inclusive institutions not only preserves what has already been achieved but also opens the door to greater inclusiveness. The odds were against the British elite of the eighteenth century maintaining their grip on political power without serious challenges. This elite had come to power by challenging the divine right of kings and opening the door to participation by the people in politics, but then they gave this right only to a small minority. It was only a matter of time until more and more of the population demanded the right to participate in the political process. And in the years leading up to 1831, they did.

The first three decades of the nineteenth century witnessed increasing social unrest in Britain, mostly in response to increasing economic inequities and demands from the disenfranchised masses for greater political representation. The Luddite Riots of 1811–1816, where workers fought against the introduction of new technologies they believed would reduce their wages, were followed by riots explicitly demanding political rights, the Spa Fields Riots of 1816 in London and the Peterloo Massacre of 1819 in Manchester. In the Swing Riots of 1830, agricultural workers protested against falling living standards as well as the introduction of new technology. Meanwhile, in Paris, the July Revolution of 1830 exploded. A consensus among elites was starting to form that the discontent was reaching the boiling point, and the only way to defuse social unrest, and turn back a revolution, was by meeting the demands of the masses and undertaking parliamentary reform.

It was no surprise then that the 1831 election was mostly about a single issue: political reform. The Whigs, almost one hundred years after Sir Robert Walpole, were much more responsive to the wishes of the common man and campaigned to extend voting rights. But this meant only a small increase in the electorate. Universal suffrage, even only for men, was not on the table. The Whigs won the election, and their leader, Earl Grey, became the prime minister. Earl Grey was no radical—far from it. He and the Whigs pushed for reform not because they thought a broader voting franchise was more just or because they wanted to share power. British democracy was not given by the elite. It was largely taken by the masses, who were empowered by the political processes that had been ongoing in England and the rest of Britain for the last several centuries. They had become emboldened by the changes in the nature of political institutions unleashed by the Glorious Revolution. Reforms were granted because the elite thought that reform was the only way to secure the continuation of their rule, albeit in a somewhat lessened form. Earl Grey, in his famous speech to Parliament in favor of political reform, said this very clearly:

> There is no-one more decided against annual Parliaments, universal suffrage and the ballot, than I am. My object is not to favour, but to put an end to such hopes and projects . . . The principle of my reform is, to prevent the necessity of revolution . . . reforming to preserve and not to overthrow.

The masses did not just want the vote for its own sake but to have a seat at the table to be able to defend their interests. This was well understood by the Chartist movement, which led the campaign for universal suffrage after 1838, taking its name from its adoption of the People's Charter, named to evoke a parallel with the Magna Carta. Chartist J. R. Stephens articulated why universal suffrage, and the vote for all citizens, was key for the masses:

The question of universal suffrage . . . is a knife and
fork question, a bread and cheese question . . . by universal suffrage I mean to say that every working man
in the land has a right to a good coat on his back, a
good hat on his head, a good roof for the shelter of his
household, a good dinner upon his table.

Stephens had well understood that universal suffrage was the most
durable way of empowering the British masses further and guarantee-
ing a coat, a hat, a roof, and a good dinner for the working man.

Ultimately, Earl Grey was successful both in ensuring the passage
of the First Reform Act and in defusing the revolutionary tides without
taking any major strides toward universal mass suffrage. The 1832
reforms were modest, only doubling the voting franchise from 8 percent to about 16 percent of the adult male population (from about 2
to 4 percent of all the population). They also got rid of rotten boroughs and gave independent representation to the new industrializing cities such as Manchester, Leeds, and Sheffield. But this still left
many issues unresolved. Hence there were soon further demands for
greater voting rights and further social unrest. In response, further
reform would follow.

Why did the British elites give in to the demands? Why did Earl
Grey feel that partial—indeed, very partial—reform was the only way
to preserve the system? Why did they have to put up with the lesser
of the two evils, reform or revolution, rather than maintaining their
power without any reform? Couldn't they just have done what the
Spanish conquistadors did in South America, what Austria-Hungarian
and Russian monarchs would do in the next several decades when
the demands for reform reached those lands, and what the British
themselves did in the Caribbean and in India: use force to put down
the demands? The answer to this question comes from the virtuous
circle. The economic and political changes that had already taken
place in Britain made using force to repress these demands both unattractive for the elite and increasingly infeasible. As E. P. Thompson
wrote:

> When the struggles of 1790–1832 signalled that this
> equilibrium had changed, the rulers of England were
> faced with alarming alternatives. They could either
> dispense with the rule of law, dismantle their elabo-
> rate constitutional structures, countermand their own
> rhetoric and rule by force; or they could submit to
> their own rules and surrender their hegemony . . . they
> took halting steps in the first direction. But in the end,
> rather than shatter their own self-image and repudiate
> 150 years of constitutional legality, they surrendered
> to the law.

Put differently, the same forces that made the British elite not wish
to tear down the edifice of the rule of law during the Black Act also
made them shun repression and rule by force, which would again risk
the stability of the entire system. If undermining the law in trying to
implement the Black Act would have weakened the system that merchants, businessmen, and the gentry had built in the Glorious Revolution, setting up a repressive dictatorship in 1832 would have entirely
undermined it. In fact, the organizers of the protests for parliamentary
reform were well aware of the importance of the rule of law and its
symbolism to the British political institutions during this period. They
used its rhetoric to bring home this point. One of the first organizations seeking parliamentary reform was called the Hampden Club,
after the member of Parliament who had first resisted Charles I over
the ship money tax, a crucial event leading up to the first major uprising against Stuart absolutism, as we saw in chapter 7.

There was also dynamic positive feedback between inclusive economic and political institutions making such a course of action attractive. Inclusive economic institutions led to the development of
inclusive markets, inducing a more efficient allocation of resources,
greater encouragement to acquire education and skills, and further
innovations in technology. All of these forces were in play in Britain
by 1831. Clamping down on popular demands and undertaking a
coup against inclusive political institutions would also destroy these

gains, and the elites opposing greater democratization and greater inclusiveness might find themselves among those losing their fortunes from this destruction.

Another aspect of this positive feedback is that under inclusive economic and political institutions, controlling power became less central. In Austria-Hungary and in Russia, as we saw in chapter 8, the monarchs and the aristocracy had much to lose from industrialization and reform. In contrast, in Britain at the beginning of the nineteenth century, thanks to the development of inclusive economic institutions, there was much less at stake: there were no serfs, relatively little coercion in the labor market, and few monopolies protected by entry barriers. Clinging to power was thus much less valuable for the British elite.

The logic of the virtuous circle also meant that such repressive steps would be increasingly infeasible, again because of the positive feedback between inclusive economic and political institutions. Inclusive economic institutions lead to a more equitable distribution of resources than extractive institutions. As such, they empower the citizens at large and thus create a more level playing field, even when it comes to the fight for power. This makes it more difficult for a small elite to crush the masses rather than to give in to their demands, or at least to some of them. The British inclusive institutions had also already unleashed the Industrial Revolution, and Britain was highly urbanized. Using repression against an urban, concentrated, and partially organized and empowered group of people would have been much harder than repressing a peasantry or dependent serfs.

The virtuous circle thus brought the First Reform Act to Britain in 1832. But this was just the beginning. There was still a long road to travel toward real democracy, because in 1832 the elite had only offered what they thought they had to and no more. The issue of parliamentary reform was taken up by the Chartist movement, whose People's Charter of 1838 included the clauses

A vote for every man twenty-one years of age, of sound mind, and not undergoing punishment for crime.

The ballot.—To protect the elector in the exercise of his vote.

No property qualification for members of Parliament—thus enabling the constituencies to return the man of their choice, be he rich or poor.

Payment of members, thus enabling an honest trades-man, working man, or other person, to serve a con-stituency, when taken from his business to attend to the interests of the Country.

Equal Constituencies, securing the same amount of repre-sentation for the same number of electors, instead of allowing small constituencies to swamp the votes of large ones.

Annual Parliaments, thus presenting the most effectual check to bribery and intimidation, since though a con-stituency might be bought once in seven years (even with the ballot), no purse could buy a constituency (under a system of universal suffrage) in each ensuing twelve-month; and since members, when elected for a year only, would not be able to defy and betray their constituents as now.

By the "ballot," they meant the secret ballot and the end of open voting, which had facilitated the buying of votes and the coercion of voters.

The Chartist movement organized a series of mass demonstrations, and throughout this period Parliament continually discussed the po-tential for further reforms. Though the Chartists disintegrated after 1848, they were followed by the National Reform Union, founded in 1864, and the Reform League, which was founded in 1865. In July 1866, major pro-reform riots in Hyde Park brought reform right to the top of the political agenda once more. This pressure bore dividends in the form of the Second Reform Act of 1867, in which the total elec-torate was doubled and working-class voters became the majority in all urban constituencies. Shortly afterward the secret ballot was introduced and moves were made to eliminate corrupt electoral practices such as "treating" (essentially buying votes in exchange for which the voter received a treat, usually money, food, or alcohol). The electorate was doubled again by the Third Reform Act of 1884, when 60 percent of adult males were enfranchised. Following the First World War, the Representation of the People Act of 1918 gave the vote to all adult males over the age of twenty-one, and to women over the age of thirty who were taxpayers or married to taxpayers. Ultimately, all women also received the vote on the same terms as men in 1928. The measures of 1918 were negotiated during the war and reflected a quid pro quo between the government and the working classes, who were needed to fight and produce munitions. The government may also have taken note of the radicalism of the Russian Revolution.

Parallel with the gradual development of more inclusive political institutions was a movement toward even more inclusive economic institutions. One major consequence of the First Reform Act was the repeal of the Corn Laws in 1846. As we saw in chapter 7, the Corn Laws banned the import of grains and cereals, keeping their prices high and ensuring lucrative profits for large landowners. The new parliamentarians from Manchester and Birmingham wanted cheap corn and low wages. They won, and the landed interests suffered a major defeat.

The changes in the electorate and other dimensions of political institutions taking place during the course of the nineteenth century were followed by further reforms. In 1871 the Liberal prime minister Gladstone opened up the civil service to public examination, making it meritocratic, and thus continuing the process of political centralization and the building of state institutions that started during the Tudor period. Liberal and Tory governments during this period introduced a considerable amount of labor market legislation. For example, the Masters and Servants Acts, which allowed employers to use the law to reduce the mobility of their workers, was repealed, changing the nature of labor relations in favor of workers. During 1906–1914, the Liberal Party, under the leadership of H. H. Asquith and David Lloyd George, began to use the state to provide far more public services, including health and unemployment insurance, government-financed pensions, minimum wages, and a commitment to redistributive taxation. As a result of these fiscal changes, taxes as a proportion of national product more than doubled in the last three decades of the nineteenth century, and then doubled again in the first three decades of the twentieth. The tax system also became more "progressive," so that wealthier people bore a heavier burden.

Meanwhile, the education system, which was previously either primarily for the elite, run by religious denominations, or required poor people to pay fees, was made more accessible to the masses; the Education Act of 1870 committed the government to the systematic provision of universal education for the first time. Education became free of charge in 1891. The school-leaving age was set at eleven in 1893. In 1899 it was increased to twelve, and special provisions for the children of needy families were introduced. As a result of these changes, the proportion of ten-year-olds enrolled in school, which stood at a disappointing 40 percent in 1870, increased to 100 percent in 1900. Finally, the Education Act of 1902 led to a large expansion in resources for schools and introduced the grammar schools, which subsequently became the foundation of secondary education in Britain.

In fact, the British example, an illustration of the virtuous circle of inclusive institutions, provides an example of a "gradual virtuous circle." The political changes were unmistakably toward more inclusive political institutions and were the result of demands from empowered masses. But they were also gradual. Every decade another step, sometimes smaller, sometimes larger, was taken toward democracy. There was conflict over each step, and the outcome of each was contingent. But the virtuous circle created forces that reduced the stakes involved in clinging to power. It also spurred the rule of law, making it harder to use force against those who were demanding what these elites had themselves demanded from Stuart monarchs. It became less likely that this conflict would turn into an all-out revolution and more likely that it would be resolved in favor of greater inclusiveness. There is great virtue in this sort of gradual change. It is less threatening to the elite than the wholesale overthrow of the system. Each step is small, and it makes sense to give in to a small demand rather than create a major showdown. This partly explains how the Corn Law was repealed without more serious conflict. By 1846 landowners could no longer control legislation in Parliament. This was an outcome of the First Reform Act. However, if in 1832 the expansion of the electorate, the reform of the rotten boroughs, and the repeal of the Corn Laws had all been on the table, landowners would have put up much more resistance. The fact that there were first limited political reforms and that repeal of the Corn Laws came on the agenda only later defused conflict.

Gradual change also prevented ventures into uncharted territories. A violent overthrow of the system means that something entirely new has to be built in place of what has been removed. This was the case with the French Revolution, when the first experiment with democracy led to the Terror and then back to a monarchy twice before finally leading to the French Third Republic in 1870. It was the case in the Russian Revolution, where the desires of many for a more equal system than that of the Russian Empire led to a one-party dictatorship that was much more violent, bloody, and vicious than what it had replaced. Gradual reform was difficult in these societies precisely because they lacked pluralism and were highly extractive. It was the pluralism emerging from the Glorious Revolution, and the rule of law that it introduced, that made gradual change feasible, and desirable, in Britain.

The conservative English commentator Edmund Burke, who steadfastly opposed the French Revolution, wrote in 1790, "It is with infinite caution that any man should venture upon pulling down an edifice, which has answered in any tolerable degree for ages the common purposes of society, or on building it up again without having models and patterns of approved utility before his eyes." Burke was wrong on the big picture. The French Revolution had replaced a rotten edifice and opened the way for inclusive institutions not only in France, but throughout much of Western Europe. But Burke's caution was not entirely off the mark. The gradual process of British political reform, which had started in 1688 and would pick up pace three decades after Burke's death, would be more effective because its gradual nature made it more powerful, harder to resist, and ultimately more durable.

BUSTING TRUSTS

Inclusive institutions in the United States had their roots in the struggles in Virginia, Maryland, and the Carolinas during the colonial period (pages 19–28). These institutions were reinforced by the Constitution of the United States, with its system of constraints and its separation of powers. But the Constitution did not mark the end of the development of inclusive institutions. Just as in Britain, these were strengthened by a process of positive feedback, based on the virtuous circle.

By the middle of the nineteenth century, all white males, though not women or blacks, could vote in the United States. Economic institutions became more inclusive—for example, with the passage of the Homestead Act in 1862 (page 37), which made frontier land available to potential settlers rather than allocating these lands to political elites. But just as in Britain, challenges to inclusive institutions were never entirely absent. The end of the U.S. Civil War initiated a rapid spurt of economic growth in the North. As railways, industry, and commerce expanded, a few people made vast fortunes. Emboldened by their economic success, these men and their companies became increasingly unscrupulous. They were called the Robber Barons because of their hard-nosed business practices aimed at consolidating monopolies and preventing any potential competitor from entering the market or doing business on an equal footing. One of the most notorious of these was Cornelius Vanderbilt, who famously remarked, "What do I care about the Law? Hain't I got the power?"

Another was John D. Rockefeller, who started the Standard Oil Company in 1870. He quickly eliminated rivals in Cleveland and attempted to monopolize the transportation and retailing of oil and oil products. By 1882 he had created a massive monopoly—in the language of the day, a trust. By 1890 Standard Oil controlled 88 percent of the refined oil flows in the United States, and Rockefeller became the world's first billionaire in 1916. Contemporary cartoons depict Standard Oil as an octopus wrapping itself around not just the oil industry but also Capitol Hill.

Almost as infamous was John Pierpont Morgan, the founder of the modern banking conglomerate J.P. Morgan, which later, after many mergers over decades, eventually became JPMorgan Chase. Along with Andrew Carnegie, Morgan founded the U.S. Steel Company in 1901, the first corporation with a capitalized value of more than $1 billion and by far the largest steel corporation in the world. In the 1890s, large trusts began to emerge in nearly every sector of the economy, and many of them controlled more than 70 percent of the market in their sector. These included several household names, such as Du Pont, Eastman Kodak, and International Harvester. Historically the United States, at least the northern and midwestern United States, had relatively competitive markets and had been more egalitarian than other parts of the country, particularly the South. But during this period, competition gave way to monopoly, and wealth inequality rapidly increased.

The pluralistic U.S. political system already empowered a broad segment of society that could stand up against such encroachments. Those who were the victims of the monopolistic practices of the Robber Barons, or who objected to their unscrupulous domination of their industries, began to organize against them. They formed the Populist and then subsequently the Progressive movements.

The Populist movement emerged out of a long-running agrarian crisis, which afflicted the Midwest from the late 1860s onward. The National Grange of the Order of Patrons of Husbandry, known as the Grangers, was founded in 1867 and began to mobilize farmers against unfair and discriminatory business practices. In 1873 and 1874, the Grangers won control of eleven midwestern state legislatures, and rural discontent culminated in the formation of the People's Party in 1892, which got 8.5 percent of the popular vote in the 1892 presidential election. In the next two elections, the Populists fell in behind the two unsuccessful Democratic campaigns by William Jennings Bryan, who made many of their issues his own. Grass-roots opposition to the spread of the trusts had now organized to try to counteract the influence that Rockefeller and other Robber Barons were exerting over national politics.

These political movements slowly began to have an impact on

political attitudes and then on legislation, particularly concerning the role of the state in the regulation of monopoly. The first important piece of legislation was the Interstate Commerce Act of 1887, which created the Interstate Commerce Commission and initiated the development of the federal regulation of industry. This was quickly followed by the Sherman Antitrust Act of 1890. The Sherman Act, which is still a major part of U.S. antitrust regulation, would become the basis for attacks on the Robber Barons' trusts. Major action against the trusts came after the election of presidents committed to reform and to limiting the power of the Robber Barons: Theodore Roosevelt, 1901–1909; William Taft, 1909–1913; and Woodrow Wilson, 1913–1921.

A key political force behind antitrust and the move to impose federal regulation of industry was again the farm vote. Early attempts by individual states in the 1870s to regulate railroads came from farmers' organizations. Indeed, nearly all the fifty-nine petitions that concerned trusts sent to Congress prior to the enactment of the Sherman Act came from farming states and emanated from organizations such as the Farmers' Union, Farmers' Alliance, Farmers' Mutual Benefit Association, and Patrons of Animal Husbandry. Farmers found a collective interest in opposing the monopolistic practices of industry.

From the ashes of the Populists, who seriously declined after throwing their weight behind the Democrats, came the Progressives, a heterogeneous reform movement concerned with many of the same issues. The Progressive movement initially gelled around the figure of Teddy Roosevelt, who was William McKinley's vice president and who assumed the presidency following McKinley's assassination in 1901. Prior to his rise to national office, Roosevelt had been an uncompromising governor of New York and had worked hard to eliminate political corruption and "machine politics." In his first address to Congress, Roosevelt turned his attention to the trusts. He argued that the prosperity of the United States was based on market economy and the ingenuity of businessmen, but at the same time,

> there are real and grave evils . . . and a . . . widespread
> conviction in the minds of the American people that
> the great corporations known as trusts are in certain of

their features and tendencies hurtful to the general welfare. This springs from no spirit of envy or uncharitableness, nor lack of pride in the great industrial achievements that have placed this country at the head of the nations struggling for commercial supremacy. It does not rest upon a lack of intelligent appreciation of the necessity of meeting changing and changed conditions of trade with new methods, nor upon ignorance of the fact that combination of capital in the effort to accomplish great things is necessary when the world's progress demands that great things be done. It is based upon sincere conviction that combination and concentration should be, not prohibited, but supervised and within reasonable limits controlled; and in my judgment this conviction is right.

He continued: "It should be as much the aim of those who seek for social betterment to rid the business world of crimes of cunning as to rid the entire body politic of crimes of violence." His conclusion was that

in the interest of the whole people, the nation should, without interfering with the power of the states in the matter itself, also assume power of supervision and regulation over all corporations doing an interstate business. This is especially true where the corporation derives a portion of its wealth from the existence of some monopolistic element or tendency in its business.

Roosevelt proposed that Congress establish a federal agency with power to investigate the affairs of the great corporations and that, if necessary, a constitutional amendment could be used to create such an agency. By 1902 Roosevelt had used the Sherman Act to break up the Northern Securities Company, affecting the interests of J.P. Morgan, and subsequent suits had been brought against Du Pont, the

American Tobacco Company, and the Standard Oil Company. Roosevelt strengthened the Interstate Commerce Act with the Hepburn Act of 1906, which increased the powers of the Interstate Commerce Commission, particularly allowing it to inspect the financial accounts of railways and extending its authority into new spheres. Roosevelt's successor, William Taft, prosecuted trusts even more assiduously, the high point of this being the breakup of the Standard Oil Company in 1911. Taft also promoted other important reforms, such as the introduction of a federal income tax, which came with the ratification of the Sixteenth Amendment in 1913.

The apogee of Progressive reforms came with the election of Woodrow Wilson in 1912. Wilson noted in his 1913 book, *The New Freedom,* "If monopoly persists, monopoly will always sit at the helm of government. I do not expect to see monopoly restrain itself. If there are men in this country big enough to own the government of the United States, they are going to own it."

Wilson worked to pass the Clayton Antitrust Act in 1914, strengthening the Sherman Act, and he created the Federal Trade Commission, which enforced the Clayton Act. In addition, under the impetus of the investigation of the Pujo Committee, led by Louisiana congressman Arsene Pujo, into the "money trust," the spread of monopoly into the financial industry, Wilson moved to increase regulation of the financial sector. In 1913 he created the Federal Reserve Board, which would regulate monopolistic activities in the financial sector.

The rise of Robber Barons and their monopoly trusts in the late nineteenth and early twentieth centuries underscores that, as we already emphasized in chapter 3, the presence of markets is not by itself a guarantee of inclusive institutions. Markets can be dominated by a few firms, charging exorbitant prices and blocking the entry of more efficient rivals and new technologies. Markets, left to their own devices, can cease to be inclusive, becoming increasingly dominated by the economically and politically powerful. Inclusive economic institutions require not just markets, but inclusive markets that create a level playing field and economic opportunities for the majority of the people. Widespread monopoly, backed by the political power of the elite, contradicts this. But the reaction to the monopoly trusts also illustrates that when political institutions are inclusive, they create a countervailing force against movements away from inclusive markets. This is the virtuous circle in action. Inclusive economic institutions provide foundations upon which inclusive political institutions can flourish, while inclusive political institutions restrict deviations away from inclusive economic institutions. Trust busting in the United States, in contrast to what we have seen in Mexico (pages 38–40), illustrates this facet of the virtuous circle. While there is no political body in Mexico restricting Carlos Slim's monopoly, the Sherman and Clayton Acts have been used repeatedly in the United States over the past century to restrict trusts, monopolies, and cartels, and to ensure that markets remain inclusive.

The U.S. experience in the first half of the twentieth century also emphasizes the important role of free media in empowering broad segments of society and thus in the virtuous circle. In 1906 Roosevelt coined the term *muckraker,* based on a literary character, the man with the muckrake in Bunyan's *Pilgrim's Progress,* to describe what he regarded as intrusive journalism. The term stuck and came to symbolize journalists who were intrusively, but also effectively, exposing the excesses of Robber Barons as well as corruption in local and federal politics. Perhaps the most famous muckraker was Ida Tarbell, whose 1904 book, *History of the Standard Oil Company,* played a key role in moving public opinion against Rockefeller and his business interests, culminating in the breakup of Standard Oil in 1911. Another key muckraker was lawyer and author Louis Brandeis, who would later be named Supreme Court justice by President Wilson. Brandeis outlined a series of financial scandals in his book *Other People's Money and How Bankers Use It,* and was highly influential on the Pujo Committee. The newspaper magnate William Randolph Hearst also played a salient role as muckraker. His serialization in his magazine *The Cosmopolitan* in 1906 of articles by David Graham Phillips, called "The Treason of the Senate," galvanized the campaign to introduce direct elections for the Senate, another key Progressive reform that happened with the enactment of the Seventeenth Amendment to the U.S. constitution in 1913.

The muckrakers played a major role in inducing politicians to take action against the trusts. The Robber Barons hated the muckrakers, but the political institutions of the United States made it impossible for them to stamp out and silence them. Inclusive political institutions allow a free media to flourish, and a free media, in turn, makes it more likely that threats against inclusive economic and political institutions will be widely known and resisted. In contrast, such freedom is impossible under extractive political institutions, under absolutism, or under dictatorships, which helps extractive regimes to prevent serious opposition from forming in the first place. The information that the free media provided was clearly key during the first half of the twentieth century in the United States. Without this information, the U.S. public would not have known the true extent of the power and abuses of the Robber Barons and would not have mobilized against their trusts.

PACKING THE COURT

Franklin D. Roosevelt, the Democratic Party candidate and cousin of Teddy Roosevelt, was elected president in 1932 in the midst of the Great Depression. He came to power with a popular mandate to implement an ambitious set of policies for combating the Great Depression. At the time of his inauguration in early 1933, one-quarter of the labor force was unemployed, with many thrown into poverty. Industrial production had fallen by over half since the Depression hit in 1929, and investment had collapsed. The policies Roosevelt proposed to counteract this situation were collectively known as the New Deal. Roosevelt had won a solid victory, with 57 percent of the popular vote, and the Democratic Party had majorities in both the Congress and Senate, enough to pass New Deal legislation. However, some of the legislation raised constitutional issues and ended up in the Supreme Court, where Roosevelt's electoral mandate cut much less ice.

One of the key pillars of the New Deal was the National Industrial Recovery Act. Title I focused on industrial recovery. President Roosevelt and his team believed that restraining industrial competition, giving workers greater rights to form trade unions, and regulating working standards were crucial to the recovery effort. Title II established the Public Works Administration, whose infrastructure projects include such landmarks as the Thirtieth Street railroad station in

Philadelphia, the Triborough Bridge, the Grand Coulee Dam, and the Overseas Highway connecting Key West, Florida, with the mainland. President Roosevelt signed the bill into law on June 16, 1933, and the National Industrial Recovery Act was put into operation. However, it immediately faced challenges in the courts. On May 27, 1935, the Supreme Court unanimously ruled that Title I of the act was unconstitutional. Their verdict noted solemnly, "Extraordinary conditions may call for extraordinary remedies. But . . . extraordinary conditions do not create or enlarge constitutional power."

Before the Court's ruling came in, Roosevelt had moved to the next step of his agenda and had signed the Social Security Act, which introduced the modern welfare state into the United States: pensions at retirement, unemployment benefits, aid to families with dependent children, and some public health care and disability benefits. He also signed the National Labor Relations Act, which further strengthened the rights of workers to organize unions, engage in collective bargaining, and conduct strikes against their employers. These measures also faced challenges in the Supreme Court. As these were making their way through the judiciary, Roosevelt was reelected in 1936 with a strong mandate, receiving 61 percent of the popular vote.

With his popularity at record highs, Roosevelt had no intention of letting the Supreme Court derail more of his policy agenda. He laid out his plans in one of his regular Fireside Chats, which was broadcast live on the radio on March 9, 1937. He started by pointing out that in his first term, much-needed policies had only cleared the Supreme Court by a whisker. He went on:

> I am reminded of that evening in March, four years ago, when I made my first radio report to you. We were then in the midst of the great banking crisis. Soon after, with the authority of the Congress, we asked the nation to turn over all of its privately held gold, dollar for dollar, to the government of the United States. Today's recovery proves how right that policy was. But when, almost two years later, it came before the Supreme Court its constitutionality was upheld

only by a five-to-four vote. The change of one vote would have thrown all the affairs of this great nation back into hopeless chaos. In effect, four justices ruled that the right under a private contract to exact a pound of flesh was more sacred than the main objectives of the Constitution to establish an enduring nation.

Obviously, this should not be risked again. Roosevelt continued:

Last Thursday I described the American form of government as a three-horse team provided by the Constitution to the American people so that their field might be plowed. The three horses are, of course, the three branches of government—the Congress, the executive, and the courts. Two of the horses, the Congress and the executive, are pulling in unison today; the third is not.

Roosevelt then pointed out that the U.S. Constitution had not actually endowed the Supreme Court with the right to challenge the constitutionality of legislation, but that it had assumed this role in 1803. At the time, Justice Bushrod Washington had stipulated that the Supreme Court should "presume in favor of [a law's] validity until its violation of the Constitution is proved beyond all reasonable doubt." Roosevelt then charged:

In the last four years the sound rule of giving statutes the benefit of all reasonable doubt has been cast aside. The Court has been acting not as a judicial body, but as a policymaking body.

Roosevelt claimed that he had an electoral mandate to change this situation and that "after consideration of what reform to propose the only method which was clearly constitutional . . . was to infuse new blood into all our courts." He also argued that the Supreme Court judges were overworked, and the load was just too much for the older justices—who happened to be the ones striking down his legislation. He then proposed that all judges should face compulsory retirement at the age of seventy and that he should be allowed to appoint up to six new justices. This plan, which Roosevelt presented as the Judiciary Reorganization Bill, would have sufficed to remove the justices who had been appointed earlier by more conservative administrations and who had most strenuously opposed the New Deal.

Though Roosevelt skillfully tried to win popular support for the measure, opinion polls suggested that only about 40 percent of the population was in favor of the plan. Louis Brandeis was now a Supreme Court justice. Though Brandeis sympathized with much of Roosevelt's legislation, he spoke against the president's attempts to erode the power of the Supreme Court and his allegations that the justices were overworked. Roosevelt's Democratic Party had large majorities in both houses of Congress. But the House of Representatives more or less refused to deal with Roosevelt's bill. Roosevelt then tried the Senate. The bill was sent to the Senate Judiciary Committee, which then held highly contentious meetings, soliciting various opinions on the bill. They ultimately sent it back to the Senate floor with a negative report, arguing that the bill was a "needless, futile and utterly dangerous abandonment of constitutional principle . . . without precedent or justification." The Senate voted 70 to 20 to send it back to committee to be rewritten. All the "court packing" elements were stripped away. Roosevelt would be unable to remove the constraints placed on his power by the Supreme Court. Even though Roosevelt's powers remained constrained, there were compromises, and the Social Security and the National Labor Relations Acts were both ruled constitutional by the Court.

More important than the fate of these two acts was the general lesson from this episode. Inclusive political institutions not only check major deviations from inclusive economic institutions, but they also resist attempts to undermine their own continuation. It was in the immediate interests of the Democratic Congress and Senate to pack the court and ensure that all New Deal legislation survived. But in the same way that British political elites in the early eighteenth century understood that suspending the rule of law would endanger the gains they had wrested from the monarchy, congressmen and senators understood that if the president could undermine the independence of the judiciary, then this would undermine the balance of power in the system that protected them from the president and ensured the continuity of pluralistic political institutions.

Perhaps Roosevelt would have decided next that obtaining legislative majorities took too much compromise and time and that he would instead rule by decree, totally undermining pluralism and the U.S. political system. Congress certainly would not have approved this, but then Roosevelt could have appealed to the nation, asserting that Congress was impeding the necessary measures to fight the Depression. He could have used the police to close Congress. Sound far-fetched? This is exactly what happened in Peru and Venezuela in the 1990s. Presidents Fujimori and Chávez appealed to their popular mandate to close uncooperative congresses and subsequently rewrote their constitutions to massively strengthen the powers of the president. The fear of this slippery slope by those sharing power under pluralistic political institutions is exactly what stopped Walpole from fixing British courts in the 1720s, and it is what stopped the U.S. Congress from backing Roosevelt's court-packing plan. Roosevelt had encountered the power of virtuous circles.

But this logic does not always play out, particularly in societies that may have some inclusive features but that are broadly extractive. We have already seen these dynamics in Rome and Venice. Another illustration comes from comparing Roosevelt's failed attempt to pack the Court with similar efforts in Argentina, where crucially the same struggles took place in the context of predominantly extractive economic and political institutions.

The 1853 constitution of Argentina created a Supreme Court with duties similar to those of the U.S. Supreme Court. An 1887 decision allowed the Argentine court to assume the same role as that of the U.S. Supreme Court in deciding whether specific laws were constitutional. In theory, the Supreme Court could have developed as one of the important elements of inclusive political institutions in Argentina, but the rest of the political and economic system remained highly extractive, and there was neither empowerment of broad segments of society nor pluralism in Argentina. As in the United States, the constitutional role of the Supreme Court would also be challenged in Argentina. In 1946 Juan Domingo Perón was democratically elected president of Argentina. Perón was a former colonel and had first come to national prominence after a military coup in 1943, which had appointed him minister of labor. In this post, he built a political coalition with trade unions and the labor movement, which would be crucial for his presidential bid.

Shortly after Perón's victory, his supporters in the Chamber of Deputies proposed the impeachment of four of the five members of the Court. The charges leveled against the Court were several. One involved unconstitutionally accepting the legality of two military regimes in 1930 and 1943—rather ironic, since Perón had played a key role in the latter coup. The other focused on legislation that the court had struck down, just as its U.S. counterpart had done. In particular, just prior to Perón's election as president, the Court had issued a decision ruling that Perón's new national labor relations board was unconstitutional. Just as Roosevelt heavily criticized the Supreme Court in his 1936 reelection campaign, Perón did the same in his 1946 campaign. Nine months after initiating the impeachment process, the Chamber of Deputies impeached three of the judges, the fourth having already resigned. The Senate approved the motion. Perón then appointed four new justices. The undermining of the Court clearly had the effect of freeing Perón from political constraints. He could now exercise unchecked power, in much the same way the military regimes in Argentina did before and after his presidency. His newly appointed judges, for example, ruled as constitutional the conviction of Ricardo Balbín, the leader of the main opposition party to Perón, the Radical Party, for disrespecting Perón. Perón could effectively rule as a dictator.

Since Perón successfully packed the Court, it has become the norm in Argentina for any new president to handpick his own Supreme Court justices. So a political institution that might have exercised some constraints on the power of the executive is gone. Perón's regime was removed from power by another coup in 1955, and was followed by a long sequence of transitions between military and civilian rule. Both new military and civilian regimes picked their own justices. But picking Supreme Court justices in Argentina was not an activity confined to transitions between military and civilian rule. In 1990 Argentina finally experienced a transition between democratically elected governments—one democratic government followed by another. Yet, by this time democratic governments did not behave much differently from military ones when it came to the Supreme Court. The incoming president was Carlos Saúl Menem of the Perónist Party. The sitting Supreme Court had been appointed after the transition to democracy in 1983 by the Radical Party president Raúl Alfonsín. Since this was a democratic transition, there should have been no reason for Menem to appoint his own court. But in the run-up to the election, Menem had already shown his colors. He continually, though not successfully, tried to encourage (or even intimidate) members of the court to resign. He famously offered Justice Carlos Fayt an ambassadorship. But he was rebuked, and Fayt responded by sending him a copy of his book *Law and Ethics,* with the note "Beware I wrote this" inscribed. Undeterred, within three months of taking office, Menem sent a law to the Chamber of Deputies proposing to expand the Court from five to nine members. One argument was the same Roosevelt used in 1937: the court was overworked. The law quickly passed the Senate and Chamber, and this allowed Menem to name four new judges. He had his majority.

Menem's victory against the Supreme Court set in motion the type of slippery-slope dynamics we mentioned earlier. His next step was to rewrite the constitution to remove the term limit so he could run for president again. After being reelected, Menem moved to rewrite the constitution again, but was stopped not by Argentina political institutions but by factions within his own Perónist Party, who fought back against his personal domination.

Since independence, Argentina has suffered from most of the institutional problems that have plagued Latin America. It has been trapped in a vicious, not a virtuous, circle. As a consequence, positive developments, such as first steps toward the creation of an independent Supreme Court, never gained a foothold. With pluralism, no group wants or dares to overthrow the power of another, for fear that its own power will be subsequently challenged. At the same time, the broad distribution of power makes such an overthrow difficult. A Supreme Court can have power if it receives significant support from broad segments of society willing to push back attempts to vitiate the Court's independence. That has been the case in the United States, but not Argentina. Legislators there were happy to undermine the Court even if they anticipated that this could jeopardize their own position. One reason is that with extractive institutions there is much to gain from overthrowing the Supreme Court, and the potential benefits are worth the risks.

POSITIVE FEEDBACK AND VIRTUOUS CIRCLES

Inclusive economic and political institutions do not emerge by themselves. They are often the outcome of significant conflict between elites resisting economic growth and political change and those wishing to limit the economic and political power of existing elites. Inclusive institutions emerge during critical junctures, such as during the Glorious Revolution in England or the foundation of the Jamestown colony in North America, when a series of factors weaken the hold of the elites in power, make their opponents stronger, and create incentives for the formation of a pluralistic society. The outcome of political conflict is never certain, and even if in hindsight we see many historical events as inevitable, the path of history is contingent. Nevertheless, once in place, inclusive economic and political institutions tend to create a virtuous circle, a process of positive feedback, making it more likely that these institutions will persist and even expand.

The virtuous circle works through several mechanisms. First, the logic of pluralistic political institutions makes usurpation of power by a dictator, a faction within the government, or even a well-meaning president much more difficult, as Franklin Roosevelt discovered when he tried to remove the checks on his power imposed by the Supreme Court, and as Sir Robert Walpole discovered when he attempted to summarily implement the Black Act. In both cases, concentrating power further in the hands of an individual or a narrow group would have started undermining the foundations of pluralistic political institutions, and the true measure of pluralism is precisely its ability to resist such attempts. Pluralism also enshrines the notion of the rule of law, the principle that laws should be applied equally to everybody—something that is naturally impossible under an absolutist monarchy. But the rule of law, in turn, implies that laws cannot simply be used by one group to encroach upon the rights of another. What's more, the principle of the rule of law opens the door for greater participation in the political process and greater inclusivity, as it powerfully introduces the idea that people should be equal not only before the law but also in the political system. This was one of the principles that made it difficult for the British political system to resist the forceful calls for greater democracy throughout the nineteenth century, opening the way to the gradual extension of the franchise to all adults.

Second, as we have seen several times before, inclusive political institutions support and are supported by inclusive economic institutions. This creates another mechanism of the virtuous circle. Inclusive economic institutions remove the most egregious extractive economic relations, such as slavery and serfdom, reduce the importance of monopolies, and create a dynamic economy, all of which reduces the economic benefits that one can secure, at least in the short run, by usurping political power. Because economic institutions had already become sufficiently inclusive in Britain by the eighteenth century, the elite had less to gain by clinging to power and, in fact, much to lose by using widespread repression against those demanding greater democracy. This facet of the virtuous circle made the gradual march of democracy in nineteenth-century Britain both less threatening to the elite and more likely to succeed. This contrasts with the situation in absolutist regimes such as the Austro-Hungarian or Russian empires, where economic institutions were still highly extractive and, in consequence, where calls for greater political inclusion later in the nineteenth century would be met by repression because the elite had too much to lose from sharing power.

Finally, inclusive political institutions allow a free media to flourish, and a free media often provides information about and mobilizes opposition to threats against inclusive institutions, as it did during the last quarter of the nineteenth century and first quarter of the twentieth century, when the increasing economic domination of the Robber Barons was threatening the essence of inclusive economic institutions in the United States.

Though the outcome of the ever-present conflicts continues to be contingent, through these mechanisms the virtuous circle creates a powerful tendency for inclusive institutions to persist, to resist challenges, and to expand as they did in both Britain and the United States. Unfortunately, as we will see in the next chapter, extractive institutions create equally strong forces toward their persistence—the process of the vicious circle.

12.

THE VICIOUS CIRCLE

YOU CAN'T TAKE THE TRAIN
TO BO ANYMORE

ALL OF THE WEST AFRICAN nation of Sierra Leone became a British colony in 1896. The capital city, Freetown, had
originally been founded in the late eighteenth century as a home for
repatriated and freed slaves. But when Freetown became a British
colony, the interior of Sierra Leone was still made up of many small
African kingdoms. Gradually, in the second half of the nineteenth
century, the British extended their rule into the interior through a long
series of treaties with African rulers. On August 31, 1896, the British
government declared the colony a protectorate on the basis of these
treaties. The British identified important rulers and gave them a new
title, paramount chief. In eastern Sierra Leone, for example, in the
modern diamond-mining district of Kono, they encountered Suluku,
a powerful warrior king. King Suluku was made Paramount Chief
Suluku, and the chieftaincy of Sandor was created as an administrative unit in the protectorate.

Though kings such as Suluku had signed treaties with a British
administrator, they had not understood that these treaties would be
interpreted as carte blanche to set up a colony. When the British tried
to levy a hut tax—a tax of five shillings to be raised from every
house—in January 1898, the chiefs rose up in a civil war that became
known as the Hut Tax Rebellion. It started in the north, but was strongest and lasted longer in the south, particularly in Mendeland, dominated by the Mende ethnic group. The Hut Tax Rebellion was soon
defeated, but it warned the British about the challenges of controlling

the Sierra Leonean hinterland. The British had already started to build a railway from Freetown into the interior. Work began in March 1896, and the line reached Songo Town in December 1898, in the midst of the Hut Tax Rebellion. British parliamentary papers from 1904 recorded that:

> In the case of the Sierra Leone Railways the Native Insurrection that broke out in February 1898 had the effect of completely stopping the works and disorganizing the staff for some time. The rebels descended upon the railway, with the result that the entire staff had to be withdrawn to Freetown . . . Rotifunk, now situated upon the railways at 55 miles from Freetown, was at that time completely in the hands of the rebels.

In fact, Rotifunk was not on the planned railway line in 1894. The route was changed after the start of the rebellion, so that instead of going to the northeast, it went south, via Rotifunk and on to Bo, into Mendeland. The British wanted quick access to Mendeland, the heart of the rebellion, and to other potentially disruptive parts of the hinterland if other rebellions were to flare up.

When Sierra Leone became independent in 1961, the British handed power to Sir Milton Margai and his Sierra Leone People's Party (SLPP), which attracted support primarily in the south, particularly Mendeland, and the east. Sir Milton was followed as prime minister by his brother, Sir Albert Margai, in 1964. In 1967 the SLPP narrowly lost a hotly contested election to the opposition, the All People's Congress Party (APC), led by Siaka Stevens. Stevens was a Limba, from the north, and the APC got most of their support from northern ethnic groups, the Limba, the Temne, and the Loko.

Though the railway to the south was initially designed by the British to rule Sierra Leone, by 1967 its role was economic, transporting most of the country's exports: coffee, cocoa, and diamonds. The farmers who grew coffee and cocoa were Mende, and the railway was Mendeland's window to the world. Mendeland had voted hugely for

Albert Margai in the 1967 election. Stevens was much more interested in holding on to power than promoting Mendeland's exports. His reasoning was simple: whatever was good for the Mende was good for the SLPP, and bad for Stevens. So he pulled up the railway line to Mendeland. He then went ahead and sold off the track and rolling stock to make the change as irreversible as possible. Now, as you drive out of Freetown to the east, you pass the dilapidated railway stations of Hastings and Waterloo. There are no more trains to Bo. Of course, Stevens's drastic action fatally damaged some of the most vibrant sectors of Sierra Leone's economy. But like many of Africa's postindependence leaders, when the choice was between consolidating power and encouraging economic growth, Stevens chose consolidating his power, and he never looked back. Today you can't take the train to Bo anymore, because like Tsar Nicholas I, who feared that the railways would bring revolution to Russia, Stevens believed the railways would strengthen his opponents. Like so many other rulers in control of extractive institutions, he was afraid of challenges to his political power and was willing to sacrifice economic growth to thwart those challenges.

Stevens's strategy at first glance contrasts with that of the British. But in fact, there was a significant amount of continuity between British rule and Stevens's regime that illustrates the logic of vicious circles. Stevens ruled Sierra Leone by extracting resources from its people using similar methods. He was still in power in 1985 not because he had been popularly reelected, but because after 1967 he set up a violent dictatorship, killing and harassing his political opponents, particularly the members of the SLPP. He made himself president in 1971, and after 1978, Sierra Leone had only one political party, Stevens's APC. Stevens thus successfully consolidated his power, even if the cost was impoverishing much of the hinterland.

During the colonial period, the British used a system of indirect rule to govern Sierra Leone, as they did with most of their African colonies. At the base of this system were the paramount chiefs, who collected taxes, distributed justice, and kept order. The British dealt with the cocoa and coffee farmers not by isolating them, but by forcing them to sell all their produce to a marketing board developed by the colonial office purportedly to help the farmers. Prices for agricultural commodities fluctuated wildly over time. Cocoa prices might be high one year but low the next. The incomes of farmers fluctuated in tandem. The justification for marketing boards was that they, not the farmers, would absorb the price fluctuations. When world prices were high, the board would pay the farmers in Sierra Leone less than the world price, but when world prices were low, they would do the opposite. It seemed a good idea in principle. The reality was very different, however. The Sierra Leone Produce Marketing Board was set up in 1949. Of course the board needed a source of revenues to function. The natural way to attain these was by paying farmers just a little less than they should have received either in good or bad years. These funds could then be used for overhead expenditures and administration. Soon the little less became a lot less. The colonial state was using the marketing board as a way of heavily taxing farmers.

Many expected the worst practices of colonial rule in sub-Saharan Africa to stop after independence, and the use of marketing boards to excessively tax farmers to come to an end. But neither happened. In fact, the extraction of farmers using marketing boards got much worse. By the mid-1960s, the farmers of palm kernels were getting 56 percent of the world price from the marketing board; cocoa farmers, 48 percent; and coffee farmers, 49 percent. By the time Stevens left office in 1985, resigning to allow his handpicked successor, Joseph Momoh, to become president, these numbers were 37, 19, and 27 percent, respectively. As pitiful as this might sound, it was better than what the farmers were getting during Stevens's reign, which had often been as low as 10 percent—that is, 90 percent of the income of the farmers was extracted by Stevens's government, and not to provide public services, such as roads or education, but to enrich himself and his cronies and to buy political support.

As part of their indirect rule, the British had also stipulated that the office of the paramount chief would be held for life. To be eligible to be a chief, one had to be a member of a recognized "ruling house." The identity of the ruling houses in a chieftaincy developed over time, but it was essentially based on the lineage of the kings in a particular area and of the elite families who signed treaties with the British in

the late nineteenth century. Chiefs were elected, but not democratically. A body called the Tribal Authority, whose members were lesser
village chiefs or were appointed by paramount chiefs, village chiefs,
or the British authorities, decided who would become the paramount
chief. One might have imagined that this colonial institution would
also have been abolished or at least reformed after independence. But
just like the marketing board, it was not, and continued unchanged.
Today paramount chiefs are still in charge of collecting taxes. It is no
longer a hut tax, but its close descendant, a poll tax. In 2005 the Tribal
Authority in Sandor elected a new paramount chief. Only candidates
from the Fasuluku ruling house, which is the only ruling house, could
stand. The victor was Sheku Fasuluku, King Suluku's great-great-
grandson.

The behavior of the marketing boards and the traditional systems
of land ownership go a long way to explain why agricultural productivity is so low in Sierra Leone and much of sub-Saharan Africa. The
political scientist Robert Bates set out in the 1980s to understand why
agriculture was so unproductive in Africa even though according to
textbook economics this ought to have been the most dynamic economic sector. He realized that this had nothing to do with geography
or the sorts of factors discussed in chapter 2 that have been claimed
to make agricultural productivity intrinsically low. Rather, it was
simply because the pricing policies of the marketing boards removed
any incentives for the farmers to invest, use fertilizers, or preserve
the soil.

The reason that the policies of the marketing boards were so un-
favorable to rural interests was that these interests had no political
power. These pricing policies interacted with other fundamental factors making tenure insecure, further undermining investment incentives. In Sierra Leone, paramount chiefs not only provide law and
order and judicial services, and raise taxes, but they are also the "cus-
todians of the land." Though families, clans, and dynasties have user
rights and traditional rights to land; at the end of the day chiefs have
the last say on who farms where. Your property rights to land are only
secure if you are connected to the chief, perhaps from the same ruling family. Land cannot be bought or sold or used as collateral for a

loan, and if you are born outside a chieftaincy, you cannot plant any perennial crop such as coffee, cocoa, or palm for fear that this will allow you to establish "de facto" property rights.

The contrast between the extractive institutions developed by the British in Sierra Leone and the inclusive institutions that developed in other colonies, such as Australia, is illustrated by the way mineral resources were managed. Diamonds were discovered in Kono in eastern Sierra Leone in January 1930. The diamonds were alluvial, that is, not in deep mines. So the primary method of mining them was by panning in rivers. Some social scientists call these "democratic diamonds," because they allow many people to become involved in mining, creating a potentially inclusive opportunity. Not so in Sierra Leone. Happily ignoring the intrinsically democratic nature of panning for diamonds, the British government set up a monopoly for the entire protectorate, called it the Sierra Leone Selection Trust, and granted it to De Beers, the giant South African diamond mining company. In 1936 De Beers was also given the right to create the Diamond Protection Force, a private army that would become larger than that of the colonial government in Sierra Leone. Even so, the widespread availability of the alluvial diamonds made the situation difficult to police. By the 1950s, the Diamond Protection Force was overwhelmed by thousands of illegal diamond miners, a massive source of conflict and chaos. In 1955 the British government opened up some of the diamond fields to licensed diggers outside the Sierra Leone Selection Trust, though the company still kept the richest areas in Yengema and Koidu and Tongo Fields. Things only got worse after independence. In 1970 Siaka Stevens effectively nationalized the Sierra Leone Selection Trust, creating the National Diamond Mining Company (Sierra Leone) Limited, in which the government, effectively meaning Stevens, had a 51 percent stake. This was the opening phase of Stevens's plan to take over diamond mining in the country.

In nineteenth-century Australia it was gold, discovered in 1851 in New South Wales and the newly created state of Victoria, not diamonds, that attracted everyone's attention. Like diamonds in Sierra Leone, the gold was alluvial, and a decision had to be made about how to exploit it. Some, such as James Macarthur, son of John Macarthur, the prominent leader of the Squatters we discussed earlier (pages 278–282), proposed that fences be placed around the mining areas and the monopoly rights auctioned off. They wanted an Australian version of the Sierra Leone Selection Trust. Yet many in Australia wanted free access to the gold mining areas. The inclusive model won, and instead of setting up a monopoly, Australian authorities allowed anyone who paid an annual mining license fee to search and dig for gold. Soon the diggers, as these adventurers came to be known, were a powerful force in Australian politics, particularly in Victoria. They played an important role in pushing forward the agenda of universal suffrage and the secret ballot.

We have already seen two pernicious effects of European expansion and colonial rule in Africa: the introduction of the transatlantic slave trade, which encouraged the development of African political and economic institutions in an extractive direction, and the use of colonial legislation and institutions to eliminate the development of African commercial agriculture that might have competed with Europeans. Slavery was certainly a force in Sierra Leone. At the time of colonization there was no strong centralized state in the interior, just many small, mutually antagonistic kingdoms continually raiding one another and capturing one another's men and women. Slavery was endemic, with possibly 50 percent of the population working as slaves. The disease environment meant that large-scale white settlement was not possible in Sierra Leone, as it was in South Africa. Hence there were no whites competing with the Africans. Moreover, the lack of a mining economy on the scale of Johannesburg meant that, in addition to the lack of demand for African labor from white farms, there was no incentive to create the extractive labor market institutions so characteristic of Apartheid South Africa.

But other mechanisms were also in play. Sierra Leone's cocoa and coffee farmers did not compete with whites, though their incomes were still expropriated via a government monopoly, the marketing board. Sierra Leone also suffered from indirect rule. In many parts of Africa where the British authorities wished to use indirect rule, they found peoples who did not have a system of centralized authority who could be taken over. For example, in eastern Nigeria the Igbo peoples had no chiefs when the British encountered them in the nineteenth century. The British then created chiefs, the warrant chiefs. In Sierra Leone, the British would base indirect rule on existing indigenous institutions and systems of authority.

Nevertheless, regardless of the historical basis for the individuals recognized as paramount chiefs in 1896, indirect rule, and the powers that it invested in paramount chiefs, completely changed the existing politics of Sierra Leone. For one, it introduced a system of social stratification—the ruling houses—where none had existed previously. A hereditary aristocracy replaced a situation that had been much more fluid and where chiefs had required popular support. Instead what emerged was a rigid system with chiefs holding office for life, beholden to their patrons in Freetown or Britain, and far less accountable to the people they ruled. The British were happy to subvert the institutions in other ways, too, for example, by replacing legitimate chiefs with people who were more cooperative. Indeed, the Margai family, which supplied the first two prime ministers of independent Sierra Leone, came to power in the Lower Banta chieftaincy by siding with the British in the Hut Tax Rebellion against the reigning chief, Nyama. Nyama was deposed, and the Margais became chiefs and held the position until 2010.

What is remarkable is the extent of continuity between colonial and independent Sierra Leone. The British created the marketing boards and used them to tax farmers. Postcolonial governments did the same extracting at even higher rates. The British created the system of indirect rule through paramount chiefs. Governments that followed independence didn't reject this colonial institution; rather, they used it to govern the countryside as well. The British set up a diamond monopoly and tried to keep out African miners. Postindependence governments did the same. It is true that the British thought that building railways was a good way to rule Mendeland, while Siaka Stevens thought the opposite. The British could trust their army and knew it could be sent to Mendeland if a rebellion arose. Stevens, on the other hand, could not do so. As in many other African nations, a strong army would have become a threat to Stevens's rule. It was for this reason that he emasculated the army, cutting it down and privatizing violence through specially created paramilitary units loyal only to him, and in the process, he accelerated the decline of the little state authority that existed in Sierra Leone. Instead of the army, first came the Internal Security Unit, the ISU, which Sierra Leone's long-suffering people knew as "I Shoot U." Then came the Special Security Division, the SSD, which the people knew as "Siaka Stevens's Dogs." In the end, the absence of an army supporting the regime would also be its undoing. It was a group of only thirty soldiers, led by Captain Valentine Strasser, that pitched the APC regime from power on April 29, 1992.

Sierra Leone's development, or lack thereof, could be best understood as the outcome of the vicious circle. British colonial authorities built extractive institutions in the first place, and the postindependence African politicians were only too happy to take up the baton for themselves. The pattern was eerily similar all over sub-Saharan Africa. There were similar hopes for postindependence Ghana, Kenya, Zambia, and many other African countries. Yet in all these cases, extractive institutions were re-created in a pattern predicted by the vicious circle—only they became more vicious as time went by. In all these countries, for example, the British creation of marketing boards and indirect rule were sustained.

There are natural reasons for this vicious circle. Extractive political institutions lead to extractive economic institutions, which enrich a few at the expense of many. Those who benefit from extractive institutions thus have the resources to build their (private) armies and mercenaries, to buy their judges, and to rig their elections in order to remain in power. They also have every interest in defending the system. Therefore, extractive economic institutions create the platform for extractive political institutions to persist. Power is valuable in regimes with extractive political institutions, because power is unchecked and brings economic riches.

Extractive political institutions also provide no checks against abuses of power. Whether power corrupts is debatable, but Lord Acton was certainly right when he argued that absolute power corrupts absolutely. We saw in the previous chapter that even when Franklin Roosevelt wished to use his presidential powers in a way that he thought would be beneficial for the society, unencumbered by constraints imposed by the Supreme Court, the inclusive U.S. political institutions prevented him from setting aside the constraints on his power. Under extractive political institutions, there is little check against the exercise of power, however distorted and sociopathic it may become. In 1980 Sam Bangura, then the governor of the central bank in Sierra Leone, criticized Siaka Stevens's policies for being profligate. He was soon murdered and thrown from the top floor of the central bank building onto the aptly named Siaka Stevens Street. Extractive political institutions thus also tend to create a vicious circle because they provide no line of defense against those who want to further usurp and misuse the powers of the state.

Yet another mechanism for the vicious circle is that extractive institutions, by creating unconstrained power and great income inequality, increase the potential stakes of the political game. Because whoever controls the state becomes the beneficiary of this excessive power and the wealth that it generates, extractive institutions create incentives for infighting in order to control power and its benefits, a dynamic that we saw played out in Maya city-states and in Ancient Rome. In this light, it is no surprise that the extractive institutions that many African countries inherited from the colonial powers sowed the seeds of power struggles and civil wars. These struggles would be very different conflicts from the English Civil War and the Glorious Revolution. They would not be fought to change political institutions, introduce constraints on the exercise of power, or create pluralism, but to capture power and enrich one group at the expense of the rest. In Angola, Burundi, Chad, Côte d'Ivoire, the Democratic Republic of Congo, Ethiopia, Liberia, Mozambique, Nigeria, Republic of Congo Brazzaville, Rwanda, Somalia, Sudan, and Uganda, and of course in Sierra Leone, as we will see in more detail in the next chapter, these conflicts would turn into bloody civil wars and would create economic ruin and unparalleled human suffering—as well as cause state failure.

FROM *ENCOMIENDA* TO LAND GRAB

On January 14, 1993, Ramiro De León Carpio was sworn in as the president of Guatemala. He named Richard Aitkenhead Castillo as his minister of finance, and Ricardo Castillo Sinibaldi as his minister of development. These three men all had something in common: all were direct descendants of Spanish conquistadors who had come to Guatemala in the early sixteenth century. De León's illustrious ancestor was Juan De León Cardona, while the Castillos were related to Bernal Díaz del Castillo, a man who wrote one of the most famous eyewitness accounts of the conquest of Mexico. In reward for his service to Hernán Cortés, Díaz del Castillo was appointed governor of Santiago de los Caballeros, which is today the city of Antigua in Guatemala. Both Castillo and De León founded dynasties along with other conquistadors, such as Pedro de Alvarado. The Guatemalan sociologist Marta Casaús Arzú identified a core group of twenty-two families in Guatemala that had ties through marriage to another twenty-six families just outside the core. Her genealogical and political study suggested that these families have controlled economic and political power in Guatemala since 1531. An even broader definition of which families were part of this elite suggested that they accounted for just over 1 percent of the population in the 1990s.

In Sierra Leone and in much of sub-Saharan Africa, the vicious circle took the form of the extractive institutions set up by colonial powers being taken over by postindependence leaders. In Guatemala, as in much of Central America, we see a simpler, more naked form of the vicious circle: those who have economic and political power structure institutions to ensure the continuity of their power, and succeed in doing so. This type of vicious circle leads to the persistence of extractive institutions and the persistence of the same elites in power together with the persistence of underdevelopment.

At the time of the conquest, Guatemala was densely settled, probably with a population of around two million Mayas. Disease and exploitation took a heavy toll as everywhere else in the Americas. It was not until the 1920s that its total population returned to this level.

As elsewhere in the Spanish Empire, the indigenous people were allocated to conquistadors in grants of *encomienda*. As we saw in the context of the colonization of Mexico and Peru, the *encomienda* was a system of forced labor, which subsequently gave way to other similar coercive institutions, particularly to the *repartimiento,* also called the *mandamiento* in Guatemala. The elite, made up of the descendants of the conquistadors and some indigenous elements, not only benefited from the various forced labor systems but also controlled and monopolized trade through a merchant guild called the Consulado de Comercio. Most of the population in Guatemala was high in the mountains and far from the coast. The high transportation costs reduced the extent of the export economy, and initially land was not very valuable. Much of it was still in the hands of indigenous peoples, who had large communal landholdings called *ejidos*. The remainder was largely unoccupied and notionally owned by the government. There was more money in controlling and taxing trade, such as it was, than in controlling the land.

Just as in Mexico, the Guatemalan elite viewed the Cadiz Constitution (pages 28–32) with hostility, which encouraged them to declare independence just as the Mexican elites did. Following a brief union with Mexico and the Central American Federation, the colonial elite ruled Guatemala under the dictatorship of Rafael Carrera from 1839 to 1865. During this period the descendants of the conquistadors and the indigenous elite maintained the extractive economic institutions of the colonial era largely unchanged. Even the organization of the Consulado did not alter with independence. Though this was a royal institution, it happily continued under a republican government.

Independence then was simply a coup by the preexisting local elite, just as in Mexico; they carried on as usual with the extractive economic institutions from which they had benefited so much. Ironically enough, during this period the Consulado remained in charge of the economic development of the country. But as had been the case pre-independence, the Consulado had its own interests at heart, not those of the country. Part of its responsibility was for the development of infrastructure, such as ports and roads, but as in Austria-

Hungary, Russia, and Sierra Leone, this often threatened creative destruction and could have destabilized the system. Therefore, the development of infrastructure, rather than being implemented, was often resisted. For example, the development of a port on the Suchitepéquez coast, bordering the Pacific Ocean, was one of the proposed projects. At the time the only proper ports were on the Caribbean coast, and these were controlled by the Consulado. The Consulado did nothing on the Pacific side because a port in that region would have provided a much easier outlet for goods from the highland towns of Mazatenango and Quezaltenango, and access to a different market for these goods would have undermined the Consulado's monopoly on foreign trade. The same logic applied to roads, where, again, the Consulado had the responsibility for the entire country. Predictably it also refused to build roads that would have strengthened competing groups or would have potentially undone its monopoly. Pressure to do so again came from western Guatemala and Quezaltenango, in the Los Altos region. But if the road between Los Altos and the Suchitepéquez coast had been improved, this could have created a merchant class, which would have been a competitor to the Consulado merchants in the capital. The road did not get improved.

As a result of this elite dominance, Guatemala was caught in a time warp in the middle of the nineteenth century, as the rest of the world was changing rapidly. But these changes would ultimately affect Guatemala. Transportation costs were falling due to technological innovations such as the steam train, the railways, and new, much faster types of ships. Moreover, the rising incomes of people in Western Europe and North America were creating a mass demand for many products that a country such as Guatemala could potentially produce.

Early in the century, some indigo and then cochineal, both natural dyes, had been produced for export, but the more profitable opportunity would become coffee production. Guatemala had a lot of land suitable for coffee, and cultivation began to spread—without any assistance from the Consulado. As the world price of coffee rose and international trade expanded, there were huge profits to be made, and the Guatemalan elite became interested in coffee. In 1871 the long-lasting regime created by the dictator Carrera was finally overthrown by a group of people calling themselves Liberals, after the worldwide movement of that name. What liberalism means has changed over time. But in the nineteenth century in the United States and Europe, it was similar to what is today called libertarianism, and it stood for freedom of individuals, limited government, and free trade. Things worked a little differently in Guatemala. Led initially by Miguel García Granados, and after 1873 by Justo Rufino Barrios, the Guatemalan Liberals were, for the most part, not new men with liberal ideals. By and large, the same families remained in charge. They maintained extractive political institutions and implemented a huge reorganization of the economy to exploit coffee. They did abolish the Consulado in 1871, but economic circumstances had changed. The focus of extractive economic institutions would now be the production and export of coffee.

Coffee production needed land and labor. To create land for coffee farms, the Liberals pushed through land privatization, in fact really a land grab in which they would be able to capture land previously held communally or by the government. Though their attempt was bitterly contested, given the highly extractive political institutions and the concentration of political power in Guatemala, the elite were ultimately victorious. Between 1871 and 1883 nearly one million acres of land, mostly indigenous communal land and frontier lands, passed into the hands of the elite, and it was only then that coffee developed rapidly. The aim was the formation of large estates. The privatized lands were auctioned off typically to members of the traditional elite or those connected with them. The coercive power of the Liberal state was then used to help large landowners gain access to labor by adapting and intensifying various systems of forced labor. In November 1876, President Barrios wrote to all the governors of Guatemala noting that

because the country has extensive areas of land that it needs to exploit by cultivation using the multitude of

workers who today remain outside the movement of
development of the nation's productive elements, you
are to give all help to export agriculture:
1. From the Indian towns of your jurisdiction provide to the owners of fincas [farms] of that department
who ask for labor the number of workers they need,
be it fifty or one hundred.

The *repartimiento,* the forced labor draft, had never been abolished after independence, but now it was increased in scope and
duration. It was institutionalized in 1877 by Decree 177, which specified that employers could request and receive from the government
up to sixty workers for fifteen days of work if the property was in the
same department, and for thirty days if it was outside it. The request
could be renewed if the employer so desired. These workers could be
forcibly recruited unless they could demonstrate from their personal
workbook that such service had recently been performed satisfacto-
rily. All rural workers were also forced to carry a workbook, called a
libreta, which included details of whom they were working for and a
record of any debts. Many rural workers were indebted to their employers, and an indebted worker could not leave his current employer
without permission. Decree 177 further stipulated that the only way
to avoid being drafted into the *repartimiento* was to show you were
currently in debt to an employer. Workers were trapped. In addition
to these laws, numerous vagrancy laws were passed so that anyone
who could not prove he had a job would be immediately recruited for
the *repartimiento* or other types of forced labor on the roads, or
would be forced to accept employment on a farm. As in nineteenth-
and twentieth-century South Africa, land policies after 1871 were also
designed to undermine the subsistence economy of the indigenous
peoples, to force them to work for low wages. The *repartimiento*
lasted until the 1920s; the *libreta* system and the full gamut of vagrancy laws were in effect until 1945, when Guatemala experienced
its first brief flowering of democracy.

Just as before 1871, the Guatemalan elite ruled via military strongmen. They continued to do so after the coffee boom took off. Jorge Ubico, president between 1931 and 1944, ruled longest. Ubico won the presidential election in 1931 unopposed, since nobody was foolish enough to run against him. Like the Consulado, he didn't approve of doing things that would have induced creative destruction and threatened both his political power and his and the elite's profits. He therefore opposed industry for the same reason that Francis I in Austria-Hungary and Nicholas I in Russia did: industrial workers would have caused trouble. In a legislation unparalleled in its paranoid repressiveness, Ubico banned the use of words such as *obreros* (workers), *sindicatos* (labor unions), and *huelgas* (strikes). You could be jailed for using any one of them. Even though Ubico was powerful, the elite pulled the strings. Opposition to his regime mounted in 1944, headed by disaffected university students who began to organize demonstrations. Popular discontent increased, and on June 24, 311 people, many of them from the elite, signed the Memorial de los 311, an open letter denouncing the regime. Ubico resigned on July 1. Though he was followed by a democratic regime in 1945, this was overthrown by a coup in 1954, leading to a murderous civil war. Guatemala democratized again after only 1986.

The Spanish conquistadors had no compunction about setting up an extractive political and economic system. That was why they had come all the way to the New World. But most of the institutions they set up were meant to be temporary. The *encomienda,* for example, was a temporary grant of rights over labor. They did not have a fully worked-out plan of how they would set up a system that would persist for another four hundred years. In fact, the institutions they set up changed significantly along the way, but one thing did not: the extractive nature of the institutions, the result of the vicious circle. The form of extraction changed, but neither the extractive nature of the institutions nor the identity of the elite did. In Guatemala the *encomienda,* the *repartimiento,* and the monopolization of trade gave way to the *libreta* and the land grab. But the majority of the indigenous Maya continued to work as low-wage laborers with little education, no rights, and no public services.

In Guatemala, as in much of Central America, in a typical pattern of the vicious circle, extractive political institutions supported extractive economic institutions, which in turn provided the basis for extractive political institutions and the continuation of the power of the same elite.

FROM SLAVERY TO JIM CROW

In Guatemala, extractive institutions persisted from colonial to modern times with the same elite firmly in control. Any change in institutions resulted from adaptations to changing environments, as was the case with the land grab by the elite motivated by the coffee boom. The institutions in the U.S. South were similarly extractive until the Civil War. Economics and politics were dominated by the southern elite, plantation owners with large land and slave holdings. Slaves had neither political nor economic rights; indeed, they had few rights of any kind.

The South's extractive economic and political institutions made it considerably poorer than the North by the middle of the nineteenth century. The South lacked industry and made relatively little investment in infrastructure. In 1860 its total manufacturing output was less than that of Pennsylvania, New York, or Massachusetts. Only 9 percent of the southern population lived in urban areas, compared with 35 percent in the Northeast. The density of railroads (i.e., miles of track divided by land area) was three times higher in the North than in southern states. The ratio of canal mileage was similar.

Map 18 (page 352) shows the extent of slavery by plotting the percentage of the population that were slaves across U.S. counties in 1840. It is apparent that slavery was dominant in the South with some counties, for example, along the Mississippi River having as much as 95 percent of the population slaves. Map 19 (page 353) then shows one of the consequences of this, the proportion of the labor force working in manufacturing in 1880. Though this was not high anywhere by twentieth-century standards, there are marked differences between the North and the South. In much of the Northeast, more than 10 percent of the labor force worked in manufacturing. In contrast in much of the South, particularly the areas with heavy concentrations of slaves, the proportion was basically zero.

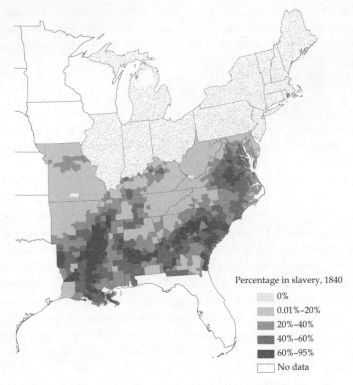

Map 18: Slavery across U.S. counties in 1840

The South was not even innovative in the sectors in which it specialized: from 1837 to 1859, the numbers of patents issued per year for innovations related to corn and wheat were on average twelve and ten, respectively; there was just one per year for the most important crop of the South, cotton. There was no indication that industrialization and economic growth would commence anytime soon. But defeat in the Civil War was followed by fundamental economic and political reform at bayonet point. Slavery was abolished, and black men were allowed to vote.

These major changes should have opened the way for a radical transformation of southern extractive institutions into inclusive ones,

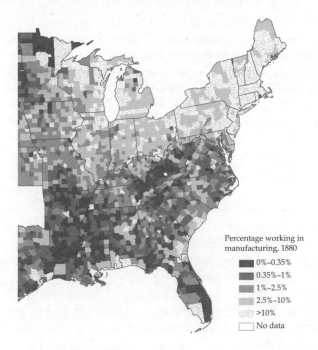

Map 19: Manufacturing employment across U.S. counties in 1880

and launched the South onto a path to economic prosperity. But in yet another manifestation of the vicious circle, nothing of the sort happened. A continuation of extractive institutions, this time of the Jim Crow kind rather than of slavery, emerged in the South. The phrase *Jim Crow*, which supposedly originated from "Jump Jim Crow," an early-nineteenth-century satire of black people performed by white performers in "blackface," came to refer to the whole gamut of segregationist legislation that was enacted in the South after 1865. These persisted for almost another century, until yet another major upheaval, the civil rights movement. In the meantime, blacks continued to be excluded from power and repressed. Plantation-type agriculture based on low-wage, poorly educated labor persisted, and southern incomes fell further relative to the U.S. average. The vicious circle of extractive institutions was stronger than many had expected at the time.

The reason that the economic and political trajectory of the South never changed, even though slavery was abolished and black men were given the right to vote, was because blacks' political power and economic independence were tenuous. The southern planters lost the war, but would win the peace. They were still organized and they still owned the land. During the war, freed slaves had been offered the promise of forty acres and a mule when slavery was abolished, and some even got it during the famous campaigns of General William T. Sherman. But in 1865, President Andrew Johnson revoked Sherman's orders, and the hoped-for land redistribution never took place. In a debate on this issue in Congress, Congressman George Washington Julian presciently noted, "Of what avail would be an act of congress totally abolishing slavery . . . if the old agricultural basis of aristocratic power shall remain?" This was the beginning of the "redemption" of the old South and the persistence of the old southern landed elite.

The sociologist Jonathan Wiener studied the persistence of the planter elite in five counties of the Black Belt, prime cotton country, of southern Alabama. Tracking families from the U.S. census and considering those with at least $10,000 of real estate, he found that of the 236 members of the planter elite in 1850, 101 maintained their position in 1870. Interestingly, this rate of persistence was very similar to that experienced in the pre–Civil War period; of the 236 wealthiest planter families of 1850, only 110 remained so a decade later. Nevertheless, of the 25 planters with the largest landholdings in 1870, 18 (72 percent) had been in the elite families in 1860; 16 had been in the 1850 elite group. While more than 600,000 were killed in the Civil War, the planter elites suffered few casualties. The law, designed by the planters and for the planters, exempted one slaveholder from military service for every twenty slaves held. As hundreds of thousands of men died to preserve the southern plantation economy, many big slaveholders and their sons sat out the war on their porches and thus were able to ensure the persistence of the plantation economy.

After the end of the war, the elite planters controlling the land were able to reexert their control over the labor force. Though the economic institution of slavery was abolished, the evidence shows a clear line of persistence in the economic system of the South based on plantation-type agriculture with cheap labor. This economic system was maintained through a variety of channels, including both control of local politics and exercise of violence. As a consequence, in the words of the African American scholar W.E.B. Du Bois, the South became "simply an armed camp for intimidating black folk."

In 1865 the state legislature of Alabama passed the Black Code, an important landmark toward the repression of black labor. Similar to Decree 177 in Guatemala, the Black Code of Alabama consisted of a vagrancy law and a law against the "enticement" of laborers. It was designed to impede labor mobility and reduce competition in the labor market, and it ensured that southern planters would still have a reliable low-cost labor pool.

Following the Civil War, the period called Reconstruction lasted from 1865 until 1877. Northern politicians, with the help of the Union Army, engineered some social changes in the South. But a systematic backlash from the southern elite in the guise of support for the so-called Redeemers, seeking the South's redemption, re-created the old system. In the 1877 presidential election, Rutherford Hayes needed southern support in the electoral college. This college, still used today, was at the heart of the indirect election for president created by the U.S. Constitution. Citizens' votes do not directly elect the president but instead elect electors who then choose the president in the electoral college. In exchange for their support in the electoral college, the southerners demanded that Union soldiers be withdrawn from the South and the region left to its own devices. Hayes agreed. With southern support, Hayes became president and pulled out the troops. The period after 1877 then marked the real reemergence of the pre–Civil War planter elite. The redemption of the South involved the introduction of new poll taxes and literacy tests for voting, which systematically disenfranchised blacks, and often also the poor white population. These attempts succeeded and created a one-party regime under the Democratic Party, with much of the political power vested in the hands of the planter elite.

The Jim Crow laws created separate, and predictably inferior, schools. Alabama, for example, rewrote its constitution in 1901 to achieve this. Shockingly, even today Section 256 of Alabama's constitution, though no longer enforced, still states:

> Duty of legislature to establish and maintain public school system; apportionment of public school fund; separate schools for white and colored children.
>
> The legislature shall establish, organize, and maintain a liberal system of public schools throughout the state for the benefit of the children thereof between the ages of seven and twenty-one years. The public school fund shall be apportioned to the several counties in proportion to the number of school children of school age therein, and shall be so apportioned to the schools in the districts or townships in the counties as to provide, as nearly as practicable, school terms of equal duration in such school districts or townships. Separate schools shall be provided for white and colored children, and no child of either race shall be permitted to attend a school of the other race.

An amendment to strike Section 256 from the constitution was narrowly defeated in the state legislature in 2004.

Disenfranchisement, the vagrancy laws such as the Black Code of Alabama, various Jim Crow laws, and the actions of the Ku Klux Klan, often financed and supported by the elite, turned the post–Civil War South into an effective apartheid society, where blacks and whites lived different lives. As in South Africa, these laws and practices were aimed at controlling the black population and its labor.

Southern politicians in Washington also worked to make sure that the extractive institutions of the South could persist. For instance, they ensured that no federal projects or public works that would have jeopardized southern elite control over the black workforce ever got approved. Consequently, the South entered the twentieth century as a largely rural society with low levels of education and backward technology, still employing hand labor and mule power virtually unassisted by mechanical implements. Though the proportion of people in urban areas increased, it was far less than in the North. In 1900, for example, 13.5 percent of the population of the South was urbanized, as compared with 60 percent in the Northeast.

All in all, the extractive institutions in the southern United States, based on the power of the landed elite, plantation agriculture, and low-wage, low-education labor, persisted well into the twentieth century. These institutions started to crumble only after the Second World War and then truly after the civil rights movement destroyed the political basis of the system. And it was only after the demise of these institutions in the 1950s and '60s that the South began its process of rapid convergence to the North.

The U.S. South shows another, more resilient side of the vicious circle: as in Guatemala, the southern planter elite remained in power and structured economic and political institutions in order to ensure the continuity of its power. But differently from Guatemala, it was faced with significant challenges after its defeat in the Civil War, which abolished slavery and reversed the total, constitutional exclusion of blacks from political participation. But there is more than one way of skinning a cat: as long as the planter elite was in control of its huge landholdings and remained organized, it could structure a new set of institutions, Jim Crow instead of slavery, to achieve the same objective. The vicious circle turned out to be stronger than many, including Abraham Lincoln, had thought. The vicious circle is based on extractive political institutions creating extractive economic institutions, which in turn support the extractive political institutions, because economic wealth and power buy political power. When forty acres and a mule was off the table, the southern planter elite's economic power remained untarnished. And, unsurprisingly and unfortunately, the implications for the black population of the South, and the South's economic development, were the same.

THE IRON LAW OF OLIGARCHY

The Solomonic dynasty in Ethiopia lasted until it was overthrown by a military coup in 1974. The coup was led by the Derg, a group of Marxist army officers. The regime that the Derg pitched from power looked like it was frozen in some earlier century, a historical anachronism. The emperor Haile Selassie would start his day by arriving in the courtyard at the Grand Palace, which had been built by Emperor Menelik II in the late nineteenth century. Outside the palace would be a crowd of dignitaries anticipating his arrival, bowing and desperately trying to get his attention. The emperor would hold court in the Audience Hall, sitting on the imperial throne. (Selassie was a small man; so that his legs were not left swinging in the air, it was the job of a special pillow bearer to accompany him wherever he went to make sure there was a suitable pillow to put under his feet. The bearer kept a stock of fifty-two pillows to cope with any situation.) Selassie presided over an extreme set of extractive institutions and ran the country as his own private property, handing out favors and patronage and ruthlessly punishing lack of loyalty. There was no economic development to speak of in Ethiopia under the Solomonic dynasty.

The Derg initially formed out of 108 representatives of different military units from all over the country. The representative of the Third Division in Harar province was a major named Mengistu Haile Mariam. Though in their initial declaration of July 4, 1974, the Derg officers declared their loyalty to the emperor, they soon started to arrest members of the government, testing how much opposition it would create. As they became more confident that the support for Selassie's regime was hollow, they moved on the emperor himself, arresting him on September 12. Then the executions began. Many politicians at the core of the old regime were swiftly killed. By December, the Derg had declared that Ethiopia was a socialist state. Selassie died, probably murdered, on August 27, 1975. In 1975 the Derg started nationalizing property, including all urban and rural land and most kinds of private property. The increasingly authoritarian behavior of the regime sparked opposition around the country. Large parts of Ethiopia were put together during the European colonial expansion in the late nineteenth and early twentieth centuries by the policies of Emperor Menelik II, the victor of the battle of Adowa, which we encountered before (page 237). These included Eritrea and Tigray in the north and the Ogaden in the east. Independence movements in response to the Derg's ruthless regime emerged in Eritrea and Tigray, while the Somali army invaded the Somali-speaking Ogaden. The Derg itself started to disintegrate and split into factions. Major Mengistu turned out to be the most ruthless and clever of them. By mid-1977 he had eliminated his major opponents and effectively taken charge of the regime, which was saved from collapse only by a huge influx of weapons and troops from the Soviet Union and Cuba later in November of that year.

In 1978 the regime organized a national celebration marking the fourth anniversary of the overthrow of Haile Selassie. By this time Mengistu was the unchallenged leader of the Derg. As his residence, the place from where he would rule Ethiopia, he had chosen Selassie's Grand Palace, left unoccupied since the monarchy was abolished. At the celebration, he sat on a gilded armchair, just like the emperors of old, watching the parade. Official functions were now held once again at the Grand Palace, with Mengistu sitting on Haile Selassie's old throne. Mengistu started to compare himself to Emperor Tewodros, who had refounded the Solomonic Dynasty in the mid-nineteenth century after a period of decline.

One of his ministers, Dawit Wolde Giorgis, recalled in his memoir:

> At the beginning of the Revolution all of us had utterly rejected anything to do with the past. We would no longer drive cars, or wear suits; neckties were considered criminal. Anything that made you look well-off or bourgeois, anything that smacked of affluence or sophistication, was scorned as part of the old order. Then, around 1978, all that began to change. Gradually materialism became accepted, then required. Designer clothes from the best European tailors were the uniform of all senior government officials and members

of the Military Council. We had the best of everything: the best homes, the best cars, the best whiskey, champagne, food. It was a complete reversal of the ideals of the Revolution.

Giorgis also vividly recorded how Mengistu changed once he became sole ruler:

> The real Mengistu emerged: vengeful, cruel and authoritarian . . . Many of us who used to talk to him with hands in our pockets, as if he were one of us, found ourselves standing stiffly to attention, cautiously respectful in his presence. In addressing him we had always used the familiar form of "you," *ante;* now we found ourselves switching to the more formal "you," *ersiwo.* He moved into a bigger, more lavish office in the Palace of Menelik . . . He began using the Emperor's cars . . . We were supposed to have a revolution of equality; now he had become the new Emperor.

The pattern of vicious circle depicted by the transition between Haile Selassie and Mengistu, or between the British colonial governors of Sierra Leone and Siaka Stevens, is so extreme and at some level so strange that it deserves a special name. As we already mentioned in chapter 4, the German sociologist Robert Michels called it the iron law of oligarchy. The internal logic of oligarchies, and in fact of all hierarchical organizations, is that, argued Michels, they will reproduce themselves not only when the same group is in power, but even when an entirely new group takes control. What Michels did not anticipate perhaps was an echo of Karl Marx's remark that history repeats itself—the first time as tragedy, the second time as farce.

It is not only that many of the postindependence leaders of Africa moved into the same residences, made use of the same patronage networks, and employed the same ways of manipulating markets and extracting resources as had the colonial regimes and the emperors they replaced; but they also made things worse. It was indeed a farce that the staunchly anticolonial Stevens would be concerned with controlling the same people, the Mende, whom the British had sought to control; that he would rely on the same chiefs whom the British had empowered and then used to control the hinterland; that he would run the economy in the same way, expropriating the farmers with the same marketing boards and controlling the diamonds under a similar monopoly. It was indeed a farce, a very sad farce indeed, that Laurent Kabila, who mobilized an army against Mobutu's dictatorship with the promise of freeing the people and ending the stifling and impoverishing corruption and repression of Mobutu's Zaire, would then set up a regime just as corrupt and perhaps even more disastrous. It was certainly farcical that he tried to start a Mobutuesque personality cult aided and abetted by Dominique Sakombi Inongo, previously Mobutu's minister of information, and that Mobutu's regime was itself fashioned on patterns of exploitation of the masses that had started more than a century previously with King Leopold's Congo Free State. It was indeed a farce that the Marxist officer Mengistu would start living in a palace, viewing himself as an emperor, and enriching himself and his entourage just like Haile Selassie and other emperors before him had done.

It was all a farce, but also more tragic than the original tragedy, and not only for the hopes that were dashed. Stevens and Kabila, like many other rulers in Africa, would start murdering their opponents and then innocent citizens. Mengistu and the Derg's policies would bring recurring famine to Ethiopia's fertile lands. History was repeating itself, but in a very distorted form. It was a famine in Wollo province in 1973 to which Haile Selassie was apparently indifferent that did so much finally to solidify opposition to his regime. Selassie had at least been only indifferent. Mengistu instead saw famine as a political tool to undermine the strength of his opponents. History was not only farcical and tragic, but also cruel to the citizens of Ethiopia and much of sub-Saharan Africa.

The essence of the iron law of oligarchy, this particular facet of the vicious circle, is that new leaders overthrowing old ones with promises of radical change bring nothing but more of the same. At some level, the iron law of oligarchy is harder to understand than other forms of the vicious circle. There is a clear logic to the persistence of the extractive institutions in the U.S. South and in Guatemala. The same groups continued to dominate the economy and the politics for centuries. Even when challenged, as the U.S. southern planters were after the Civil War, their power remained intact and they were able to keep and re-create a similar set of extractive institutions from which they would again benefit. But how can we understand those who come to power in the name of radical change re-creating the same system? The answer to this question reveals, once again, that the vicious circle is stronger than it first appears.

Not all radical changes are doomed to failure. The Glorious Revolution was a radical change, and it led to what perhaps turned out to be the most important political revolution of the past two millennia. The French Revolution was even more radical, with its chaos and excessive violence and the ascent of Napoleon Bonaparte, but it did not re-create the *ancien régime*.

Three factors greatly facilitated the emergence of more inclusive political institutions following the Glorious Revolution and the French Revolution. The first was new merchants and businessmen wishing to unleash the power of creative destruction from which they themselves would benefit; these new men were among the key members of the revolutionary coalitions and did not wish to see the development of yet another set of extractive institutions that would again prey on them.

The second was the nature of the broad coalition that had formed in both cases. For example, the Glorious Revolution wasn't a coup by a narrow group or a specific narrow interest, but a movement backed by merchants, industrialists, the gentry, and diverse political groupings. The same was largely true for the French Revolution.

The third factor relates to the history of English and French political institutions. They created a background against which new, more inclusive regimes could develop. In both countries there was a tradition of parliaments and power sharing going back to the Magna Carta in England and to the Assembly of Notables in France. Moreover, both revolutions happened in the midst of a process that had already weakened the grasp of the absolutist, or aspiring absolutist, regimes.

In neither case would these political institutions make it easy for a new set of rulers or a narrow group to take control of the state and usurp existing economic wealth and build unchecked and durable political power. In the aftermath of the French Revolution, a narrow group under the leadership of Robespierre and Saint-Just did take control, with disastrous consequences, but this was temporary and did not derail the path toward more inclusive institutions. All this contrasts with the situation of societies with long histories of extreme extractive economic and political institutions, and no checks on the power of rulers. In these societies, there would be no new strong merchants or businessmen supporting and bankrolling the resistance against the existing regime in part to secure more inclusive economic institutions; no broad coalitions introducing constraints against the power of each of their members; no political institutions inhibiting new rulers intent on usurping and exploiting power.

In consequence, in Sierra Leone, Ethiopia, and the Congo, the vicious circle would be far harder to resist, and moves toward inclusive institutions far more unlikely to get under way. There were also no traditional or historical institutions that could check the power of those who would take control of the state. Such institutions had existed in some parts of Africa, and some, as in Botswana, even survived the colonial era. But they were much less prominent throughout Sierra Leone's history, and to the extent that they existed, they were warped by indirect rule. The same was true in other British colonies in Africa, such as Kenya and Nigeria. They never existed in the absolutist kingdom of Ethiopia. In the Congo, indigenous institutions were emasculated by Belgian colonial rule and the autocratic policies of Mobutu. In all these societies, there were also no new merchants, businessmen, or entrepreneurs supporting the new regimes and demanding secure property rights and an end to previous extractive institutions. In fact, the extractive economic institutions of the colonial period meant that there was not much entrepreneurship or business left at all.

The international community thought that postcolonial African independence would lead to economic growth through a process of state planning and cultivation of the private sector. But the private sector was not there—except in rural areas, which had no representation in the new governments and would thus be their first prey. Most important perhaps, in most of these cases there were enormous benefits from holding power. These benefits both attracted the most unscrupulous men, such as Stevens, who wished to monopolize this power, and brought the worst out of them once they were in power. There was nothing to break the vicious circle.

NEGATIVE FEEDBACK AND VICIOUS CIRCLES

Rich nations are rich largely because they managed to develop inclusive institutions at some point during the past three hundred years. These institutions have persisted through a process of virtuous circles. Even if inclusive only in a limited sense to begin with, and sometimes fragile, they generated dynamics that would create a process of positive feedback, gradually increasing their inclusiveness. England did not become a democracy after the Glorious Revolution of 1688. Far from it. Only a small fraction of the population had formal representation, but crucially, she was pluralistic. Once pluralism was enshrined, there was a tendency for the institutions to become more inclusive over time, even if this was a rocky and uncertain process.

In this, England was typical of virtuous circles: inclusive political institutions create constraints against the exercise and usurpation of power. They also tend to create inclusive economic institutions, which in turn make the continuation of inclusive political institutions more likely.

Under inclusive economic institutions, wealth is not concentrated in the hands of a small group that could then use its economic might to increase its political power disproportionately. Furthermore, under inclusive economic institutions there are more limited gains from holding political power, thus weaker incentives for every group and every ambitious, upstart individual to try to take control of the state. A confluence of factors at a critical juncture, including interplay between existing institutions and the opportunities and challenges brought by the critical juncture, is generally responsible for the onset of inclusive institutions, as the English case demonstrates. But once these inclusive institutions are in place, we do not need the same confluence of factors for them to survive. Virtuous circles, though still subject to significant contingency, enable the institutions' continuity and often even unleash dynamics taking society toward greater inclusiveness.

As virtuous circles make inclusive institutions persist, vicious circles create powerful forces toward the persistence of extractive institutions. History is not destiny, and vicious circles are not unbreakable, as we will see further in chapter 14. But they are resilient. They create a powerful process of negative feedback, with extractive political institutions forging extractive economic institutions, which in turn create the basis for the persistence of extractive political institutions. We saw this most clearly in the case of Guatemala, where the same elite held power, first under colonial rule, then in independent Guatemala, for more than four centuries; extractive institutions enrich the elite, and their wealth forms the basis for the continuation of their domination.

The same process of the vicious circle is also apparent in the persistence of the plantation economy in the U.S. South, except that it also showcases the vicious circle's great resilience in the face of challenges. U.S. southern planters lost their formal control of economic and political institutions after their defeat in the Civil War. Slavery, which was the basis of the plantation economy, was abolished, and blacks were given equal political and economic rights. Yet the Civil War did not destroy the political power of the planter elite or its economic basis, and they were able to restructure the system, under a different guise but still under their own local political control, and to achieve the same objective: abundance of low-cost labor for the plantations.

This form of the vicious circle, where extractive institutions persist because the elite controlling them and benefiting from them persists, is not its only form. At first a more puzzling, but no less real and no less vicious, form of negative feedback shaped the political and economic development of many nations, and is exemplified by the experiences of much of sub-Saharan Africa, in particular Sierra Leone and Ethiopia. In a form that the sociologist Robert Michels would recognize as the iron law of oligarchy, the overthrow of a regime presiding over extractive institutions heralds the arrival of a new set of masters to exploit the same set of pernicious extractive institutions.

The logic of this type of vicious circle is also simple to understand in hindsight: extractive political institutions create few constraints on the exercise of power, so there are essentially no institutions to restrain the use and abuse of power by those overthrowing previous dictators and assuming control of the state; and extractive economic institutions imply that there are great profits and wealth to be made merely by controlling power, expropriating the assets of others, and setting up monopolies.

Of course, the iron law of oligarchy is not a true law, in the sense that the laws of physics are. It does not chart an inevitable path, as the Glorious Revolution in England or the Meiji Restoration in Japan illustrate.

A key factor in these episodes, which saw a major turn toward inclusive institutions, was the empowerment of a broad coalition that could stand up against absolutism and would replace the absolutist institutions by more inclusive, pluralistic ones. A revolution by a broad coalition makes the emergence of pluralistic political institutions much more likely. In Sierra Leone and Ethiopia, the iron law of oligarchy was made more likely not only because existing institutions were highly extractive but also because neither the independence movement in the former nor the Derg coup in the latter were revolutions led by such broad coalitions, but rather by individuals and groups seeking power so that they could do the extracting.

There is yet another, even more destructive facet of the vicious circle, anticipated by our discussion of the Maya city-states in chapter 5. When extractive institutions create huge inequalities in society and great wealth and unchecked power for those in control, there will be many wishing to fight to take control of the state and institutions. Extractive institutions then not only pave the way for the next regime, which will be even more extractive, but they also engender continuous infighting and civil wars. These civil wars then cause more human suffering and also destroy even what little state centralization these societies have achieved. This also often starts a process of descent into lawlessness, state failure, and political chaos, crushing all hopes of economic prosperity, as the next chapter will illustrate.

13.

WHY NATIONS FAIL TODAY

IT WAS JANUARY 2000 in Harare, Zimbabwe. Master of Ceremonies Fallot Chawawa was in charge of drawing the winning ticket for the national lottery organized by a partly state-owned bank, the Zimbabwe Banking Corporation (Zimbank). The lottery was open to all clients who had kept five thousand or more Zimbabwe dollars in their accounts during December 1999. When Chawawa drew the ticket, he was dumfounded. As the public statement of Zimbank put it, "Master of Ceremonies Fallot Chawawa could hardly believe his eyes when the ticket drawn for the Z$100,000 prize was handed to him and he saw His Excellency RG Mugabe written on it."

President Robert Mugabe, who had ruled Zimbabwe by hook or by crook, and usually with an iron fist, since 1980, had won the lottery, which was worth a hundred thousand Zimbabwe dollars, about five times the annual per capita income of the country. Zimbank claimed that Mr. Mugabe's name had been drawn from among thousands of eligible customers. What a lucky man! Needless to say he didn't really need the money. Mugabe had in fact only recently awarded himself and his cabinet salary hikes of up to 200 percent.

The lottery ticket was just one more indication of Zimbabwe's extractive institutions. One could call this corruption, but it is just a symptom of the institutional malaise in Zimbabwe. The fact that Mugabe could even win the lottery if he wanted showed how much control he had over matters in Zimbabwe, and gave the world a glimpse of the extent of the country's extractive institutions.

The most common reason why nations fail today is because they have extractive institutions. Zimbabwe under Mugabe's regime vividly illustrates the economic and social consequences. Though the national statistics in Zimbabwe are very unreliable, the best estimate is that by 2008, Zimbabwe's per capita income was about half of what it was when the country gained its independence in 1980. Dramatic as this sounds, it does not in fact begin to capture the deterioration in living standards in Zimbabwe. The state has collapsed and more or less stopped providing any basic public services. In 2008–2009 the deterioration in the health systems led to an outbreak of cholera across the country. As of January 10, 2010, there have been 98,741 reported cases and 4,293 deaths, making it the deadliest cholera outbreak in Africa over the previous fifteen years. In the meantime, mass unemployment has also reached unprecedented levels. In early 2009, the UN Office for the Coordination of Humanitarian Affairs claimed that the unemployment rate had hit an incredible 94 percent.

The roots of many economic and political institutions in Zimbabwe, as is the case for much of sub-Saharan Africa, can be traced back to the colonial period. In 1890 Cecil Rhodes's British South Africa Company sent a military expedition into the then-kingdom of the Ndebele, based in Matabeleland, and also into the neighboring Mashonaland. Their superior weaponry quickly suppressed African resistance, and by 1901 the colony of Southern Rhodesia, named after Rhodes, had been formed in the area that is currently Zimbabwe. Now that the area was a privately owned concession of the British South Africa Company, Rhodes anticipated making money there through prospecting and mining for precious minerals. The ventures never got off the ground, but the very rich farmlands began attracting white migration. These settlers soon annexed much of the land. By 1923 they had freed themselves from the rule of the British South Africa Company and persuaded the British government to grant them self-government. What then occurred is very similar to what had happened in South Africa a decade or so previously. The 1913 Natives Land Act (pages 265–266) created a dual economy in South Africa. Rhodesia passed very similar laws, and inspired by the South African model, a white-only apartheid state was constructed soon after 1923.

As the European colonial empires collapsed in the late 1950s and early 1960s, the white elite in Rhodesia, led by Ian Smith, comprising possibly 5 percent of the population, declared independence from Britain in 1965. Few international governments recognized Rhodesia's independence, and the United Nations levied economic and political sanctions against it. The black citizens organized a guerrilla war from bases in the neighboring countries of Mozambique and Zambia. International pressure and the rebellion waged by the two main groups, Mugabe's ZANU (the Zimbabwe African National Union) and ZAPU (the Zimbabwe African People's Union), led by Joshua Nkomo, resulted in a negotiated end to white rule. The state of Zimbabwe was created in 1980.

After independence, Mugabe quickly established his personal control. He either violently eliminated his opponents or co-opted them. The most egregious acts of violence happened in Matabeleland, the heartland of support for ZAPU, where as many as twenty thousand people were killed in the early 1980s. By 1987 ZAPU had merged with ZANU to create ZANU-PF, and Joshua Nkomo was sidelined politically. Mugabe was able to rewrite the constitution he had inherited as a part of the independence negotiation, making himself president (he had started as prime minister), abolishing white voter rolls that were part of the independence agreement, and eventually, in 1990, getting rid of the Senate altogether and introducing positions in the legislature that he could nominate. A de facto one-party state headed by Mugabe was the result.

Upon independence, Mugabe took over a set of extractive economic institutions created by the white regime. These included a host of regulations on prices and international trade, state-run industries, and the obligatory agricultural marketing boards. State employment expanded rapidly, with jobs given to supporters of ZANU-PF. The tight government regulation of the economy suited the ZANU-PF elites because it made it difficult for an independent class of African businessmen, who might then have challenged the former's political monopoly, to emerge. This was very similar to the situation we saw in Ghana in the 1960s in chapter 2 (pages 64–68). Ironically, of course, this left whites as the main business class. During this period the main strengths of the white economy, particularly the highly productive agricultural export sector, was left untouched. But this would last only until Mugabe became unpopular.

The model of regulation and market intervention gradually became unsustainable, and a process of institutional change, with the support of the World Bank and the International Monetary Fund, began in 1991 after a severe fiscal crisis. The deteriorating economic performance finally led to the emergence of a serious political opposition to ZANU-PF's one-party rule: the Movement for Democratic Change (MDC). The 1995 parliamentary elections were far from competitive. ZANU-PF won 81 percent of the vote and 118 out of the 120 seats. Fifty-five of these members of Parliament were elected unopposed. The presidential election the following year showed even more signs of irregularities and fraud. Mugabe won 93 percent of the vote, but his two opponents, Abel Muzorewa and Ndabaningi Sithole, had already withdrawn their candidacy prior to the election, accusing the government of coercion and fraud.

After 2000, despite all the corruption, ZANU-PF's grip was weakening. It took only 49 percent of the popular vote, and only 63 seats. All were contested by the MDC, who took every seat in the capital, Harare. In the presidential election of 2002, Mugabe scraped home with only 56 percent of the vote. Both sets of elections went ZANU-PF's way only because of violence and intimidation, coupled with electoral fraud.

The response of Mugabe to the breakdown of his political control was to intensify both the repression and the use of government policies to buy support. He unleashed a full-scale assault on white landowners. Starting in 2000, he encouraged and supported an extensive series of land occupations and expropriations. They were often led by war veterans' associations, groups supposedly comprised of former combatants in the war of independence. Some of the expropriated land was given to these groups, but much of it also went to the ZANU-PF elites. The insecurity of property rights wrought by Mugabe and ZANU-PF led to a collapse of agricultural output and productivity. As the economy crumbled, the only thing left was to print money to buy support, which led to enormous hyperinflation. In January 2009, it became legal to use other currencies, such as the South African rand, and the Zimbabwean dollar vanished from circulation, a worthless piece of paper.

What happened in Zimbabwe after 1980 was commonplace in sub-Saharan Africa since independence. Zimbabwe inherited a set of highly extractive political and economic institutions in 1980. For the first decade and a half, these were maintained relatively untouched. While elections took place, political institutions were anything but inclusive. Economic institutions changed somewhat; for example, there was no longer explicit discrimination against blacks. But on the whole the institutions remained extractive, with the only difference being that instead of Ian Smith and the whites doing the extracting, it was Robert Mugabe and the ZANU-PF elites filling their pockets. Over time the institutions became even more extractive, and incomes in Zimbabwe collapsed. The economic and political failure in Zimbabwe is yet another manifestation of the iron law of oligarchy—in this instance, with the extractive and repressive regime of Ian Smith being replaced by the extractive, corrupt, and repressive regime of Robert Mugabe. Mugabe's fake lottery win in 2000 was then simply the tip of a very corrupt and historically shaped iceberg.

NATIONS FAIL TODAY because their extractive economic institutions do not create the incentives needed for people to save, invest, and innovate. Extractive political institutions support these economic institutions by cementing the power of those who benefit from the extraction. Extractive economic and political institutions, though their details vary under different circumstances, are always at the root of this failure. In many cases, for example, as we will see in Argentina, Colombia, and Egypt, this failure takes the form of lack of sufficient economic activity, because the politicians are just too happy to extract resources or quash any type of independent economic activity that threatens themselves and the economic elites. In some extreme cases, as in Zimbabwe and Sierra Leone, which we discuss next, extractive institutions pave the way for complete state failure, destroying not only law and order but also even the most basic economic incentives. The result is economic stagnation and—as the recent history of

Angola, Cameroon, Chad, the Democratic Republic of Congo, Haiti, Liberia, Nepal, Sierra Leone, Sudan, and Zimbabwe illustrates—civil wars, mass displacements, famines, and epidemics, making many of these countries poorer today than they were in the 1960s.

A CHILDREN'S CRUSADE?

On March 23, 1991, a group of armed men under the leadership of Foday Sankoh crossed the border from Liberia into Sierra Leone and attacked the southern frontier town of Kailahun. Sankoh, formerly a corporal in the Sierra Leonean army, had been imprisoned after taking part in an abortive coup against Siaka Stevens's government in 1971. After being released, he eventually ended up in Libya, where he entered a training camp that the Libyan dictator Colonel Qaddafi ran for African revolutionaries. There he met Charles Taylor, who was plotting to overthrow the government in Liberia. When Taylor invaded Liberia on Christmas Eve 1989, Sankoh was with him, and it was with a group of Taylor's men, mostly Liberians and Burkinabes (citizens of Burkina Faso), that Sankoh invaded Sierra Leone. They called themselves the RUF, the Revolutionary United Front, and they announced that they were there to overthrow the corrupt and tyrannical government of the APC.

As we saw in the previous chapter, Siaka Stevens and his All People's Congress, the APC, took over and intensified the extractive institutions of colonial rule in Sierra Leone, just as Mugabe and ZANU-PF did in Zimbabwe. By 1985, when Stevens, ill with cancer, brought in Joseph Momoh to replace him, the economy was collapsing. Stevens, apparently without irony, used to enjoy quoting the aphorism "The cow eats where it is tethered." And where Stevens had once eaten, Momoh now gorged. The roads fell to pieces, and schools disintegrated. National television broadcasts stopped in 1987, when the transmitter was sold by the minister of information, and in 1989 a radio tower that relayed radio signals outside Freetown fell down, ending transmissions outside the capital. An analysis published in a newspaper in the capital city of Freetown in 1995 rings very true:

by the end of Momoh's rule he had stopped paying civil servants, teachers and even Paramount Chiefs. Central government had collapsed, and then of course we had border incursions, "rebels" and all the automatic weapons pouring over the border from Liberia. The NPRC, the "rebels" and the "sobels" [soldiers turned rebels] all amount to the chaos one expects when government disappears. None of them are the causes of our problems, but they are symptoms.

The collapse of the state under Momoh, once again a consequence of the vicious circle unleashed by the extreme extractive institutions under Stevens, meant that there was nothing to stop the RUF from coming across the border in 1991. The state had no capacity to oppose it. Stevens had already emasculated the military, because he worried they might overthrow him. It was then easy for a relatively small number of armed men to create chaos in most of the country. They even had a manifesto called "Footpaths to Democracy," which started with a quote from the black intellectual Frantz Fanon: "Each generation must, out of relative obscurity, discover its mission, fulfill it or betray it." The section "What Are We Fighting For?" begins:

> We continue to fight because we are tired of being perpetual victims of state sponsored poverty and human degradation visited on us by years of autocratic rule and militarism. But, we shall exercise restraint and continue to wait patiently at the rendezvous of peace— where we shall all be winners. We are committed to peace, by any means necessary, but what we are not committed to is becoming victims of peace. We know our cause to be just and God/Allah will never abandon us in our struggle to reconstruct a new Sierra Leone.

Though Sankoh and other RUF leaders may have started with political grievances, and the grievances of the people suffering under the APC's extractive institutions may have encouraged them to join the movement early on, the situation quickly changed and spun out of control. The "mission" of the RUF plunged the country into agony, as in the testimony of a teenager from Geoma, in the south of Sierra Leone:

> They gathered some of us . . . They chose some of our friends and killed them, two of them. These were people whose fathers were the chiefs, and they had soldiers' boots and property in their houses. They were shot, for no other reason than that they were accused of harbouring soldiers. The chiefs were also killed—as part of the government. They chose someone to be the new chief. They were still saying they had come to free us from the APC. After a point, they were not choosing people to kill, just shooting people.

In the first year of the invasion, any intellectual roots that the RUF may have had were completely extinguished. Sankoh executed those who criticized the mounting stream of atrocities. Soon, few voluntarily joined the RUF. Instead they turned to forcible recruitment, particularly of children. Indeed, all sides did this, including the army. If the Sierra Leonean civil war was a crusade to build a better society, in the end it was a children's crusade. The conflict intensified with massacres and massive human rights abuses, including mass rapes and the amputation of hands and ears. When the RUF took over areas, they also engaged in economic exploitation. It was most obvious in the diamond mining areas, where they press-ganged people into diamond mining, but was widespread elsewhere as well.

The RUF wasn't alone in committing atrocities, massacres, and organized forced labor. The government did so as well. Such was the collapse of law and order that it became difficult for people to tell who was a soldier and who was a rebel. Military discipline completely vanished. By the time the war ended in 2001, probably eighty thousand people had died and the whole country had been devastated. Roads, houses, and buildings were entirely destroyed. Today, if you go to Koidu, a major diamond-producing area in the east, you'll still see rows of burned-out houses scarred with bullet holes.

By 1991 the state in Sierra Leone had totally failed. Think of what King Shyaam started with the Bushong (pages 133–136): he set up extractive institutions to cement his power and extract the output the rest of society would produce. But even extractive institutions with central authority concentrated in his hands were an improvement over the situation without any law and order, central authority, or property rights that characterized the Lele society on the other side of the river Kasai. Such lack of order and central authority has been the fate of many African nations in recent decades, partly because the process of political centralization was historically delayed in much of sub-Saharan Africa, but also because the vicious circle of extractive institutions reversed any state centralization that existed, paving the way for state failure.

Sierra Leone during her bloody civil war of ten years, from 1991 to 2001, was a typical case of a failed state. It started out as just another country marred by extractive institutions, albeit of a particularly vicious and inefficient type. Countries become failed states not because of their geography or their culture, but because of the legacy of extractive institutions, which concentrate power and wealth in the hands of those controlling the state, opening the way for unrest, strife, and civil war. Extractive institutions also directly contribute to the gradual failing of the state by neglecting investment in the most basic public services, exactly what happened in Sierra Leone.

Extractive institutions that expropriate and impoverish the people and block economic development are quite common in Africa, Asia, and South America. Charles Taylor helped to start the civil war in Sierra Leone while at the same time initiating a savage conflict in Liberia, which led to state failure there, too. The pattern of extractive institutions collapsing into civil war and state failure has happened elsewhere in Africa; for example, in Angola, Côte d'Ivoire, the Democratic Republic of Congo, Mozambique, Republic of Congo, Somalia, Sudan, and Uganda. Extraction paves the way for conflict, not unlike the conflict that the highly extractive institutions of the Maya city-states generated almost a thousand years ago. Conflict precipitates state failure. So another reason why nations fail today is that their states fail. This, in turn, is a consequence of decades of rule under extractive economic and political institutions.

Who Is the State?

The cases of Zimbabwe, Somalia, and Sierra Leone, even if typical of poor countries in Africa, and perhaps even some in Asia, seem rather extreme. Surely Latin American countries do not have failed states? Surely their presidents are not brazen enough to win the lottery?

In Colombia, the Andean Mountains gradually merge to the north with a large coastal plain that borders the Caribbean Ocean. Colombians call this the *tierra caliente,* the "hot country," as distinct from the Andean world of the *tierra fria,* the "cold country." For the last fifty years, Colombia has been regarded by most political scientists and governments as a democracy. The United States feels happy to negotiate a potential free trade agreement with the country and pours all kinds of aid into it, particularly military aid. After a short-lived military government, which ended in 1958, elections have been regularly held, even though until 1974 a pact rotated political power and the presidency between the two traditional political parties, the Conservatives and the Liberals. Still, this pact, the National Front, was itself ratified by the Colombian people via a plebiscite, and this all seems democratic enough.

Yet while Colombia has a long history of democratic elections, it does not have inclusive institutions. Instead, its history has been marred by violations of civil liberties, extrajudicial executions, violence against civilians, and civil war. Not the sort of outcomes we expect from a democracy. The civil war in Colombia is different from that in Sierra Leone, where the state and society collapsed and chaos reigned. But it is a civil war nonetheless and one that has caused far more casualties. The military rule of the 1950s was itself partially in response to a civil war known in Spanish simply as La Violencia, or "The Violence." Since that time quite a range of insurgent groups, mostly communist revolutionaries, have plagued the countryside, kidnapping and murdering. To avoid either of these unpleasant options in rural Colombia, you have to pay the *vacuna*, literally "the vaccination," meaning that you have to vaccinate yourself against being murdered or kidnapped by paying off some group of armed thugs each month.

Not all armed groups in Colombia are communists. In 1981 members of the main communist guerrilla group in Colombia, the Fuerzas Armadas Revolucionarias de Colombia (the FARC—the Revolutionary Armed Forces of Colombia) kidnapped a dairy farmer, Jesus Castaño, who lived in a small town called Amalfi in the hot country in the northeastern part of the department of Antioquia. The FARC demanded a ransom amounting to $7,500, a small fortune in rural Colombia. The family raised it by mortgaging the farm, but their father's corpse was found anyway, chained to a tree. Enough was enough for three of Castaño's sons, Carlos, Fidel, and Vicente. They founded a paramilitary group, Los Tangueros, to hunt down members of the FARC and avenge this act. The brothers were good at organizing, and soon their group grew and began to find a common interest with other similar paramilitary groups that had developed from similar causes. Colombians in many areas were suffering at the hands of left-wing guerrillas, and right-wing paramilitaries formed in opposition. Paramilitaries were being used by landowners to defend themselves against the guerrillas, but they were also involved in drug trafficking, extortion, and the kidnapping and murder of citizens.

By 1997 the paramilitaries, under the leadership of the Castaño brothers, had managed to form a national organization for paramilitaries called the Autodefensas Unidas de Colombia (the AUC—United Self-Defense Forces of Colombia). The AUC expanded into large parts of the country, particularly into the hot country, in the departments of Córdoba, Sucre, Magdalena, and César. By 2001 the AUC may have had as many as thirty thousand armed men at its disposal and was organized into different blocks. In Córdoba, the paramilitary Bloque Catatumbo was led by Salvatore Mancuso. As its power continued to grow, the AUC made a strategic decision to get involved in politics. Paramilitaries and politicians courted each other. Several of the leaders of the AUC organized a meeting with prominent politicians in the town of Santa Fé de Ralito in Córdoba. A joint document, a pact, calling for the "refounding of the country" was issued and signed by leading members of the AUC, such as "Jorge 40" (the nickname for Rodrigo Tovar Pupo), Adolfo Paz (a nom de guerre for Diego Fernando "Don Berna" Murillo), and Diego Vecino (real name: Edwar Cobo Téllez), along with politicians, including national senators William Montes and Miguel de la Espriella. By this point the AUC was running large tracts of Colombia, and it was easy for them to fix who got elected in the 2002 elections for the Congress and Senate. For example, in the municipality of San Onofre, in Sucre, the election was arranged by the paramilitary leader Cadena ("chain"). One eyewitness described what happened as follows:

> The trucks sent by Cadena went around the neighborhoods, corregimientos and rural areas of San Onofre picking people up. According to some inhabitants . . . for the 2002 elections hundreds of peasants were taken to the corregimiento Plan Parejo so they could see the faces of the candidates they had to vote for in the parliamentarian elections: Jairo Merlano for Senate and Muriel Benito Rebollo for Congress.
>
> Cadena put in a bag the names of the members of the municipal council, took out two and said that he would kill them and other people chosen randomly if Muriel did not win.

The threat seems to have worked: each candidate obtained forty thousand votes in the whole of Sucre. It is no surprise that the mayor of San Onofre signed the pact of Santa Fé de Ralito. Probably one-third of the congressmen and senators owed their election in 2002 to paramilitary support, and Map 20 (page 380), which depicts the areas of Colombia under paramilitary control, shows how widespread their hold was. Salvatore Mancuso himself put it in an interview in the following way:

> 35 percent of the Congress was elected in areas where there were states of the Self-Defense groups, in those

states we were the ones collecting taxes, we delivered justice, and we had the military and territorial control of the region and all the people who wanted to go into politics had to come and deal with the political representatives we had there.

It is not difficult to imagine the effect of this extent of paramilitary control of politics and society on economic institutions and public policy. The expansion of the AUC was not a peaceful affair. The

Map 20: Paramilitary presence across Colombia, 1997–2005

group not only fought against the FARC, but also murdered innocent civilians and terrorized and displaced hundreds of thousands of people from their homes. According to the Internal Displacement Monitoring Centre (IDMC) of the Norwegian Refugee Council, in early 2010 around 10 percent of Colombia's population, nearly 4.5 million people, was internally displaced. The paramilitaries also, as Mancuso suggested, took over the government and all its functions, except that the taxes they collected were just expropriation for their own pockets. An extraordinary pact between the paramilitary leader Martín Llanos (real name: Héctor Germán Buitrago) and the mayors of the municipalities of Tauramena, Aguazul, Maní, Villanueva, Monterrey, and Sabanalarga, in the department of Casanare in eastern Colombia, lists the following rules to which the mayors had to adhere by order of the "Paramilitary Peasants of Casanare":

9) Give 50 percent of the municipality budget to be managed by the Paramilitary Peasants of Casanare.
10) 10 percent of each and every contract of the municipality [to be given to the Paramilitary Peasants of Casanare].
11) Mandatory assistance to all the meetings called by the Paramilitary Peasants of Casanare.
12) Inclusion of the Paramilitary Peasants of Casanare in every infrastructure project.
13) Affiliation to the new political party formed by the Paramilitary Peasants of Casanare.
14) Accomplishment of his/hers governance program.

Casanare is not a poor department. On the contrary, it has the highest level of per capita income of any Colombian department, because it has significant oil deposits, just the kind of resources that attract paramilitaries. In fact, once they gained power, the paramilitaries intensified their systematic expropriation of property. Mancuso himself reputedly accumulated $25 million worth of urban and rural property. Estimates of land expropriated in Colombia by paramilitaries are as high as 10 percent of all rural land.

Colombia is not a case of a failed state about to collapse. But it is a state without sufficient centralization and with far-from-complete authority over all its territory. Though the state is able to provide security and public services in large urban areas such as Bogotá and Barranquilla, there are significant parts of the country where it provides few public services and almost no law and order. Instead, alternative groups and people, such as Mancuso, control politics and resources. In parts of the country, economic institutions function quite well, and there are high levels of human capital and entrepreneurial skill; in other parts the institutions are highly extractive, even failing to provide a minimal degree of state authority.

It might be hard to understand how a situation like this can sustain itself for decades, even centuries. But in fact, the situation has a logic of its own, as a type of vicious circle. Violence and the absence of centralized state institutions of this type enter into a symbiotic relationship with politicians running the functional parts of the society. The symbiotic relationship arises because national politicians exploit the lawlessness in peripheral parts of the country, while paramilitary groups are left to their own devices by the national government.

This pattern became particularly apparent in the 2000s. In 2002 the presidential election was won by Álvaro Uribe. Uribe had something in common with the Castaño brothers: his father had been killed by the FARC. Uribe ran a campaign repudiating the attempts of the previous administration to try to make peace with the FARC. In 2002 his vote share was 3 percentage points higher in areas with paramilitaries than without them. In 2006, when he was reelected, his vote share was 11 percentage points higher in such areas. If Mancuso and his partners could deliver the vote for Congress and the Senate, they could do so in presidential elections as well, particularly for a president strongly aligned with their worldview and likely to be lenient on them. As Jairo Angarita, Salvatore Mancuso's deputy and the former leader of the AUC's Sinú and San Jorge blocs, declared in September 2005, he was proud to work for the "reelection of the best president we have ever had."

Once elected, the paramilitary senators and congressmen voted for what Uribe wanted, in particular changing the constitution so that he could be reelected in 2006, which had not been allowed at the time of his first election, in 2002. In exchange, President Uribe delivered a highly lenient law that allowed the paramilitaries to demobilize. Demobilization did not mean the end of paramilitarism, simply its institutionalization in large parts of Colombia and the Colombian state, which the paramilitaries had taken over and were allowed to keep.

In Colombia many aspects of economic and political institutions have become more inclusive over time. But certain major extractive elements remain. Lawlessness and insecure property rights are endemic in large swaths of the country, and this is a consequence of the lack of control by the national state in many parts of the country, and the particular form of lack of state centralization in Colombia. But this state of affairs is not an inevitable outcome. It is itself a consequence of dynamics mirroring the vicious circle: political institutions in Colombia do not generate incentives for politicians to provide public services and law and order in much of the country and do not put enough constraints on them to prevent them from entering into implicit or explicit deals with paramilitaries and thugs.

EL CORRALITO

Argentina was in the grip of an economic crisis in late 2001. For three years, income had been falling, unemployment had been rising, and the country had accumulated a massive international debt. The policies leading to this situation were adopted after 1989 by the government of Carlos Menem, to stop hyperinflation and stabilize the economy. For a time they were successful.

In 1991 Menem tied the Argentine peso to the U.S. dollar. One peso was equal to one dollar by law. There was to be no change in the exchange rate. End of story. Well, almost. To convince people that the government really meant to stick to the law, it persuaded people to open bank accounts in U.S. dollars. Dollars could be used in the shops of the capital city of Buenos Aires and withdrawn from cash machines all over the city. This policy may have helped stabilize the economy, but it had one big drawback. It made Argentine exports very expensive and foreign imports very cheap. Exports dribbled to a halt; imports gushed in. The only way to pay for them was to borrow. It was an unsustainable situation. As more people began worrying about the sustainability of the peso, they put more of their wealth into dollar accounts at banks. After all, if the government ripped up the law and devalued the peso, they would be safe with dollar accounts, right? They were right to be worried about the peso. But they were too optimistic about their dollars.

On December 1, 2001, the government froze all bank accounts, initially for ninety days. Only a small amount of cash was allowed for withdrawal on a weekly basis. First it was 250 pesos, still worth $250; then 300 pesos. But this was allowed to be withdrawn only from peso accounts. Nobody was allowed to withdraw money from their dollar accounts, unless they agreed to convert the dollars into pesos. Nobody wanted to do so. Argentines dubbed this situation El Corralito, "the Little Corral": depositors were hemmed into a corral like cows, with nowhere to go. In January the devaluation was finally enacted, and instead of there being one peso for one dollar, there were soon four pesos for one dollar. This should have been a vindication of those who thought that they should put their savings in dollars. But it wasn't, because the government then forcibly converted all the dollar bank accounts into pesos, but at the old one-for-one exchange rate. Someone who had had $1,000 saved suddenly found himself with only $250. The government had expropriated three-quarters of people's savings.

For economists, Argentina is a perplexing country. To illustrate how difficult it was to understand Argentina, the Nobel Prize–winning economist Simon Kuznets once famously remarked that there were four sorts of countries: developed, underdeveloped, Japan, and Argentina. Kuznets thought so because, around the time of the First World War, Argentina was one of the richest countries in the world. It then began a steady decline relative to the other rich countries in Western Europe and North America, which turned, in the 1970s and '80s, into an absolute decline. On the surface of it, Argentina's economic performance is puzzling, but the reasons for its decline become clearer when looked at through the lens of inclusive and extractive institutions.

It is true that before 1914, Argentina experienced around fifty years of economic growth, but this was a classic case of growth under extractive institutions. Argentina was then ruled by a narrow elite heavily invested in the agricultural export economy. The economy grew by exporting beef, hides, and grain in the middle of a boom in the world prices of these commodities. Like all such experiences of growth under extractive institutions, it involved no creative destruction and no innovation. And it was not sustainable. Around the time of the First World War, mounting political instability and armed revolts induced the Argentine elites to try to broaden the political system, but this led to the mobilization of forces they could not control, and in 1930 came the first military coup. Between then and 1983, Argentina oscillated backward and forward between dictatorship and democracy and between various extractive institutions. There was mass repression under military rule, which peaked in the 1970s with at least nine thousand people and probably far more being illegally executed. Hundreds of thousands were imprisoned and tortured.

During the periods of civilian rule there were elections—a democracy of sorts. But the political system was far from inclusive. Since the rise of Perón in the 1940s, democratic Argentina has been dominated by the political party he created, the Partido Justicialista, usually just called the Perónist Party. The Perónists won elections thanks to a huge political machine, which succeeded by buying votes, dispensing patronage, and engaging in corruption, including government contracts and jobs in exchange for political support. In a sense this was a democracy, but it was not pluralistic. Power was highly concentrated in the Perónist Party, which faced few constraints on what it could do, at least in the period when the military restrained from throwing it from power. As we saw earlier (pages 329–332), if the Supreme Court challenged a policy, so much the worse for the Supreme Court.

In the 1940s, Perón had cultivated the labor movement as a political base. When it was weakened by military repression in the 1970s and '80s, his party simply switched to buying votes from others instead. Economic policies and institutions were designed to deliver income to their supporters, not to create a level playing field. When President Menem faced a term limit that kept him from being re-elected in the 1990s, it was just more of the same; he could simply rewrite the constitution and get rid of the term limit. As El Corralito shows, even if Argentina has elections and popularly elected governments, the government is quite able to override property rights and expropriate its own citizens with impunity. There is little check on Argentine presidents and political elites, and certainly no pluralism.

What puzzled Kuznets, and no doubt many others who visit Buenos Aires, is that the city seems so different from Lima, Guatemala City, or even Mexico City. You do not see indigenous people, and you do not see the descendants of former slaves. Mostly you see the glorious architecture and buildings put up during the Belle Epoch, the years of growth under extractive institutions. But in Buenos Aires you see only part of Argentina. Menem, for example, was not from Buenos Aires. He was born in Anillaco, in the province of La Rioja, in the mountains far to the northwest of Buenos Aires, and he served three terms as governor of the province. At the time of the conquest of the Americas by the Spanish, this area of Argentina was an outlying part of the Inca Empire and had a dense population of indigenous people (see Map 1 on page 17). The Spanish created *encomiendas* here, and a highly extractive economy developed growing food and breeding mules for the miners in Potosí to the north. In fact, La Rioja was much more like the area of Potosí in Peru and Bolivia than it was like Buenos Aires. In the nineteenth century, La Rioja produced the famous warlord Facundo Quiroga, who ruled the area lawlessly and marched his army on Buenos Aires. The story about the development of Argentine political institutions is a story about how the interior provinces, such as La Rioja, reached agreements with Buenos Aires. These agreements were a truce: the warlords of La Rioja agreed to leave Buenos Aires alone so that it could make money. In return, the Buenos Aires elites gave up on reforming the institutions of "the interior." So Argentina at first appears a world apart from Peru or Bolivia, but it is really not so different once you leave the elegant boulevards of Buenos Aires. That the preferences and the politics of the interior got embedded into Argentine institutions is the reason why the country has experienced a very similar institutional path to those of other extractive Latin American countries.

That elections have not brought either inclusive political or economic institutions is the typical case in Latin America. In Colombia, paramilitaries can fix one-third of national elections. In Venezuela today, as in Argentina, the democratically elected government of Hugo Chávez attacks its opponents, fires them from public-sector jobs, closes down newspapers whose editorials it doesn't like, and expropriates property. In whatever he does, Chávez is much more powerful and less constrained than Sir Robert Walpole was in Britain in the 1720s, when he was unable to condemn John Huntridge under the Black Act (pages 302–308). Huntridge would have fared much less well in present-day Venezuela or Argentina.

While the democracy emerging in Latin America is in principle diametrically opposed to elite rule, and in rhetoric and action it tries to redistribute rights and opportunities away from at least a segment of the elite, its roots are firmly based in extractive regimes in two senses. First, inequities persisting for centuries under extractive regimes make voters in newly emerging democracies vote in favor of politicians with extreme policies. It is not that Argentinians are just naïve and think that Juan Perón or the more recent Perónist politicians such as Menem or the Kirchners are selfless and looking out for their interests, or that Venezuelans see their salvation in Chávez. Instead, many Argentinians and Venezuelans recognize that all other politicians and parties have for so long failed to give them voice, to provide them with the most basic public services, such as roads and education, and to protect them from exploitation by local elites. So many Venezuelans today support the policies that Chávez is adopting even if these come with corruption and waste in the same way that many Argentinians supported Perón's policies in the 1940s and 1970s. Second, it is again the underlying extractive institutions that make politics so attractive to, and so biased in favor of, strongmen such as Perón and Chávez, rather than an effective party system producing socially desirable alternatives. Perón, Chávez, and dozens of other strongmen in Latin America are just another facet of the iron law of oligarchy, and as the name suggests, the roots of this iron law lies in the underlying elite-controlled regimes.

THE NEW ABSOLUTISM

In November 2009, the government of North Korea implemented what economists call a currency reform. Severe bouts of inflation are often the reasons for such reforms. In France in January 1960, a currency reform introduced a new franc that was equal to 100 of the existing francs. Old francs continued in circulation and people even quoted prices in them as the change to the new francs was gradually made. Finally, old francs ceased to be legal tender in January 2002, when France introduced the euro. The North Korean reform looked similar on the face of it. Like the French in 1960, the North Korean government decided to take two zeros off the currency. One hundred old wons, the currency of North Korea, were to be worth one new won. Individuals were allowed to come forward to exchange their old currency for the newly printed currency, though this had to be done in one week, rather than forty-two years, as in the French case. Then came the catch: the government announced that no one could convert more than 100,000 won, though it later relaxed this to 500,000. One hundred thousand won was about $40 at the black market exchange rate. In one stroke, the government had wiped out a huge fraction of North Korean citizens' private wealth; we do not know exactly how much, but it is probably greater than that expropriated by the Argentine government in 2002.

The government in North Korea is a communist dictatorship opposed to private property and markets. But it is difficult to control black markets, and black markets make transactions in cash. Of course quite a bit of foreign exchange is involved, particularly Chinese currency, but many transactions use won. The currency reform was designed to punish people who used these markets and, more specifically, to make sure that they did not become too wealthy or powerful enough to threaten the regime. Keeping them poor was safer. Black markets are not the whole story. People in North Korea also keep their savings in wons because there are few banks in Korea, and they are all owned by the government. In effect, the government used the currency reform to expropriate much of people's savings.

Though the government says it regards markets as bad, the North Korean elite rather like what markets can produce for them. The previous leader, Kim Jong-Il, had a seven-story pleasure palace equipped with a bar, a karaoke machine, and a mini movie theater. The ground floor had an enormous swimming pool with a wave machine, where Kim liked to use a body board fitted with a small motor. When in 2006 the United States placed sanctions on North Korea, it knew how to really hit the regime where it hurt. It made it illegal to export more than sixty luxury items to North Korea, including yachts, water scooters, racing cars, motorcycles, DVD players, and televisions larger than twenty-nine inches. There would be no more silk scarves, designer fountain pens, furs, or leather luggage. These were exactly the items collected by Kim and his Communist Party elites. One scholar used sales figures from the French company Hennessy to estimate that Kim's annual cognac budget before the sanctions could have been as high as $800,000 a year.

It is impossible to understand many of the poorest regions of the world at the end of the twentieth century without understanding the new absolutism of the twentieth century: communism. Marx's vision was a system that would generate prosperity under more humane conditions and without inequality. Lenin and his Communist Party were inspired by Marx, but the practice could not have been more different from the theory. The Bolshevik Revolution of 1917 was a bloody affair, and there was no humane aspect to it. Equality was not part of the equation, either, since the first thing Lenin and his entourage did was to create a new elite, themselves, at the head of the Bolshevik Party. In doing so, they purged and murdered not only non-communist elements, but also other communists who could have threatened their power. But the real tragedies were yet to come: first with the Civil War, and then under Stalin's collectivization and his all-too-frequent purges, which may have killed as many as forty million people. Russian communism was brutal, repressive, and bloody, but not unique. The economic consequences and the human suffering were quite typical of what happened elsewhere—for example, in Cambodia in the 1970s under the Khmer Rouge, in China, and in North Korea. In all cases communism brought vicious dictatorships and widespread human rights abuses. Beyond the human suffering and carnage, the communist regimes all set up various types of extractive institutions. The economic institutions, with or without markets, were designed to extract resources from the people, and by entirely abhorring property rights, they often created poverty instead of prosperity. In the Soviet case, as we saw in chapter 5, the Communist system at first generated rapid growth, but then faltered and led to stagnation. The consequences were much more devastating in China under Mao, in Cambodia under the Khmer Rouge, and in North Korea, where the Communist economic institutions led to economic collapse and famine.

The Communist economic institutions were in turn supported by extractive political institutions, concentrating all power in the hands of Communist parties and introducing no constraints on the exercise of this power. Though these were different extractive institutions in form, they had similar effects on the livelihoods of the people as the extractive institutions in Zimbabwe and Sierra Leone.

KING COTTON

Cotton accounts for about 45 percent of the exports of Uzbekistan, making it the most important crop since the country established independence at the breakup of the Soviet Union in 1991. Under Soviet communism all farmland in Uzbekistan was under the control of 2,048 state-owned farms. These were broken up and the land distributed after 1991. But that didn't mean farmers could act independently. Cotton was too valuable to the new government of Uzbekistan's first, and so far only, president, Islam Karimov. Instead, regulations were introduced that determined what farmers could plant and exactly how much they could sell it for. Cotton was a valuable export, and farmers were paid a small fraction of world market prices for their crop, with the government taking the rest. Nobody would have grown cotton at the prices paid, so the government forced them. Every farmer now has to allocate 35 percent of his land to cotton. This caused many problems, difficulties with machinery being one. At the time of independence, about 40 percent of the harvest was picked by combine harvesters. After 1991, not surprisingly, given the incentives that President Karimov's regime created for farmers, they were not willing to buy these or maintain them. Recognizing the problem, Karimov came up with a solution, in fact, a cheaper option than combine harvesters: schoolchildren.

The cotton bolls start to ripen and are ready to be picked in early September, at about the same time that children return to school. Karimov issued orders to local governors to send cotton delivery quotas to schools. In early September the schools are emptied of 2.7 million children (2006 figures). Teachers, instead of being instructors, became labor recruiters. Gulnaz, a mother of two of these children, explained what happens:

> At the beginning of each school year, approximately at the beginning of September, the classes in school are suspended, and instead of classes children are sent to the cotton harvest. Nobody asks for the consent of parents. They don't have weekend holidays [during the harvesting season]. If a child is for any reason left at home, his teacher or class curator comes over and denounces the parents. They assign a plan to each child, from 20 to 60 kg per day depending on the child's age. If a child fails to fulfil this plan then next morning he is lambasted in front of the whole class.

The harvest lasts for two months. Rural children lucky enough to be assigned to farms close to home can walk or are bused to work. Children farther away or from urban areas have to sleep in the sheds or storehouses with the machinery and animals. There are no toilets or kitchens. Children have to bring their own food for lunch.

The main beneficiaries from all this forced labor are the political elites, led by President Karimov, the de facto king of all Uzbeki cotton. The schoolchildren are supposedly paid for their labor, but only supposedly. In 2006, when the world price of cotton was around $1.40 (U.S.) per kilo, the children were paid about $0.03 for their daily quota of twenty to sixty kilos. Probably 75 percent of the cotton harvest is now picked by children. In the spring, school is closed for compulsory hoeing, weeding, and transplanting.

How did it all come to this? Uzbekistan, like the other Soviet Socialist Republics, was supposed to gain its independence after the collapse of the Soviet Union and develop a market economy and democracy. As in many other Soviet Republics, this is not what happened, however. President Karimov, who began his political career in the Communist Party of the old Soviet Union, rising to the post of first secretary for Uzbekistan at the opportune moment of 1989, just as the Berlin Wall was collapsing, managed to reinvent himself as a nationalist. With the crucial support of the security forces, in December 1991 he won Uzbekistan's first-ever presidential election. After taking power, he cracked down on the independent political opposition. Opponents are now in prison or exile. There is no free media in Uzbekistan, and no nongovernmental organizations are allowed. The apogee of the intensifying repression came in 2005, when possibly 750, maybe more, demonstrators were murdered by the police and army in Andijon.

Using this command of the security forces and total control of the media, Karimov first extended his presidential term for five years, through a referendum, and then won reelection for a new seven-year term in 2000, with 91.2 percent of the vote. His only opponent declared that he had voted for Karimov! In his 2007 reelection, widely regarded as fraudulent, he won 88 percent of the vote. Elections in Uzbekistan are similar to those that Joseph Stalin used to organize in the heyday of the Soviet Union. One in 1937 was famously covered by *New York Times* correspondent Harold Denny, who reproduced a translation from *Pravda*, the newspaper of the Communist Party, which was meant to convey the tension and excitement of Soviet elections:

Midnight has struck. The twelfth of December, the day of the first general, equal and direct elections to the Supreme Soviet, has ended. The result of the voting is about to be announced.

The commission remains alone in its room. It is quiet, and the lamps are shining solemnly. Amid the general attentive and intense expectation the chairman performs all the necessary formalities before counting of the ballots—checking up by list how many voters there were and how many have voted—and the result is 100 per cent. 100 per cent! What election in what country for what candidate has given a 100 per cent response?

The main business starts now. Excitedly the chairman inspects the seals on the boxes. Then the members of the commission inspect them. The seals are intact and are cut off. The boxes are opened.

It is quiet. They sit attentively and seriously, these election inspectors and executives.

Now it is time to open the envelopes. Three members of the commission take scissors. The chairman rises. The tellers have their copybooks ready. The first envelope is slit. All eyes are directed to it. The chairman takes out two slips—white [for a candidate for the Soviet of the Union] and blue [for a candidate for the Soviet of Nationalities]—and reads loudly and distinctly, "Comrade Stalin."

Instantly the solemnity is broken. Everybody in the room jumps up and applauds joyously and stormily for the first ballot of the first general secret election under the Stalinist Constitution—a ballot with the name of the Constitution's creator.

This mood would have captured the suspense surrounding the reelections of Karimov, who appears an apt pupil of Stalin when it comes to repression and political control and seems to organize elections that compete with those of Stalin in their surrealism.

Under Karimov, Uzbekistan is a country with very extractive political and economic institutions. And it is poor. Probably one-third of the people live in poverty, and the average annual income is around $1,000. Not all the development indicators are bad. According to World Bank data, school enrollment is 100 percent . . . well, except possibly during the cotton picking season. Literacy is also very high, though apart from controlling all the media, the regime also bans books and censors the Internet. While most people are paid only a few cents a day to pick cotton, the Karimov family and former communist cadres who reinvented themselves after 1989 as the new economic and political elites of Uzbekistan have become fabulously wealthy.

The family economic interests are run by Karimov's daughter Gulnora, who is expected to succeed her father as president. In a country so untransparent and secretive, nobody knows exactly what the Karimov family controls or how much money they earn, but the experience of the U.S. company Interspan is indicative of what has happened in the Uzbek economy in the last two decades. Cotton is not the only agricultural crop; parts of the country are ideal for growing tea, and Interspan decided to invest. By 2005 it had taken over 30 percent of the local market, but then it ran into trouble. Gulnora decided that the tea industry looked economically promising. Soon Interspan's local personnel started to be arrested, beaten up, and tortured. It became impossible to operate, and by August 2006 the company had pulled out. Its assets were taken over by the Karimov families' rapidly expanding tea interests, at the time representing 67 percent of the market, up from 2 percent a couple of years earlier.

Uzbekistan in many ways looks like a relic from the past, a forgotten age. It is a country languishing under the absolutism of a single family and the cronies surrounding them, with an economy based on forced labor—in fact, the forced labor of children. Except that it isn't. It's part of the current mosaic of societies failing under extractive institutions, and unfortunately it has many commonalities with other former Soviet Socialist Republics, ranging from Armenia and Azerbaijan to Kyrgyzstan, Tajikistan, and Turkmenistan, and reminds us that even in the twenty-first century, extractive economic and political institutions can take an unashamed atrociously extractive form.

KEEPING THE PLAYING FIELD AT AN ANGLE

The 1990s were a period of reform in Egypt. Since the military coup that removed the monarchy in 1954, Egypt had been run as a quasi-socialist society in which the government played a central role in the economy. Many sectors of the economy were dominated by state-owned enterprises. Over the years, the rhetoric of socialism lapsed, markets opened, and the private sector developed. Yet these were not inclusive markets, but markets controlled by the state and by a handful of businessmen allied with the National Democratic Party (NDP), the political party founded by President Anwar Sadat in 1978. Businessmen became more and more involved with the party, and the party became more and more involved with them under the government of Hosni Mubarak. Mubarak, who became president in 1981 following Anwar Sadat's assassination, ruled with the NDP until being forced from power by popular protests and the military in February 2011, as we discussed in the Preface (page 1).

Major businesspeople were appointed to key government posts in areas closely related to their economic interests. Rasheed Mohamed Rasheed, former president of Unilever AMET (Africa, Middle East, and Turkey), became minister of foreign trade and industry; Mohamed Zoheir Wahid Garana, the owner and managing director of Garana Travel Company, one of the largest in Egypt, became minister of tourism; Amin Ahmed Mohamed Osman Abaza, founder of the Nile Cotton Trade Company, the largest cotton-exporting company in Egypt, became minister of agriculture.

In many sectors of the economy, businessmen persuaded the government to restrict entry through state regulation. These sectors included the media, iron and steel, the automotive industry, alcoholic beverages, and cement. Each sector was very concentrated with high entry barriers protecting the politically connected businessmen and firms. Big businessmen close to the regime, such as Ahmed Ezz (iron and steel), the Sawiris family (multimedia, beverages, and telecommunications), and Mohamed Nosseir (beverages and telecommunications) received not only protection from the state but also government contracts and large bank loans without needing to put up collateral. Ahmed Ezz was both the chairman of Ezz Steel, the largest company in the country's steel industry, producing 70 percent of Egypt's steel, and also a high-ranking member of the NDP, the chairman of the People's Assembly Budget and Planning Committee, and a close associate of Gamal Mubarak, one of President Mubarak's sons.

The economic reforms of the 1990s promoted by international financial institutions and economists were aimed at freeing up markets and reducing the role of the state in the economy. A key pillar of such reforms everywhere was the privatization of state-owned assets. Mexican privatization (pages 38–40), instead of increasing competition, simply turned state-owned monopolies into privately owned monopolies, in the process enriching politically connected businessmen such as Carlos Slim. Exactly the same thing took place in Egypt. The businesspeople connected to the regime were able to heavily influence implementation of Egypt's privatization program so that it favored the wealthy business elite—or the "whales," as they are known locally. At the time that privatization began, the economy was dominated by thirty-two of these whales.

One was Ahmed Zayat, at the helm of the Luxor Group. In 1996 the government decided to privatize Al Ahram beverages (ABC), which was the monopoly maker of beer in Egypt. A bid came in from a consortium of the Egyptian Finance Company, led by real estate developer Farid Saad, along with the first venture capital company formed in Egypt in 1995. The consortium included Fouad Sultan, former minister of tourism, Mohamed Nosseir, and Mohamed Ragab, another elite businessman. The group was well connected, but not well connected enough. Its bid of 400 million Egyptian pounds was turned down as too low. Zayat was better connected. He didn't have the money to purchase ABC, so he came up with a scheme of Carlos Slim–type ingenuity. ABC shares were floated for the first time on the

London Stock Exchange, and the Luxor Group acquired 74.9 percent of those shares at 68.5 Egyptian pounds per share. Three months later the shares were then split in two, and the Luxor Group was able to sell all of them at 52.5 pounds each, netting a 36 percent profit, with which Zayat was able to fund the purchase of ABC for 231 million pounds the next month. At the time, ABC was making an annual profit of around 41.3 million Egyptian pounds and had cash reserves of 93 million Egyptian pounds. It was quite a bargain. In 1999 the newly privatized ABC extended its monopoly from beer into wine by buying the privatized national wine monopoly Gianaclis. Gianaclis was a very profitable company, nestling behind a 3,000 percent tariff imposed on imported wines, and it had a 70 percent profit margin on what it sold. In 2002 the monopoly changed hands again when Zayat sold ABC to Heineken for 1.3 billion Egyptian pounds. A 563 percent profit in five years.

Mohamed Nosseir hadn't always been on the losing side. In 1993 he purchased the privatized El Nasr Bottling Company, which had the monopoly rights to bottle and sell Coca-Cola in Egypt. Nosseir's relations with the then-minister of the public business sector, Atef Ebeid, allowed him to make the purchase with little competition. Nosseir then sold the company after two years for more than three times the acquisition price. Another example was the move in the late 1990s to involve the private sector in the state cinema industry. Again political connections implied that only two families were allowed to bid for and operate the cinemas—one of whom was the Sawiris family.

Egypt today is a poor nation—not as poor as most countries to the south, in sub-Saharan Africa, but still one where around 40 percent of the population is very poor and lives on less than two dollars a day. Ironically, as we saw earlier (pages 61–62), in the nineteenth century Egypt was the site of an initially successful attempt at institutional change and economic modernization under Muhammad Ali, who did generate a period of extractive economic growth before it was effectively annexed to the British Empire. From the British colonial period a set of extractive institutions emerged, and were continued by the military after 1954. There was some economic growth and investment in education, but the majority of the population had few economic opportunities, while the new elite could benefit from their connections to the government.

These extractive economic institutions were again supported by extractive political institutions. President Mubarak planned to begin a political dynasty, grooming his son Gamal to replace him. His plan was cut short only by the collapse of his extractive regime in early 2011 in the face of widespread unrest and demonstrations during the so-called Arab Spring. During the period when Nasser was president, there were some inclusive aspects of economic institutions, and the state did open up the education system and provide some opportunities that the previous regime of King Farouk had not. But this was an example of an unstable combination of extractive political institutions with some inclusivity of economic institutions.

The inevitable outcome, which came during Mubarak's reign, was that economic institutions became more extractive, reflecting the distribution of political power in society. In some sense the Arab Spring was a reaction to this. This was true not just in Egypt but also in Tunisia. Three decades of Tunisian growth under extractive political institutions started to go into reverse as President Ben Ali and his family began to prey more and more on the economy.

WHY NATIONS FAIL

Nations fail economically because of extractive institutions. These institutions keep poor countries poor and prevent them from embarking on a path to economic growth. This is true today in Africa, in places such as Zimbabwe and Sierra Leone; in South America, in countries such as Colombia and Argentina; in Asia, in countries such as North Korea and Uzbekistan; and in the Middle East, in nations such as Egypt. There are notable differences among these countries. Some are tropical, some are in temperate latitudes. Some were colonies of Britain; others, of Japan, Spain, and Russia. They have very different histories, languages, and cultures. What they all share is extractive institutions. In all these cases the basis of these institutions is an elite who design economic institutions in order to enrich themselves and perpetuate their power at the expense of the vast majority of people in society. The different histories and social structures of the countries lead to the differences in the nature of the elites and in the details of the extractive institutions. But the reason why these extractive institutions persist is always related to the vicious circle, and the implications of these institutions in terms of impoverishing their citizens are similar—even if their intensity differs.

In Zimbabwe, for example, the elite comprise Robert Mugabe and the core of ZANU-PF, who spearheaded the anticolonial fight in the 1970s. In North Korea, they are the clique around Kim Jong-Il and the Communist Party. In Uzbekistan it is President Islam Karimov, his family, and his reinvented Soviet Union–era cronies. These groups are obviously very different, and these differences, along with the variegated polities and economies they govern, mean that the specific form the extractive institutions take differs. For instance, because North Korea was created by a communist revolution, it takes as its political model the one-party rule of the Communist Party. Though Mugabe did invite the North Korean military into Zimbabwe in the 1980s to massacre his opponents in Matabeleland, such a model for extractive political institutions is not applicable in Zimbabwe. Instead, because of the way he came to power in the anticolonial struggle, Mugabe had to cloak his rule with elections, even if for a while he managed actually to engineer a constitutionally sanctified one-party state.

In contrast, Colombia has had a long history of elections, which emerged historically as a method for sharing power between the Liberal and Conservative parties in the wake of independence from Spain. Not only is the nature of elites different, but their numbers are. In Uzbekistan, Karimov could hijack the remnants of the Soviet state, which gave him a strong apparatus to suppress and murder alternative elites. In Colombia, the lack of authority of the central state in parts of the country has naturally led to much more fragmented elites—in fact, so much so that they sometimes murder one another. Nevertheless, despite these variegated elites and political institutions, these institutions often manage to cement and reproduce the power of the elite that created them. But sometimes the infighting they induce leads to the collapse of the state, as in Sierra Leone.

Just as different histories and structures mean that the identity of elites and the details of extractive political institutions differ, so do the details of the extractive economic institutions that the elites set up. In North Korea, the tools of extraction were again inherited from the communist toolkit: the abolition of private property, state-run farms, and industry.

In Egypt, the situation was quite similar under the avowedly socialist military regime created by Colonel Nasser after 1952. Nasser sided with the Soviet Union in the cold war, expropriating foreign investments, such as the British-owned Suez Canal, and took into public ownership much of the economy. However, the situation in Egypt in the 1950s and '60s was very different from that in North Korea in the 1940s. It was much easier for the North Koreans to create a more radically communist-style economy, since they could expropriate former Japanese assets and build on the economic model of the Chinese Revolution.

In contrast, the Egyptian Revolution was more a coup by a group of military officers. When Egypt changed sides in the cold war and became pro-Western, it was therefore relatively easy, as well as expedient, for the Egyptian military to change from central command to crony capitalism as a method of extraction. Even so, the better economic performance of Egypt compared with North Korea was a consequence of the more limited extractive nature of Egyptian institutions. For one thing, lacking the stifling control of the North Korean Communist Party, the Egyptian regime had to placate its population in a way that the North Korean regime does not. For another, even crony capitalism generates some incentives for investment, at least among those favored by the regime, that are totally absent in North Korea.

Though these details are all important and interesting, the more critical lessons are in the big picture, which reveals that in each of these cases, extractive political institutions have created extractive economic institutions, transferring wealth and power toward the elite.

The intensity of extraction in these different countries obviously varies and has important consequences for prosperity. In Argentina, for example, the constitution and democratic elections do not work well to promote pluralism, but they do function much better than in Colombia. At least the state can claim the monopoly of violence in Argentina. Partly as a consequence, income per capita in Argentina is double that of Colombia. The political institutions of both countries do a much better job of restraining elites than those in Zimbabwe and Sierra Leone, and as a result, Zimbabwe and Sierra Leone are much poorer than Argentina and Colombia.

The vicious circle also implies that even when extractive institutions lead to the collapse of the state, as in Sierra Leone and Zimbabwe, this doesn't put a conclusive end to the rule of these institutions. We have already seen that civil wars and revolutions, while they may occur during critical junctures, do not necessarily lead to institutional change. The events in Sierra Leone since the civil war ended in 2002 vividly illustrate this possibility.

In 2007 in a democratic election, the old party of Siaka Stevens, the APC, returned to power. Though the man who won the presidential election, Ernest Bai Koroma, had no association with the old APC governments, many of his cabinet did. Two of Stevens's sons, Bockarie and Jengo, were even made ambassadors to the United States and Germany. In a sense this is a more volatile version of what we saw happen in Colombia. There the lack of state authority in many parts of the country persists over time because it is in the interests of part of the national political elite to allow it to do so, but the core state institutions are also strong enough to prevent this disorder from turning into complete chaos. In Sierra Leone, partly because of the more extractive nature of economic institutions and partly because of the country's history of highly extractive political institutions, the society has not only suffered economically but has also tipped between complete disorder and some sort of order. Still, the long-run effect is the same: the state all but remains absent, and institutions are extractive.

In all these cases there has been a long history of extractive institutions since at least the nineteenth century. Each country is trapped in a vicious circle. In Colombia and Argentina, they are rooted in the institutions of Spanish colonial rule (pages 9–19). Zimbabwe and Sierra Leone originated in British colonial regimes set up in the late nineteenth century. In Sierra Leone, in the absence of white settlers, these regimes built extensively on precolonial extractive structures of political power and intensified them. These structures themselves were the outcome of a long vicious circle that featured lack of political centralization and the disastrous effects of the slave trade. In Zimbabwe, there was much more of a construction of a new form of extractive institutions, because the British South Africa Company created a dual economy. Uzbekistan could take over the extractive institutions of the Soviet Union and, like Egypt, modify them into crony capitalism. The Soviet Union's extractive institutions themselves were in many ways a continuation of those of the tsarist regime, again in a pattern predicated on the iron law of oligarchy. As these various vicious circles played out in different parts of the world over the past 250 years, world inequality emerged, and persists.

The solution to the economic and political failure of nations today is to transform their extractive institutions toward inclusive ones. The vicious circle means that this is not easy. But it is not impossible, and the iron law of oligarchy is not inevitable. Either some preexisting inclusive elements in institutions, or the presence of broad coalitions leading the fight against the existing regime, or just the contingent nature of history, can break vicious circles. Just like the civil war in Sierra Leone, the Glorious Revolution in 1688 was a struggle for power. But it was a struggle of a very different nature than the civil war in Sierra Leone. Conceivably some in Parliament fighting to remove James II in the wake of the Glorious Revolution imagined themselves playing the role of the new absolutist, as Oliver Cromwell did after the English Civil War. But the fact that Parliament was already powerful and made up of a broad coalition consisting of different economic interests and different points of view made the iron law of oligarchy less likely to apply in 1688. And it was helped by the fact that luck was on the side of Parliament against James II. In the next chapter, we will see other examples of countries that have managed to break the mold and transform their institutions for the better, even after a long history of extractive institutions.

14.

BREAKING THE MOLD

THREE AFRICAN CHIEFS

ON SEPTEMBER 6, 1895, the ocean liner *Tantallon Castle* docked at Plymouth on the southern coast of England. Three African chiefs, Khama of the Ngwato, Bathoen of the Ngwaketse, and Sebele of the Kwena, disembarked and took the 8:10 express train to Paddington Station, London. The three chiefs had come to Britain on a mission: to save their and five other Tswana states from Cecil Rhodes. The Ngwato, Ngwaketse, and Kwena were three of the eight Tswana states comprising what was then known as Bechuanaland, which would become Botswana after independence in 1966.

The tribes had been trading with Europeans for most of the nineteenth century. In the 1840s, the famous Scottish missionary David Livingstone had traveled extensively in Bechuanaland and converted King Sechele of the Kwena to Christianity. The first translation of the Bible into an African language was in Setswana, the language of the Tswana. In 1885 Britain had declared Bechuanaland a protectorate. The Tswana were content with the arrangement, as they thought this would bring them protection from further European invasions, particularly from the Boers, with whom they had been clashing since the Great Trek in 1835, a migration of thousands of Boers into the interior to escape from British colonialism. The British, on the other hand, wanted control of the area to block both further expansions by the Boers (pages 260–261) and possible expansions by Germans, who had annexed the area of southwest Africa corresponding to today's Namibia. The British did not think that a full-scale colonization was worthwhile. The high commissioner Rey summarized the attitudes of the British government in 1885 clearly: "We have no interest in the country to the north of the Molope [the Bechuanaland protectorate], except as a road to the interior; we might therefore confine ourselves for the present to preventing that part of the Protectorate being occupied by either filibusters or foreign powers doing as little in the way of administration or settlement as possible."

But things changed for the Tswana in 1889 when Cecil Rhodes's British South Africa Company started expanding north out of South Africa, expropriating great swaths of land that would eventually become Northern and Southern Rhodesia, now Zambia and Zimbabwe. By 1895, the year of the three chiefs' visit to London, Rhodes had his eye on territories to the southwest of Rhodesia, Bechuanaland. The chiefs knew that only disaster and exploitation lay ahead for territories if they fell under the control of Rhodes. Though it was impossible for them to defeat Rhodes militarily, they were determined to fight him any way they could. They decided to opt for the lesser of two evils: greater control by the British rather than annexation by Rhodes. With the help of the London Missionary Society, they traveled to London to try to persuade Queen Victoria and Joseph Chamberlain, then colonial secretary, to take greater control of Bechuanaland and protect it from Rhodes.

On September 11, 1895, they had their first meeting with Chamberlain. Sebele spoke first, then Bathoen, and finally Khama. Chamberlain declared that he would consider imposing British control to protect the tribes from Rhodes. In the meantime, the chiefs quickly embarked on a nationwide speaking tour to drum up popular support for their requests. They visited and spoke at Windsor and Reading, close to London; in Southampton on the south coast; and in Leicester and Birmingham, in Chamberlain's political support base, the Midlands. They went north to industrial Yorkshire, to Sheffield, Leeds, Halifax, and Bradford; they also went west to Bristol and then up to Manchester and Liverpool.

Meanwhile, back in South Africa, Cecil Rhodes was making preparations for what would become the disastrous Jameson Raid, an armed assault on the Boer Republic of the Transvaal, despite Chamberlain's strong objections. These events likely made Chamberlain much more sympathetic to the chiefs' plight than he might have been otherwise. On November 6, they met with him again in London. The chiefs spoke through an interpreter:

> **Chamberlain:** I will speak about the lands of the Chiefs, and about the railway, and about the law which is to be observed in the territory of the Chiefs . . . Now let us look at the map . . . We will take the land that we want for the railway, and no more.
>
> **Khama:** I say, that if Mr. Chamberlain will take the land himself, I will be content.
>
> **Chamberlain:** Then tell him that I will make the railway myself by the eyes of one whom I will send and I will take only as much as I require, and will give compensation if what I take is of value.
>
> **Khama:** I would like to know how [i.e., where] the railway will go.
>
> **Chamberlain:** It shall go through his territory but shall be fenced in, and we will take no land.
>
> **Khama:** I trust that you will do this work as for myself, and treat me fairly in this matter.
>
> **Chamberlain:** I will guard your interests.

The next day, Edward Fairfield, at the Colonial Office, explained Chamberlain's settlement in more detail:

> Each of the three chiefs, Khama, Sebele and Bathoen, shall have a country within which they shall live as hitherto under the protection of the Queen. The Queen shall appoint an officer to reside with them. The chiefs will rule their own people much as at present.

Rhodes's reaction to being outmaneuvered by the three African chiefs was predictable. He cabled to one of his employees, saying, "I do object to being beaten by three canting natives."

The chiefs in fact had something valuable that they had protected from Rhodes and would subsequently protect from British indirect rule. By the nineteenth century, the Tswana states had developed a core set of political institutions. These involved both an unusual degree, by sub-Saharan African standards, of political centralization and collective decision-making procedures that can even be viewed as a nascent, primitive form of pluralism. Just as the Magna Carta enabled the participation of barons into the political decision-making process and put some restrictions on the actions of the English monarchs, the political institutions of the Tswana, in particular the *kgotla,* also encouraged political participation and constrained chiefs. The South African anthropologist Isaac Schapera describes how the *kgotla* worked as follows:

> all matters of tribal policy are dealt with finally before a general assembly of the adult males in the chief's kgotla (council place). Such meetings are very frequently held . . . among the topics discussed . . . are tribal disputes, quarrels between the chief and his relatives, the imposition of new levies, the undertaking of new public works, the promulgation of new decrees by the chief . . . it is not unknown for the tribal assembly to overrule the wishes of the chief. Since anyone may speak, these meetings enable him to ascertain the feelings of the people generally, and provide the latter with an opportunity of stating their grievances. If the occasion calls for it, he and his advisers may be taken severely to task, for the people are seldom afraid to speak openly and frankly.

Beyond the *kgotla,* the Tswana chieftaincy was not strictly hereditary but open to any man demonstrating significant talent and ability. Anthropologist John Comaroff studied in detail the political history of another of the Tswana states, the Rolong. He showed that though in appearance the Tswana had clear rules stipulating how the chieftancy was to be inherited, in practice these rules were interpreted to remove bad rulers and allow talented candidates to become chief. He showed that winning the chieftancy was a matter of achievement, but was then rationalized so that the successful competitor appeared to be the rightful heir. The Tswana captured this idea with a proverb, with a tinge of constitutional monarchy: *kgosi ke kgosi ka morafe,* "The king is king by the grace of the people."

The Tswana chiefs continued in their attempts to maintain their independence from Britain and preserve their indigenous institutions after their trip to London. They conceded the construction of railways in Bechuanaland, but limited the intervention of the British in other aspects of economic and political life. They were not opposed to the construction of the railways, certainly not for the same reasons as the Austro-Hungarian and Russian monarchs blocked railways. They just realized that railways, like the rest of the policies of the British, would not bring development to Bechuanaland as long as it was under colonial control. The early experience of Quett Masire, president of independent Botswana from 1980 to 1998, explains why. Masire was an enterprising farmer in the 1950s; he developed new cultivation techniques for sorghum and found a potential customer in Vryburg Milling, a company located across the border in South Africa. He went to the railway station master at Lobatse in Bechuanaland and asked to rent two rail trucks to move his crop to Vryburg. The station master refused. Then he got a white friend to intervene. The station master reluctantly agreed, but quoted Masire four times the rate for whites. Masire gave up and concluded, "It was the practice of the whites, not just the laws prohibiting Africans from owning freehold land or holding trading licenses that kept blacks from developing enterprises in Bechuanaland."

All in all, the chiefs, and the Tswana people, had been lucky. Perhaps against all odds, they succeeded in preventing Rhodes's takeover. As Bechuanaland was still marginal for the British, the establishment of indirect rule there did not create the type of vicious circle playing out in Sierra Leone (pages 335–344). They also avoided the kind of colonial expansion that went on in the interior of South Africa that would turn those lands into reservoirs of cheap labor for white miners or farmers. The early stages of the process of colonization are a critical juncture for most societies, a crucial period during which events that will have important long-term consequences for their economic and political development transpire. As we discussed in chapter 9, most societies in sub-Saharan Africa, just as those in South America and South Asia, witnessed the establishment or intensification of extractive institutions during colonization. The Tswana would instead avoid both intense indirect rule and the far worse fate that would have befallen them had Rhodes succeeded in annexing their lands. This was not just blind luck, however. It was once again a result of the interplay between the existing institutions, shaped by the institutional drift of the Tswana people, and the critical juncture brought about by colonialism. The three chiefs had made their own luck by taking the initiative and traveling to London, and they were able to do this because they had an unusual degree of authority, compared with other tribal leaders in sub-Saharan Africa, owing to the political centralization the Tswana tribes had achieved, and perhaps they also had an unusual degree of legitimacy, because of the modicum of pluralism embedded in their tribal institutions.

Another critical juncture at the end of the colonial period would be more central to the success of Botswana, enabling it to develop inclusive institutions. By the time Bechuanaland became independent in 1966 under the name Botswana, the lucky success of chiefs Sebele, Bathoen, and Khama was long in the past. In the intervening years, the British invested little in Bechuanaland. At independence, Botswana was one of the poorest countries in the world; it had a total of twelve kilometers of paved roads, twenty-two citizens who had graduated from university, and one hundred from secondary school. To top it all off, it was almost completely surrounded by the white regimes of South Africa, Namibia, and Rhodesia, all of which were hostile to independent African countries run by blacks. It would have been on few people's list of countries most likely to succeed. Yet over the next forty-five years, Botswana would become one of the fastest-growing countries in the world. Today Botswana has the highest per capita income in sub-Saharan Africa, and is at the same level as successful Eastern European countries such as Estonia and Hungary, and the most successful Latin American nations, such as Costa Rica.

How did Botswana break the mold? By quickly developing

inclusive economic and political institutions after independence. Since
then, it has been democratic, holds regular and competitive elections,
and has never experienced civil war or military intervention. The government set up economic institutions enforcing property rights, ensuring macroeconomic stability, and encouraging the development of
an inclusive market economy. But of course, the more challenging
question is, how did Botswana manage to establish a stable democracy and pluralistic institutions, and choose inclusive economic institutions, while most other African countries did the opposite? To
answer this, we have to understand how a critical juncture, this time
the end of colonial rule, interacted with Botswana's existing institutions.

In most of sub-Saharan Africa—for example, for Sierra Leone and
Zimbabwe—independence was an opportunity missed, accompanied
by the re-creation of the same type of extractive institutions that existed during the colonial period. Early stages of independence would
play out very differently in Botswana, again largely because of the
background created by Tswana historical institutions. In this, Botswana exhibited many parallels to England on the verge of the Glorious Revolution. England had achieved rapid political centralization
under the Tudors and had the Magna Carta and the tradition of Parliament that could at least aspire to constrain monarchs and ensure
some degree of pluralism. Botswana also had some amount of state
centralization and relatively pluralistic tribal institutions that survived
colonialism. England had a newly forming broad coalition, consisting
of Atlantic traders, industrialists, and the commercially minded gentry,
that was in favor of well-enforced property rights. Botswana had its
coalition in favor of secure procedure rights, the Tswana chiefs, and
elites who owned the major assets in the economy, cattle. Even
though land was held communally, cattle was private property in the
Tswana states, and the elites were similarly in favor of well-enforced
property rights. All this of course is not denying the contingent path
of history. Things would have turned out very differently in England
if parliamentary leaders and the new monarch had attempted to use
the Glorious Revolution to usurp power. Similarly, things could have
turned out very differently in Botswana, especially if it hadn't been so

fortunate as to have leaders such as Seretse Khama, or Quett Masire, who decided to contest power in elections rather than subvert the electoral system, as many postindependence leaders in sub-Saharan Africa did.

At independence the Tswana emerged with a history of institutions enshrining limited chieftaincy and some degree of accountability of chiefs to the people. The Tswana were of course not unique in Africa for having institutions like this, but they were unique in the extent to which these institutions survived the colonial period unscathed. British rule had been all but absent. Bechuanaland was administered from Mafeking, in South Africa, and it was only during the transition to independence in the 1960s that the plans for the capital of Gaborone were laid out. The capital and the new structures there were not meant to expunge the indigenous institutions, but to build on them; as Gaborone was constructed, new *kgotlas* were planned along with it.

Independence was also a relatively orderly affair. The drive for independence was led by the Botswana Democratic Party (BDP), founded in 1960 by Quett Masire and Seretse Khama. Khama was the grandson of King Khama III; his given name, Seretse, means "the clay that binds together." It was to be an extraordinarily apt name. Khama was the hereditary chief of the Ngwato, and most of the Tswana chiefs and elites joined the Botswana Democratic Party. Botswana didn't have a marketing board, because the British had been so uninterested in the colony. The BDP quickly set one up in 1967, the Botswana Meat Commission. But instead of expropriating the ranchers and cattle owners, the Meat Commission played a central role in developing the cattle economy; it put up fences to control foot-and-mouth disease and promoted exports, which would both contribute to economic development and increase the support for inclusive economic institutions.

Though the early growth in Botswana relied on meat exports, things changed dramatically when diamonds were discovered. The management of natural resources in Botswana also differed markedly from that in other African nations. During the colonial period, the Tswana chiefs had attempted to block prospecting for minerals in

Bechuanaland because they knew that if Europeans discovered precious metals or stones, their autonomy would be over. The first big diamond discovery was under Ngwato land, Seretse Khama's traditional homeland. Before the discovery was announced, Khama instigated a change in the law so that all subsoil mineral rights were vested in the nation, not the tribe. This ensured that diamond wealth would not create great inequities in Botswana. It also gave further impetus to the process of state centralization as diamond revenues could now be used for building a state bureaucracy and infrastructure and for investing in education. In Sierra Leone and many other sub-Saharan African nations, diamonds fueled conflict between different groups and helped to sustain civil wars, earning the label Blood Diamonds for the carnage brought about by the wars fought over their control. In Botswana, diamond revenues were managed for the good of the nation.

The change in subsoil mineral rights was not the only policy of state building that Seretse Khama's government implemented. Ultimately, the Chieftaincy Act of 1965 passed by the legislative assembly prior to independence, and the Chieftaincy Amendment Act of 1970 would continue the process of political centralization, enshrining the power of the state and the elected president by removing from chiefs the right to allocate land and enabling the president to remove a chief from office if necessary. Another facet of political centralization was the effort to unify the country further, for example, with legislation ensuring that only Setswana and English were to be taught in school. Today Botswana looks like a homogenous country, without the ethnic and linguistic fragmentation associated with many other African nations. But this was an outcome of the policy to have only English and a single national language, Setswana, taught in schools to minimize conflict between different tribes and groups within society. The last census to ask questions about ethnicity was the one taken in 1946, which revealed considerable heterogeneity in Botswana. In the Ngwato reserve, for example, only 20 percent of the population identified themselves as pure Ngwato; though there were other Tswana tribes present, there were also many non-Tswana groups whose first language was not Setswana. This underlying heterogeneity has been modulated both by the policies of the postindependence government and by the relatively inclusive institutions of the Tswana tribes in the same way as heterogeneity in Britain, for example, between the English and the Welsh, has been modulated by the British state. The Botswanan state did the same. Since independence, the census in Botswana has never asked about ethnic heterogeneity, because in Botswana everyone is Tswana.

Botswana achieved remarkable growth rates after independence because Seretse Khama, Quett Masire, and the Botswana Democratic Party led Botswana onto a path of inclusive economic and political institutions. When the diamonds came on stream in the 1970s, they did not lead to civil war, but provided a strong fiscal base for the government, which would use the revenues to invest in public services. There was much less incentive to challenge or overthrow the government and control the state. Inclusive political institutions bred political stability and supported inclusive economic institutions. In a pattern familiar from the virtuous circle described in chapter 11, inclusive economic institutions increased the viability and durability of inclusive political institutions.

Botswana broke the mold because it was able to seize a critical juncture, postcolonial independence, and set up inclusive institutions. The Botswana Democratic Party and the traditional elites, including Khama himself, did not try to form a dictatorial regime or set up extractive institutions that might have enriched them at the expense of society. This was once again an outcome of the interplay between a critical juncture and existing institutions. As we have seen, differently from almost anywhere else in sub-Saharan Africa, Botswana already had tribal institutions that had achieved some amount of centralized authority and contained important pluralistic features. Moreover, the country had economic elites who themselves had much to gain from secure property rights.

No less important, the contingent path of history worked in Botswana's favor. It was particularly lucky because Seretse Khama and Quett Masire were not Siaka Stevens and Robert Mugabe. The former worked hard and honestly to build inclusive institutions on the foundations of the Tswanas' tribal institutions. All this made it more likely that Botswana would succeed in taking a path toward inclusive institutions, whereas much of the rest of sub-Saharan Africa did not even try, or failed outright.

THE END OF THE SOUTHERN EXTRACTION

It was December 1, 1955. The city of Montgomery, Alabama, arrest warrant lists the time that the offense occurred as 6:06 p.m. James Blake, a bus driver, was having trouble, he called the police, and Officers Day and Mixon arrived on the scene. They noted in their report:

> We received a call upon arrival the bus operator said
> he had a colored female sitting in the white section of
> the bus, and would not move back. We . . . also saw
> her. The bus operator signed a warrant for her. Rosa
> Parks (cf) was charged with chapter 6 section 11 of
> the Montgomery City Code.

Rosa Parks's offense was to sit in a section of the Cleveland Avenue bus reserved for whites, a crime under Alabama's Jim Crow laws. Parks was fined ten dollars in addition to court fees of four dollars. Rosa Parks wasn't just anybody. She was already the secretary of the Montgomery chapter of the National Association for the Advancement of Colored People, the NAACP, which had long been struggling to change the institutions of the U.S. South. Her arrest triggered a mass movement, the Montgomery Bus Boycott, masterminded by Martin Luther King, Jr. By December 3, King and other black leaders had organized a coordinated bus boycott, convincing all black people that they should not ride on any bus in Montgomery. The boycott was successful and it lasted until December 20, 1956. It set in motion a process that culminated in the U.S. Supreme Court ruling that the laws that segregated buses in Alabama and Montgomery were unconstitutional.

The Montgomery Bus Boycott was a key moment in the civil rights movement in the U.S. South. This movement was part of a series of events and changes that finally broke the mold in the South and led to a fundamental change of institutions. As we saw in chapter 12, after the Civil War, southern landowning elites had managed to re-create the extractive economic and political institutions that had dominated the South before the Civil War. Though the details of these institutions changed—for example, slavery was no longer possible—the negative impact on economic incentives and prosperity in the South was the same. The South was notably poorer than the rest of the United States.

Starting in the 1950s, southern institutions would begin to move the region onto a much faster growth trajectory. The type of extractive institutions ultimately eliminated in the U.S. South were different from the colonial institutions of pre-independence Botswana. The type of critical juncture that started the process of their downfall was also different but shared several commonalities. Starting in the 1940s, those who bore the brunt of the discrimination and the extractive institutions in the South, people such as Rosa Parks, started to become much better organized in their fight against them. At the same time, the U.S. Supreme Court and the federal government finally began to intervene systematically to reform the extractive institutions in the South. Thus a main factor creating a critical juncture for change in the South was the empowerment of black Americans there and the end of the unchallenged domination of the southern elites.

The southern political institutions, both before the Civil War and after, had a clear economic logic, not too different from the South African Apartheid regime: to secure cheap labor for the plantations. But by the 1950s, this logic became less compelling. For one, significant mass outmigration of blacks from the South was already under way, a legacy of both the Great Depression and the Second World War. In the 1940s and '50s, this reached an average of a hundred thousand people per year. Meanwhile, technological innovation in agriculture, though adopted only slowly, was reducing the dependence of the plantation owners on cheap labor. Most labor in the plantations was used for picking cotton. In 1950 almost all southern cotton was still picked by hand. But the mechanization of cotton picking was reducing the demand for this type of work. By 1960, in the key states of Alabama, Louisiana, and Mississippi, almost half of production had become mechanized. Just as blacks became harder to trap in the South, they also became no longer indispensable for the plantation owners. There was thus less reason for elites to fight vigorously to maintain the old extractive economic institutions. This did not mean that they would accept the changes in institutions willingly, however. Instead, a protracted conflict ensued. An unusual coalition, between southern blacks and the inclusive federal institutions of the United States, created a powerful force away from southern extraction and toward equal political and civil rights for southern blacks, which would finally remove the significant barriers to economic growth in the U.S. South.

The most important impetus for change came from the civil rights movement. It was the empowerment of blacks in the South that led the way, as in Montgomery, by challenging extractive institutions around them, by demanding their rights, and by protesting and mobilizing in order to obtain them. But they weren't alone in this, because the U.S. South was not a separate country and the southern elites did not have free rein as did Guatemalan elites, for example. As part of the United States of America, the South was subject to the U.S. Constitution and federal legislation. The cause for fundamental reform in the South would finally receive support from the U.S. executive, legislature, and Supreme Court partly because the civil rights movement was able to have its voice heard outside the South, thereby mobilizing the federal government.

Federal intervention to change the institutions in the South started with the decision of the Supreme Court in 1944 that primary elections where only white people could stand were unconstitutional. As we have seen, blacks had been politically disenfranchised in the 1890s with the use of poll taxes and literacy tests (pages 351–357). These tests were routinely manipulated to discriminate against black people, while still allowing poor and illiterate whites to vote. In a famous example from the early 1960s, in Louisiana a white applicant was judged literate after giving the answer "FRDUM FOOF SPETGH" to a question about the state constitution. The Supreme Court decision in 1944 was the opening salvo in the longer battle to open up the political system to blacks, and the Court understood the importance of loosening white control of political parties.

That decision was followed by *Brown v. Board of Education* in 1954, in which the Supreme Court ruled that state-mandated segregation of schools and other public sites was unconstitutional. In 1962 the Court knocked away another pillar of the political dominance of white elites: legislative malapportionment. When a legislature is malapportioned—as were the "rotten boroughs" in England before the First Reform Act—some areas or regions receive much greater representation than they should based on their share of the relevant population. Malapportionment in the South meant that the rural areas, the heartland of the southern planter elite, were heavily overrepresented relative to urban areas. The Supreme Court put an end to this in 1962 with its decision in the *Baker v. Carr* case, which introduced the "one-person, one-vote" standard.

But all the rulings from the Supreme Court would have amounted to little if they hadn't been implemented. In the 1890s, in fact, federal legislation enfranchising southern blacks was not implemented, because local law enforcement was under the control of the southern elite and the Democratic Party, and the federal government was happy to go along with this state of affairs. But as blacks started rising up against the southern elite, this bastion of support for Jim Crow crumbled, and the Democratic Party, led by its non-southern elements, turned against racial segregation. The renegade southern Democrats regrouped under the banner of the States' Rights Democratic Party and competed in the 1948 presidential election. Their candidate, Strom Thurmond, carried four states and gained thirty-nine votes in the Electoral College. But this was a far cry from the power of the unified Democratic Party in national politics and the capture of that party by the southern elites. Strom Thurmond's campaign was centered on his challenge to the ability of the federal government to intervene in the institutions of the South. He stated his position forcefully: "I wanna tell you, ladies and gentlemen, that there's not enough troops in the army to force the Southern people to break down segregation and admit the nigra race into our theaters, into our swimming pools, into our homes, and into our churches."

He would be proved wrong. The rulings of the Supreme Court meant that southern educational facilities had to be desegregated, including the University of Mississippi in Oxford. In 1962, after a long legal battle, federal courts ruled that James Meredith, a young black air force veteran, had to be admitted to "Ole Miss." Opposition to the implementation of this ruling was orchestrated by the so-called Citizens' Councils, the first of which had been formed in Indianola, Mississippi, in 1954 to fight desegregation of the South. State governor Ross Barnett publicly rejected the court-ordered desegregation on television on September 13, announcing that state universities would close before they agreed to be desegregated. Finally, after much negotiation between Barnett and President John Kennedy and Attorney General Robert Kennedy in Washington, the federal government intervened forcibly to implement this ruling. A day was set when U.S. marshals would bring Meredith to Oxford. In anticipation, white supremacists began to organize. On September 30, the day before Meredith was due to appear, U.S. marshals entered the university campus and surrounded the main administration building. A crowd of about 2,500 came to protest, and soon a riot broke out. The marshals used tear gas to disperse the rioters, but soon came under fire. By 10:00 p.m. that night, federal troops were moved into the city to restore order. Soon there were 20,000 troops and 11,000 National Guardsmen in Oxford. In total, 300 people would be arrested. Meredith decided to stay on campus, where, protected from death threats by U.S. marshals and 300 soldiers, he eventually graduated.

Federal legislation was pivotal in the process of institutional reform in the South. During the passage of the first Civil Rights Act in 1957, Strom Thurmond, then a senator, spoke nonstop for twenty-four hours and eighteen minutes to prevent, or at least delay, passage of the act. During his speech he read everything from the Declaration of Independence to various phone books. But to no avail. The 1957 act culminated in the Civil Rights Act of 1964 outlawing a whole gamut of segregationist state legislation and practices. The Voting Rights Act of 1965 declared the literacy tests, poll taxes, and other methods used for disenfranchising southern blacks to be illegal. It also extended a great deal of federal oversight into state elections.

The impact of all these events was a significant change in economic and legal institutions in the South. In Mississippi, for example, only about 5 percent of eligible black people were voting in 1960. By 1970 this figure had increased to 50 percent. In Alabama and South Carolina, it went from around 10 percent in 1960 to 50 percent in 1970. These patterns changed the nature of elections, both for local and national offices. More important, the political support from the dominant Democratic Party for the extractive institutions discriminating against blacks eroded. The way was then open for a range of changes in economic institutions. Prior to the institutional reforms of the 1960s, blacks had been almost entirely excluded from jobs in textile mills. In 1960 only about 5 percent of employees in southern textile mills were black. Civil rights legislation stopped this discrimination. By 1970 this proportion had increased to 15 percent; by 1990 it was at 25 percent. Economic discrimination against blacks began to decline, the educational opportunities for blacks improved significantly, and the southern labor market became more competitive. Together with inclusive institutions came more rapid economic improvements in the South. In 1940 southern states had only about 50 percent of the level of per capita income of the United States. This started to change in the late 1940s and '50s. By 1990 the gap had basically vanished.

As in Botswana, the key in the U.S. South was the development of inclusive political and economic institutions. This came at the juxtaposition of the increasing discontent among blacks suffering under southern extractive institutions and the crumbling of the one-party rule of the Democratic Party in the South. Once again, existing institutions shaped the path of change. In this case, it was pivotal that southern institutions were situated within the inclusive federal institutions of the United States, and this allowed southern blacks finally to mobilize the federal government and institutions for their cause. The whole process was also facilitated by the fact that, with the massive outmigration of blacks from the South and the mechanization of cotton production, economic conditions had changed so that southern elites were less willing to put up more of a fight.

420 · WHY NATIONS FAIL

REBIRTH IN CHINA

The Communist Party under the leadership of Mao Zedong finally overthrew the Nationalists, led by Chiang Kai-shek, in 1949. The People's Republic of China was proclaimed on October 1. The political and economic institutions created after 1949 were highly extractive. Politically, they featured the dictatorship of the Chinese Communist Party. No other political organization has been allowed in China since then. Until his death in 1976, Mao entirely dominated the Communist Party and the government. Accompanying these authoritarian, extractive political institutions were highly extractive economic institutions. Mao immediately nationalized land and abolished all kinds of property rights in one fell swoop. He had landlords, as well as other segments he deemed to be against the regime, executed. The market economy was essentially abolished. People in rural areas were gradually organized onto communal farms. Money and wages were replaced by "work points," which could be traded for goods. Internal passports were introduced in 1956 forbidding travel without appropriate authorization, in order to increase political and economic control. All industry was similarly nationalized, and Mao launched an ambitious attempt to promote the rapid development of industry through the use of "five-year plans," modeled on those in the Soviet Union.

As with all extractive institutions, Mao's regime was attempting to extract resources from the vast country he was now controlling. As in the case of the government of Sierra Leone with its marketing board, the Chinese Communist Party had a monopoly over the sale of produce, such as rice and grain, which was used to heavily tax farmers. The attempts at industrialization turned into the infamous Great Leap Forward after 1958 with the roll-out of the second five-year plan. Mao announced that steel output would double in a year based on small-scale "backyard" blast furnaces. He claimed that in fifteen years, China would catch up with British steel production. The only problem was that there was no feasible way of meeting these targets. To meet the plan's goals, scrap metal had to be found, and people would have to melt down their pots and pans and even their agricultural implements such as hoes and plows. Workers who ought to have been tending the fields were making steel by destroying their plows, and thus their future ability to feed themselves and the country. The result was a calamitous famine in the Chinese countryside. Though scholars debate the role of Mao's policy compared with the impact of droughts at the same time, nobody doubts the central role of the Great Leap Forward in contributing to the death of between twenty and forty million people. We don't know precisely how many, because China under Mao did not collect the numbers that would have documented the atrocities. Per capita income fell by around one-quarter.

One consequence of the Great Leap Forward was that a senior member of the Communist Party, Deng Xiaoping, a very successful general during the revolution, who led an "anti-rightist" campaign resulting in the execution of many "enemies of the revolution," had a change of heart. At a conference in Guangzhou in the south of China in 1961, Deng argued, "No matter whether the cat is black or white, if it catches mice, it's a good cat." It did not matter whether policies appeared communist or not; China needed policies that would encourage production so that it could feed its people.

Yet Deng was soon to suffer for his newfound practicality. On May 16, 1966, Mao announced that the revolution was under threat from "bourgeois" interests that were undermining China's communist society and wishing to re-create capitalism. In response, he announced the Great Proletarian Cultural Revolution, usually referred to as the Cultural Revolution. The Cultural Revolution was based on sixteen points. The first started:

> Although the bourgeoisie has been overthrown, it is still trying to use the old ideas, culture, and customs, and habits of the exploiting classes to corrupt the masses, capture their minds, and endeavor to stage a comeback. The proletariat must do just the opposite: it must meet head-on every challenge of the bourgeoisie in the ideological field and use the new ideas, culture, customs, and habits of the proletariat to change the mental outlook of the whole of society. At present our

objective is to struggle against and crush those persons in authority who are taking the capitalist road, to criticize and repudiate the reactionary bourgeois academic authorities and the ideology of the bourgeoisie and all other exploiting classes and transform education, literature, and art and all other parts of the superstructure that do not correspond to the socialist economic base, so as to facilitate the consolidation and development of the socialist system.

Soon the Cultural Revolution, just like the Great Leap Forward, would start wrecking both the economy and many human lives. Units of Red Guards were formed across the country: young, enthusiastic members of the Communist Party who were used to purge opponents of the regime. Many people were killed, arrested, or sent into internal exile. Mao himself retorted to concerns about the extent of the violence, stating, "This man Hitler was even more ferocious. The more ferocious, the better, don't you think? The more people you kill, the more revolutionary you are."

Deng found himself labeled number-two capitalist roader, was jailed in 1967, and then was exiled to Jiangxi province in 1969, to work in a rural tractor factory. He was rehabilitated in 1974, and Mao was persuaded by Premier Zhou Enlai to make Deng first vice-premier. Already in 1975, Deng supervised the composition of three party documents that would have charted a new direction had they been adopted. They called for a revitalization of higher education, a return to material incentives in industry and agriculture, and the removal of "leftists" from the party. At the time, Mao's health was deteriorating and power was increasingly concentrated in the hands of the very leftists whom Deng Xiaoping wanted to remove from power. Mao's wife, Jiang Qing, and three of her close associates, collectively known as the Gang of Four, had been great supporters of the Cultural Revolution and the resulting repression. They intended to continue using this blueprint to run the country under the dictatorship of the Communist Party. On April 5, a spontaneous celebration of the life of Zhou Enlai in Tiananmen Square turned into a protest against the government. The Gang of Four blamed Deng for the demonstrations, and he was once more stripped of all his positions and dismissed. Instead of achieving the removal of the leftists, Deng found that the leftists had removed him. After the death of Zhou Enlai, Mao had appointed Hua Guofeng as the acting premier instead of Deng. In the relative power vacuum of 1976, Hua was able to accumulate a great deal of personal power.

In September there was a critical juncture: Mao died. The Chinese Communist Party had been under Mao's domination, and the Great Leap Forward and the Cultural Revolution had been largely his initiatives. With Mao gone, there was a true power vacuum, which resulted in a struggle between those with different visions and different beliefs about the consequences of change. The Gang of Four intended to continue with the policies of the Cultural Revolution as the only way of consolidating theirs and the Communist Party's power. Hua Guofeng wanted to abandon the Cultural Revolution, but he could not distance himself too much from it, because he owed his own rise in the party to its effects. Instead, he advocated a return to a more balanced version of Mao's vision, which he encapsulated in the "Two Whatevers," as the *People's Daily,* the newspaper of the Chinese Communist Party, put it in 1977. Hua argued, "We will resolutely uphold whatever policy decisions Chairman Mao made, and unswervingly follow whatever instructions Chairman Mao gave."

Deng Xiaoping did not wish to abolish the communist regime and replace it with inclusive markets any more than Hua did. He, too, was part of the same group of people brought to power by the communist revolution. But he and his supporters thought that significant economic growth could be achieved without endangering their political control: they had a model of growth under extractive political institutions that would not threaten their power, because the Chinese people were in dire need of improved living standards and because all meaningful opposition to the Communist Party had been obliterated during Mao's reign and the Cultural Revolution. To achieve this, they wished to repudiate not just the Cultural Revolution but also much of the Maoist institutional legacy. They realized that economic growth would be possible only with significant moves toward inclusive economic institutions. They thus wished to reform the economy and bolster the role of market forces and incentives. They also wanted to expand the scope for private ownership and reduce the role of the Communist Party in society and the administration, getting rid of such concepts as class struggle. Deng's group was also open to foreign investment and international trade, and wished to pursue a much more aggressive policy of integrating with the international economy. Still, there were limits, and building truly inclusive economic institutions and significantly lessening the grip the Communist Party had on the economy weren't even options.

The turning point for China was Hua Guofeng's power and his willingness to use it against the Gang of Four. Within a month of Mao's death, Hua mounted a coup against the Gang of Four, having them all arrested. He then reinstated Deng in March 1977. There was nothing inevitable either about this course of events or about the next significant steps, which resulted from Hua himself being politically outmaneuvered by Deng Xiaoping. Deng encouraged public criticism of the Cultural Revolution and began to fill key positions in the Communist Party at all levels with people who, like him, had suffered during this period. Hua could not repudiate the Cultural Revolution, and this weakened him. He was also a comparative newcomer to the centers of power, and he lacked the web of connections and informal relations that Deng had built up over many years. In a series of speeches, Deng began to criticize Hua's policies. In September 1978, he explicitly attacked the Two Whatevers, noting that rather than let whatever Mao had said determine policy, the correct approach was to "seek truth from facts."

Deng also brilliantly began to bring public pressure to bear on Hua, which was reflected most powerfully in the Democracy Wall movement in 1978, in which people posted complaints about the country on a wall in Beijing. In July of 1978, one of Deng's supporters, Hu Qiaomu, presented some basic principles of economic reform. These included the notions that firms should be given greater initiative and authority to make their own production decisions. Prices should be allowed to bring supply and demand together, rather than just being set by the government, and the state regulation of the economy more generally ought to be reduced. These were radical suggestions, but Deng was gaining influence. In November and December 1978, the Third Plenum of the Eleventh Central Party Committee produced a breakthrough. Over Hua's objections, it was decided that, from then on, the focus of the party would be not class struggle but economic modernization. The plenum announced some tentative experiments with a "household responsibility system" in some provinces, which was an attempt to roll back collective agriculture and introduce economic incentives into farming. By the next year, the Central Committee was acknowledging the centrality of the notion of "truth from facts" and declaring the Cultural Revolution to have been a great calamity for the Chinese people. Throughout this period, Deng was securing the appointment of his own supporters to important positions in the party, army, and government. Though he had to move slowly against Hua's supporters in the Central Committee, he created parallel bases of power. By 1980 Hua was forced to step down from the premiership, to be replaced by Zhao Ziyang. By 1982 Hua had been removed from the Central Committee. But Deng did not stop there. At the Twelfth National Congress in 1982, and then in the National People's Congress in September 1985, he achieved an almost complete reshuffling of the party leadership and senior cadres. In came much younger, reform-minded people. If one compares 1980 to 1985, then by the latter date, twenty-one of the twenty-six members of the Politburo, eight of the eleven members of the Communist Party secretariat, and ten of the eighteen vice-premiers had been changed.

Now that Deng and the reformers had consummated their political revolution and were in control of the state, they launched a series of further changes in economic institutions. They began in agriculture: By 1983, following the ideas of Hu Qiaomu, the household responsibility system, which would provide economic incentives to farmers, was universally adopted. In 1985 the mandatory state purchasing of grain was abandoned and replaced by a system of more voluntary contracts. Administrative control of agricultural prices was greatly relaxed in 1985. In the urban economy, state enterprises were given more autonomy, and fourteen "open cities" were identified and given the ability to attract foreign investment.

It was the rural economy that took off first. The introduction of incentives led to a dramatic increase in agricultural productivity. By 1984 grain output was one-third higher than in 1978, though fewer people were involved in agriculture. Many had moved into employment in new rural industries, the so-called Township Village Enterprises. These had been allowed to grow outside the system of state industrial planning after 1979, when it was accepted that new firms could enter and compete with state-owned firms. Gradually economic incentives were also introduced into the industrial sector, in particular into the operation of state-run enterprises, though at this stage there was no hint at privatization, which had to wait until the mid-1990s.

The rebirth of China came with a significant move away from one of the most extractive set of economic institutions and toward more inclusive ones. Market incentives in agriculture and industry, then followed by foreign investment and technology, would set China on a path to rapid economic growth. As we will discuss further in the next chapter, this was growth under extractive political institutions, even if they were not as repressive as they had been under the Cultural Revolution and even if economic institutions were becoming partially inclusive. All of this should not understate the degree to which the changes in economic institutions in China were radical. China broke the mold, even if it did not transform its political institutions. As in Botswana and the U.S. South, the crucial changes came during a critical juncture—in the case of China, following Mao's death. They were also contingent, in fact highly contingent, as there was nothing inevitable about the Gang of Four losing the power struggle; and if they had not, China would not have experienced the sustained economic growth it has seen in the last thirty years. But the devastation and human suffering that the Great Leap Forward and the Cultural Revolution caused generated sufficient demand for change that Deng Xiaoping and his allies were able to win the political fight.

BOTSWANA, CHINA, and the U.S. South, just like the Glorious Revolution in England, the French Revolution, and the Meiji Restoration in Japan, are vivid illustrations that history is not destiny. Despite the vicious circle, extractive institutions can be replaced by inclusive ones. But it is neither automatic nor easy. A confluence of factors, in particular a critical juncture coupled with a broad coalition of those pushing for reform or other propitious existing institutions, is often necessary for a nation to make strides toward more inclusive institutions. In addition some luck is key, because history always unfolds in a contingent way.

15.

UNDERSTANDING PROSPERITY
AND POVERTY

HISTORICAL ORIGINS

THERE ARE HUGE DIFFERENCES in living standards around the world. Even the poorest citizens of the United States have incomes and access to health care, education, public services, and economic and social opportunities that are far superior to those available to the vast mass of people living in sub-Saharan Africa, South Asia, and Central America. The contrast of South and North Korea, the two Nogaleses, and the United States and Mexico reminds us that these are relatively recent phenomena. Five hundred years ago, Mexico, home to the Aztec state, was certainly richer than the polities to the north, and the United States did not pull ahead of Mexico until the nineteenth century. The gap between the two Nogaleses is even more recent. South and North Korea were economically, as well as socially and culturally, indistinguishable before the country was divided at the 38th parallel after the Second World War. Similarly, most of the huge economic differences we observe around us today emerged over the last two hundred years.

Did this all need to be so? Was it historically—or geographically or culturally or ethnically—predetermined that Western Europe, the United States, and Japan would become so much richer than sub-Saharan Africa, Latin America, and China over the last two hundred years or so? Was it inevitable that the Industrial Revolution would get under way in the eighteenth century in Britain, and then spread to

Western Europe and Europe's offshoots in North America and Australasia? Is a counterfactual world where the Glorious Revolution and the Industrial Revolution take place in Peru, which then colonizes Western Europe and enslaves whites, possible, or is it just a form of historical science fiction?

To answer—in fact, even to reason about—these questions, we need a theory of why some nations are prosperous while others fail and are poor. This theory needs to delineate both the factors that create and retard prosperity and their historical origins. This book has proposed such a theory. Any complex social phenomenon, such as the origins of the different economic and political trajectories of hundreds of polities around the world, likely has a multitude of causes, making most social scientists shun monocausal, simple, and broadly applicable theories and instead seek different explanations for seemingly similar outcomes emerging in different times and areas. Instead we've offered a simple theory and used it to explain the main contours of economic and political development around the world since the Neolithic Revolution. Our choice was motivated not by a naïve belief that such a theory could explain everything, but by the belief that a theory should enable us to focus on the parallels, sometimes at the expense of abstracting from many interesting details. A successful theory, then, does not faithfully reproduce details, but provides a useful and empirically well-grounded explanation for a range of processes while also clarifying the main forces at work.

Our theory has attempted to achieve this by operating on two levels. The first is the distinction between extractive and inclusive economic and political institutions. The second is our explanation for why inclusive institutions emerged in some parts of the world and not in others. While the first level of our theory is about an institutional interpretation of history, the second level is about how history has shaped institutional trajectories of nations.

Central to our theory is the link between inclusive economic and political institutions and prosperity. Inclusive economic institutions that enforce property rights, create a level playing field, and encourage investments in new technologies and skills are more conducive to economic growth than extractive economic institutions that are structured to extract resources from the many by the few and that fail to protect property rights or provide incentives for economic activity. Inclusive economic institutions are in turn supported by, and support, inclusive political institutions, that is, those that distribute political power widely in a pluralistic manner and are able to achieve some amount of political centralization so as to establish law and order, the foundations of secure property rights, and an inclusive market economy. Similarly, extractive economic institutions are synergistically linked to extractive political institutions, which concentrate power in the hands of a few, who will then have incentives to maintain and develop extractive economic institutions for their benefit and use the resources they obtain to cement their hold on political power.

These tendencies do not imply that extractive economic and political institutions are inconsistent with economic growth. On the contrary, every elite would, all else being equal, like to encourage as much growth as possible in order to have more to extract. Extractive institutions that have achieved at least a minimal degree of political centralization are often able to generate some amount of growth. What is crucial, however, is that growth under extractive institutions will not be sustained, for two key reasons. First, sustained economic growth requires innovation, and innovation cannot be decoupled from creative destruction, which replaces the old with the new in the economic realm and also destabilizes established power relations in politics. Because elites dominating extractive institutions fear creative destruction, they will resist it, and any growth that germinates under extractive institutions will be ultimately short lived. Second, the ability of those who dominate extractive institutions to benefit greatly at the expense of the rest of society implies that political power under extractive institutions is highly coveted, making many groups and individuals fight to obtain it. As a consequence, there will be powerful forces pushing societies under extractive institutions toward political instability.

The synergies between extractive economic and political institutions create a vicious circle, where extractive institutions, once in place, tend to persist. Similarly, there is a virtuous circle associated with inclusive economic and political institutions. But neither the vicious nor the virtuous circle is absolute. In fact, some nations live under inclusive institutions today because, though extractive institutions have been the norm in history, some societies have been able to break the mold and transition toward inclusive institutions. Our explanation for these transitions is historical, but not historically predetermined. Major institutional change, the requisite for major economic change, takes place as a result of the interaction between existing institutions and critical junctures. Critical junctures are major events that disrupt the existing political and economic balance in one or many societies, such as the Black Death, which killed possibly as much as half the population of most areas in Europe during the fourteenth century; the opening of Atlantic trade routes, which created enormous profit opportunities for many in Western Europe; and the Industrial Revolution, which offered the potential for rapid but also disruptive changes in the structure of economies around the world.

Existing institutional differences among societies themselves are a result of past institutional changes. Why does the path of institutional change differ across societies? The answer to this question lies in institutional drift. In the same way that the genes of two isolated populations of organisms will drift apart slowly because of random mutations in the so-called process of evolutionary or genetic drift, two otherwise similar societies will also drift apart institutionally—albeit, again, slowly. Conflict over income and power, and indirectly over institutions, is a constant in all societies. This conflict often has a contingent outcome, even if the playing field over which it transpires is not level. The outcome of this conflict leads to institutional drift. But this is not necessarily a cumulative process. It does not imply that the small differences that emerge at some point will necessarily become larger over time. On the contrary, as our discussion of Roman Britain in chapter 6 illustrates, small differences open up, and then disappear, and then reappear again. However, when a critical juncture arrives, these small differences that have emerged as a result of institutional drift may be the small differences that matter in leading otherwise quite similar societies to diverge radically.

We saw in chapters 7 and 8 that despite the many similarities between England, France, and Spain, the critical juncture of the Atlantic trade had the most transformative impact on England because of such small differences—the fact that because of developments during the fifteenth and sixteenth centuries, the English Crown could not control all overseas trade, as this trade was mostly under Crown monopoly in France and Spain. As a result, in France and Spain, it was the monarchy and the groups allied with it who were the main beneficiaries of the large profits created by Atlantic trade and colonial expansion, while in England it was groups strongly opposed to the monarchy who gained from economic opportunities thrown open by this critical juncture. Though institutional drift leads to small differences, its interplay with critical junctures leads to institutional divergence, and thus this divergence then creates the now more major institutional differences that the next critical juncture will affect.

History is key, since it is historical processes that, via institutional drift, create the differences that may become consequential during critical junctures. Critical junctures themselves are historical turning points. And the vicious and virtuous circles imply that we have to study history to understand the nature of institutional differences that have been historically structured. Yet our theory does not imply historical determinism—or any other kind of determinism. It is for this reason that the answer to the question we started with in this chapter is no: there was no historical necessity that Peru end up so much poorer than Western Europe or the United States.

To start with, in contrast with the geography and culture hypotheses, Peru is not condemned to poverty because of its geography or culture. In our theory, Peru is so much poorer than Western Europe and the United States today because of its institutions, and to understand the reasons for this, we need to understand the historical process of institutional development in Peru. As we saw in the second chapter, five hundred years ago the Inca Empire, which occupied contemporary Peru, was richer, more technologically sophisticated, and more politically centralized than the smaller polities occupying North America. The turning point was the way in which this area was colonized and how this contrasted with the colonization of North

America. This resulted not from a historically predetermined process but as the contingent outcome of several pivotal institutional developments during critical junctures. At least three factors could have changed this trajectory and led to very different long-run patterns.

First, institutional differences within the Americas during the fifteenth century shaped how these areas were colonized. North America followed a different institutional trajectory than Peru because it was sparsely settled before colonization and attracted European settlers who then successfully rose up against the elite whom entities such as the Virginia Company and the English Crown had tried to create. In contrast, Spanish conquistadors found a centralized, extractive state in Peru they could take over and a large population they could put to work in mines and plantations. There was also nothing geographically predetermined about the lay of the land within the Americas at the time the Europeans arrived. In the same way that the emergence of a centralized state led by King Shyaam among the Bushong was a result of a major institutional innovation, or perhaps even of political revolution, as we saw in chapter 5, the Inca civilization in Peru and the large populations in this area resulted from major institutional innovations. These could instead have taken place in North America, in places such as the Mississippi Valley or even the northeastern United States. Had this been the case, Europeans might have encountered empty lands in the Andes and centralized states in North America, and the roles of Peru and the United States could have been reversed. Europeans would then have settled in areas around Peru, and the conflict between the majority of settlers and the elite could have led to the creation of inclusive institutions there instead of in North America. The subsequent paths of economic development would then likely have been different.

Second, the Inca Empire might have resisted European colonialism, as Japan did when Commodore Perry's ships arrived in Edo Bay. Though the greater extractiveness of the Inca Empire in contrast with Tokugawa, Japan, certainly made a political revolution akin to the Meiji Restoration less likely in Peru, there was no historical necessity that the Inca completely succumb to European domination. If they had been able to resist and even institutionally modernize in response to the threats, the whole path of the history of the New World, and with it the entire history of the world, could have been different.

Third and most radically, it is not even historically or geographically or culturally predetermined that Europeans should have been the ones colonizing the world. It could have been the Chinese or even the Incas. Of course, such an outcome is impossible when we look at the world from the vantage point of the fifteenth century, by which time Western Europe had pulled ahead of the Americas, and China had already turned inward. But Western Europe of the fifteenth century was itself an outcome of a contingent process of institutional drift punctuated by critical junctures, and nothing about it was inevitable. Western European powers could not have surged ahead and conquered the world without several historic turning points. These included the specific path that feudalism took, replacing slavery and weakening the power of monarchs on the way; the fact that the centuries following the turn of the first millennium in Europe witnessed the development of independent and commercially autonomous cities; the fact that European monarchs were not as threatened by, and consequently did not try to discourage, overseas trade as the Chinese emperors did during the Ming dynasty; and the arrival of the Black Death, which shook up the foundations of the feudal order. If these events had transpired differently, we could be living in a very different world today, one in which Peru might be richer than Western Europe or the United States.

NATURALLY, THE PREDICTIVE POWER of a theory where both small differences and contingency play key roles will be limited. Few would have predicted in the fifteenth or even the sixteenth centuries, let alone in the many centuries following the fall of the Roman Empire, that the major breakthrough toward inclusive institutions would happen in Britain. It was only the specific process of institutional drift and the nature of the critical juncture created by the opening of Atlantic trade that made this possible. Neither would many have believed in the midst of the Cultural Revolution during the 1970s that China would soon be on a path toward radical changes in its economic institutions and subsequently on a breakneck growth trajectory. It is similarly impossible to predict with any certainty what the lay of the land will be in five hundred years. Yet these are not shortcomings of our theory. The historical account we have presented so far indicates that any approach based on historical determinism—based on geography, culture, or even other historical factors—is inadequate. Small differences and contingency are not just part of our theory; they are part of the shape of history.

Even if making precise predictions about which societies will prosper relative to others is difficult, we have seen throughout the book that our theory explains the broad differences in the prosperity and poverty of nations around the world fairly well. We will see in the rest of this chapter that it also provides some guidelines as to what types of societies are more likely to achieve economic growth over the next several decades.

First, vicious and virtuous circles generate a lot of persistence and sluggishness. There should be little doubt that in fifty or even a hundred years, the United States and Western Europe, based on their inclusive economic and political institutions, will be richer, most likely considerably richer, than sub-Saharan Africa, the Middle East, Central America, or Southeast Asia. However, within these broad patterns there will be major institutional changes in the next century, with some countries breaking the mold and transitioning from poor to rich.

Nations that have achieved almost no political centralization, such as Somalia and Afghanistan, or those that have undergone a collapse of the state, such as Haiti did over the last several decades—long before the massive earthquake there in 2010 led to the devastation of the country's infrastructure—are unlikely either to achieve growth under extractive political institutions or to make major changes toward inclusive institutions. Instead, nations likely to grow over the next several decades—albeit probably under extractive institutions—are those that have attained some degree of political centralization. In sub-Saharan Africa this includes Burundi, Ethiopia, Rwanda, nations with long histories of centralized states, and Tanzania, which has managed to build such centralization, or at least put in place some of the prerequisites for centralization, since independence. In Latin America, it includes Brazil, Chile, and Mexico, which have not only achieved political centralization but also made significant strides toward nascent pluralism. Our theory would suggest that sustained economic growth is very unlikely in Colombia.

Our theory also suggests that growth under extractive political institutions, as in China, will not bring sustained growth, and is likely to run out of steam. Beyond these cases, there is much uncertainty. Cuba, for example, might transition toward inclusive institutions and experience a major economic transformation, or it may linger on under extractive political and economic institutions. The same is true of North Korea and Burma (Myanmar) in Asia. Thus, while our theory provides the tools for thinking about how institutions change and the consequences of such changes, the nature of this change—the role of small differences and contingency—makes more precise predictions difficult.

Even greater caution is necessary in drawing policy recommendations from this broad account of the origins of prosperity and poverty. In the same way that the impact of critical junctures depends on existing institutions, how a society will respond to the same policy intervention depends on the institutions that are in place. Of course, our theory is all about how nations can take steps toward prosperity—by transforming their institutions from extractive to inclusive. But it also makes it very clear from the outset that there are no easy recipes for achieving such a transition. First, the vicious circle implies that changing institutions is much harder than it first appears. In particular, extractive institutions can re-create themselves under different guises, as we saw with the iron law of oligarchy in chapter 12. Thus the fact that the extractive regime of President Mubarak was overturned by popular protest in February 2011 does not guarantee that Egypt will move onto a path to more inclusive institutions. Instead extractive institutions may re-create themselves despite the vibrant and hopeful pro-democracy movement. Second, because the contingent path of history implies that it is difficult to know whether a particular interplay of critical junctures and existing institutional differences will lead toward more inclusive or extractive institutions, it would be heroic to formulate general policy recommendations to encourage change toward inclusive institutions. Nevertheless, our theory is still useful for policy analysis, as it enables us to recognize bad policy advice, based on either incorrect hypotheses or inadequate understanding of how institutions can change. In this, as in most things, avoiding the worst mistakes is as important as—and more realistic than—attempting to develop simple solutions. Perhaps this is most clearly visible when we consider current policy recommendations encouraging "authoritarian growth" based on the successful Chinese growth experience of the last several decades. We next explain why these policy recommendations are misleading and why Chinese growth, as it has unfolded so far, is just another form of growth under extractive political institutions, unlikely to translate into sustained economic development.

THE IRRESISTIBLE CHARM OF
AUTHORITARIAN GROWTH

Dai Guofang recognized the coming urban boom in China early on. New highways, business centers, residences, and skyscrapers were sprawling everywhere around China in the 1990s, and Dai thought this growth would only pick up speed in the next decade. He reasoned that his company, Jinagsu Tieben Iron and Steel, could capture a large market as a low-cost producer, especially compared with the inefficient state-owned steel factories. Dai planned to build a true steel giant, and with support from the local party bosses in Changzhou, he started building in 2003. By March 2004, however, the project had been stopped by order of the Chinese Communist Party in Beijing, and Dai was arrested for reasons never clearly articulated. The authorities may have presumed that they would find some incriminating evidence in Dai's accounts. In the event, he spent the next five years in jail and home detention, and was found guilty on a minor charge in 2009. His real crime was to start a large project that would compete with state-sponsored companies and do so without the approval of the higher-ups in the Communist Party. This was certainly the lesson that others drew from the case.

The Communist Party's reaction to entrepreneurs such as Dai should not be a surprise. Chen Yun, one of Deng Xiaoping's closest associates and arguably the major architect behind the early market reforms, summarized the views of most party cadres with a "bird in a cage" analogy for the economy: China's economy was the bird; the party's control, the cage, had to be enlarged to make the bird healthier and more dynamic, but it could not be unlocked or removed, lest the bird fly away. Jiang Zemin, shortly after becoming general secretary of the Communist Party in 1989, the most powerful position in China, went even further and summarized the party's suspicion of entrepreneurs by characterizing them as "self-employed traders and peddlers [who] cheat, embezzle, bribe and evade taxation." Throughout the 1990s, even as foreign investment was pouring into China and state-owned enterprises were encouraged to expand, private entrepreneurship was greeted with suspicion, and many entrepreneurs were expropriated or even jailed. Jiang Zemin's view of entrepreneurs, though in relative decline, is still widespread in China. In the words of a Chinese economist, "Big state companies can get involved in huge projects. But when private companies do so, especially in competition with the state, then trouble comes from every corners [sic]."

While scores of private companies are now profitably operating in China, many elements of the economy are still under the party's command and protection. Journalist Richard McGregor reports that on the desk of the head of each of the biggest state companies in China stands a red phone. When it rings, it is the party calling with orders on what the company should do, where it should invest, and what its targets will be. These giant companies are still under the command of the party, a fact we are reminded of when the party decides to shuffle their chief executives, fire them, or promote them, with little explanation.

These stories of course do not deny that China has made great strides toward inclusive economic institutions, strides that underpin its spectacular growth rates over the past thirty years. Most entrepreneurs have some security, not least because they cultivate the support of local cadres and Communist Party elites in Beijing. Most state-owned enterprises seek profits and compete in international markets. This is a radical change from the China of Mao. As we saw in the previous chapter, China was first able to grow because under Deng Xiaoping there were radical reforms away from the most extractive economic institutions and toward inclusive economic institutions. Growth has continued as Chinese economic institutions have been on a path toward greater inclusiveness, albeit at a slow pace. China is also greatly benefiting from its large supply of cheap labor and its access to foreign markets, capital, and technologies.

Even if Chinese economic institutions are incomparably more inclusive today than three decades ago, the Chinese experience is an example of growth under extractive political institutions. Despite the recent emphasis in China on innovation and technology, Chinese growth is based on the adoption of existing technologies and rapid investment, not creative destruction. An important aspect of this is that property rights are not entirely secure in China. Every now and then, just like Dai, some entrepreneurs are expropriated. Labor mobility is tightly regulated, and the most basic of property rights, the right to sell one's own labor in the way one wishes, is still highly imperfect. The extent to which economic institutions are still far from being truly inclusive is illustrated by the fact that only a few businessmen and -women would even venture into any activity without the support of the local party cadre or, even more important, of Beijing. The connection between business and the party is highly lucrative for both. Businesses supported by the party receive contracts on favorable terms, can evict ordinary people to expropriate their land, and violate laws and regulations with impunity. Those who stand in the path of this business plan will be trampled and can even be jailed or murdered.

The all-too-present weight of the Communist Party and extractive institutions in China remind us of the many similarities between Soviet growth in the 1950s and '60s and Chinese growth today, though there are also notable differences. The Soviet Union achieved growth under extractive economic institutions and extractive political institutions because it forcibly allocated resources toward industry under a centralized command structure, particularly armaments and heavy industry. Such growth was feasible partly because there was a lot of catching up to be done. Growth under extractive institutions is easier when creative destruction is not a necessity. Chinese economic institutions are certainly more inclusive than those in the Soviet Union, but China's political institutions are still extractive. The Communist Party is all-powerful in China and controls the entire state bureaucracy, the armed forces, the media, and large parts of the economy. Chinese people have few political freedoms and very little participation in the political process.

Many have long believed that growth in China would bring democracy and greater pluralism. There was a real sense in 1989 that the Tiananmen Square demonstrations would lead to greater opening and perhaps even the collapse of the communist regime. But tanks were unleashed on the demonstrators, and instead of a peaceful revolution, history books now call it the Tiananmen Square Massacre. In many ways, Chinese political institutions became more extractive in the aftermath of Tiananmen; reformers such as Zhao Ziyang, who as general secretary of the Communist Party lent his support to the students in Tiananmen Square, were purged, and the party clamped down on civil liberties and press freedom with greater zeal. Zhao Ziyang was put under house arrest for more than fifteen years, and his public record was gradually erased, so that he would not be even a symbol for those who supported political change.

Today the party's control over the media, including the Internet, is unprecedented. Much of this is achieved through self-censorship: media outlets know that they should not mention Zhao Ziyang or Liu Xiaobo, the government critic demanding greater democratization, who is still languishing in prison even after he was awarded the Nobel Peace Prize. Self-censorship is supported by an Orwellian apparatus that can monitor conversations and communications, close Web sites and newspapers, and even selectively block access to individual news stories on the Internet. All of this was on display when news about corruption charges against the son of the general secretary of the party since 2002, Hu Jintao, broke out in 2009. The party's apparatus immediately sprang into action and was not only able to prevent Chinese media from covering the case but also managed to selectively block stories about the case on the *New York Times* and *Financial Times* Web sites.

Because of the party's control over economic institutions, the extent of creative destruction is heavily curtailed, and it will remain so until there is radical reform in political institutions. Just as in the Soviet Union, the Chinese experience of growth under extractive political institutions is greatly facilitated because there is a lot of catching up to do. Income per capita in China is still a fraction of that in the United States and Western Europe. Of course, Chinese growth is considerably more diversified than Soviet growth; it doesn't rely on only armaments or heavy industry, and Chinese entrepreneurs are showing a lot of ingenuity. All the same, this growth will run out of steam unless extractive political institutions make way for inclusive institutions. As long as political institutions remain extractive, growth will be inherently limited, as it has been in all other similar cases.

The Chinese experience does raise several interesting questions about the future of Chinese growth and, more important, the desirability and viability of authoritarian growth. Such growth has become a popular alternative to the "Washington consensus," which emphasizes the importance of market and trade liberalization and certain forms of institutional reform for kick-starting economic growth in many less developed parts of the world. While part of the appeal of authoritarian growth comes as a reaction to the Washington consensus, perhaps its greater charm—certainly to the rulers presiding over extractive institutions—is that it gives them free rein in maintaining and even strengthening their hold on power and legitimizes their extraction.

As our theory highlights, particularly in societies that have undergone some degree of state centralization, this type of growth under extractive institutions is possible and may even be the most likely scenario for many nations, ranging from Cambodia and Vietnam to Burundi, Ethiopia, and Rwanda. But it also implies that like all examples of growth under extractive political institutions, it will not be sustained.

In the case of China, the growth process based on catch-up, import of foreign technology, and export of low-end manufacturing products is likely to continue for a while. Nevertheless, Chinese growth is also likely to come to an end, particularly once China reaches the standards of living level of a middle-income country. The most likely scenario may be for the Chinese Communist Party and the increasingly powerful Chinese economic elite to manage to maintain their very tight grip on power in the next several decades. In this case, history and our theory suggest that growth with creative destruction and true innovation will not arrive, and the spectacular growth rates in China will slowly evaporate. But this outcome is far from preordained; it can be avoided if China transitions to inclusive political institutions before its growth under extractive institutions reaches its limit. Nevertheless, as we will see next, there is little reason to expect that a transition in China toward more inclusive political institutions is likely or that it will take place automatically and painlessly.

Even some voices within the Chinese Communist Party are recognizing the dangers on the road ahead and are throwing around the idea that political reform—that is, a transition to more inclusive political institutions, to use our terminology—is necessary. The powerful premier Wen Jiabao has recently warned of the danger that economic growth will be hampered unless political reform gets under way. We think Wen's analysis is prescient, even if some people doubt his sincerity. But many in the West do not agree with Wen's pronouncements. To them, China reveals an alternative path to sustained economic growth, one under authoritarianism rather than inclusive economic and political institutions. But they are wrong. We have already seen the important salient roots of Chinese success: a radical change in economic institutions away from rigidly communist ones and toward institutions that provide incentives to increase productivity and to trade. Looked at from this perspective, there is nothing fundamentally different about China's experience relative to that of countries that have managed to take steps away from extractive and toward inclusive economic institutions, even when this takes place under extractive political institutions, as in the Chinese case. China has thus achieved economic growth not thanks to its extractive political institutions, but despite them: its successful growth experience over the last three decades is due to a radical shift away from extractive economic institutions and toward significantly more inclusive economic institutions, which was made more difficult, not easier, by the presence of highly authoritarian, extractive political institutions.

A DIFFERENT TYPE of endorsement of authoritarian growth recognizes its unattractive nature but claims that authoritarianism is just a passing stage. This idea goes back to one of the classical theories of political sociology, the theory of modernization, formulated by Seymour Martin Lipset. Modernization theory maintains that all societies, as they grow, are headed toward a more modern, developed, and civilized existence, and in particular toward democracy. Many followers of modernization theory also claim that, like democracy, inclusive institutions will emerge as a by-product of the growth process. Moreover, even though democracy is not the same as inclusive political institutions, regular elections and relatively unencumbered political competition are likely to bring forth the development of inclusive political institutions. Different versions of modernization theory also claim that an educated workforce will naturally lead to democracy and better institutions. In a somewhat postmodern version of modernization theory, *New York Times* columnist Thomas Friedman went so far as to suggest that once a country got enough McDonald's restaurants, democracy and institutions were bound to follow. All this paints an optimistic picture. Over the past sixty years, most countries, even many of those with extractive institutions, have experienced some growth, and most have witnessed notable increases in the educational attainment of their workforces. So, as their incomes and educational levels continue to rise, one way or another, all other good things, such as democracy, human rights, civil liberties, and secure property rights, should follow.

Modernization theory has a wide following both within and outside academia. Recent U.S. attitudes toward China, for example, have been shaped by this theory. George H. W. Bush summarized U.S. policy toward Chinese democracy as "Trade freely with China and time is on our side." The idea was that as China traded freely with the West, it would grow, and that growth would bring democracy and better institutions in China, as modernization theory predicted. Yet the rapid increase in U.S.-China trade since the mid-1980s has done little for Chinese democracy, and the even closer integration that is likely to follow during the next decade will do equally little.

The attitudes of many about the future of Iraqi society and democracy in the aftermath of the U.S.-led invasion were similarly optimistic because of modernization theory. Despite its disastrous economic performance under Saddam Hussein's regime, Iraq was not as poor in 2002 as many sub-Saharan African nations, and it had a comparatively well-educated population, so it was believed to be ripe ground for the development of democracy and civil liberties, and perhaps even what we would describe as pluralism. These hopes were quickly dashed as chaos and civil war descended upon Iraqi society.

Modernization theory is both incorrect and unhelpful for thinking about how to confront the major problems of extractive institutions in failing nations. The strongest piece of evidence in favor of modernization theory is that rich nations are the ones that have democratic regimes, respect civil and human rights, and enjoy functioning markets and generally inclusive economic institutions. Yet interpreting this association as supporting modernization theory ignores the major effect of inclusive economic and political institutions on economic growth. As we have argued throughout this book, it is the societies with inclusive institutions that have grown over the past three hundred years and have become relatively rich today. That this accounts for what we see around us is shown clearly if we look at the facts slightly differently: while nations that have built inclusive economic and political institutions over the last several centuries have achieved sustained economic growth, authoritarian regimes that have grown more rapidly over the past sixty or one hundred years, contrary to what Lipset's modernization theory would claim, have not become more democratic. And this is in fact not surprising. Growth under extractive institutions is possible precisely because it doesn't necessarily or automatically imply the demise of these very institutions. In fact, it is often generated because those in control of the extractive institutions view economic growth as not a threat but a support to their regime, as the Chinese Communist Party has done since the 1980s. It is also not surprising that growth generated by increases in the value of the natural resources of a nation, such as in Gabon, Russia, Saudi Arabia, and Venezuela, is unlikely to lead to a fundamental transformation of these authoritarian regimes toward inclusive institutions.

The historical record is even less generous to modernization theory. Many relatively prosperous nations have succumbed to and supported repressive dictatorships and extractive institutions. Both Germany and Japan were among the richest and most industrialized nations in the world in the first half of the twentieth century, and had comparatively well-educated citizens. This did not prevent the rise of the National Socialist Party in Germany or a militaristic regime intent on territorial expansion via war in Japan—making both political and economic institutions take a sharp turn toward extractive institutions. Argentina was also one of the richest countries in the world in the nineteenth century, as rich as or even richer than Britain, because it was the beneficiary of the worldwide resource boom; it also had the most educated population in Latin America. But democracy and pluralism were no more successful, and were arguably less successful, in Argentina than in much of the rest of Latin America. One coup followed another, and as we saw in chapter 11, even democratically elected leaders acted as rapacious dictators. Even more recently there has been little progress toward inclusive economic institutions, and as we saw in chapter 13, twenty-first-century Argentinian governments can still expropriate their citizens' wealth with impunity.

All of this highlights several important ideas. First, growth under authoritarian, extractive political institutions in China, though likely to continue for a while yet, will not translate into sustained growth, supported by truly inclusive economic institutions and creative destruction. Second, contrary to the claims of modernization theory, we should not count on authoritarian growth leading to democracy or inclusive political institutions. China, Russia, and several other authoritarian regimes currently experiencing some growth are likely to reach the limits of extractive growth before they transform their political institutions in a more inclusive direction—and in fact, probably before there is any desire among the elite for such changes or any strong opposition forcing them to do so. Third, authoritarian growth is neither desirable nor viable in the long run, and thus should not receive the endorsement of the international community as a template for nations in Latin America, Asia, and sub-Saharan Africa, even if it is a path that many nations will choose precisely because it is sometimes consistent with the interests of the economic and political elites dominating them.

YOU CAN'T ENGINEER PROSPERITY

Unlike the theory we have developed in this book, the ignorance hypothesis comes readily with a suggestion about how to "solve" the problem of poverty: if ignorance got us here, enlightening and informing rulers and policymakers can get us out, and we should be able to "engineer" prosperity around the world by providing the right advice and by convincing politicians of what is good economics. In chapter 2, when we discussed this hypothesis, we showed how the experience of Ghana's prime minister Kofi Busia in the early 1970s underscored the fact that the main obstacle to the adoption of policies that would reduce market failures and encourage economic growth is not the ignorance of politicians, but the incentives and constraints they face from the political and economic institutions in their societies. Nevertheless, the ignorance hypothesis still rules supreme in Western policymaking circles, which, almost to the exclusion of anything else, focus on how to engineer prosperity.

These engineering attempts come in two flavors. The first, often advocated by international organizations such as the International Monetary Fund, recognizes that poor development is caused by bad economic policies and institutions, and then proposes a list of improvements these international organizations attempt to induce poor countries to adopt. (The Washington consensus makes up one such list.) These improvements focus on sensible things such as macroeconomic stability and seemingly attractive macroeconomic goals such as a reduction in the size of the government sector, flexible exchange rates, and capital account liberalization. They also focus on more microeconomic goals, such as privatization, improvements in the efficiency of public service provision, and perhaps also suggestions as to how to improve the functioning of the state itself by emphasizing anticorruption measures. Though on their own many of these reforms might be sensible, the approach of international organizations in Washington, London, Paris, and elsewhere is still steeped in an incorrect perspective that fails to recognize the role of political institutions and the constraints they place on policymaking. Attempts by international institutions to engineer economic growth by hectoring poor countries into adopting better policies and institutions are not successful because they do not take place in the context of an explanation of why bad policies and institutions are there in the first place, except that the leaders of poor countries are ignorant. The consequence is that the policies are not adopted and not implemented, or are implemented in name only.

For example, many economies around the world ostensibly implementing such reforms, most notably in Latin America, stagnated throughout the 1980s and '90s. In reality, such reforms were foisted upon these countries in contexts where politics went on as usual. Hence, even when reforms were adopted, their intent was subverted, or politicians used other ways to blunt their impact. All this is illustrated by the "implementation" of one of the key recommendations of international institutions aimed at achieving macroeconomic stability, central bank independence. This recommendation either was implemented in theory but not in practice or was undermined by the use of other policy instruments. It was quite sensible in principle. Many politicians around the world were spending more than they were raising in tax revenue and were then forcing their central banks to make up the difference by printing money. The resulting inflation was creating instability and uncertainty. The theory was that independent central banks, just like the Bundesbank in Germany, would resist political pressure and put a lid on inflation. Zimbabwe's president Mugabe decided to heed international advice; he declared the Zimbabwean central bank independent in 1995. Before this, the inflation rate in Zimbabwe was hovering around 20 percent. By 2002 it had reached 140 percent; by 2003, almost 600 percent; by 2007, 66,000 percent; and by 2008, 230 million percent! Of course, in a country where the president wins the lottery (pages 368–373), it should surprise nobody that passing a law making the central bank independent means nothing. The governor of the Zimbabwean central bank probably knew how his counterpart in Sierra Leone had "fallen" from the top floor of the central bank building when he disagreed with Siaka Stevens (page 344). Independent or not, complying with the president's demands was the prudent choice for his personal health, even if not for the health of the economy. Not all countries are like Zimbabwe. In Argentina and Colombia, central banks were also made independent in the 1990s, and they actually did their job of reducing inflation. But since in neither country was politics changed, political elites could use other ways to buy votes, maintain their interests, and reward themselves and their followers. Since they couldn't do this by printing money anymore, they had to use a different way. In both countries the introduction of central bank independence coincided with a big expansion in government expenditures, financed largely by borrowing.

The second approach to engineering prosperity is much more in vogue nowadays. It recognizes that there are no easy fixes for lifting a nation from poverty to prosperity overnight or even in the course of a few decades. Instead, it claims, there are many "micro-market failures" that can be redressed with good advice, and prosperity will result if policymakers take advantage of these opportunities—which, again, can be achieved with the help and vision of economists and others. Small market failures are everywhere in poor countries, this approach claims—for example, in their education systems, health care delivery, and the way their markets are organized. This is undoubtedly true. But the problem is that these small market failures may be only the tip of the iceberg, the symptom of deeper-rooted problems in a society functioning under extractive institutions. Just as it is not a coincidence that poor countries have bad macroeconomic policies, it is not a coincidence that their educational systems do not work well. These market failures may not be due solely to ignorance.

The policymakers and bureaucrats who are supposed to act on well-intentioned advice may be as much a part of the problem, and the many attempts to rectify these inefficiencies may backfire precisely because those in charge are not grappling with the institutional causes of the poverty in the first place.

These problems are illustrated by intervention engineered by the nongovernmental organization (NGO) Seva Mandir to improve health care delivery in the state of Rajasthan in India. The story of health care delivery in India is one of deep-rooted inefficiency and failure. Government-provided health care is, at least in theory, widely available and cheap, and the personnel are generally qualified. But even the poorest Indians do not use government health care facilities, opting instead for the much more expensive, unregulated, and sometimes even deficient private providers. This is not because of some type of irrationality: people are unable to get any care from government facilities, which are plagued by absenteeism. If an Indian visited his government-run facility, not only would there be no nurses there, but he would probably not even be able to get in the building, because health care facilities are closed most of the time.

In 2006 Seva Mandir, together with a group of economists, designed an incentive scheme to encourage nurses to turn up for work in the Udaipur district of Rajasthan. The idea was simple: Seva Mandir introduced time clocks that would stamp the date and time when nurses were in the facility. Nurses were supposed to stamp their time cards three times a day, to ensure that they arrived on time, stayed around, and left on time. If such a scheme worked, and increased the quality and quantity of health care provision, it would be a strong illustration of the theory that there were easy solutions to key problems in development.

In the event, the intervention revealed something very different. Shortly after the program was implemented, there was a sharp increase in nurse attendance. But this was very short lived. In a little more than a year, the local health administration of the district deliberately undermined the incentive scheme introduced by Seva Mandir. Absenteeism was back to its usual level, yet there was a sharp increase in "exempt days," which meant that nurses were not actually around—but this was officially sanctioned by the local health administration. There was also a sharp increase in "machine problems," as the time clocks were broken. But Seva Mandir was unable to replace them because local health ministers would not cooperate.

Forcing nurses to stamp a time clock three times a day doesn't seem like such an innovative idea. Indeed, it is a practice used throughout the industry, even Indian industry, and it must have occurred to health administrators as a potential solution to their problems. It seems unlikely, then, that ignorance of such a simple incentive scheme was what stopped its being used in the first place. What occurred during the program simply confirmed this. Health administrators sabotaged the program because they were in cahoots with the nurses and complicit in the endemic absenteeism problems. They did not want an incentive scheme forcing nurses to turn up or reducing their pay if they did not.

What this episode illustrates is a micro version of the difficulty of implementing meaningful changes when institutions are the cause of the problems in the first place. In this case, it was not corrupt politicians or powerful businesses undermining institutional reform, but rather, the local health administration and nurses who were able to sabotage Seva Mandir's and the development economists' incentive scheme. This suggests that many of the micro-market failures that are apparently easy to fix may be illusory: the institutional structure that creates market failures will also prevent implementation of interventions to improve incentives at the micro level. Attempting to engineer prosperity without confronting the root cause of the problems—extractive institutions and the politics that keeps them in place—is unlikely to bear fruit.

THE FAILURE OF FOREIGN AID

Following the September 11, 2001, attacks by Al Qaeda, U.S.-led forces swiftly toppled the repressive Taliban regime in Afghanistan, which was harboring and refusing to hand over key members of Al Qaeda. The Bonn Agreement of December 2001 between leaders of the former Afghan mujahideen who had cooperated with the U.S.

forces and key members of the Afghan diaspora, including Hamid Karzai, created a plan for the establishment of a democratic regime. A first step was the nationwide grand assembly, the Loya Jirga, which elected Karzai to lead the interim government. Things were looking up for Afghanistan. A majority of the Afghan people were longing to leave the Taliban behind. The international community thought that all that Afghanistan needed now was a large infusion of foreign aid. Representatives from the United Nations and several leading NGOs soon descended on the capital, Kabul.

What ensued should not have been a surprise, especially given the failure of foreign aid to poor countries and failed states over the past five decades. Surprise or not, the usual ritual was repeated. Scores of aid workers and their entourages arrived in town with their own private jets, NGOs of all sorts poured in to pursue their own agendas, and high-level talks began between governments and delegations from the international community. Billions of dollars were now coming to Afghanistan. But little of it was used for building infrastructure, schools, or other public services essential for the development of inclusive institutions or even for restoring law and order. While much of the infrastructure remained in tatters, the first tranche of the money was used to commission an airline to shuttle around UN and other international officials. The next thing they needed were drivers and interpreters. So they hired the few English-speaking bureaucrats and the remaining teachers in Afghan schools to chauffeur and chaperone them around, paying them multiples of current Afghan salaries. As the few skilled bureaucrats were shunted into jobs servicing the foreign aid community, the aid flows, rather than building infrastructure in Afghanistan, started by undermining the Afghan state they were supposed to build upon and strengthen.

Villagers in a remote district in the central valley of Afghanistan heard a radio announcement about a new multimillion-dollar program to restore shelter to their area. After a long while, a few wooden beams, carried by the trucking cartel of Ismail Khan, famous former warlord and member of the Afghan government, were delivered. But they were too big to be used for anything in the district, and the villagers put them to the only possible use: firewood. So what had happened to the millions of dollars promised to the villagers? Of the promised money, 20 percent of it was taken as UN head office costs in Geneva. The remainder was subcontracted to an NGO, which took another 20 percent for its own head office costs in Brussels, and so on, for another three layers, with each party taking approximately another 20 percent of what was remaining. The little money that reached Afghanistan was used to buy wood from western Iran, and much of it was paid to Ismail Khan's trucking cartel to cover the inflated transport prices. It was a bit of a miracle that those oversize wooden beams even arrived in the village.

What happened in the central valley of Afghanistan is not an isolated incident. Many studies estimate that only about 10 or at most 20 percent of aid ever reaches its target. There are dozens of ongoing fraud investigations into charges of UN and local officials siphoning off aid money. But most of the waste resulting from foreign aid is not fraud, just incompetence or even worse: simply business as usual for aid organizations.

The Afghan experience with aid was in fact probably a qualified success compared to others. Throughout the last five decades, hundreds of billions of dollars have been paid to governments around the world as "development" aid. Much of it has been wasted in overhead and corruption, just as in Afghanistan. Worse, a lot of it went to dictators such as Mobutu, who depended on foreign aid from his Western patrons both to buy support from his clients to shore up his regime and to enrich himself. The picture in much of the rest of sub-Saharan Africa was similar. Humanitarian aid given for temporary relief in times of crises, for example, most recently in Haiti and Pakistan, has certainly been more useful, even though its delivery, too, has been marred in similar problems.

Despite this unflattering track record of "development" aid, foreign aid is one of the most popular policies that Western governments, international organizations such as the United Nations, and NGOs of different ilk recommend as a way of combating poverty around the world. And of course, the cycle of the failure of foreign aid repeats itself over and over again. The idea that rich Western countries should provide large amounts of "developmental aid" in order to solve the problem of poverty in sub-Saharan Africa, the Caribbean, Central America, and South Asia is based on an incorrect understanding of what causes poverty. Countries such as Afghanistan are poor because of their extractive institutions—which result in lack of property rights, law and order, or well-functioning legal systems and the stifling dominance of national and, more often, local elites over political and economic life. The same institutional problems mean that foreign aid will be ineffective, as it will be plundered and is unlikely to be delivered where it is supposed to go. In the worst-case scenario, it will prop up the regimes that are at the very root of the problems of these societies. If sustained economic growth depends on inclusive institutions, giving aid to regimes presiding over extractive institutions cannot be the solution. This is not to deny that, even beyond humanitarian aid, considerable good comes out of specific aid programs that build schools in areas where none existed before and that pay teachers who would otherwise go unpaid. While much of the aid community that poured into Kabul did little to improve life for ordinary Afghans, there have also been notable successes in building schools, particularly for girls, who were entirely excluded from education under the Taliban and even before.

One solution—which has recently become more popular, partly based on the recognition that institutions have something to do with prosperity and even the delivery of aid—is to make aid "conditional." According to this view, continued foreign aid should depend on recipient governments meeting certain conditions—for example, liberalizing markets or moving toward democracy. The George W. Bush administration undertook the biggest step toward this type of conditional aid by starting the Millennium Challenge Accounts, which made future aid payments dependent on quantitative improvements in several dimensions of economic and political development. But the effectiveness of conditional aid appears no better than the unconditional kind. Countries failing to meet these conditions typically receive as much aid as those that do. There is a simple reason: they have a greater need for aid of either the developmental or humanitarian kind. And quite predictably, conditional aid seems to have little effect on a nation's institutions. After all, it would have been quite surprising for somebody such as Siaka Stevens in Sierra Leone or Mobutu in the Congo suddenly to start dismantling the extractive institutions on which he depended just for a little more foreign aid. Even in sub-Saharan Africa, where foreign aid is a significant fraction of many governments' total budget, and even after the Millennium Challenge Accounts, which increased the extent of conditionality, the amount of additional foreign aid that a dictator can obtain by undermining his own power is both small and not worth the risk either to his continued dominance over the country or to his life.

But all this does not imply that foreign aid, except the humanitarian kind, should cease. Putting an end to foreign aid is impractical and would likely lead to additional human suffering. It is impractical because citizens of many Western nations feel guilt and unease about the economic and humanitarian disasters around the world, and foreign aid makes them believe that something is being done to combat the problems. Even if this something is not very effective, their desire for doing it will continue, and so will foreign aid. The enormous complex of international organizations and NGOs will also ceaselessly demand and mobilize resources to ensure the continuation of the status quo. Also, it would be callous to cut the aid given to the neediest nations. Yes, much of it is wasted. But if out of every dollar given to aid, ten cents makes it to the poorest people in the world, that is ten cents more than they had before to alleviate the most abject poverty, and it might still be better than nothing.

There are two important lessons here. First, foreign aid is not a very effective means of dealing with the failure of nations around the world today. Far from it. Countries need inclusive economic and political institutions to break out of the cycle of poverty. Foreign aid can typically do little in this respect, and certainly not with the way that it is currently organized. Recognizing the roots of world inequality and poverty is important precisely so that we do not pin our hopes on false promises. As those roots lie in institutions, foreign aid, within the framework of given institutions in recipient nations, will do little to spur sustained growth. Second, since the development of inclusive economic and political institutions is key, using the existing flows of foreign aid at least in part to facilitate such development would be useful. As we saw, conditionality is not the answer here, as it requires existing rulers to make concessions. Instead, perhaps structuring foreign aid so that its use and administration bring groups and leaders otherwise excluded from power into the decision-making process and empowering a broad segment of population might be a better prospect.

EMPOWERMENT

May 12, 1978, seemed as if it were going to be a normal day at the Scânia truck factory in the city of São Bernardo in the Brazilian state of São Paulo. But the workers were restless. Strikes had been banned in Brazil since 1964, when the military overthrew the democratic government of President João Goulart. But news had just broken that the government had been fixing the national inflation figures so that the rise in the cost of living had been underestimated. As the 7:00 a.m. shift began, workers put down their tools. At 8:00 a.m., Gilson Menezes, a union organizer working at the plant, called the union. The president of the São Bernardo Metalworkers was a thirty-three-year-old activist called Luiz Inácio Lula da Silva ("Lula"). By noon Lula was at the factory. When the company asked him to persuade the employees to go back to work, he refused.

The Scânia strike was the first in a wave of strikes that swept across Brazil. On the face of it these were about wages, but as Lula later noted,

> I think we can't separate economic and political factors. . . . The . . . struggle was over wages, but in struggling for wages, the working class won a political victory.

The resurgence of the Brazilian labor movement was just part of a much broader social reaction to a decade and a half of military rule. The left-wing intellectual Fernando Henrique Cardoso, like Lula destined to become president of Brazil after the re-creation of democracy, argued in 1973 that democracy would be created in Brazil by the

456 • WHY NATIONS FAIL

many social groups that opposed the military coming together. He said that what was needed was a "reactivation of civil society . . . the professional associations, the trade unions, the churches, the student organizations, the study groups and the debating circles, the social movements"—in other words, a broad coalition with the aim of re-creating democracy and changing Brazilian society.

The Scânia factory heralded the formation of this coalition. By late 1978, Lula was floating the idea of creating a new political party, the Workers' Party. This was to be the party not just of trade unionists, however. Lula insisted that it should be a party for all wage earners and the poor in general. Here the attempts of union leaders to organize a political platform began to coalesce with the many social movements that were springing up. On August 18, 1979, a meeting was held in São Paulo to discuss the formation of the Workers' Party, which brought together former opposition politicians, union leaders, students, intellectuals, and people representing one hundred diverse social movements that had begun to organize in the 1970s across Brazil. The Workers' Party, launched at the São Judas Tadeo restaurant in São Bernardo in October 1979, would come to represent all these diverse groups.

The party quickly began to benefit from the political opening that the military was reluctantly organizing. In the local elections of 1982, it ran candidates for the first time, and won two races for mayor. Throughout the 1980s, as democracy was gradually re-created in Brazil, the Workers' Party began to take over more and more local governments. By 1988 it controlled the governments in thirty-six municipalities, including large cities such as São Paulo and Porto Alegre. In 1989, in the first free presidential elections since the military coup, Lula won 16 percent of the vote in the first round as the party's candidate. In the runoff race with Fernando Collor, he won 44 percent.

In taking over many local governments, something that accelerated in the 1990s, the Workers' Party began to enter into a symbiotic relationship with many local social movements. In Porto Alegre the first Workers' Party administration after 1988 introduced "participatory budgeting," which was a mechanism for bringing ordinary citizens into the formulation of the spending priorities of the city. It created a system that has become a world model for local government accountability and responsiveness, and it went along with huge improvements in public service provision and the quality of life in the city. The successful governance structure of the party at the local level mapped into greater political mobilization and success at the national level. Though Lula was defeated by Fernando Henrique Cardoso in the presidential elections of 1994 and 1998, he was elected president of Brazil in 2002. The Workers' Party has been in power ever since.

The formation of a broad coalition in Brazil as a result of the coming together of diverse social movements and organized labor has had a remarkable impact on the Brazilian economy. Since 1990 economic growth has been rapid, with the proportion of the population in poverty falling from 45 percent to 30 percent in 2006. Inequality, which rose rapidly under the military, has fallen sharply, particularly after the Workers' Party took power, and there has been a huge expansion of education, with the average years of schooling of the population increasing from six in 1995 to eight in 2006. Brazil has now become part of the BRIC nations (Brazil, Russia, India, and China), the first Latin American country actually to have weight in international diplomatic circles.

THE RISE OF BRAZIL since the 1970s was not engineered by economists of international institutions instructing Brazilian policymakers on how to design better policies or avoid market failures. It was not achieved with injections of foreign aid. It was not the natural outcome of modernization. Rather, it was the consequence of diverse groups of people courageously building inclusive institutions. Eventually these led to more inclusive economic institutions. But the Brazilian transformation, like that of England in the seventeenth century, began with the creation of inclusive political institutions. But how can society build inclusive political institutions?

History, as we have seen, is littered with examples of reform movements that succumbed to the iron law of oligarchy and replaced one set of extractive institutions with even more pernicious ones. We have seen that England in 1688, France in 1789, and Japan during the Meiji Restoration of 1868 started the process of forging inclusive political institutions with a political revolution. But such political revolutions generally create much destruction and hardship, and their success is far from certain. The Bolshevik Revolution advertised its aim as replacing the exploitative economic system of tsarist Russia with a more just and efficient one that would bring freedom and prosperity to millions of Russians. Alas, the outcome was the opposite, and much more repressive and extractive institutions replaced those of the government the Bolsheviks overthrew. The experiences in China, Cuba, and Vietnam were similar. Many noncommunist, top-down reforms fared no better. Nasser vowed to build a modern egalitarian society in Egypt, but this led only to Hosni Mubarak's corrupt regime, as we saw in chapter 13. Robert Mugabe was viewed by many as a freedom fighter ousting Ian Smith's racist and highly extractive Rhodesian regime. But Zimbabwe's institutions became no less extractive, and its economic performance has been even worse than before independence.

What is common among the political revolutions that successfully paved the way for more inclusive institutions and the gradual institutional changes in North America, in England in the nineteenth century, and in Botswana after independence—which also led to significant strengthening of inclusive political institutions—is that they succeeded in empowering a fairly broad cross-section of society. Pluralism, the cornerstone of inclusive political institutions, requires political power to be widely held in society, and starting from extractive institutions that vest power in a narrow elite, this requires a process of empowerment. This, as we emphasized in chapter 7, is what sets apart the Glorious Revolution from the overthrow of one elite by another. In the case of the Glorious Revolution, the roots of pluralism were in the overthrow of James II by a political revolution led by a broad coalition consisting of merchants, industrialists, the gentry, and even many members of the English aristocracy not allied with the Crown. As we have seen, the Glorious Revolution was facilitated by the prior mobilization and empowerment of a broad coalition, and more important, it in turn led to the further empowerment of an even broader segment of society than what came before—even though clearly this segment was much less broad than the entire society, and England would remain far from a true democracy for more than another two hundred years. The factors leading to the emergence of inclusive institutions in the North American colonies were also similar, as we saw in the first chapter. Once again, the path starting in Virginia, Carolina, Maryland, and Massachusetts and leading up to the Declaration of Independence and to the consolidation of inclusive political institutions in the United States was one of empowerment for increasingly broader segments in society.

The French Revolution, too, is an example of empowerment of a broader segment of society, which rose up against the *ancien régime* in France and managed to pave the way for a more pluralistic political system. But the French Revolution, especially the interlude of the Terror under Robespierre, a repressive and murderous regime, also illustrates how the process of empowerment is not without its pitfalls. Ultimately, however, Robespierre and his Jacobin cadres were cast aside, and the most important inheritance from the French Revolution became not the guillotine but the far-ranging reforms that the revolution implemented in France and other parts of Europe.

There are many parallels between these historical processes of empowerment and what took place in Brazil starting in the 1970s. Though one root of the Workers' Party is the trade union movement, right from its early days, leaders such as Lula, along with the many intellectuals and opposition politicians who lent their support to the party, sought to make it into a broad coalition. These impulses began to fuse with local social movements all over the country, as the party took over local governments, encouraging civic participation and causing a sort of revolution in governance throughout the country. In Brazil, in contrast with England in the seventeenth century or France at the turn of the eighteenth century, there was no radical revolution igniting the process of transforming political institutions at one fell swoop. But the process of empowerment that started in the factories of São Bernardo was effective in part because it translated into fundamental political change at the national level—for example, the transitioning out of military rule to democracy. More important, empowerment at the grass-roots level in Brazil ensured that the transition to democracy corresponded to a move toward inclusive political institutions, and thus was a key factor in the emergence of a government committed to the provision of public services, educational expansion, and a truly level playing field. As we have seen, democracy is no guarantee that there will be pluralism. The contrast of the development of pluralistic institutions in Brazil to the Venezuelan experience is telling in this context. Venezuela also transitioned to democracy after 1958, but this happened without empowerment at the grassroots level and did not create a pluralistic distribution of political power. Instead, corrupt politics, patronage networks, and conflict persisted in Venezuela, and in part as a result, when voters went to the polls, they were even willing to support potential despots such as Hugo Chávez, most likely because they thought he alone could stand up to the established elites of Venezuela. In consequence, Venezuela still languishes under extractive institutions, while Brazil broke the mold.

WHAT CAN BE DONE to kick-start or perhaps just facilitate the process of empowerment and thus the development of inclusive political institutions? The honest answer of course is that there is no recipe for building such institutions. Naturally there are some obvious factors that would make the process of empowerment more likely to get off the ground. These would include the presence of some degree of centralized order so that social movements challenging existing regimes do not immediately descend into lawlessness; some preexisting political institutions that introduce a modicum of pluralism, such as the traditional political institutions in Botswana, so that broad coalitions can form and endure; and the presence of civil society institutions that can coordinate the demands of the population so that opposition movements can neither be easily crushed by the current elites nor inevitably turn into a vehicle for another group to take control of existing extractive institutions. But many of these factors are historically predetermined and change only slowly. The Brazilian case illustrates how civil society institutions and associated party organizations can be built from the ground up, but this process is slow, and how successful it can be under different circumstances is not well understood.

One other actor, or set of actors, can play a transformative role in the process of empowerment: the media. Empowerment of society at large is difficult to coordinate and maintain without widespread information about whether there are economic and political abuses by those in power. We saw in chapter 11 the role of the media in informing the public and coordinating their demands against forces undermining inclusive institutions in the United States. The media can also play a key role in channeling the empowerment of a broad segment of society into more durable political reforms, again as illustrated in our discussion in chapter 11, particularly in the context of British democratization.

Pamphlets and books informing and galvanizing people played an important role during the Glorious Revolution in England, the French Revolution, and the march toward democracy in nineteenth-century Britain. Similarly, media, particularly new forms based on advances in information and communication technology, such as Web blogs, anonymous chats, Facebook, and Twitter, played a central role in Iranian opposition against Ahmadinejad's fraudulent election in 2009 and subsequent repression, and they seem to be playing a similarly central role in the Arab Spring protests that are ongoing as this manuscript is being completed.

Authoritarian regimes are often aware of the importance of a free media, and do their best to fight it. An extreme illustration of this comes from Alberto Fujimori's rule in Peru. Though originally democratically elected, Fujimori soon set up a dictatorial regime in Peru, mounting a coup while still in office in 1992. Thereafter, though elections continued, Fujimori built a corrupt regime and ruled through repression and bribery. In this he relied heavily on his right-hand man, Valdimiro Montesinos, who headed the powerful national intelligence service of Peru. Montesinos was an organized man, so he kept good records of how much the administration paid different individuals to buy their loyalty, even videotaping many actual acts of bribery. There was a logic to this. Beyond just recordkeeping, this evidence made sure that the accomplices were now on record and would be considered as guilty as Fujimori and Montesinos. After the fall of the regime, these records fell into the hands of journalists and authorities. The amounts are revealing about the value of the media to a dictatorship. A Supreme Court judge was worth between $5,000 and $10,000 a month, and politicians in the same or different parties were paid similar amounts. But when it came to newspapers and TV stations, the sums were in the millions. Fujimori and Montesinos paid $9 million on one occasion and more than $10 million on another to control TV stations. They paid more than $1 million to a mainstream newspaper, and to other newspapers they paid any amount between $3,000 and $8,000 per headline. Fujimori and Montesinos thought that controlling the media was much more important than controlling politicians and judges. One of Montesinos's henchmen, General Bello, summed this up in one of the videos by stating, "If we do not control the television we do not do anything."

The current extractive institutions in China are also crucially dependent on Chinese authorities' control of the media, which, as we have seen, has become frighteningly sophisticated. As a Chinese commentator summarized, "To uphold the leadership of the Party in political reform, three principles must be followed: that the Party controls the armed forces; the Party controls cadres; and the Party controls the news."

But of course a free media and new communication technologies can help only at the margins, by providing information and coordinating the demands and actions of those vying for more inclusive institutions. Their help will translate into meaningful change only when a broad segment of society mobilizes and organizes in order to effect political change, and does so not for sectarian reasons or to take control of extractive institutions, but to transform extractive institutions into more inclusive ones. Whether such a process will get under way and open the door to further empowerment, and ultimately to durable political reform, will depend, as we have seen in many different instances, on the history of economic and political institutions, on many small differences that matter and on the very contingent path of history.

ACKNOWLEDGMENTS

THIS BOOK IS the culmination of fifteen years of collaborative research, and along the way we have accumulated a great deal of practical and intellectual debts. Our greatest debt is to our long-term collaborator Simon Johnson, who coauthored many of the key scientific papers that shaped our understanding of comparative economic development.

Our other coauthors, with whom we have worked on related research projects, played a significant role in the development of our views, and we would like to particularly thank in this capacity Philippe Aghion, Jean-Marie Baland, María Angélica Bautista, Davide Cantoni, Isaías Chaves, Jonathan Conning, Melissa Dell, Georgy Egorov, Leopoldo Fergusson, Camilo García-Jimeno, Tarek Hassan, Sebastián Mazzuca, Jeffrey Nugent, Neil Parsons, Steve Pincus, Pablo Querubín, Rafael Santos, Konstantin Sonin, Davide Ticchi, Ragnar Torvik, Juan Fernando Vargas, Thierry Verdier, Andrea Vindigni, Alex Wolitzky, Pierre Yared, and Fabrizio Zilibotti.

Many other people played very important roles in encouraging, challenging, and critiquing us over the years. We would particularly like to thank Lee Alston, Abhijit Banerjee, Robert Bates, Timothy Besley, John Coatsworth, Jared Diamond, Richard Easterlin, Stanley Engerman, Peter Evans, Jeff Frieden, Peter Gourevitch, Stephen Haber, Mark Harrison, Elhanan Helpman, Peter Lindert, Karl Ove Moene, Dani Rodrik, and Barry Weingast.

Two people played a particularly significant role in shaping our views and encouraging our research, and we would like to take this opportunity to express our intellectual debt and our sincere gratitude to them: Joel Mokyr, and Ken Sokoloff, who unfortunately passed away before this book was written. Ken is sorely missed by us both.

We are also very grateful to the scholars who attended a conference we organized in February 2010 on an early version of our book manuscript at the Institute for Quantitative Social Science at Harvard. We would particularly like to thank the co-organizers, Jim Alt and Ken Shepsle, and our discussants at the conference: Robert Allen, Abhijit Banerjee, Robert Bates, Stanley Engerman, Claudia Goldin, Elhanan Helpman, Joel Mokyr, Ian Morris, Şevket Pamuk, Steve Pincus, and Peter Temin. We are also grateful to Melissa Dell, Jesús Fernández-Villaverde, Sándor László, Suresh Naidu, Roger Owen, Dan Trefler, Michael Walton, and Noam Yuchtman, who gave us extensive comments at the conference and at many other times.

We are also grateful to Charles Mann, Leandro Prados de la Escosura, and David Webster for their expert advice.

During much of the process of researching and writing this book we were both members of the Canadian Institute for Advanced Research's (CIFAR) program on Institutions, Organizations, and Growth. We presented research related to this book many times at CIFAR meetings and have benefited hugely from the support of this wonderful organization and the scholars that it brings together.

We also received comments from literally hundreds of people in various seminars and conferences on the material developed in this book, and we apologize for failing to attribute properly any suggestion, idea, or insight that we got from those presentations and discussions.

We are also very grateful to María Angélica Bautista, Melissa Dell, and Leander Heldring for their superb research assistance on this project.

Last, but certainly not least, we have been very fortunate to have a wonderful, insightful, and extremely supportive editor, John Mahaney. John's comments and suggestions have greatly improved our book, and his support and enthusiasm for the project made the last year and a half much more pleasant and less taxing than it might have been.

BIBLIOGRAPHICAL ESSAY
AND SOURCES

PREFACE

Mohamed ElBaradei's views can be found at twitter.com/#!/ElBaradei.

Mosaab El Shami and Noha Hamed quotes are from Yahoo! news 2/6/2011, at news.yahoo.com/s/yblog_exclusive/20110206/ts_yblog_exclusive/egyptian-voices-from-tahrir-square.

On the twelve immediate demands posted on Wael Khalil's blog, see alethonews.wordpress.com/2011/02/27/egypt-reviewing-the-demands/.

Reda Metwaly is quoted on Al Jazeera, 2/1/2011, at english.aljazeera.net/news/middleeast/2011/02/2011212597913527.html.

CHAPTER 1: SO CLOSE AND YET SO DIFFERENT

A good discussion of the Spanish exploration of the Rio de La Plata is Rock (1992), chap. 1. On the discovery and colonization of the Guaraní, see Ganson (2003). The quotations from de Sahagún are from de Sahagún (1975), pp. 47–49. Gibson (1963) is fundamental on the Spanish conquest of Mexico and the institutions they structured. The quotations from de las Casas come from de las Casas (1992), pp. 39, 117–18, and 107, respectively.

On Pizarro in Peru, see Hemming (1983). Chaps. 1–6 cover the meeting at Cajamarca and the march south and the capture of the Inca capital, Cuzco. See Hemming (1983), chap. 20, on de Toledo. Bakewell (1984) gives an overview of the functioning of the Potosí *mita,* and Dell (2010) provides statistical evidence that shows how it has had persistent effects over time.

The quote from Arthur Young is reproduced from Sheridan (1973), p. 8. There are many good books that describe the early history of Jamestown: for example, Price (2003), and Kupperman (2007). Our treatment is heavily influenced by Morgan (1975) and Galenson (1996). The quote from Anas Todkill comes from p. 38 of Todkill (1885). The quotes from John Smith are from Price (2003), p. 77 ("Victuals . . ."), p. 93 ("If your king . . ."), and p. 96 ("When you send . . ."). The Charter of Maryland, the Fundamental Constitutions of Carolina, and other colonial constitutions have been put on the Internet by Yale University's Avalon Project, at avalon.law.yale.edu/17th_century.

Bakewell (2009), chap. 14, discusses the independence of Mexico and the constitution. See Stevens (1991) and Knight (2011) on postindependence political instability and presidents. Coatsworth (1978) is the seminal paper on the evidence on economic decline in Mexico after independence. Haber (2010) presents the comparison of the development of banking in Mexico and the United States. Sokoloff (1988) and Sokoloff and Khan (1990) provide evidence on the social background of innovators in the United States who filed patents. See Israel (2000) for a biography of Thomas Edison. Haber, Maurer, and Razo (2003) proposes an interpretation of the political economy of the regime of Porfirio Díaz very much in the spirit of our discussion. Haber, Klein, Maurer, and Middlebrook (2008) extend this treatment of Mexico's political economy into the twentieth century. On the differential allocation of frontier lands in North and Latin America, see Nugent and Robinson (2010) and García-Jimeno and Robinson (2011). Hu-DeHart (1984) discusses the deportation of the Yaqui people in chap. 6. On the fortune of Carlos Slim and how it was made, see Relea (2007) and Martinez (2002).

Our interpretation of comparative economic development of the Americas builds on our own previous research with Simon Johnson, particularly Acemoglu, Johnson, and Robinson (2001, 2002), and has also been heavily influenced by Coatsworth (1978, 2008) and Engerman and Sokoloff (1997).

CHAPTER 2: THEORIES THAT DON'T WORK

Jared Diamond's views on world inequality are laid out in his book *Guns, Germs and Steel* (1997). Sachs (2006) sets out his own version of geographical determinism. Views about culture are widely spread throughout the academic literature but have never been brought together in one work. Weber (2002) argued that it was the Protestant Reformation that explained why it was Europe that had the Industrial Revolution. Landes (1999) proposed that

Northern Europeans developed a unique set of cultural attitudes that led them to work hard, save, and be innovative. Harrison and Huntington, eds. (2000), is a forceful statement of the importance of culture for comparative economic development. The notion that there is some sort of superior British culture or superior set of British institutions is widespread and used to explain U.S. exceptionalism (Fisher, 1989) and also patterns of comparative development more generally (La Porta, Lopez-de-Silanes, and Shleifer, 2008). The works of Banfield (1958) and Putnam, Leonardi, and Nanetti (1994) are very influential cultural interpretations of how one aspect of culture, or "social capital," as they call it, makes the south of Italy poor. For a survey of how economists use notions of culture, see Guiso, Sapienza, and Zingales (2006). Tabellini (2010) examines the correlation between the extent to which people trust each other in Western Europe and levels of annual income per capita. Nunn and Wantchekon (2010) show how the lack of trust and social capital in Africa is correlated with the historical intensity of the slave trade.

The relevant history of the Kongo is presented in Hilton (1985) and Thornton (1983). On the historical backwardness of African technology, see the works of Goody (1971), Law (1980), and Austen and Headrick (1983).

The definition of economics proposed by Robbins is from Robbins (1935), p. 16.

The quote from Abba Lerner is in Lerner (1972), p. 259. The idea that ignorance explains comparative development is implicit in most economic analyses of economic development and policy reform: for example, Williamson (1990); Perkins, Radelet, and Lindauer (2006); and Aghion and Howitt (2009). A recent, forceful version of this view is developed in Banerjee and Duflo (2011).

Acemoglu, Johnson, and Robinson (2001, 2002) provide a statistical analysis of the relative role of institutions, geography, and culture, showing that institutions dominate the other two types of explanations in accounting for differences in per capita income today.

CHAPTER 3: THE MAKING OF PROSPERITY AND POVERTY

The reconstruction of the meeting between Hwang Pyŏng-Wŏn and his brother is taken from James A. Foley's interview of Hwang transcribed in Foley (2003), pp. 197–203.

The notion of extractive institutions originates from Acemoglu, Johnson, and Robinson (2001). The terminology of inclusive institutions was suggested to us by Tim Besley. The terminology of economic losers and the distinction between them and political losers comes from Acemoglu and Robinson (2000b). The data on Barbados comes from Dunn (1969). Our treatment of the Soviet economy relies on Nove (1992) and Davies (1998). Allen (2003) provides an alternative and more positive interpretation of Soviet economic history.

In the social science literature there is a great deal of research related to our theory and argument. See Acemoglu, Johnson, and Robinson (2005b) for an overview of this literature and our contribution to it. The institutional view of comparative development builds on a number of important works. Particularly notable is the work of North; see North and Thomas (1973), North (1982), North and Weingast (1989), and North, Wallis, and Weingast (2009). Olson (1984) also provided a very influential account of the political economy of economic growth. Mokyr (1990) is a fundamental book that links economic losers to comparative technological change in world history. The notion of economic losers is very widespread in social science as an explanation for why efficient institutional and policy outcomes do not occur. Our interpretation, which builds on Robinson (1998) and Acemoglu and Robinson (2000b, 2006b), differs by emphasizing the idea that the most important barrier to the emergence of inclusive institutions is elites' fear that they will lose their political power. Jones (2003) provides a rich comparative history emphasizing similar themes, and Engerman and Sokoloff's (1997) important work on the Americas also emphasizes these ideas. A seminal political economy interpretation of African underdevelopment was developed by Bates (1981, 1983, 1989), whose work heavily influenced ours. Seminal studies by Dalton (1965) and Killick (1978) emphasize the role of politics in African development and particularly how the fear of losing political power influences economic policy. The notion of political losers was previously implicit in other theoretical work in political economy, for instance, Besley and Coate (1998) and Bourguignon and Verdier (2000). The role of political centralization and state institutions in development has been most heavily emphasized by historical sociologists following the work by Max Weber. Notable is the work of Mann (1986, 1993), Migdal (1988), and Evans (1995). In Africa, work on the connection between the state and development is emphasized by Herbst (2000) and Bates (2001). Economists have recently begun to contribute to this literature; for example, Acemoglu (2005) and Besley and Persson (2011). Finally, Johnson (1982), Haggard (1990), Wade (1990), and Amsden (1992) emphasized how it was the particular political economy of East Asian nations that allowed them to be so economically successful. Finley (1965) made a seminal argument that slavery was responsible for the lack of technological dynamism in the classical world.

The idea that growth under extractive institutions is possible but is also likely to run out of steam is emphasized in Acemoglu (2008).

CHAPTER 4: SMALL DIFFERENCES AND CRITICAL JUNCTURES

Benedictow (2004) provides a definitive overview of the Black Death, though his assessments of how many people the plague killed are controversial. The quotations from Boccaccio and Ralph of Shrewsbury are reproduced from Horrox (1994). Hatcher (2008) provides a compelling account of the anticipation and arrival of the plague in England. The text of the Statute of Laborers is available online from the Avalon Project, at avalon.law.yale.edu/medieval/statlab.asp

The fundamental works on the impact of the Black Death on the divergence of Eastern and Western Europe are North and Thomas (1973) and particularly Brenner (1976), whose analysis of how the initial distribution of political power affected the consequences of the plague has greatly influenced our thinking. See DuPlessis (1997) on the Second Serfdom in Eastern Europe. Conning (2010) and Acemoglu and Wolitzky (2011) develop formalizations of Brenner's thesis. The quote from James Watt is reproduced from Robinson (1964), pp. 223–24.

In Acemoglu, Johnson, and Robinson (2005a) we first presented the argument that it was the interaction between Atlantic trade and initial institutional differences that led to the divergence of English institutions and ultimately the Industrial Revolution. The notion of the iron law of oligarchy is due to Michels (1962). The notion of a critical juncture was first developed by Lipset and Rokkan (1967).

On the role of institutions in the long-run development of the Ottoman Empire, the research of Owen (1981), Owen and Pamuk (1999), and Pamuk (2006) is fundamental.

CHAPTER 5: "I'VE SEEN THE FUTURE, AND IT WORKS"

On Steffens's mission to Russia and his words to Baruch, see Steffens (1931), chap. 18, pp. 790–802. For the number of people who starved in the 1930s, we use the figures of Davies and Wheatcroft (2004). On the 1937 census numbers, see Wheatcroft and Davies (1994a, 1994b). The nature of innovation in the Soviet economy is studied in Berliner (1976). Our discussion of how Stalinism, and particularly economic planning, really worked is based on Gregory and Harrison (2005). On how writers of U.S. economics textbooks continually got Soviet economic growth wrong, see Levy and Peart (2009).

Our treatment and interpretation of the Lele and the Bushong is based on the research of Douglas (1962, 1963) and Vansina (1978).

On the concept of the Long Summer, see Fagan (2003). An accessible introduction to the Natufians and archaeological sites we mention can be found in Mithen (2006) and Barker (2006). The seminal work on Abu Hureyra is Moore, Hillman, and Legge (2000), which documents how sedentary life and institutional innovation appeared prior to farming. See Smith (1998) for a general overview of the evidence that sedentary life preceded farming, and see Bar-Yosef and Belfer-Cohen (1992) for the case of the Natufians. Our approach to the Neolithic Revolution is inspired by Sahlins (1972), which also has the anecdote about the Yir Yoront.

Our discussion of Maya history follows Martin and Grube (2000) and Webster (2002). The reconstruction of the population history of Copán comes from Webster, Freter, and Gonlin (2000). The number of dated monuments is from Sidrys and Berger (1979).

CHAPTER 6: DRIFTING APART

The discussion of the Venetian case follows Puga and Trefler (2010), and chaps. 8 and 9 of Lane (1973).

The material on Rome is contained in any standard history. Our interpretation of Roman economic institutions follows Finlay (1999) and Bang (2008). Our account of Roman decline follows Ward-Perkins (2006) and Goldsworthy (2009). On institutional changes in the late Roman Empire, see Jones (1964). The anecdotes about Tiberius and Hadrian are from Finley (1999).

The evidence from shipwrecks was first used by Hopkins (1980). See De Callataÿ (2005) and Jongman (2007) for an overview of this and the Greenland Ice Core Project.

The Vindolanda tablets are available online at vindolanda.csad.ox.ac.uk/. The quote we use comes from TVII Pub. no.: 343.

The discussion of the factors that led to the decline of Roman Britain follows Cleary (1989), chap. 4; Faulkner (2000), chap. 7; Dark (1994), chap. 2.

On Aksum, see Munro-Hay (1991). The seminal work on European feudalism and its origins is Bloch (1961); see Crummey (2000) on Ethiopian feudalism. Phillipson (1998) makes the comparison between the collapse of Aksum and the collapse of the Roman Empire.

CHAPTER 7: THE TURNING POINT

The story of Lee's machine and meeting with Queen Elizabeth I is available at calverton.homestead.com/willlee.html.

Allen (2009b) presents the data on real wages using Diocletian's Edict on Maximum Prices.

Our argument about the causes of the Industrial Revolution is highly influenced by the arguments made in North and Thomas (1973), North and Weingast (1989), Brenner (1993), Pincus (2009), and Pincus and Robinson (2010). These scholars in turn were inspired by earlier Marxist interpretations of British institutional change and the emergence of capitalism; see Dobb (1963) and Hill (1961, 1980). See also Tawney's (1941) thesis about how the state building project of Henry VIII changed the English social structure.

The text of the Magna Carta is available online at the Avalon Project, at avalon.law.yale.edu/medieval/magframe.asp.

Elton (1953) is the seminal work on the development of state institutions under Henry VIII, and Neale (1971) relates these to the evolution of parliament.

On the Peasants' Revolt, see Hilton (2003). The quote from Hill on monopolies is from Hill (1961), p. 25. On Charles I's period of "personal rule," we follow Sharp (1992). Our evidence on how different groups and regions sided either for or against Parliament comes from Brunton and Pennington (1954), Hill (1961), and Stone (2001). Pincus (2009) is fundamental on the Glorious Revolution and discusses many of the specific changes in policies and economic institutions; for example, the repeal of the Hearth Tax and the creation of the Bank of England. See also Pincus and Robinson (2010). Pettigrew (2007, 2009) discusses the attack on monopolies, including the Royal African Company, and our data on petitioning comes from his papers. Knights (2010) emphasizes the political importance of petitioning. Our information on Hoare's Bank comes from Temin and Voth (2008).

Our information about Superviser Cowperthwaite and the excise tax bureaucracy comes from Brewer (1988).

Our overview of the economic history of the Industrial Revolution rests on Mantoux (1961), Daunton (1995), Allen (2009a), and Mokyr (1990, 2009), who provide details on the famous inventors and inventions we discuss. The story about the Baldwyn family is from Bogart and Richardson (2009, 2011), who stress the connection between the Glorious Revolution, the reorganization of property rights, and the construction of roads and canals. On the Calicoe Acts and Manchester Acts, see O'Brien, Griffiths, and Hunt (1991), which is the source of the quotes from the legislation. On the dominance of new people in industry, see Daunton (1995), chap. 7, and Crouzet (1985).

Our account of why the major institutional changes first took place in England is based on Acemoglu, Johnson, and Robinson (2005a) and Brenner (1976). The data on the number of independent merchants and their political preferences come from Zahedieh (2010).

CHAPTER 8: NOT ON OUR TURF

On the opposition to the printing press in the Ottoman Empire, see Savage-Smith (2003) pp. 656–59. Comparative historical literacy comes from Easterlin (1981).

Our discussion of political institutions of Spain follows Thompson (1994a, 1994b). For evidence on the economic decline of Spain over this period, see Nogal and Prados de la Escosura (2007).

Our discussion of the impediments to economic development in Austria-Hungary follows Blum (1943), Freudenberger (1967), and Gross (1973). The quotation from Maria Theresa comes from Freudenberger, p. 495. All other quotations from Count Hartig and Francis I are from Blum. Francis's reply to the delegates from the Tyrol is quoted from Jászi (1929), pp. 80–81. The comment of Friedrich von Gentz to Robert Owen is also quoted from Jászi (1929), p. 80. The experience of the Rothschilds in Austria is discussed in chap. 2 of Corti (1928).

Our analysis of Russia follows Gerschenkron (1970). The quotation from Kropotkin is from p. 60 of the 2009 edition of his book. The conversation between Nicholas and Mikhail is quoted from Saunders (1992), p. 117. Kankrin's quote on railways is in Owen (1991), pp. 15–16.

The speech by Nicholas to the manufacturers is reproduced from Pintner (1967), p. 100.

The quote from A. A. Zakrevskii is from Pintner (1967), p. 235.

On Admiral Zheng, see Dreyer (2007). The economic history of early Modern China is covered by Myers and Wang (2002). The quote from T'ang Chen is quoted from Myers and Wang, pp. 564–65.

See Zewde (2002) for an overview of the relevant Ethiopian history. The data on how extractive Ethiopia has been historically come from Pankhurst (1961), as do all the quotes we reproduce here.

Our description of Somali institutions and history follows Lewis (1961, 2002). The *beer* of the Hassan Ugaas is reproduced on p.177 of Lewis (1961); our description of a feud comes from chap. 8 of Lewis (1961), where he reports many other examples. On the Kingdom of Taqali and writing, see Ewald (1988).

CHAPTER 9: REVERSING DEVELOPMENT

Our discussion of the takeover of Ambon and Banda by the Dutch East India Company and the company's negative effect on the development of Southeast Asia follows Hanna (1978) and particularly Reid (1993), chap. 5. The quotes from Reid on Tomé Pires are from p. 271; the Dutch factor in

Maguindanao, p. 299; the sultan of Maguindanao, pp. 299–300. Data on the impact of the Dutch East India Company on the price of spices come from O'Rourke and Williamson (2002).

A definitive overview of slavery in African society and the impact of the slave trade is Lovejoy (2000). Lovejoy, p. 47, Table 31, reports consensus estimates of the extent of the slave trade. Nunn (2008) provided the first quantitative estimates of the impact of the slave trade on African economic institutions and economic growth. The data on firearms and gunpowder imports are from Inikori (1977). The testimony of Francis Moore is quoted from Lovejoy (2000), pp. 89–90. Law (1977) is a seminal study of the expansion of the Oyo state. The estimates of the impact of the slave trade on population in Africa are taken from Manning (1990). Lovejoy (2000), chap. 8, the essays in Law (1995), and the important book of Austin (2005) are the basis for our discussion of the analysis of the period of "legitimate commerce." Data on the proportion of Africans who were slaves in Africa comes from Lovejoy (2000), e.g., p. 192, Table 9.2.

Data on labor in Liberia is from Clower, Dalton, Harwitz, and Walters (1966).

The dual economy idea was developed by Lewis (1954). Fergusson (2010) develops a mathematical model of the dual economy. The notion that this was a creation of colonialism was first proposed in the seminal collection of essays edited by Palmer and Parsons (1977). Our account of South Africa is based on Bundy (1979) and Feinstein (2005).

The Moravian missionary is quoted in Bundy (1979), p. 46, and John Hemming is quoted in Bundy, p. 72. The spread of land ownership in Griqualand East is from Bundy, p. 89; the exploits of Stephen Sonjica are from Bundy, p. 94; the quote from Matthew Blyth is from p. 97; and the quote from a European observer in Fingoland 1884 is from Bundy, pp. 100–101. George Albu is quoted in Feinstein (2005), p. 63; secretary for native affairs is quoted from Feinstein, p. 45; and Verwoerd is quoted from Feinstein, p. 159. Data on the real wages of African gold miners are from p. 66 of Wilson (1972). G. Findlay is quoted in Bundy (1979), p. 242.

The notion that the development of the rich countries of the West is the mirror image of the underdevelopment of the rest of the world was originally developed by Wallertsein (1974–2011), though he emphasizes very different mechanisms than we do.

CHAPTER 10: THE DIFFUSION OF PROSPERITY

This chapter builds heavily on our previous research with Simon Johnson and Davide Cantoni: Acemoglu, Johnson, and Robinson (2002) and Acemoglu, Cantoni, Johnson, and Robinson (2010, 2011).

Our discussion of the development of early institutions in Australia follows the seminal work of Hirst (1983, 1988, 2003) and Neal (1991). The original manuscript of the writ issued to Judge Collins is available (thanks to the Macquarie University Law School in Australia) at www.law.mq.edu.au/scnsw/html/Cable%20v%20Sinclair,%201788.htm.

Macarthur's characterization of Wentworth's supporters is quoted from Melbourne (1963), pp. 131–32.

Our discussion of the origins of the Rothschilds follows Ferguson (1998); Mayer Rothschild's remark to his son is reproduced from Ferguson, p. 76.

Our discussion of the impact of the French on European institutions is taken from Acemoglu, Cantoni, Johnson, and Robinson (2010, 2011) and the references therein. See Doyle (2002) for a standard overview of the French Revolution. Information on the feudal dues in Nassau-Usingen is from Lenger (2004), p. 96. Ogilivie (2011) overviews the historical impact of guilds on European development.

For a treatment of the life of Ōkubo Toshimichi, see Iwata (1964). Sakamoto Ryūma's eight-point plan is reproduced from Jansen (2000), p. 310.

CHAPTER 11: THE VIRTUOUS CIRCLE

Our discussion of the Black Act follows Thompson (1975). Baptist Nunn's report of June 27 is from Thompson (1975), pp. 65–66. The other quotes are from Thompson's section on the rule of law, pp. 258–69, which is well worth reading in its entirety.

Our approach to democratization in England is based on Acemoglu and Robinson (2000a, 2001, and 2006a). Earl Grey's speech is quoted from Evans (1996), p. 223. Stephens's comment about democracy is quoted in Briggs (1959), p. 34. Thompson's quote is from Thompson (1975), p. 269.

The entire text of the People's Charter can be found in Cole and Filson (1951) and at web.bham.ac.uk/1848/document/peoplech.htm.

The quote from Burke is taken from Burke (1790/1969), p. 152.

Lindert (2004, 2009) is a seminal treatment of the coevolution of democracy and public policy over the past two hundred years.

Keyssar (2009) is a seminal introduction to the evolution of political rights in the United States. Vanderbilt is quoted in Josephson (1934), p. 15. The text of Roosevelt's address is at www.theodore-roosevelt.com/sotu1.html.

The quote from Woodrow Wilson is from Wilson (1913), p. 286.

The text of President Roosevelt's Fireside Chat can be found at miller-center.org/scripps/archive/speeches/detail/3309.

Data on the relative tenure of Supreme Court justices in Argentina and the United States is presented in Iaryczower, Spiller, and Tommasi (2002). Helmke (2004) discusses the history of court packing in Argentina and quotes Justice Carlos Fayt.

CHAPTER 12: THE VICIOUS CIRCLE

This chapter heavily relies on our theoretical and empirical research on institutional persistence, particularly Acemoglu, Johnson, and Robinson (2005b) and Acemoglu and Robinson (2008a). Heath (1972) and Kelley and Klein (1980) made a seminal application of the iron law of oligarchy to the 1952 Bolivian Revolution.

The quote from the British parliamentary papers is reproduced from p. 15 of House of Commons (1904). The early political history of postindependence Sierra Leone is well told in Cartwright (1970). Though interpretations differ as to why Siaka Stevens pulled up the railway line, the salient one is that he did this to isolate Mendeland. In this we follow Abraham and Sesay (1993), p. 120; Richards (1996), pp. 42–43; and Davies (2007), pp. 684–85. Reno (1995, 2003) are the best treatments of Stevens's regime. The data on the agricultural marketing boards comes from Davies (2007). On the murder of Sam Bangura by defenestration, see Reno (1995), pp. 137–41. Jackson (2004), p. 63, and Keen (2005), p. 17, discuss the acronyms ISU and SSD.

Bates (1981) is the seminal analysis of how marketing boards destroyed agricultural productivity in postindependence Africa, see Goldstein and Udry (2009) on how political connections to chiefs determine property rights to land in Ghana.

On the relation between politicians in 1993 and the conquistadors, see Dosal (1995), chap. 1, and Casaús Arzú (2007). Our discussion of the policies of the Consulado de Comercio follows Woodward (1966). The quote from President Barrios is from McCreery (1994), pp. 187–88. Our discussion of the regime of Jorge Ubico follows Grieb (1979).

Our discussion of the underdevelopment of the U.S. South follows Acemoglu and Robinson (2008b). See Wright (1978) on the pre–Civil War development of the slave economy, and Bateman and Weiss (1981) on the dearth of industry. Fogel and Engerman (1974) give a different and controversial interpretation. Wright (1986) and Ransom and Sutch (2001) give overviews of the extent to which the southern economy after 1865 really changed. Congressman George Washington Julian is quoted in Wiener (1978), p. 6. The same book contains the analysis of the persistence of the southern landed elite after the Civil War. Naidu (2009) examines the impact of the introduction of poll taxes and literacy tests in the 1890s in southern states. The quotation from W.E.B. Du Bois is in his book Du Bois (1903), p. 88. Clause 256 of the Alabama constitution can be found at www.legislature.state.al.us/CodeOfAlabama/Constitution/1901/CA-245806.htm.

Alston and Ferrie (1999) discuss how southern politicians blocked federal legislation they thought would disrupt the South's economy. Woodward (1955) gives a seminal overview of the creation of Jim Crow.

Overviews of the Ethiopian revolution are provided in Halliday and Molyneux (1981). On the Emperor's cushions, see Kapuściński (1983). The quotes from Dawit Wolde Giorgis are from Dawit Wolde Giorgis (1989), pp. 49 and 48, respectively.

CHAPTER 13: WHY NATIONS FAIL TODAY

For the BBC report on Mugabe's lottery success, including the public statement of Zimbank, see news.bbc.co.uk/2/hi/africa/621895.stm.

Our treatment of the creation of white rule in Rhodesia follows Palmer (1977) and Alexander (2006). Meredith (2007) provides a good overview of more recent Zimbabwean politics.

Our account of the civil war in Sierra Leone follows Richards (1996), Truth and Reconciliation Commission (2004), and Keen (2005). The analysis published in a newspaper in the capital city of Freetown in 1995 is quoted from Keen (2005), p. 34. The text of the RUF's "Footpaths to Democracy" can we found at www.sierra-leone.org/AFRC-RUF/footpaths.html.

The quotation from the teenager from Geoma is from Keen (2005), p. 42.

Our discussion of the Colombian paramilitaries follows Acemoglu, Robinson, and Santos (2010) and Chaves and Robinson (2010), which in turn heavily rely on the extensive work by Colombian scholars, particularly Romero (2003), the essays in Romero (2007), and López (2010). León (2009) is an accessible and balanced account of the nature of contemporary conflicts in Colombia. Also fundamental is the Web site run by the weekly newspaper *Semana,* www.verdadabierta.com/. All the quotes come from Acemoglu, Robinson, and Santos (2010). The contract between Martín Llanos and the mayors in Casanare is available in Spanish at www.verdadabierta .com/victimarios/los-jefes/714-perfil-hector-german-buitrago-alias-martin -llanos.

The origins and consequences of El Corralito are well presented in a series of articles in *The Economist* magazine, available at www.economist.com/ search/apachesolr_search/corralito.

On the role of the interior in Argentine development, see Sawers (1996).

Hassig and Oh (2009) provides an excellent, valuable account of life in North Korea. Chap. 2 covers the luxurious lifestyle of the leadership, and chaps. 3 and 4, the economic realities that most people face. The BBC coverage of the currency reform can be found at news.bbc.co.uk/2/hi/8500017 .stm.

On the pleasure palace and brandy consumption, see chap. 12 of Post (2004).

Our discussion of child labor and its use for picking cotton in Uzbeksitan follows Kandiyoti (2008), available at www.soas.ac.uk/cccac/events/cotton- sector-in-central-asia-2005/file49842.pdf. The quote from Gulnaz is on p. 20 of Kandiyoti. On the Andijon uprising, see International Crisis Group (2005). The description of the election of Joseph Stalin in the Soviet Union is reproduced from Denny (1937).

Our analysis of "crony capitalism" in Egypt follows Sfakianakis (2004).

CHAPTER 14: BREAKING THE MOLD

Our treatment of Botswana follows Acemoglu, Johnson, and Robinson (2003); Robinson and Parsons (2006); and Leith (2005). Schapera (1970) and Parsons, Henderson, and Tlou (1995) are fundamental works. High Commissioner Rey is quoted in Acemoglu, Johnson, and Robinson (2003), p. 96. The discussion of the three chiefs' visit to England follows Parsons (1998), and all quotes relating to this come from his book: Chamberlain, pp. 206–7; Fairfield, p. 209; and Rhodes, p. 223. Schapera is quoted from Schapera (1940), p. 72. The quote from Quett Masire is from Masire (2006), p. 43. On the ethnic composition of the Tswana tribes, see Schapera (1952).

Our treatment of change in the U.S. South follows Acemoglu and Robinson (2008b). On the population movement out of the U.S. South, see Wright (1999); on the mechanization of cotton picking, Heinicke (1994). "FRDUM FOOF SPETGH" is quoted from Mickey (2008), p. 50. Thurmond's 1948 speech is taken from www.slate.com/id/2075151/, where you also can listen to the audio recording. On James Meredith and Oxford, Mississippi, see Doyle (2001). See Wright (1999) on the impact of civil rights legislation on black voting in the South.

On the nature and politics of China's political transition after the death of Mao, see Harding (1987) and MacFarquhar and Schoenhals (2008). Deng's quote about the cat is from Harding, p. 58. The first point of the Cultural Revolution is from Schoenhals (1996), p. 33; Mao on Hitler is from MacFarquhar and Schoenhals, p. 102; Hua on the "Two Whatevers" is from Harding, p. 56.

CHAPTER 15: UNDERSTANDING PROSPERITY AND POVERTY

For the story of Dai Guofang, see McGregor (2010), pp. 219–26. The story of red telephones is also from McGregor, chap. 1. On the control of the party over media, see Pan (2008), chap. 9, and McGregor (2010), pp. 64–69 and 235–62. The quotes on the party's attitudes toward entrepreneurs are from McGregor (2010), pp. 200–201 and 223. For Wen Jiabao's comments on political reforms in China, see www.guardian.co.uk/world/2010/aug/29/wen-jiabao-china-reform.

The modernization hypothesis is clearly articulated in Lipset (1959). The evidence against it is discussed in detail in Acemoglu, Johnson, Robinson, and Yared (2008, 2009). George H. W. Bush's quote is from news.bbc.co .uk/2/hi/business/752224.stm.

Our discussion of NGO activity and foreign aid in Afghanistan after

December 2001 draws on Ghani and Lockhart (2008). See also Reinikka and Svensson (2004) and Easterly (2006) on problems of foreign aid.

Our discussion of problems of macroeconomic reform and inflation in Zimbabwe is from Acemoglu, Johnson, Robinson, and Querubín (2008). The Seva Mandir discussion is drawn from Banerjee, Duflo, and Glennerster (2008).

The formation of the Workers' Party in Brazil is covered in Keck (1992); on the Scânia strike, see chap. 4. The quote from Cardoso is from Keck, pp. 44–45; the quote from Lula is on Keck, p. 65.

The discussion of the efforts of Fujimori and Montesinos to control the media is from McMillan and Zoido (2004), and the quote on the Chinese Communist Party's control is from McGregor (2010), p. 69.

SOURCES FOR THE MAPS

Map 1: The Inca Empire and road system are adapted from John V. Murra (1984), "Andean Societies before 1532," in Leslie Bethell, ed., *The Cambridge History of Latin America,* vol. 1 (New York: Cambridge University Press). The map of the *mita* catchment area is taken from Melissa Dell (2010), "The Persistent Effects of Peru's Mining *Mita*," *Econometrica* 78:6, 1863–1903.

Map 2: Drawn using data from Miriam Bruhn and Francisco Gallego (2010), "The Good, the Bad, and the Ugly: Do They Matter for Economic Development?" forthcoming in the *Review of Economics and Statistics.*

Map 3: Drawn using data from World Development Indicators (2008), the World Bank.

Map 4: Map of wild pigs adapted from W. L. R. Oliver; I. L. Brisbin, Jr.; and S. Takahashi (1993), "The Eurasian Wild Pig (*Sus scrofa*)," in W. L. R. Oliver, ed., *Pigs, Peccaries, and Hippos: Status Survey and Action Plan* (Gland, Switzerland: IUCN), pp. 112–21. Wild cattle adapted from map of aurochs from Cis van Vuure (2005), *Retracing the Aurochs* (Sofia: Pensoft Publishers), p. 41.

Map 5: Adapted from Daniel Zohary and Maria Hopf (2001), *The Domestication of Plants in the Old World,* 3rd edition (New York: Oxford University Press), wheat map 4, p. 56; barley map 5, p. 55. Map of rice distribution adapted from Te-Tzu Chang (1976), "The Origin, Evolution, Cultivation, Dissemination, and Diversification of Asian and African Rices," *Euphytica* 25, 425–41, figure 2, p. 433.

Map 6: The Kuba Kingdom is based on Jan Vansina (1978), *The Children of Woot* (Madison: University of Wisconsin Press), map 2, p. 8. Kongo based on Jan Vansina (1995), "Equatorial Africa Before the Nineteenth Century," in Philip Curtin, Steven Feierman, Leonard Thompson, and Jan Vansina, *African History: From Earliest Times to Independence* (New York: Longman), map 8.4, p. 228.

Map 7: Drawn using data from the Defense Meteorological Satellite Program's Operational Linescan System (DMSP-OLS), which reports images of the Earth at night captured from 20:00 to 21:30 local time from an altitude of 830 km (http://www.ngdc.noaa.gov/dmsp/sensors/ols.html).

Map 8: Constructed from data in Jerome Blum (1998), *The End of the Old Order in Rural Europe* (Princeton: Princeton University Press).

Map 9: Adapted from the maps in Colin Martin and Geoffrey Parker (1988), *The Spanish Armada* (London: Hamilton), pp. i–ii, 243.

Map 10: Adapted from Simon Martin and Nikolai Gribe (2000), *Chronicle of the Maya Kings and Queens: Deciphering the Dynasties of the Ancient Maya* (London: Thames and Hudson), p. 21.

Map 11: Map adapted from Mark A. Kishlansky, Patrick Geary, and Patricia O'Brien (1991), *Civilization in the West* (New York: HarperCollins Publishers), p. 151.

Map 12: Somali clan families adapted from Ioan M. Lewis (2002), *A Modern History of Somalia* (Oxford: James Currey), map of "Somali ethnic and clan-family distribution 2002"; map of Aksum adapted from Kevin Shillington (1995), *History of Africa*, 2nd edition (New York: St. Martin's Press), map 5.4, p. 69.

Map 13: J. R. Walton (1998), "Changing Patterns of Trade and Interaction Since 1500," in R. A. Butlin and R. A. Dodgshon, eds., *An Historical Geography of Europe* (Oxford: Oxford University Press), figure 15.2, p. 326.

Map 14: Adapted from Anthony Reid (1988), *Southeast Asia in the Age of Commerce, 1450–1680: Volume 1, The Land Below the Winds* (New Haven: Yale University Press), map 2, p. 9.

Map 15: Drawn from data taken from Nathan Nunn (2008), "The Long Term Effects of Africa's Slave Trades," *Quarterly Journal of Economics* 123, no. 1, 139–76.

Map 16: Maps based on the following maps: for South Africa, A. J. Christopher (2001), *The Atlas of Changing South Africa* (London: Routledge), figure 1.19, p. 31; for Zimbabwe, Robin Palmer (1977), *Land and Racial Domination in Rhodesia* (Berkeley: University of California Press), map 5, p. 245.

Map 17: Adapted from Alexander Grab (2003), *Napoleon and the Transformation of Europe* (London: Palgrave Macmillan), map 1, p. 17; map 2, p. 91.

Map 18: Drawn using data from the 1840 U.S. Census, downloadable at the National Historical Geographic Information System: http://www.nhgis .org/.

Map 19: Drawn using data from the 1880 U.S. Census, downloadable at the National Historical Geographic Information System: http://www.nhgis .org/.

Map 20: Daron Acemoglu, James A. Robinson, and Rafael J. Santos (2010), "The Monopoly of Violence: Evidence from Colombia," at http://scholar .harvard.edu/jrobinson/files/jr_formationofstate.pdf.

References

Abraham, Arthur, and Habib Sesay (1993). "Regional Politics and Social Service Provision Since Independence." In C. Magbaily Fyle, ed. *The State and the Provision of Social Services in Sierra Leone Since Independence, 1961–1991.* Oxford, U.K.: Codesaria.

Acemoglu, Daron (2005). "Politics and Economics in Weak and Strong States." *Journal of Monetary Economics* 52: 1199–226.

—— (2008). "Oligarchic Versus Democratic Societies." *Journal of European Economic Association* 6: 1–44.

Acemoglu, Daron, Davide Cantoni, Simon Johnson, and James A. Robinson (2010). "From Ancien Régime to Capitalism: The Spread of the French Revolution as a Natural Experiment." In Jared Diamond and James A. Robinson, eds. *Natural Experiments in History.* Cambridge, Mass.: Harvard University Press.

—— (2011). "Consequences of Radical Reform: The French Revolution." *American Economic Review*, forthcoming.

Acemoglu, Daron, Simon Johnson, and James A. Robinson (2001). "The Colonial Origins of Comparative Development: An Empirical Investigation." *American Economic Review* 91: 1369–1401.

—— (2002). "Reversal of Fortune: Geography and Institutions in the Making of the Modern World Income Distribution." *Quarterly Journal of Economics* 118: 1231–94.

—— (2003). "An African Success Story: Botswana." In Dani Rodrik, ed. *In Search of Prosperity: Analytic Narratives on Economic Growth*. Princeton, N.J.: Princeton University Press.

—— (2005a). "Rise of Europe: Atlantic Trade, Institutional Change and Economic Growth." *American Economic Review* 95: 546–79.

—— (2005b). "Institutions as the Fundamental Cause of Long-Run Growth." In Philippe Aghion and Steven Durlauf, eds. *Handbook of Economic Growth*. Amsterdam: North-Holland.

Acemoglu, Daron, Simon Johnson, James A. Robinson, and Pablo Querubín (2008). "When Does Policy Reform Work? The Case of Central Bank Independence." *Brookings Papers in Economic Activity*, 351–418.

Acemoglu, Daron, Simon Johnson, James A. Robinson, and Pierre Yared (2008). "Income and Democracy." *American Economic Review* 98: 808–42.

—— (2009). "Reevaluating the Modernization Hypothesis." *Journal of Monetary Economics* 56: 1043–58 .

Acemoglu, Daron, and James A. Robinson (2000a). "Why Did the West Extend the Franchise? Growth, Inequality and Democracy in Historical Perspective." *Quarterly Journal of Economics* 115: 1167–99.

—— (2000b). "Political Losers as Barriers to Economic Development." *American Economic Review* 90: 126–30.

—— (2001). "A Theory of Political Transitions." *American Economic Review* 91: 938–63.

—— (2006a). *Economic Origins of Dictatorship and Democracy*. New York: Cambridge University Press.

—— (2006b). "Economic Backwardness in Political Perspective." *American Political Science Review* 100: 115–31.

—— (2008a). "Persistence of Power, Elites and Institutions." *American Economic Review* 98: 267–93.

—— (2008b). "The Persistence and Change of Institutions in the Americas." *Southern Economic Journal* 75: 282–99.

Acemoglu, Daron, James A. Robinson, and Rafael Santos (2010). "The Monopoly of Violence: Evidence from Colombia." Unpublished.

Acemoglu, Daron, and Alex Wolitzky (2010). "The Economics of Labor Coercion." *Econometric*, 79: 555–600.

Aghion, Philippe, and Peter Howitt (2009). *The Economics of Growth*. Cambridge, Mass.: MIT Press.

Alexander, Jocelyn (2006). *The Unsettled Land: State-making and the Politics of Land in Zimbabwe, 1893–2003*. Oxford, U.K.: James Currey.

Allen, Robert C. (2003). *Farm to Factory: A Reinterpretation of the Soviet Industrial Revolution*. Princeton, N.J.: Princeton University Press.

—— (2009a). *The British Industrial Revolution in Global Perspective*. New York: Cambridge University Press.

—— (2009b). "How Prosperous Were the Romans? Evidence from Diocletian's Price Edict (301 AD)." In Alan Bowman and Andrew Wilson, eds. *Quantifying the Roman Economy: Methods and Problems*. Oxford, U.K.: Oxford University Press.

Alston, Lee J., and Joseph P. Ferrie (1999). *Southern Paternalism and the Rise of the American Welfare State: Economics, Politics, and Institutions in the South*. New York: Cambridge University Press.

Amsden, Alice H. (1992). *Asia's Next Giant*, New York: Oxford Universty Press.

Austen, Ralph A., and Daniel Headrick (1983). "The Role of Technology in the African Past." *African Studies Review* 26: 163–84.

Austin, Gareth (2005). *Labour, Land and Capital in Ghana: From Slavery to Free Labour in Asante, 1807–1956*. Rochester, N.Y.: University of Rochester Press.

Bakewell, Peter J. (1984). *Miners of the Red Mountain: Indian Labor in Potosí, 1545–1650*. Albuquerque: University of New Mexico Press.

—— (2009). *A History of Latin America to 1825*. Hoboken, N.J.: Wiley-Blackwell.

Banerjee, Abhijit V., and Esther Duflo (2011). *Poor Economics: A Radical Rethinking of the Way to Fight Global Poverty*. New York: Public Affairs.

Banerjee, Abhijit V., Esther Duflo, and Rachel Glennerster (2008). "Putting a Band-Aid on a Corpse: Incentives for Nurses in the Indian Public Health Care System." *Journal of the European Economic Association* 7: 487–500.

Banfield, Edward C. (1958). *The Moral Basis of a Backward Society*. Glencoe, N.Y.: Free Press.

Bang, Peter (2008). *The Roman Bazaar*. New York: Cambridge University Press.

Barker, Graeme (2006). *The Agricultural Revolution in Prehistory: Why Did Foragers Become Farmers?* New York: Oxford University Press.

Bar-Yosef, Ofer, and Avner Belfer-Cohen (1992). "From Foraging to Farming in the Mediterranean Levant." In A. B. Gebauer and T. D. Price, eds. *Transitions to Agriculture in Prehistory*. Madison, Wisc.: Prehistory Press.

Bateman, Fred, and Thomas Weiss (1981). *A Deplorable Scarcity: The Failure of Industrialization in the Slave Economy*. Chapel Hill: University of North Carolina Press.

Bates, Robert H. (1981). *Markets and States in Tropical Africa*. Berkeley: University of California Press.

—— (1983). *Essays in the Political Economy of Rural Africa*. New York: Cambridge University Press.

—— (1989). *Beyond the Miracle of the Market*. New York: Cambridge University Press.

—— (2001). *Prosperity and Violence: The Political Economy of Development*. New York: W.W. Norton.

Benedictow, Ole J. (2004). *The Black Death, 1346–1353: The Complete History*. Rochester, N.Y.: Boydell Press.

Berliner, Joseph S. (1976). *The Innovation Decision in Soviet Industry*. Cambridge, Mass.: Harvard University Press.

Besley, Timothy, and Stephen Coate (1998). "Sources of Inefficiency in a Representative Democracy: A Dynamic Analysis." *American Economic Review* 88: 139–56.

Besley, Timothy, and Torsten Persson (2011). *Pillars of Prosperity: The Political Economics of Development Clusters*. Princeton, N.J.: Princeton University Press.

Bloch, Marc L. B. (1961). *Feudal Society.* 2 vols. Chiacgo: University of Chicago Press.

Blum, Jerome (1943). "Transportation and Industry in Austria, 1815–1848." *The Journal of Modern History* 15: 24–38.

Bogart, Dan, and Gary Richardson (2009). "Making Property Productive: Reorganizing Rights to Real and Equitable Estates in Britain, 1660 to 1830." *European Review of Economic History* 13: 3–30.

——— (2011). "Did the Glorious Revolution Contribute to the Transport Revolution? Evidence from Investment in Roads and Rivers." *Economic History Review*. Forthcoming.

Bourguignon, François, and Thierry Verdier (1990). "Oligarchy, Democracy, Inequality and Growth." *Journal of Development Economics* 62: 285–313.

Brenner, Robert (1976). "Agrarian Class Structure and Economic Development in Preindustrial Europe." *Past and Present* 70: 30–75.

——— (1993). *Merchants and Revolution*. Princeton, N.J.: Princeton University Press.

Brenner, Robert, and Christopher Isett (2002). "England's Divergence from China's Yangzi Delta: Property Relations, Microeconomics, and Patterns of Development." *Journal of Asian Studies* 61: 609–62.

Brewer, John (1988). *The Sinews of Power: War, Money and the English State, 1688–1773*. Cambridge, Mass.: Harvard University Press.

Briggs, Asa (1959). *Chartist Studies*. London: Macmillan.

Brunton, D., and D. H. Pennignton (1954). *Members of the Long Parliament*. London: George Allen and Unwin.

Bundy, Colin (1979). *The Rise and Fall of the South African Peasantry*. Berkeley: University of California Press.

Burke, Edmund (1790/1969). *Reflections of the Revolution in France*. Baltimore, Md.: Penguin Books.

Cartwright, John R. (1970). *Politics in Sierra Leone 1947–67*. Toronto: University of Toronto Press.

Casaús Arzú, Marta (2007). *Guatemala: Linaje y Racismo*. 3rd ed., rev. y ampliada. Guatemala City: F&G Editores.

Chaves, Isaías, and James A. Robinson (2010). "Political Consequences of Civil Wars." Unpublished.

Cleary, A. S. Esmonde (1989). *The Ending of Roman Britain*. London: B.T. Batsford Ltd.

Clower, Robert W., George H. Dalton, Mitchell Harwitz, and Alan Walters (1966). *Growth Without Development; an Economic Survey of Liberia*. Evanston: Northwestern University Press.

Coatsworth, John H. (1974). "Railroads, Landholding and Agrarian Protest in the Early Porfiriato." *Hispanic American Historical Review* 54: 48–71.

—— (1978). "Obstacles to Economic Growth in Nineteenth-Century Mexico." *American Historical Review* 83: 80–100.

—— (2008). "Inequality, Institutions and Economic Growth in Latin America." *Journal of Latin American Studies* 40: 545–69.

Cole, G.D.H., and A. W. Filson, eds. (1951). *British Working Class Movements: Select Documents 1789–1875*. London: Macmillan.

Conning, Jonathan (2010). "On the Causes of Slavery or Serfdom and the Roads to Agrarian Capitalism: Domar's Hypothesis Revisited." Unpublished, Department of Economics, Hunter College, CUNY.

Corti, Egon Caeser (1928). *The Reign of the House of Rothschild*. New York: Cosmopolitan Book Corporation.

Crouzet, François (1985). *The First Industrialists: The Problem of Origins*. New York: Cambridge University Press.

Crummey, Donald E. (2000). *Land and Society in the Christian Kingdom of Ethiopia: From the Thirteenth to the Twentieth Century*. Urbana: University of Illinois Press.

Dalton, George H. (1965). "History, Politics and Economic Development in Liberia." *Journal of Economic History* 25: 569–91.

Dark, K. R. (1994). *Civitas to Kingdom: British Political Continuity 300–800*. Leicester, U.K.: Leicester University Press.

Daunton, Martin J. (1995). *Progress and Poverty: An Economic and Social History of Britain, 1700–1850*. Oxford, U.K.: Oxford University Press.

Davies, Robert W. (1998). *Soviet Economic Development from Lenin to Khrushchev*. New York: Cambridge University Press.

Davies, Robert W., and Stephen G. Wheatcroft (2004). *The Years of Hunger: Soviet Agriculture, 1931–33*. New York: Palgrave Macmillan.

Davies, Victor A. B. (2007). "Sierra Leone's Economic Growth Performance, 1961–2000." In Benno J. Ndulu et al., eds. *The Political Economy of Growth in Africa, 1960–2000*. Vol. 2. New York: Cambridge University Press.

Dawit Wolde Giorgis (1989). *Red Teas: War, Famine and Revolution in Ethiopia*. Trenton, N.J.: Red Sea Press.

De Callataÿ, François (2005). "The Graeco-Roman Economy in the Super Longrun: Lead, Copper, and Shipwrecks." *Journal of Roman Archaeology* 18: 361–72.

de las Casas, Bartolomé (1992). *A Short Account of the Destruction of the Indies*. New York: Penguin Books.

Dell, Melissa (2010). "The Persistent Effects of Peru's Mining *Mita*." *Econometrica* 78: 1863–903.

Denny, Harold (1937). "Stalin Wins Poll by a Vote of 1005." *New York Times*, December 14, 1937, p. 11.

de Sahagún, Bernardino (1975). *Florentine Codex: General History of the Things of New Spain. Book 12: The Conquest of Mexico*. Santa Fe, N.M.: School of American Research.

Diamond, Jared (1997). *Guns, Germs and Steel*. New York: W.W. Norton and Co.

Dobb, Maurice (1963). *Studies in the Development of Capitalism*. Rev. ed. New York: International Publishers.

Dosal, Paul J. (1995). *Power in Transition: The Rise of Guatemala's Industrial Oligarchy, 1871–1994*. Westport, Conn.: Praeger.

Douglas, Mary (1962). "Lele Economy Compared to the Bushong." In Paul Bohannan and George Dalton, eds. *Markets in Africa*. Evanston, Ill.: Northwestern University Press.

——— (1963). *The Lele of the Kasai*. London: Oxford University Press.

Doyle, William (2001). *An American Insurrection: The Battle of Oxford Mississippi*. New York: Doubleday.

——— (2002). *The Oxford History of the French Revolution*. 2nd ed. New York: Oxford University Press.

Dreyer, Edward L. (2007). *Zheng He: China and the Oceans in the Early Ming Dynasty, 1405–1433*. New York: Pearson Longman.

Du Bois, W.E.B. (1903). *The Souls of Black Folk*. New York: A.C. McClurg & Company.

Dunn, Richard S. (1969). "The Barbados Census of 1680: Profile of the Richest Colony in English America." *William and Mary Quarterly* 26: 3–30.

DuPlessis, Robert S. (1997). *Transitions to Capitalism in Early Modern Europe*. New York: Cambridge University Press.

Easterly, William (2006). *The White Man's Burden: Why the West's Efforts to Aid the Rest Have Done So Much Ill and So Little Good*. New York: Oxford University Press.

Elton, Geoffrey R. (1953). *The Tudor Revolution in Government*. New York: Cambridge University Press.

Engerman, Stanley L. (2007). *Slavery, Emancipation & Freedom: Comparative Perspectives*. Baton Rouge: University of Lousiana Press.

Engerman, Stanley L., and Kenneth L. Sokoloff (1997). "Factor Endowments, Institutions, and Differential Paths of Growth Among New World Economies." In Stephen H. Haber, ed. *How Latin America Fell Behind*. Stanford, Calif.: Stanford University Press.

—— (2005). "The Evolution of Suffrage Institutions in the New World." *Journal of Economic History* 65: 891–921.

Evans, Eric J. (1996). *The Forging of the Modern State: Early Industrial Britain, 1783–1870*. 2nd ed. New York: Longman.

Evans, Peter B. (1995). *Embedded Autonomy: States and Industrial Transformation*. Princeton, N.J.: Princeton University Press.

Ewald, Janet (1988). "Speaking, Writing and Authority: Explorations in and from the Kingdom of Taqali." *Comparative Studies in History and Society* 30: 199–224.

Fagan, Brian (2003). *The Long Summer: How Climate Changed Civilization*. New York: Basic Books.

Faulkner, Neil (2000). *The Decline and Fall of Roman Britain*. Stroud, U.K.: Tempus Publishers.

Feinstein, Charles H. (2005). *An Economic History of South Africa: Conquest, Discrimination and Development*. New York: Cambridge University Press.

Ferguson, Niall (1998). *The House of Rothschild: Vol. 1: Money's Prophets, 1798–1848*. New York: Viking.

Fergusson, Leopoldo (2010). "The Political Economy of Rural Property Rights and the Persistance of the Dual Economy." Unpublished. http://economia .uniandes.edu.co.

Finley, Moses (1965). "Technical Innovation and Economic Progress in the Ancient World." *Economic History Review* 18: 29–4.

——— (1999). *The Ancient Economy*. Berkeley: University of California Press.

Fischer, David H. (1989). *Albion's Seed: Four British Folkways in America*. New York: Oxford University Press.

Fogel, Robert W., and Stanley L. Engerman (1974). *Time on the Cross: The Economics of American Negro Slavery*. Boston: Little, Brown.

Foley, James A. (2003). *Korea's Divided Families: Fifty Years of Separation*. New York: Routledge.

Freudenberger, Herman (1967). "The State as an Obstacle to Economic Growth in the Hapsburg Monarchy." *Journal of Economic History* 27: 493–509.

Galenson, David W. (1996). "The Settlement and Growth of the Colonies: Population, Labor and Economic Development." In Stanley L. Engerman and Robert E. Gallman, eds. *The Cambridge Economic History of the United States, Volume I: The Colonial Era*. New York: Cambridge University Press.

Ganson, Barbara (2003). *The Guaraní Under Spanish Rule in the Río de la Plata*. Palo Alto, Calif.: Stanford University Press.

García-Jimeno, Camilo, and James A. Robinson (2011). "The Myth of the Frontier." In Dora L. Costa and Naomi R. Lamoreaux, eds. *Understanding Long-Run Economic Growth*. Chicago: University of Chicago Press.

Gerschenkron, Alexander (1970). *Europe in the Russian Mirror*. New York: Cambridge University Press.

Ghani, Ashraf, and Clare Lockhart (2008). *Fixing Failed States: A Framework for Rebuilding a Fractured World*. New York: Oxford University Press.

Gibson, Charles (1963). *The Aztecs Under Spanish Rule*. New York: Cambridge University Press.

Goldstein, Marcus, and Christopher Udry (2008). "The Profits of Power: Land Rights and Agricultural Investment in Ghana." *Journal of Political Economy* 116: 981–1022.

Goldsworthy, Adrian K. (2009). *How Rome Fell: Death of a Superpower*. New Haven, Conn.: Yale University Press.

Goody, Jack (1971). *Technology, Tradition and the State in Africa*. New York: Cambridge University Press.

Gregory, Paul R., and Mark Harrison (2005). "Allocation Under Dictatorship: Research in Stalin's Archives." *Journal of Economic Literature* 43: 721–61.

Grieb, Kenneth J. (1979). *Guatemalan Caudillo: The Regime of Jorge Ubico, 1931–1944*. Athens: Ohio University Press.

Gross, Nachum T. (1973). "The Habsburg Monarchy, 1750–1914." In Carlo M. Cipolla, ed. *The Fontana Economic History of Europe*. Glasgow, U.K.: William Collins Sons and Co.

Guiso, Luigi, Paola Sapienza, and Luigi Zingales (2006). "Does Culture Affect Economic Outcomes?" *Journal of Economic Perspectives* 20: 23–48.

Haber, Stephen H. (2010). "Politics, Banking, and Economic Development: Evidence from New World Economies." In Jared Diamond and James A. Robinson, eds. *Natural Experiments of History*. Cambridge, Mass.: Belknap Press of Harvard University Press.

Haber, Stephen H., Herbert S. Klein, Noel Maurer, and Kevin J. Middlebrook (2008). *Mexico Since 1980*. New York: Cambridge University Press.

Haber, Stephen H., Noel Maurer, and Armando Razo (2003). *The Politics of Property Rights: Political Instability, Credible Commitments, and Economic Growth in Mexico, 1876–1929*. New York: Cambridge University Press.

Haggard, Stephan (1990). *Pathways from the Periphery: The Politics of Growth in the Newly Industrializing Countries*. Ithaca, N.Y.: Cornell University Press.

Halliday, Fred, and Maxine Molyneux (1981). *The Ethiopian Revolution*. London: Verso.

Hanna, Willard (1978). *Indonesian Banda: Colonialism and Its Aftermath in the Nutmeg Islands*. Philadelphia: Institute for the Study of Human Issues.

Harding, Harry (1987). *China's Second Revolution: Reform After Mao*. Washington, D.C.: Brookings Institution Press.

Harrison, Lawrence E., and Samuel P. Huntington, eds. (2000). *Culture Matters: How Values Shape Human Progress*. New York: Basic Books.

Hassig, Ralph C., and Kongdan Oh (2009). *The Hidden People of North Korea: Everyday Life in the Hermit Kingdom*. Lanham, Md.: Rowman and Littlefield Publishers.

Hatcher, John (2008). *The Black Death: A Personal History*. Philadelphia: Da Capo Press.

Heath, Dwight (1972). "New Patrons for Old: Changing Patron-Client Relations in the Bolivian Yungas." In Arnold Strickton and Sidney Greenfield, eds. *Structure and Process in Latin America*. Albuquerque: University of New Mexico Press.

Heinicke, Craig (1994). "African-American Migration and Mechanized Cotton Harvesting, 1950–1960." *Explorations in Economic History* 31: 501–20.

Helmke, Gretchen (2004). *Courts Under Constraints: Judges, Generals, and Presidents in Argentina*. New York: Cambridge University Press.

Hemming, John (1983). *The Conquest of the Incas*. New York: Penguin Books.

Herbst, Jeffrey I. (2000). *States and Power in Africa*. Princeton, N.J.: Princeton University Press.

Hill, Christopher (1961). *The Century of Revolution, 1603–1714*. New York: W. W. Norton and Co.

—— (1980). "A Bourgeois Revolution?" In Lawrence Stone, ed. *The British Revolutions: 1641, 1688, 1776*. Princeton, N.J.: Princeton University Press.

Hilton, Anne (1985). *The Kingdom of Kongo*. New York: Oxford University Press.

Hilton, Rodney (2003). *Bond Men Made Free: Medieval Peasant Movements and the English Rising of 1381*. 2nd ed. New York: Routledge.

Hirst, John B. (1983). *Convict Society and Its Enemies: A History of Early New South Wales.* Boston: Allen and Unwin.

—— (1988). *The Strange Birth of Colonial Democracy: New South Wales, 1848–1884.* Boston: Allen and Unwin.

—— (2003). *Australia's Democracy: A Short History.* London: Allen and Unwin.

Hopkins, Anthony G. (1973). *An Economic History of West Africa.* New York: Addison Wesley Longman.

Hopkins, Keith (1980). "Taxes and Trade in the Roman Empire, 200 BC–400 AD." *Journal of Roman Studies* LXX: 101–25.

Horrox, Rosemary, ed. (1994). *The Black Death.* New York: St. Martin's Press.

House of Commons (1904). "Papers Relating to the Construction of Railways in Sierra Leone, Lagos and the Gold Coast."

Hu-DeHart, Evelyn (1984). *Yaqui Resistance and Survival: The Struggle for Land and Autonomy, 1821–1910.* Madison: University of Wisconsin Press.

Iaryczower, Matías, Pablo Spiller, and Mariano Tommasi (2002). "Judicial Independence in Unstable Environments: Argentina 1935–1998." *American Journal of Political Science* 46: 699–716.

Inikori, Joseph (1977). "The Import of Firearms into West Africa, 1751–1807." *Journal of African History* 18: 339–68.

International Crisis Group (2005). "Uzbekistan: The Andijon Uprising," Asia Briefing No. 38, www.crisisgroup.org/en/regions/asia/central-asia/uzbekistan/B038-uzbekistan-the-andijon-uprising.aspx.

Israel, Paul (2000). *Edison: A Life of Invention.* Hoboken, N.J.: John Wiley and Sons.

Iwata, Masakazu (1964). *Ōkubo Toshimichi: The Bismarck of Japan.* Berkeley: University of California Press.

Jackson, Michael (2004). *In Sierra Leone*. Durham, N.C.: Duke University Press.

Jansen, Marius B. (2000). *The Making of Modern Japan*. Cambridge, Mass.: Harvard University Press.

Jászi, Oscar (1929). *The Dissolution of the Habsburg Monarchy*. Chicago: University of Chicago Press.

Johnson, Chalmers A. (1982). *MITI and the Japanese Miracle: The Growth of Industrial Policy, 1925–1975*. Palo Alto, Calif.: Stanford University Press.

Jones, A.M.H. (1964). *The Later Roman Empire*. Volume 2. Oxford, U.K.: Basil Blackwell.

Jones, Eric L. (2003). *The European Miracle: Environments, Economies and Geopolitics in the History of Europe and Asia*. 3rd ed. New York: Cambridge University Press.

Jongman, Willem M. (2007). "Gibbon Was Right: The Decline and Fall of the Roman Economy." In O. Hekster et al., eds. *Crises and the Roman Empire*. Leiden, the Netherlands: BRILL.

Josephson, Matthew (1934). *The Robber Barons*. Orlando, Fla.: Harcourt.

Kandiyoti, Deniz (2008). "Invisible to the World? The Dynamics of Forced Child Labour in the Cotton Sector of Uzbekistan." Unpublished. School of Oriental and Africa Studies.

Kapuściński, Ryszard (1983). *The Emperor: Downfall of an Autocrat*. San Diego: Harcourt Brace Jovanovich.

Keck, Margaret E. (1992). *The Workers' Party and Democratization in Brazil*. New Haven, Conn.: Yale University Press.

Keen, David (2005). *Conflict and Collusion in Sierra Leone*. New York: Palgrave Macmillan.

Kelley, Jonathan, and Herbert S. Klein (1980). *Revolution and the Rebirth of Inequality: A Theory of Inequality and Inherited Privilege Applied to the Bolivian National Revolution*. Berkeley: University of California Press.

Keyssar, Alexander (2009). *The Right to Vote: The Contested History of Democracy in the United States*. Revised Edition. New York: Basic Books.

Killick, Tony (1978). *Development Economics in Action*. London: Heinemann.

Knight, Alan (2011). *Mexico: The Nineteenth and Twentieth Centuries*. New York: Cambridge University Press.

Knights, Mark (2010). "Participation and Representation Before Democracy: Petitions and Addresses in Premodern Britain." In Ian Shapiro, Susan C. Stokes, Elisabeth Jean Wood, and Alexander S. Kirshner, eds. *Political Representation*. New York: Cambridge University Press.

Kropotkin, Peter (2009). *Memoirs of a Revolutionary*. New York: Cosimo.

Kupperman, Karen O. (2007). *The Jamestown Project*. Cambridge, Mass.: Belknap Press of Harvard University Press.

Landes, David S. (1999). *The Wealth and Poverty of Nations: Why Some Are So Rich and Some So Poor*. New York: W. W. Norton and Co.

Lane, Frederick C. (1973). *Venice: A Maritime Republic*. Baltimore, Md.: Johns Hopkins University Press.

La Porta, Rafael, Florencio Lopez-de-Silanes, and Andrei Shleifer (2008). "The Economic Consequences of Legal Origins." *Journal of Economic Literature* 46: 285–332.

Law, Robin C. (1977). *The Oyo Empire, c.1600–c.1836: West African Imperialism in the Era of the Atlantic Slave Trade*. Oxford, UK: The Clarendon Press.

—— (1980). "Wheeled Transportation in Pre-Colonial West Africa." *Africa* 50: 249–62.

——, ed. (1995). *From Slave Trade to "Legitimate" Commerce: The Commercial Transition in Nineteenth-century West Africa*. New York: Cambridge University Press.

Leith, Clark J. (2005). *Why Botswana Prospered*. Montreal: McGill University Press.

Lenger, Friedrich (2004). "Economy and Society." In Jonathan Sperber, ed. *The Shorter Oxford History of Germany: Germany 1800–1870*. New York: Oxford University Press.

León, Juanita (2009). *Country of Bullets: Chronicles of War*. Albuquerque: University of New Mexico Press.

Lerner, Abba P. (1972). "The Economics and Politics of Consumer Sovereignty." *American Economic Review* 62: 258–66.

Levy, David M., and Sandra J. Peart (2009). "Soviet Growth and American Textbooks." Unpublished.

Lewis, I. M. (1961). *A Pastoral Democracy*. Oxford, U.K.: Oxford University Press.

—— (2002). *A Modern History of the Somali*. 4th ed. Oxford, U.K.: James Currey.

Lewis, W. Arthur (1954). "Economic Development with Unlimited Supplies of Labour." *Manchester School of Economic and Social Studies* 22: 139–91.

Lindert, Peter H. (2004). *Growing Public. Volume 1: Social Spending and Economic Growth Since the Eighteenth Century*. New York: Cambridge University Press.

—— (2009). *Growing Public. Volume 2: Further Evidence: Social Spending and Economic Growth Since the Eighteenth Century*. New York: Cambridge University Press.

Lipset, Seymour Martin (1959). "Some Social Requisites of Democracy: Economic Development and Political Legitimacy." *American Political Science Review* 53: 69–105.

Lipset, Seymour Martin, and Stein Rokkan, eds. (1967). *Party System and Voter Alignments*. New York: Free Press.

López, Claudia, ed. (2010). *Y Refundaron la Patria . . . de cómo mafiosos y políticos reconfiguraron el Estado Colombiano*. Bogotá: Corporación Nuevo Arco Iris: Intermedio.

Lovejoy, Paul E. (2000). *Transformations in Slavery: A History of Slavery in Africa*. 2nd ed. New York: Cambridge University Press.

MacFarquhar, Roderick, and Michael Schoenhals (2008). *Mao's Last Revolution*. Cambridge, Mass.: Harvard University Press.

Mann, Michael (1986). *The Sources of Social Power. Volume 1: A History of Power from the Beginning to A.D. 1760*. New York: Cambridge University Press.

—— (1993). *The Sources of Social Power. Volume 2: The Rise of Classes and Nation-states, 1760–1914*. New York: Cambridge University Press.

Manning, Patrick (1990). *Slavery and African Life: Occidental, Oriental, and African Slave Trades*. New York: Cambridge University Press.

Mantoux, Paul (1961). *The Industrial Revolution in the Eighteenth Century*. Rev. ed. New York: Harper and Row.

Martin, Simon, and Nikolai Grube (2000). *Chronicle of the Maya Kings and Queens: Deciphering the Dynasties of the Ancient Maya*. New York: Thames and Hudson.

Martinez, José (2002). *Carlos Slim: Retrato Inédito*. Mexico City: Editorial Oceano.

Masire, Quett K. J. (2006). *Very Brave or Very Foolish? Memoirs of an African Democrat*. Gaborone, Botswana: Macmillan.

McCreery, David J. (1994). *Rural Guatemala, 1760–1940*. Palo Alto, Calif.: Stanford University Press.

McGregor, Richard (2010). *The Party: The Secret World of China's Communist Rulers*. New York: Harper.

McMillan, John, and Pablo Zoido (2004). "How to Subvert Democracy: Montesinos in Peru." *Journal of Economic Perspectives* 18: 69–92.

Melbourne, Alexander C. V. (1963). *Early Constitutional Development in Australia: New South Wales 1788–1856; Queensland 1859–1922*. With notes to 1963 by the editor. Edited and introduced by R. B. Joyce. 2nd ed. St. Lucia: University of Queensland Press.

Meredith, Martin (2007). *Mugabe: Power, Plunder, and the Struggle for Zimbabwe's Future*. New York: Public Affairs Press.

Michels, Robert (1962). *Political Parties: A Sociological Study of the Oligarchical Tendencies of Modern Democracy*. New York: Free Press.

Mickey, Robert W. (2008). *Paths out of Dixie: The Democratization of Authoritarian Enclaves in America's Deep South, 1944–1972*. Unpublished book manuscript.

Migdal, Joel S. (1988). *Strong Societies and Weak States: State-Society Relations and State Capabilities in the Third World*. Princeton, N.J.: Princeton University Press.

Mithen, Stephen (2006). *After the Ice: A Global Human History 20,000–5000 BC*. Cambridge, Mass.: Harvard University Press.

Mokyr, Joel (1990). *The Lever of Riches: Technological Creativity and Economic Progress*. New York: Oxford University Press.

—— (2009). *The Enlightened Economy*. New York: Penguin.

Moore, Andrew M. T., G. C. Hillman, and A. J. Legge (2000). *Village on the Euphrates: From Foraging to Farming at Abu Hureyra*. New York: Oxford University Press.

Morgan, Edmund S. (1975). *American Slavery, American Freedom: The Ordeal of Colonial Virginia*. New York: W. W. Norton and Co.

Munro-Hay, Stuart C. (1991). *Aksum: An African Civilisation of Late Antiquity*. Edinburgh: Edinburgh University Press.

Myers, Ramon H., and Yeh-Chien Wang (2002). "Economic Developments, 1644–1800." In Willard J. Peterson, ed. *The Cambridge History of China. Volume 9, Part 1: The Ch'ing Empire to 1800*. New York: Cambridge University Press.

Naidu, Suresh (2009). "Suffrage, Schooling, and Sorting in the Post-Bellum South." Unpublished. Department of Economics, Columbia University. Available at tuvalu.santafe.edu/~snaidu/papers/suffrage_sept_16_2010_combined.pdf.

Narayan, Deepa, ed. (2002). *Empowerment and Poverty Reduction: A Sourcebook.* Washington, D.C.: The World Bank.

Neal, David (1991). *The Rule of Law in a Penal Colony.* New York: Cambridge University Press.

Neale, J. E. (1971). *Elizabeth I and Her Parliaments, 1559–1581.* London: Cape.

Nogal, C. Álvarez, and Leandro Prados de la Escosura (2007). "The Decline of Spain (1500–1850): Conjectural Estimates." *European Review of Economic History* 11: 319–66.

North, Douglass C. (1982). *Structure and Change in Economic History.* New York: W. W. Norton and Co.

North, Douglass C., and Robert P. Thomas (1973). *The Rise of the Western World: A New Economic History.* New York: Cambridge University Press.

North, Douglass C., John J. Wallis, and Barry R. Weingast (1989). *Violence and Social Orders: A Conceptual Framework for Interpreting Recorded Human History.* Princeton, N.J.: Princeton University Press.

North, Douglass C., and Barry R. Weingast (1989). "Constitutions and Commitment: Evolution of Institutions Governing Public Choice in 17th Century England." *Journal of Economic History* 49: 803–32.

Nove, Alec (1992). *An Economic History of the USSR 1917–1991.* 3rd ed. New York: Penguin Books.

Nugent, Jeffrey B., and James A. Robinson (2010). "Are Endowments Fate? On the Political Economy of Comparative Institutional Development." *Revista de Historia Económica* (*Journal of Iberian and Latin American Economic History*) 28: 45–82.

Nunn, Nathan (2008). "The Long-Term Effects of Africa's Slave Trades." *Quarterly Journal of Economics* 123: 139–76.

Nunn, Nathan, and Leonard Wantchekon (2011). "The Slave Trade and the Origins of Mistrust in Africa," forthcoming in the *American Economic Review.*

O'Brien, Patrick K., Trevor Griffiths, and Philip Hunt (1991). "Political Components of the Industrial Revolution: Parliament and the English Cotton Textile Industry, 1660–1774." *Economic History Review*, New Series 44: 395–423.

Ogilvie, Sheilagh (2011). *Institutions and European Trade: Merchant Guilds 1000–1500*. New York: Cambridge University Press.

Olson, Mancur C. (1984). *The Rise and Decline of Nations: Economic Growth, Stagflation, and Social Rigidities*. New Haven, Conn.: Yale University Press.

O'Rourke, Kevin H., and Jeffrey G. Williamson (2002). "After Columbus: Explaining the Global Trade Boom 1500–1800." *Journal of Economic History* 62: 417–56.

Owen, E. Roger (1981). *The Middle East in the World Economy, 1800–1914*. London: Methuen and Co.

Owen, E. Roger, and Şevket Pamuk (1999). *A History of Middle East Economies in the Twentieth Century*. Cambridge, Mass.: Harvard University Press.

Owen, Thomas C. (1991). *The Corporation Under Russian Law, 1800–1917*. New York: Cambridge University Press.

Palmer, Robin H. (1977). *Land and Racial Domination in Rhodesia*. Berkeley: University of California Press.

Palmer, Robin H., and Q. Neil Parsons, eds. (1977). *The Roots of Rural Poverty in Central and Southern Africa*. London: Heinemann Educational.

Pamuk, Şevket (2006). "Estimating Economic Growth in the Middle East Since 1820." *Journal of Economic History* 66: 809–28.

Pan, Philip P. (2008). *Out Of Mao's Shadow: The Struggle for the Soul of a New China*. New York: Simon & Schuster.

Pankhurst, Richard (1961). *An Introduction to the Economic History of Ethiopia, from Early Times to 1800*. London: Lalibela House.

Parsons, Q. Neil (1998). *King Khama, Emperor Joe and the Great White Queen*. Chicago: University of Chicago Press.

Parsons, Q. Neil, Willie Henderson, and Thomas Tlou (1995). *Seretse Khama, 1921–1980*. Bloemfontein, South Africa: Macmillan.

Perkins, Dwight H., Steven Radelet, and David L. Lindauer (2006). *Development Economics*. 6th ed. New York: W. W. Norton and Co.

Pettigrew, William (2007). "Free to Enslave: Politics and the Escalation of Britain's Transatlantic Slave Trade, 1688–1714." *William and Mary Quarterly,* 3rd ser., LXIV: 3–37.

—— (2009). "Some Underappreciated Connections Between Constitutional Change and National Economic Growth in England, 1660–1720." Unpublished paper. Department of History, University of Kent, Canterbury.

Phillipson, David W. (1998). *Ancient Ethiopia: Aksum, Its Antecedents and Successors*. London: British Museum Press.

Pincus, Steven C. A. (2009). *1688: The First Modern Revolution*. New Haven, Conn.: Yale University Press.

Pincus, Steven C. A., and James A. Robinson (2010). "What Really Happened During the Glorious Revolution?" Unpublished. http://scholar.harvard.edu/jrobinson.

Pintner, Walter M. (1967). *Russian Economic Policy Under Nicholas I*. Ithaca, N.Y.: Cornell University Press.

Post, Jerrold M. (2004). *Leaders and Their Followers in a Dangerous World: The Psychology of Political Behavior*. Ithaca, N.Y.: Cornell University Press.

Price, David A. (2003). *Love and Hate in Jamestown: John Smith, Pocahontas, and the Heart of a New Nation*. New York: Knopf.

Puga, Diego, and Daniel Trefler (2010). "International Trade and Domestic Institutions: The Medieval Response to Globalization." Unpublished. Department of Economics, University of Toronto.

Putnam, Robert H., Robert Leonardi, and Raffaella Y. Nanetti (1994). *Making Democracy Work: Civic Traditions in Modern Italy*. Princeton, N.J.: Princeton University Press.

Ransom, Roger L., and Richard Sutch (2001). *One Kind of Freedom: The Economic Consequences of Emancipation.* 2nd ed. New York: Cambridge University Press.

Reid, Anthony (1993). *Southeast Asia in the Age of Commerce, 1450–1680. Volume 2: Expansion and Crisis.* New Haven, Conn.: Yale University Press.

Reinikka, Ritva, and Jacob Svensson (2004). "Local Capture: Evidence from a Central Government Transfer Program in Uganda." *Quarterly Journal of Economics,* 119: 679–705.

Relea, Francesco (2007). "Carlos Slim, Liderazgo sin Competencia." In Jorge Zepeda Patterson, ed. *Los amos de México: los juegos de poder a los que sólo unos pocos son invitados.* Mexico City: Planeta Mexicana.

Reno, William (1995). *Corruption and State Politics in Sierra Leone.* New York: Cambridge University Press.

——— (2003). "Political Networks in a Failing State: The Roots and Future of Violent Conflict in Sierra Leone," *IPG* 2: 44–66.

Richards, Paul (1996). *Fighting for the Rainforest: War, Youth and Resources in Sierra Leone.* Oxford, U.K.: James Currey.

Robbins, Lionel (1935). *An Essay on the Nature and Significance of Economic Science.* 2nd ed. London: Macmillan.

Robinson, Eric (1964). "Matthew Boulton and the Art of Parliamentary Lobbying." *The Historical Journal* 7: 209–29.

Robinson, James A. (1998). "Theories of Bad Policy." *Journal of Policy Reform* 1, 1–46.

Robinson, James A, and Q. Neil Parsons (2006). "State Formation and Governance in Botswana." *Journal of African Economies* 15, AERC Supplement (2006): 100–140.

Rock, David (1992). *Argentina 1516–1982: From Spanish Colonization to the Falklands War.* Berkeley: University of California Press.

Romero, Mauricio (2003). *Paramilitares y autodefensas, 1982–2003.* Bogotá: Editorial Planeta Colombiana.

——, ed. (2007). *Para Política: La Ruta de la Expansión Paramilitar y los Acuerdos Políticos*, Bogotá: Corporación Nuevo Arco Iris: Intermedio.

Sachs, Jeffery B. (2006). *The End of Poverty: Economic Possibilities for Our Time*. New York: Penguin.

Sahlins, Marshall (1972). *Stone Age Economics*. Chicago: Aldine.

Saunders, David (1992). *Russia in the Age of Reaction and Reform, 1801–1881*. New York: Longman.

Savage-Smith, Emily (2003). "Islam." In Roy Porter, ed. *The Cambridge History of Science. Volume 4: Eighteenth-Century Science*. New York: Cambridge University Press.

Sawers, Larry (1996). *The Other Argentina: The Interior and National Development*. Boulder: Westview Press.

Schapera, Isaac (1940). "The Political Organization of the Ngwato of Bechuanaland Protectorate." In E. E. Evans-Pritchard and Meyer Fortes, eds. *African Political Systems*. Oxford, U.K.: Oxford University Press.

—— (1952). *The Ethnic Composition of the Tswana Tribes*. London: London School of Economics and Political Science.

—— (1970). *Tribal Innovators: Tswana Chiefs and Social Change 1795–1940*. London: The Athlone Press.

Schoenhals, Michael, ed. (1996). *China's Cultural Revolution, 1966–1969*. Armonk, N.Y.: M.E. Sharpe.

Sfakianakis, John (2004). "The Whales of the Nile: Networks, Businessmen and Bureaucrats During the Era of Privatization in Egypt." In Steven Heydemann, ed. *Networks of Privilege in the Middle East*. New York: Palgrave Macmillan.

Sharp, Kevin (1992). *The Personal Rule of Charles I*. New Haven, Conn.: Yale University Press.

Sheridan, Richard B. (1973). *Sugar and Slaves: An Economic History of the British West Indies 1623–1775*. Baltimore, Md.: Johns Hopkins University Press.

Sidrys, Raymond, and Rainer Berger (1979). "Lowland Maya Radiocarbon Dates and the Classic Maya Collapse." *Nature* 277: 269–77.

Smith, Bruce D. (1998). *Emergence of Agriculture*. New York: Scientific American Library.

Sokoloff, Kenneth L. (1988). "Inventive Activity in Early Industrial America: Evidence from Patent Records, 1790–1846." *Journal of Economic History* 48: 813–30.

Sokoloff, Kenneth L., and B. Zorina Khan (1990). "The Democratization of Invention During Early Industrialization: Evidence from the United States, 1790–1846." *Journal of Economic History* 50: 363–78.

Steffens, Lincoln (1931). *The Autobiography of Lincoln Steffens*. New York: Harcourt, Brace and Company.

Stevens, Donald F. (1991). *Origins of Instability in Early Republican Mexico*. Durham, N.C.: Duke University Press.

Stone, Lawrence (2001). *The Causes of the English Revolution, 1529–1642*. New York: Routledge.

Tabellini, Guido (2010). "Culture and Institutions: Economic Development in the Regions of Europe." *Journal of the European Economic Association* 8, 677–716.

Tarbell, Ida M. (1904). *The History of the Standard Oil Company*. New York: McClure, Phillips.

Tawney, R. H. (1941). "The Rise of the Gentry." *Economic History Review* 11: 1–38.

Temin, Peter, and Hans-Joachim Voth (2008). "Private Borrowing During the Financial Revolution: Hoare's Bank and Its Customers, 1702–24." *Economic History Review* 61: 541–64.

Thompson, E. P. (1975). *Whigs and Hunters: The Origin of the Black Act*. New York: Pantheon Books.

Thompson, I.A.A. (1994a). "Castile: Polity, Fiscality and Fiscal Crisis." In Philip T. Hoffman and Kathryn Norberg, eds. *Fiscal Crisis, Liberty, and Representative Government 1450–1789*. Palo Alto, Calif.: Stanford University Press.

—— (1994b). "Castile: Absolutism, Constitutionalism and Liberty." In Philip T. Hoffman and Kathryn Norberg, eds. *Fiscal Crisis, Liberty, and Representative Government 1450–1789*. Palo Alto, Calif.: Stanford University Press.

Thornton, John (1983). *The Kingdom of Kongo: Civil War and Transition, 1641–1718*. Madison: University of Wisconsin Press.

Todkill, Anas (1885). *My Lady Pocahontas: A True Relation of Virginia. Writ by Anas Todkill, Puritan and Pilgrim*. Boston: Houghton, Mifflin and Company.

Truth and Reconciliation Commission (2004). *Final Report of the Truth and Reconciliation Commission of Sierra Leone*. Freetown.

Vansina, Jan (1978). *The Children of Woot: A History of the Kuba People*. Madison: University of Wisconsin Press.

Wade, Robert H. (1990). *Governing the Market: Economic Theory and the Role of Government in East Asian Industrialization*. Princeton, N.J.: Princeton University Press.

Wallerstein, Immanuel (1974–2011). *The Modern World System*. 4 Vol. New York: Academic Press.

Ward-Perkins, Bryan (2006). *The Fall of Rome and the End of Civilization*. New York: Oxford University Press.

Weber, Max (2002). *The Protestant Ethic and the Spirit of Capitalism*. New York: Penguin.

Webster, David L. (2002). *The Fall of the Ancient Maya*. New York: Thames and Hudson.

Webster, David L., Ann Corinne Freter, and Nancy Gonlin (2000). *Copan: The Rise and Fall of an Ancient Maya Kingdom*. Fort Worth, Tex.: Harcourt College Publishers.

Wheatcroft, Stephen G., and Robert W. Davies (1994a). "The Crooked Mirror of Soviet Economic Statistics." In Robert W. Davies, Mark Harrison, and Stephen G. Wheatcroft, eds. *The Economic Transformation of the Soviet Union, 1913–1945.* New York: Cambridge University Press.

—— **(1994b).** "Population." In Robert W. Davies, Mark Harrison, and Stephen G. Wheatcroft, eds. *The Economic Transformation of the Soviet Union, 1913–1945.* New York: Cambridge University Press.

Wiener, Jonathan M. (1978). *Social Origins of the New South: Alabama, 1860–1885.* Baton Rouge: Louisiana State University Press.

Williamson, John (1990). *Latin American Adjustment: How Much Has Happened?* Washington, D.C.: Institute of International Economics.

Wilson, Francis (1972). *Labour in the South African Gold Mines, 1911–1969.* New York: Cambridge University Press.

Wilson, Woodrow (1913). *The New Freedom: A Call for the Emancipation of the Generous Energies of a People.* New York: Doubleday.

Woodward, C. Vann (1955). *The Strange Career of Jim Crow.* New York: Oxford University Press.

Woodward, Ralph L. (1966). *Class Privilege and Economic Development: The Consulado de Comercio of Guatemala, 1793–1871.* Chapel Hill: University of North Carolina Press.

Wright, Gavin (1978). *The Political Economy of the Cotton South: Households, Markets, and Wealth in the Nineteenth Century.* New York: Norton.

—— **(1986).** *Old South, New South: Revolutions in the Southern Economy Since the Civil War.* New York: Basic Books.

—— **(1999).** "The Civil Rights Movement as Economic History." *Journal of Economic History* 59: 267–89.

Zahedieh, Nuala (2010). *The Capital and the Colonies: London and the Atlantic Economy, 1660–1700.* New York: Cambridge University Press.

Zewde, Bahru (2002). *History of Modern Ethiopia, 1855–1991*. Athens: Ohio University Press.

Zohary, Daniel, and Maria Hopf (2001). *Domestication of Plants in the Old World: The Origin and Spread of Cultivated Plants in West Asia, Europe, and the Nile Valley* Third Edition, New York: Oxford University Press.

INDEX

Note: Page numbers in *italics* refer to maps or charts.